AI-Powered English Teaching

Ankit Shukla
Rajamangala University of Technology, Thailand

Benjaporn Meeprom
Rajamangala University of Technology, Thayaburi, Thailand

Kongkiat Khunasathitchai
Rajamangala University of Technology, Thailand

Nagendra Yadav
Welcomgroup Graduate School of Hotel Administration, Manipal Academy of Higher Education, India

IGI Global
Scientific Publishing
Publishing Tomorrow's Research Today

Vice President of Editorial Melissa Wagner
Director of Acquisitions Mikaela Felty
Director of Book Development Jocelynn Hessler
Production Manager Mike Brehm
Cover Design Jose Rosado

Published in the United States of America by
IGI Global Scientific Publishing
701 East Chocolate Avenue
Hershey, PA, 17033, USA
Tel: 717-533-8845
Fax: 717-533-7115
Website: https://www.igi-global.com E-mail: cust@igi-global.com

Library of Congress Cataloging-in-Publication Data

Names: Shukla, Ankit, 1992- editor | Meeprom, Benjaporn, 1981- editor | Khunsathitchai, Kongkiat, 1985- editor | Yadav, Nagendra, 1990- editor
Title: AI-powered English teaching / edited by: Ankit Shukla, Benjaporn Meeprom, Kongkiat Khunsathitchai, and Nagendra Yadav.
Description: Hershey PA : IGI Global Scientific Publishing, [2026] | Includes bibliographical references. | Summary: "The primary goal of this book is to provide educators, researchers, and policymakers with a comprehensive understanding of how artificial intelligence (AI) can revolutionize the teaching and learning of English"-- Provided by publisher.
Identifiers: LCCN 2025005861 (print) | LCCN 2025005862 (ebook) | ISBN 9798337319520 hardcover | ISBN 9798337319537 paperback | ISBN 9798337319544 ebook
Subjects: LCSH: English language--Computer-assisted instruction for foreign speakers | English language--Study and teaching--Technological innovations | Artificial intelligence--Educational applications | LCGFT: Essays
Classification: LCC PE1128.3 .A44 2025 (print) | LCC PE1128.3 (ebook) | DDC 428.0078/563--dc23/eng/20250515
LC record available at https://lccn.loc.gov/2025005861
LC ebook record available at https://lccn.loc.gov/2025005862

British Cataloguing in Publication Data
A Cataloguing in Publication record for this book is available from the British Library.

Table of Contents

Detailed Table of Contents

This chapter explores the transformative impact of artificial intelligence on English language teaching and learning, examining both theoretical frameworks and practical applications. Beginning with an analysis of the historical progression from Computer-Assisted Language Learning (CALL) to AI-Enhanced Language Learning (AIELL), the chapter investigates how machine learning algorithms, natural language processing, and adaptive learning systems are reshaping traditional pedagogical approaches. Through examination of empirical studies and case implementations across various educational contexts, the research reveals significant improvements in personalized learning experiences, assessment precision, and learner engagement. Particular attention is given to intelligent tutoring systems, automated feedback mechanisms, and AI-driven content creation tools that support both independent study and classroom instruction.

This chapter explores the transformative role of artificial intelligence (AI) in English language education, focusing on its potential to personalize learning and enhance language acquisition. AI-powered tools have revolutionized traditional language learning models by offering individualized learning experiences that cater to the unique needs, strengths, and preferences of each student. Through intelligent tutoring systems, AI-driven chatbots, speech recognition technologies, and adaptive learning platforms, AI provides learners with real-time feedback, tailored exercises, and immersive environments for language practice. These advancements shift the traditional one-size-fits-all approach to a more student-centered model that promotes deeper engagement and improved proficiency. The chapter also examines

Guide for English Educators," provides an in-depth overview of AI tools and their applications, including lesson planning, personalized learning, real-time feedback, and student engagement activities. It uses practical examples and case studies to illustrate how AI can simplify administrative tasks, address diverse learners' needs, and promote interactive learning environments. The chapter also addresses challenges like technical accessibility, pedagogical balance, and ethical issues like data privacy and algorithmic bias. It offers actionable strategies for meaningful AI integration, allowing educators to see AI as an opportunity for collaborative partnership in the teaching process. The final chapter envisions a future where AI supports inclusivity, creativity, and innovation in English education.

Chapter 9
Preparing Educators for the Future: Navigating AI Tools in English Language Teaching 267
Mustafa Kayyali, HE Higher Education Ranking, Idlib, Syria

The use of Artificial Intelligence (AI) in English Language Teaching (ELT) is set to transform educators' methodologies in language education and students' involvement in language learning. As AI technologies progress, they provide a diverse range of tools and resources aimed at improving teaching methods and learning results. To enable AI to significantly influence the future of language teaching, it is crucial to provide instructors with the knowledge to comprehend, maneuver, and proficiently incorporate these technologies into their classrooms. This chapter examines the diverse AI tools accessible to English language instructors, emphasizing their potential to provide customized, dynamic, and interactive learning experiences. By comprehending the function of AI, educators may adeptly maneuver through the difficulties of these technologies and leverage their capabilities to enhance the language acquisition process, cultivating a more efficient and stimulating educational atmosphere for learners.

Chapter 10
The Effect of Artificial Intelligence on English Learners' Anxiety Levels 309
Farzaneh Kazemi, University of Tabriz, Iran

With the development of communication, acquiring a second language different from one's first language has become of great significance. Moreover, as the current era is known for the prevalence of technology being an integral part of individual lifestyles, the phenomenon of artificial intelligence (AI) has turned into one of the central issues in language teaching and learning. The chapter explores the concept of second language anxiety as a key phenomenon. As per the literature, AI has been reported to have several benefits, such as lower cognitive load, improved language output, a higher level of motivation, adaptive learning environment, provision of personalized feedback, and reduced demotivation. However, it is not free from

shortcomings, such as unfamiliarity with computer skills can cause even more L2 anxiety in language learners. Therefore, it is concluded that the over-reliance on this technology may not be as advantageous as it may seem. The chapter is set to provide practical implications for the stakeholders in the realm of language education.

Preface

INTRODUCTION

The rapid integration of Artificial Intelligence (AI) into education has revolutionized teaching and learning processes across disciplines. Among the most dynamically transformed fields is English language education, where AI is reshaping pedagogy, assessment, communication, and learner engagement. This book, AI-Powered English Teaching, provides an in-depth examination of how AI technologies are influencing English Language Teaching (ELT), from classroom interactions to curriculum design and beyond.

By collecting cutting-edge research, case studies, and practical insights, this volume addresses the intersection of AI and English education in both theory and practice. It explores the use of AI-driven tools to improve language acquisition, facilitate formative assessment, personalize learning pathways, and enhance digital literacy. It also touches upon AI's role in specific domains like journalism, business, and the culinary arts, all while maintaining a strong focus on learner psychology, such as motivation and anxiety reduction.

Moreover, this book emphasizes the ethical and pedagogical implications of integrating AI into language classrooms, ensuring that technology enhances rather than hinders human connection and critical thinking. It considers the evolving role of English teachers in an AI-mediated environment and offers guidance for professional development in this new educational landscape. By bridging theory with real-world applications, it aims to support both novice and experienced educators in adapting to AI-enhanced instruction. This work also highlights the importance of AI literacy for both teachers and learners, positioning it as a vital skill in the 21st-century educational toolkit. Through its comprehensive scope, *AI-Powered English Teaching* aspires to shape future-ready educators capable of leveraging AI for meaningful language learning outcomes.

The Relevance of the Topic in the World Today

In today's globalized, digitized, and multilingual world, the demand for effective English language instruction is at an all-time high. Simultaneously, AI is becoming an integral part of educational ecosystems, offering unprecedented support for teachers and learners. The COVID-19 pandemic accelerated the need for flexible, scalable, and remote learning solutions, further cementing AI's role in language education.

AI tools like chatbots, intelligent tutoring systems, automated assessment platforms, and speech recognition apps are enabling educators to offer personalized, responsive, and culturally sensitive instruction. These technologies are not merely enhancing instruction—they are redefining what it means to teach and learn English in the 21st century. Understanding, leveraging, and critiquing these tools is no longer optional—it is essential.

This book aims to provide educators, researchers, policymakers, and edtech developers with the necessary insights to navigate and shape this fast-evolving landscape.

As education systems worldwide strive to become more inclusive and adaptable, AI offers promising solutions for addressing diverse learner needs, language barriers, and resource constraints. The integration of AI also aligns with global trends toward lifelong learning and skills-based education, making English proficiency more accessible across socio-economic backgrounds. Furthermore, AI's data-driven insights can empower educators to make informed pedagogical decisions, improving learning outcomes at scale. The ethical, cultural, and pedagogical considerations surrounding AI use in ELT are increasingly coming to the forefront, demanding thoughtful engagement and critical reflection. In this context, the topic of AI-powered English teaching stands not only as relevant but also as transformative for the future of education.

Target Audience

This book is designed for a diverse audience that includes:

- **English language teachers** seeking practical guidance on incorporating AI into their classrooms.
- **Education researchers** interested in the pedagogical, psychological, and sociocultural impacts of AI on English learning.
- **Instructional designers** and **curriculum developers** aiming to build AI-integrated language programs.
- **EdTech entrepreneurs and developers** looking for real-world use cases and pedagogical grounding for AI-powered tools.

- **Policy makers and administrators** tasked with shaping institutional responses to digital transformation in education.
- **Graduate students and scholars** focused on applied linguistics, language acquisition, and technology in education.

• Additionally, this book will benefit language learners themselves who wish to better understand the AI tools available to support their studies and take ownership of their learning journeys. Teacher trainers and professional development coordinators will find valuable frameworks and strategies to prepare educators for AI-enhanced teaching environments. Moreover, those working in interdisciplinary fields—such as computational linguistics, cognitive science, and digital humanities—will gain insights into the evolving relationship between language education and artificial intelligence. By addressing this broad spectrum of readers, the book fosters a collaborative dialogue among stakeholders dedicated to advancing effective, ethical, and innovative English language teaching practices. Ultimately, it aims to bridge gaps between theory, technology, and practice to empower all who engage with AI in education.

CHAPTER SUMMARIES

Chapter 1: AI in Education: Revolutionizing English Learning

This opening chapter provides a foundational overview of how AI is transforming English language education. It discusses key AI technologies—such as machine learning, NLP, and intelligent tutoring systems—and their applications in ELT. The chapter lays the groundwork for the rest of the book by mapping the technological landscape and highlighting future directions.

Chapter 2: Demystifying Artificial Intelligence: Comprehensive Guide for Non-Native Speakers

Targeted at both educators and learners, this chapter explains AI in accessible terms. It decodes technical jargon and situates AI within the context of everyday life and learning. It is especially valuable for non-native speakers and educators unfamiliar with AI, offering them a gateway into more technical or pedagogical discussions

Chapter 3: Transforming Language Acquisition: AI-Powered Approaches to English Language Teaching and Learning

This chapter delves into innovative AI-enhanced methodologies for teaching English, such as adaptive learning algorithms, intelligent feedback systems, and real-time pronunciation tools. It bridges cognitive theories of language acquisition with modern AI practices.

Chapter 4: The Role of AI in Personalized English Language Learning

Focusing on learner-centered education, this chapter explores how AI supports differentiated instruction. It presents case studies on platforms that tailor learning materials, pace, and feedback according to individual student needs and profiles.

Chapter 5: AI-Facilitated Formative Assessment: Reimagining Feedback in the English Language Classroom

This chapter discusses AI's capacity to transform assessment by providing instant, detailed, and personalized feedback. It examines tools like automated essay scoring and error detection systems and considers implications for both formative and summative assessment practices.

Chapter 6: Automated Feedback Effect on Foreign Language Writing Motivation and Anxiety

This chapter investigates how AI-generated feedback affects learners' emotional responses, particularly motivation and anxiety. It highlights both the benefits and potential drawbacks of replacing human feedback with automated alternatives.

Chapter 7: Using AI to Enhance Receptive Foreign Language Skills

The focus here is on listening and reading—skills that are often underrepresented in discussions of AI in education. The chapter explores how AI can support these receptive skills through tools such as speech recognition, audiobooks with adaptive playback, and intelligent reading assistants.

Chapter 8: AI-Assisted English Learning: Unlocking New Pathways for Student Success

Combining research and classroom anecdotes, this chapter emphasizes how AI can identify struggling students early and provide customized learning pathways, thereby promoting student success, inclusivity, and retention.

Chapter 9: Enhancing English Language Teaching with AI: Practical Case Studies, Challenges, and Pedagogical Insights

This practical chapter presents real-world examples of AI implementation in ELT. It discusses the outcomes, challenges, and best practices observed, serving as a field guide for educators venturing into AI adoption.

Chapter 10: Leveraging AI on Social Media & Digital Platforms to Enhance English Language Teaching and Learning

This chapter explores the use of AI algorithms on platforms like YouTube, TikTok, and Twitter for educational content creation, learner engagement, and content curation. It also addresses digital literacy and ethical considerations.

CONCLUSION: IMPACT AND CONTRIBUTION TO THE FIELD

This book serves as both a comprehensive guide and a critical exploration of AI's integration into English language teaching. By presenting a balance of theoretical depth, practical applications, and empirical research, AI-Powered English Teaching fills a crucial gap in ELT literature. It promotes a future-ready mindset among educators, fosters learner empowerment, and encourages innovation in curriculum development and pedagogy.

Moreover, the book acts as a bridge between disciplines—linking linguistics, technology, education, and psychology—thus contributing holistically to the field of AI-enhanced education. As AI continues to evolve, the insights and frameworks presented here will remain valuable resources for those shaping the next generation of English language learners and teachers.

Importantly, this volume highlights both the opportunities and challenges posed by AI, advocating for responsible and ethical implementation to ensure equitable access and cultural sensitivity. It encourages ongoing dialogue about the role of human agency in AI-mediated learning environments, reminding readers that technology is a tool to support, not replace, the human elements of teaching. By documenting diverse case studies and innovative practices, the book offers inspiration and practical models for adapting to rapidly changing educational contexts. It also emphasizes the need for continuous professional development to keep pace with technological advancements. Ultimately, AI-Powered English Teaching contributes to a more inclusive, personalized, and effective approach to language education. It aims to empower educators and learners alike to harness AI's potential thoughtfully and creatively, preparing them for an interconnected and technology-rich future. Through this contribution, the book aspires to influence policy, practice, and research in meaningful ways, fostering a vibrant and forward-looking ELT community.

Ankit Shukla
Rajamangala University of Technology, Thanyaburi, Thailand

Benjaporn Meeprom
Rajamangala University of Technology Thayaburi, Thailand

Kongkiat Khunasathitchai
Rajamangala University of Technology, Thanyaburi, Thailand

Nagendra Yadav
Welcomgroup Graduate School of Hotel Administration, Manipal Academy of Higher Education, India

Acknowledgment

I would like to express my deepest gratitude to all the contributing authors whose scholarly efforts, critical insights, and dedication have shaped this book, *AI-Powered English Teaching*, into a meaningful contribution to the intersection of artificial intelligence and language education. Your work represents a diverse range of perspectives, methodologies, and innovations that will undoubtedly inform and inspire educators, researchers, and policymakers alike.

My heartfelt thanks go to the editorial and production team at IGI Global, whose professionalism, patience, and technical guidance ensured that this book was brought to fruition with excellence. Your consistent support throughout the proposal, review, and publication stages made this process both efficient and enriching.

I am also deeply thankful to the peer reviewers and academic advisors who provided rigorous and constructive feedback on each chapter. Your insights helped uphold the scholarly standards and clarity that define this volume.

To my colleagues, collaborators, and mentors, thank you for your unwavering encouragement and for inspiring me to explore the potential of AI in reshaping English language instruction. Your belief in the relevance and urgency of this work kept me grounded and focused throughout the editorial journey.

A special thanks to my wife Dipika and my family for supporting me in this journey. In addition special note of appreciation goes to the academic institutions, research groups, and professional communities working tirelessly to advance AI literacy and equitable education. Your pioneering work laid the foundation upon which this book stands.

Finally, I dedicate this work to the educators and learners around the world who continue to adapt, innovate, and grow in a rapidly changing educational landscape. Your resilience, curiosity, and willingness to embrace technology for meaningful learning serve as the true inspiration for this book.

Ankit Shukla

Editor, *AI-Powered English Teaching*

Chapter 1
AI in Education:
Revolutionizing English Learning

Saddam Hossain
https://orcid.org/0009-0001-9996-4963
Khulna University, Bangladesh

Farhana Yeasmin
https://orcid.org/0000-0002-0954-7489
Jashore University of Science and Technology, Bangladesh

Shahjahan Kabir
Khulna University, Bangladesh

ABSTRACT

Today, English has emerged as a medium of instruction, communication, and job opportunities worldwide. As it has been acknowledged that ordinary means of language learning cannot help to address the diverse needs of all learners, AI has revolutionized the approach to English education. The major apps, including Duolingo, Babbel, and ELSA Speak, integrate AI that caters to the lessons depending on each individual's fluency, accent, and speed level. Tools like Carnegie Learning's MATHia, ITS, and NLP give feedback using naturally processed language. Other applications, such as AR, VR, Grammarly, and Turnitin, facilitate giving feedback in the classroom. AI also has the positive effect of universal learning, as seen with Google Translate. However, inequality, insufficient access to devices, and privacy issues must be resolved. The inability of AI to preserve interpersonal communication should not be ignored, and the ethical issues related to the aid of AI must not be downplayed.

DOI: 10.4018/979-8-3373-1952-0.ch001

I. INTRODUCTION

Integrating artificial intelligence (AI) into education represents a transformative shift in how languages, mainly English, are taught and learned. As a global *lingua franca*, English is pivotal for academic achievement, career advancement, and intercultural communication. However, traditional language teaching methods and approaches often fail to accommodate diverse learner needs, cultural contexts, and varied proficiency levels. These negatively affect the degree of learning a language, especially English. Most significant approaches to language teaching leave little room for their individuality, cultural background, and different learning abilities. By leveraging AI, educators can address these challenges, creating personalized, interactive, and effective learning experiences that cater to individual students' requirements (Aybirdi, 2023; Negrila, 2023). AI in education is a revolutionary phenomenon for learning languages and, generally, the English language. English is an important medium of communication and is considered the key to success in academic sessions, professional careers, and intercultural business and commerce. With the help of AI, one can design personal, universal, and progressive learning spaces. New technologies in natural language processing will help distinguish figures of speech and dialects, among other linguistic barriers, to make the growth of language lessons and instructions more contextual. Also, using AI and VR/AR technologies will give students more realistic experiences that will help them speak more fluently, especially when the test requires them to act out real-life situations (Freeman et al., 2009; Zhao & Liu, 2022). This innovation also enhances cross-cultural understanding, a valuable tool in an increasingly interconnected world.

Dedicated and innovative technologies like NLP and deep learning have enriched English language teaching and learning (ELT). These tools give direct feedback so the learners know how to correct their syntactical, grammatical, and pronunciation mistakes. For example, Grammarly and ProWritingAid help students with the coherence and style of writing and relieve teachers of the work of manual evaluation (Schmidt & Strasser, 2022). Similarly, speech recognition tools such as ELSA Speak offer learners instant feedback on pronunciation as they work on their fluency patterns and strike down anxiety as a barrier in oral communication (Rusmiyanto et al., 2023). These kinds of tools help the learners in their tasks and encourage them so they are not left behind, which is important for learners with language barriers. One of AI's most important promises in ELT is personalization capability. Artificial intelligence processes the student information to generate relevant content and exercises based on each student's capabilities. For instance, Duolingo and Babbel personalize lessons according to the learner's fluency, accent, and rate; they ensure the materials are comprehensible. These systems also apply learner rewards and control and create learning challenges to enhance learner interest and compliance (Chen et al., 2021; Solak, 2024).

Artificial intelligence makes it possible to produce individual learning experiences that are fun and efficient for every learner (Aybirdi, 2023; Negrila, 2023). An ITS, Carnegie Learning's MATHia, uses NLP to enable the students to practice conversational grammar and vocabulary. The systems offer specific motivation and rate of accomplishment that offer consistent language proficiency enhancement (Litman, 2016; Negrila, 2023). It is important to note that such adaptive learning technologies help provide unique learning solutions to various students to close the achievement gap and provide equal opportunities for all students to learn meaningfully. In this way, ITS eventually encourages learners to be independent and responsible—fundamental qualities necessary to achieve learning prospects.

New interactive technologies such as VR and AR are helpful in English education in providing a realistic environment and engaging lessons. These tools enable the students to use language in context, for example, when going through a 'virtual airport' or ordering food in a 'mock 'restaurant.'. A nice feature contributing to the acquired language is that such experiences make learning more realistic and playful (Zhao & Liu, 2022; Negrila, 2023). For example, a student rehearsing an organized, professional interview in a virtual reality environment can use language skills practically and, at the same time, become more confident when meeting unexpected situations. Also, conversational applications, including Chatbots like ChatGPT, offer learners opportunities to have real-life conversations (Klayklung et al., 2023). AI chatbots implement elements of game-based learning for students and ensure increased engagement and interest in language learning (Haristiani, 2019). These Chatbots can also meet culturally appropriate responses and thereby help learners get ready for social and professional transactions.

PROMs (Patient-Reported Outcome Measures) have enhanced the effectiveness of educational practice as repetitive procedures are performed by computers while the teachers themselves develop the creativity of pedagogical processes. For example, integrated unit grading systems such as Turnitin and intelligent assessment applications ease the grading system by giving accurate and consistent feedback to the learners. These save the educator time and guarantee that the learners get constructive feedback on time (Guo, 2021a; Solak, 2024). Moreover, through the help of automation, the subjectivity of the grader can be eliminated. It also helps reduce any possibility of bias inherent in artificial assessment practices.

In addition, utilizing AI to support data collection provides educators with recommendations on individual student performance and areas that require additional attention on the part of the educator. These tools help educators shift the focus of classroom teaching and learning to use quantifiable evidence, ultimately improving educational standards (Negrila, 2023). On the same note, insight from data also helps the teachers to plan for remedial lessons, which should not leave anyone behind. Performance measures can keep the teaching process evolving by using the most relevant strategies by educators that are most suitable for students.

Nevertheless, using AI in ELT has several ethical and accessibility issues. Even with the myriad benefits the implementation of AI in ELT possesses, it has unique problems regarding ethical issues and accessibility. The first issue is data protection, as most artificial intelligence applications process and store clients' compliance with learner data with the General Data Protection Regulation (GDPR). It is crucial to protect the learners and build their trust in the applications of AI (Owoc et al., 2019; Zawacki-Richter et al., 2019). Institutions must also develop policies when handling learner data to ensure accountability at all institutional levels.

There is another problem that is directly connected with inequality—the digital divide. Underprivileged students do not own the devices needed for AI-based learning; they cannot afford the Internet even if they have the devices. This challenge calls for infrastructure and policy efforts to match potential users with technology (Lai & Kritsonis, 2006; Klayklung et al., 2023). Steps like offering community-based digital literacy programs will assist in reducing this gap by assisting disadvantaged learners to use AI-effective tools. Furthermore, inexpensive solutions compatible with offline access can be created to address such places.

The advancement in technology through the development of artificial intelligence has played a key role in transforming English language teaching, especially from conventional methods and developing more innovative techniques. As a result, AI should be used to its fullest potential. To do this, educators and policymakers should work together to create rules that will make it possible to use AI's partials effectively. Therefore, there is a clear need for increased support in enhancing teachers, promoting digital literacy, and addressing ethical concerns. Eventually, emphasizing the student perspective—AI can revolutionize English learning to prepare learners for the interconnected world (Goldenberg & Coleman, 2010; Solak, 2024). There is, therefore, the need for teacher professional development in the ability to incorporate AI into the teaching-learning process continuously.

According to this study, using AI in teaching and learning can interest students, boost success, and help teachers support diversity. However, social problems and equal rights must be fixed before AI can reach its full potential. The future development of the theory and application of AI in English education depends on the cooperation among educators, researchers, and policymakers. Therefore, AI has to be integrated, considering some of the best moral practices, equality, and, importantly, student-centered learning.

II. THEORETICAL FOUNDATIONS

Artificial intelligence (AI) is transforming language acquisition through real-time feedback, tailored instruction, and the design of adaptive learning environments. Theories like Vygotsky's Zone of Proximal Development (ZPD), Krashen's Input Hypothesis, Affective Filter Hypothesis, and the Feedback and Interaction Hypotheses provide invaluable insights into how AI aids language learners.

Vygotsky's Zone of Proximal Development (ZPD) centralizes instruction on tasks situated at the learner's next developmental level under the facilitation and guidance of a teacher, fellow learner, or an AI system. Regarding AI in ELL, AI applications like Duolingo and Babbel entail learning environments that constantly push students past their comfort zone so that they are prompted to practice how to develop the next level of their language proficiency, and the system gives feedback immediately to support or correct students' actions. AI can determine the competency level of the specific learner and deliver the content in form and breadth within the ZPD, making the learning process more efficient. AI's algorithms and feedback are flexible and allow the students to work in this zone to enhance their learning by improving language learning efficiency. Duolingo and Babbel, for instance, challenge students with progressively complex tasks, ensuring continual skill development through real-time feedback (Aybirdi, 2023).

AI-powered platforms align with Krashen's theory by providing comprehensible input that is slightly more advanced than the learner's current level (i+1). ITS and NLP-based applications like Grammarly and ELSA Speak offer real-time feedback, reinforcing language structures effectively (Chen et al., 2021; Solak, 2024). Krashen's comprehension hypothesis proposes that the learners gain most of the language proficiently when they get a kind of material slightly beyond their understandability, referred to as "i + 1". ITS and speech recognition tools that are specific to learning enable the learners to be trained with software that produces input that is comprehensible for the learner but simultaneously challenging enough to enable the learner to build the language structures progressively. Thus, through personalization, the input supply demanded by the learner can be regulated, and learners, therefore, experience the appropriate value of file input, which gives language acquisition. Grammarly or ELSA Speak are two applications that use NLP technologies and provide instant correction and, hopefully, a repetition of what the learner should have been learning for a long time.

Krashen's Affective Filter Hypothesis means that affective variables ranging from motivation and anxiety to self-confidence influence language acquisition in a certain way. Specifically, the applications employed to minimize anxiety, including speech recognition applications that supply feedback as soon as a mistake is made, help the learner have a low affective filter, thus enabling him or her to learn the new language. For instance, applications such as ELSA Speak reduce the fear of speaking since the application offers feedback on pronunciation and permits the learners to speak confidently without worrying about being laughed at. This leads to a higher level of learners' self-esteem, and motivation to learn is also boosted. Furthermore, using gamification features in AI applications, like badges and rewards, increases the learners' self-motivation as learning becomes fun to accomplish specified goals, hence reducing the emotional congestion of the learner. AI reduces learning anxiety by creating a supportive, non-judgmental environment. Speech recognition tools such as ELSA Speak help learners practice pronunciation confidently, while gamification elements in AI applications motivate through rewards and challenges (Haristiani, 2019; Rusmiyanto et al., 2023).

The Interaction Hypothesis (Long, 1983) and the Feedback Hypothesis highlight the need for meaningful conversation and corrective feedback in language learning, two concepts AI-powered resources successfully incorporate into English instruction. Real-time feedback on grammar, pronunciation, and fluency is provided by AI-driven programs such as Grammarly, ELSA Speak, and ChatGPT, which enable learners to improve their language proficiency immediately (Klayklung et al., 2023; Schmidt & Strasser, 2022). Through interactive dialogues that mimic real-world conversations, AI Chatbots and virtual tutors help students improve their understanding and communication skills. Learners receive constant feedback and practice because of AI's capacity to identify mistakes, provide tailored corrections, and build immersive interaction settings. This makes learning English more effective, engaging, and tailored to each learner's needs.

III. AI-DRIVEN LEARNING TECHNOLOGIES

Adaptive Learning

Adaptive learning leverages AI to tailor the learning experience to individual student needs, adjusting content based on performance to maintain engagement and optimize learning. Platforms like Duolingo and Babbel apply adaptive algorithms, ensuring learners progress appropriately (Aybirdi, 2023). AI can personalize lectures to keep students engaged and help them learn languages (Krashen, 1982). Students can repair mistakes quickly and retain more with real-time feedback from AI systems (Vygotsky, 1978). Adaptive learning systems can also include students with different proficiency levels (Aybirdi, 2023). Games like points and badges motivate and engage users on these sites (Christian, 2019). These tools allow pupils to set their own learning pace (Negrila, 2023). These adaptable tools assist poor children in reducing achievement gaps and receive personalized guidance (Aybirdi, 2023).

Finally, AI-powered adaptive learning systems are essential for creating personalized, scalable, and efficient language learning environments that adapt lectures to student progress and ensure a proper learning pace. Duolingo and Babbel automatically mix old and new content to keep users interested (Fitria, 2021a). Gamification motivates and reinforces learning (Goldenberg, 2008).

To provide individualized and engaging material, AI systems such as Babbel and Duolingo use adaptive learning algorithms to modify the level of difficulty of lessons according to student performance. With gamified incentives and progressive challenges, these resources assist students in moving at their own speed. However, advanced students looking for more sophisticated language abilities may not have the depth required. Despite this, their capacity for adaptation guarantees ongoing participation and advancement (Aybirdi, 2023; Negrila, 2023).

Duolingo or Babbel

Duolingo and Babbel apps employ complicated algorithms to identify learners' strengths and weaknesses, accents, and pace of learning. Courses are developed to ensure the balance between the known and the unknown, with corresponding levels of comfort for the learners. For example, a learner with specific difficulties in grammar knowledge would perform exercises that strengthen those sections. A learner, on the other hand, would work with advanced syntax and lexis. This adaptability helps learners progress without prescripts but meet incremental goals compatible with their needs (Rusmiyanto et al., 2023).

The adaptation of AI learning content also includes gamification features and innovative tools. Engagement involves breaking learning-related activities into segments commonly associated with game playing, including incentives, tasks, scores, and stages. For example, in Duolingo, the learners earn virtual coins and achievement badges when they finish the lessons or sustain a streak (Fitria, 2021 a). This LMX (Learning Motivation and Experience) concept makes learning different languages by repetitive tasks. Rewards encourage the learner psychologically because acknowledging one's efforts in a specific area is crucial to giving a sense of accomplishment (Goldenberg, 2008).

Interaction is also present in AI-powered platforms. Here, learners may be offered different role-play scenarios to master. For illustration, Babbel has been designed with dialogues that resemble normal life incidences, such as ordering a meal at a restaurant or getting to know directions. These practical language uses enable learners to gain functional language while reinforcing their speaking and comprehension skills (Jiang, 2022).

Gemini

Gemini, made by Google DeepMind, helps people learn English by improving their communication skills and understanding of what is going on around them. It gives real-time input on words, spelling, and speech based on the learner's level of skill. Gemini helps people get better at speaking and become more confident by mimicking real-life situations like job interviews and social talks. Its machine learning techniques let it keep getting better, so each person can get personalized, fun language practice that fits their needs.

Interactive Learning

Google Translate, ELSA Speak, and ChatGPT improve interactive learning by giving instant feedback. ChatGPT facilitates lively discussions that mimic real-world exchanges, while ELSA Speak provides instant voice feedback to enhance pronunciation. Although Google Translate may have trouble with idiomatic or complex sentences, it helps learners with pronunciation checks and rapid translations. By enabling language practice in a positive, engaging setting, these resources help learners feel less anxious and more confident (Haristiani, 2019; Rusmiyanto et al., 2023).

Interactive learning enhances language acquisition by engaging students actively in real-world scenarios. AI tools like AR/VR create immersive environments where learners practice language skills in simulated contexts (Zhao & Liu, 2022). These interactive experiences provide meaningful opportunities for learners to apply their language knowledge in authentic settings, reinforcing vocabulary and grammar (Nicolaidou et al., 2021). NLP-driven Chatbots, such as those found in language learning apps like Duolingo and Babbel, simulate real-time conversations, offering immediate feedback to improve pronunciation and fluency (Annamalai et al., 2023). These tools reduce learner anxiety and increase confidence by providing instant corrections and fostering spontaneous speech production. Gamified elements, such as challenges and rewards, increase engagement, making interactive learning more motivating and enjoyable (Saleem et al., 2020). Interactive learning promotes deeper cognitive processing by actively encouraging students to use language in dynamic, context-rich settings (Zhao & Liu, 2022). The integration of speech recognition technology allows learners to practice speaking with AI feedback, further enhancing verbal communication skills (Rusmiyanto et al., 2023). This hands-on learning approach supports extrinsic and intrinsic motivation, keeping students engaged (Dichev & Dicheva, 2017). Overall, interactive learning via AI tools facilitates language practice in ways that traditional methods cannot, offering more personalized and compelling learning experiences.

Gamified Learning

Gamification is one of the effective paradigms in the process of learners' engagement that emerged from the field of game design. The idea behind this stems from the effort to make learning fun and engaging; thus, students are motivated to learn more. Through these game mechanics, students' extrinsic motivation is ratcheted up, while at the same time, their intrinsic motivation is also being furthered through engaging more actively with learning content. Gamification has held promise in promoting continuous participation, task completion, and problem determination predominantly when the student can see the elaboration of their success in real-time (Llorens-Largo et al., 2016; Dichev & Dicheva, 2017). Gamification also encourages critical thinking, collaboration, and time management skills as students struggle to navigate tasks and challenges to develop these competencies (Landers, 2015; Saleem et al., 2020).

With these mechanics, gamified learning creates a dynamic atmosphere where students are likelier to stick to the process, finish work, and overcome efforts for rewards. Such an approach enhances the learning process, making it more enjoyable and challenging (Dichev & Dicheva, 2017).

Augmented Reality (AR) and Virtual Reality (VR)

Augmented Reality overlaps digital components onto the existing real-world environment in which the user situates himself or herself in images, audio, or text. AR/VR enhances language immersion, providing contextualized learning experiences. Nicolaidou et al. (2021) and Zhao & Liu (2022) say that simulations like virtual business talks and buying food in a restaurant help people become more fluent and improve their confidence. It lets people interact with digital content, making learning more enjoyable. AR is commonly used through devices such as smartphones, tablets, or AR glasses, and these systems position virtual objects in the real environment. More specifically, the objects interact with the viewers via an augmented view. AR can benefit education, particularly when students are given interactive possibilities to influence virtual environments related to real objects. Students can picture past events or geographical features in their classroom or look at scientific models as if they did not have their tools. Mixing the real and the virtual makes learning more engaging and active (Azuma et al., 2001).

Virtual Reality (VR) goes even further in creating an environment by replacing the actual environment with a computer-generated three-dimensional environment. The users use VR headsets in which they are confined in a box, and through their interaction with objects or environments of their choice, it feels like they are in a real environment. Because VR exposes the learner to educational content that was not possible before, the students can go on historical tours, tour other planets, or even handle restricted experiments or projects all within the VR environment. Compared with AR, which starts from the real world constructing it, VR tends to construct a new one in which the learner is fully involved. This is particularly handy in situations involving a lot of interaction or learning by doing, as in medical students, architects, or language learning (Rojas et al., 2023).

The skills of AR and VR can be grouped into knowledge competencies, technical abilities, and cognitive competencies. In supporting acknowledgeable learning outcomes, virtual environments improve cognitive skills like spatial orientation and problem-solving abilities. Furthermore, these technologies foster constructional creativity in designing aspects that entail designing a virtual architecture or a simulation. AR and VR improve learners' engagement and encourage technical and cognitive competency skills (Li & Wong, 2021).

AI Chatbots

AI Chatbots are interactive selling tools embedded with NLP and machine learning. These tools mimic human interpersonal communication. They proactively respond to input from users and independently support all learning situations. Using Chatbots helps to avoid pausing learners which could occur in practice with peers or instructors, creating comfort in a self-learning environment. To that capacity, their zeal for assimilating more gamification elements strengthens enthusiasm. Also, such intelligent Chatbots bring in cost-efficient and bespoke learning solutions that are flexible to students' skills and learning capabilities for the best learning solutions (Haristiani, 2019; Annamalai et al., 2023). NLP-driven Chatbots simulate real-world conversations, offering instant feedback and promoting communication proficiency (Annamalai et al., 2023).

ChatGPT

OpenAI made ChatGPT, an advanced AI language model that can be used as an engaging robot to talk with students in real-time. It uses natural language processing (NLP) to make meaningful contact easier and allow language trainees to use their skills in a real-life social setting. In addition to providing easy answers, ChatGPT can understand the situation and provide personalized comments. This makes it a valuable tool for improving reading speed, understanding, and language because it lets students study complicated topics, ask questions, and get personalized replies. ChatGPT in ELL systems keeps students more interested by modeling honest conversations and letting them talk in various situations, from relaxed chats to more serious discussions.

Google Translate

Apart from helping to learn one learner at a time, the AI system has a critical function of promoting diversity. Microsoft, for instance, has an Immersive Reader that incorporates artificial intelligence to support learners with language difficulties due to their linguistic or socioeconomic backgrounds. Specifically, text-to-speech, translation, and simple text can help disabled people or people who only received elementary education to read English articles (Zawacki-Richter et al., 2019). Learning resources are available throughout the population; hence, the democratization of English language education gets to everyone regardless of social standing (Goldenberg & Coleman, 2010).

Google Translate is a popular tool that helps people translate text, documents, and websites from over a hundred languages. As a translation tool, this tool has proven most helpful in enhancing reading and writing skills through translated real-time word meanings, grammar structures, and sentence patterns in the learning language among learners (Afiliani et al., 2024). The feature in Google Translate is called neural machine translation – (NMT), which improves automatically through machine learning. It is highly beneficial for students studying a foreign language as it aims at language development and communication since translations are provided instantly (Medvedev, 2016). Also, it helps to work with pronunciation with the synthesized voice.

Turnitin

By identifying plagiarism and encouraging original work, Turnitin is a potent artificial intelligence program that is often used in academic contexts to maintain academic integrity. Turnitin is essential for teaching students about appropriate citation styles and the value of originality in writing while learning English as a second language (Gaoat et al., 2023). The application looks for similarities and possible cases of plagiarism by comparing submitted papers to a vast database of scholarly sources, publications, and earlier submissions. Turnitin helps students improve their language abilities by offering real-time comments on grammar, structure, writing style, and plagiarism detection. In addition to improving language skills, this criticism teaches students how to write better academically using more precise sentences, more coherent writing, and accurate citations.

ELSA Speak

The usual learning session is no longer a generic one, as it considers different language abilities, competency levels, and grasping powers. For instance, a concept such as pronunciation, likely to present many difficulties to a beginning-level language learner, can be supplemented by the following speech recognition instruments implemented into such platforms. One of the remarkable features is that such applications as ELSA Speak indicate inevitable mistakes concerning pronunciation, and they also show where precisely a student went wrong and how to pronounce the word correctly (Haristiani, 2019). This makes it possible for each learner to be supported when s/he has a challenge, thus helping her/him to overcome it (Nghi et al., 2019). The proposed mobile application is designed with exercises that focus on the distinct sounds of the vowels and consonants, intonation, stress on a word, syllable, and overall fluency (Fitria, 2021b; Rinaepi et al., 2022). This gives the learner immediate feedback on their errors and makes it easier for them to learn features of correct pronunciation.

ELSA Speak individualizes the exercise process by setting the difficulty level depending on the learner's achievements. With the top-up feature, the application guarantees that no learner will fall behind his/her peers during the application's usage, regardless of his/her level when he/she initially started learning the language.

Personalized Learning

Claude, ProWritingAid, and Grammarly all offer personalized learning methods with targeted comments. Grammarly and ProWritingAid focus on improving writing by giving real-time, context-based advice on language and style. To get better at speaking, Claude uses verbal feedback that is adapted to his needs. Grammarly and ProWritingAid are great for improving written language, but Claude is very good at speaking. Thus, they are appropriate for various parts of language learning (Fitria, 2021 b; Perdana et al., 2021). Personalized learning leverages AI to provide individualized educational experiences, tailoring content and feedback to meet the specific needs of each learner. AI tools such as Grammarly and ELSA Speak use Natural Language Processing (NLP) to offer real-time, personalized feedback on grammar, pronunciation, and writing style (Haristiani, 2019). These systems evaluate students' development and modify courses of instruction to guarantee that they get materials at a suitable degree of complexity (Negrila, 2023). Personalized learning encourages learner autonomy by customizing the learning process, enabling pupils to concentrate on areas where they most require development (Vygotsky, 1978). Adaptive algorithms in platforms like Duolingo and Babbel modify lesson difficulty based on individual performance, ensuring a balanced progression (Aybirdi, 2023). AI tools offer continuous assessment and provide immediate, actionable feedback, reinforcing learning and improving language skills (Chen et al., 2021). Personalized learning paths let students advance quickly, boosting their confidence (Aybirdi, 2023). This strategy helps students overcome their particular difficulties—related to grammar, vocabulary, or speaking fluency (Krashen, 1982). Encouragement of self-regulation and intrinsic motivation via personalized learning helps promote long-term involvement with language teaching (Rusmiyanto et al., 2023). Personalized learning by artificial intelligence provides customized educational support for different learners, enhancing motivation and linguistic competency.

ϖ Claude

Anthropic made a model called Claude, a talking AI that uses advanced machine learning methods to mimic how people naturally talk to each other. The best thing about Claude is that it was made with safety and user purpose in mind, which makes it a trusted tool for ELL situations where upholding moral standards is very important. This AI can talk logically, even about complicated topics. This makes it a great partner for language learners who want to improve their speaking. Claude is great at answering students' language, speech, and context questions. It gives trainees immediate, personalized feedback that helps them improve their language skills in various settings. Claude can also look at speech patterns and suggest ways to improve grammar and consistency, which helps English learners improve their writing and speaking. Because it focuses on user-driven learning, it works well in personalized learning settings and gives students feedback about their level and needs.

ProWritingAid

The cutting-edge AI-powered writing assistant ProWritingAid gives students detailed comments on their language, style, punctuation, and sentence structure to help them get better at writing. It will help students if they want to make their English writing more consistent and clear. ProWritingAid provides in-depth analysis, detecting repetitions, odd wording, and style problems that impede clear communication, in contrast to simple grammar checkers. The tool may be used for several writing assignments, such as creative writing, professional communication, and academic essays. Because its feedback is divided into particular recommendations, students may concentrate on areas that need work, including argumentation clarity or verb tense consistency. ProWritingAid is useful in ELL settings because it gives students the tools they need to become more self-reliant and confident writers by offering thorough explanations and practical recommendations.

Grammarly

Grammarly is a strong and highly developed language solution that helps users in many aspects of writing – grammar, spelling, punctuation, syntax, and style. It uses modern NLP and Machine Learning to explore and analyze the text and offers instant feedback on possible writing mistakes. Grammarly also incorporates context in that its mission as a language improvement tool is to assist users in making corrections whose details are provided based on the context in which the user is writing. This application can also be adapted for academic, professional, and personal writing abilities. While the errors relating to grammar are corrected and suggestions are made to improve the writing flow, using Grammarly improves users' language abilities over time (Fitria, 2021 b). As such, Grammarly offers real-time correction and helps develop a student's lasting positive habits regarding their writing. This is because the particular application offers an instant correction of written text, vitamins, and minerals on grammar, spelling issues, and punctuation as the user continues to write.

Bard

Bard, an AI program made by Google, has changed how people communicate. This program focuses on writing like a person using user input. Using this live language model, one can have real-time chats with students. Bard has many detailed context-based interactions that improve both language use and understanding. Its advanced NLP skills ensure that students get correct feedback and valuable explanations.

It stands out because it works so well with Google's other tools. This makes it easy for students to use a variety of devices. Bard ensures that each student's learning experience fits their needs by giving them personalized suggestions based on their progress and problems. Bard creates a space where language learners can try out new words and get instant feedback on their mistakes, whether it is through engaging stories, grammar tasks, or word lists.

■ Intelligent Tutoring System (ITS) and Natural Language Processing (NLP)

ITS (Intelligent Tutoring System) offers personalized, hands-on assistance, which is the best feature of tutor services. Like Carnegie Learning's MATHia, this system uses features such as natural language processing NLP (Natural Language Processing) to practice conversational grammar and pronunciation. For English learners, ITS provides a comfortable space for students to perform and be corrected regarding phrase/idiom/sentence/verb usage, etc., and stores and employs data on time to provide progress results, frequency of errors, and corresponding exercises. NLP and ITS have been applied in language learning, focusing on English as a Second Language (ESL) and changing how learners interact with the language.

NLP can be described as a set of computational tools that can help to process, analyze, and even generate comprehension of natural language. NLP lets artificial intelligence produce and examine human language. Grammarly and other tools in language education employ NLP to evaluate sentence structure, grammar, and syntax, providing real-time comments to enable students to write better. NLP allows artificial intelligence to provide context-aware, customized suggestions, enhancing understanding of language standards. This technology helps students by making language learning more dynamic and suited to their unique needs by providing targeted rapid feedback. Cambria and White (2014) describe that NLP has moved forward from the initial computational approach that might take a few minutes to analyze a simple sentence to the existing systems, such as Google, that analyze millions of pages within some seconds. This change in computing capacity has made NLP an adequate support system in educationally relevant ITS for language learning. As Meera and Geerthik (2022) explain, NLP involves two main components: NLU (Natural Language Understanding) and NLG (Natural Language Generation). NLU deals with the conversion of understanding input text or speech. On the other hand, NLG's takeover of this understanding puts down comprehensible and contextual responses.

Revell and Norman (1997) note that NLP's three referential models, visual, auditory, and kinaesthetic (VAK), are the key to establishing learners' perceptions. This understanding enables educators to modify teaching practices so that the lessons on language find a warm place in the hearts of the learners. For example, at the end of the lesson, one learner may have to write what he or she has learned in graphical form, while another learner may have to recreate what the teacher said in a poetic form.

ITS helps to deliver personalized learning using NLP. Marouf et al. (2024) reveal that ITS systems employ NLP for conversational grammar and pronunciation correction, allowing learners to receive immediate feedback. Celaj and Jani (2023) noted that ITS tools such as Carnegie Learning MATHia are based on natural language processing where student and teacher dialogues are provided on conversational linguistics and accent corrections. Such systems develop an environment for interaction with English learners, in which it is possible to correct syntax and usage of phrases immediately. This instruction system applies to English learners since they experience many difficulties in learning grammar, idioms, and pronunciation. ITS platforms such as Carnegie Learning's MATHia let learners do exercises more suited to their needs, allowing them to practice in small, incremental steps until fluency and error-free mastery are achieved.

As Druckman (1988) pointed out, NLP in education focuses on behavioral and speech patterns to develop teaching solutions that match learners' learning styles. All these make using this data-driven approach noble in facilitating learners' ability to process and store linguistic information. What is more important, in an ITS environment, is that the feedback is not only instant but also targeted at the set knowledge deficiency. For instance, an ITS may recognize that the learner has consistently made mistakes in using verb tenses and feed him/her exercises in this area.

IV. ADVANTAGES OF INTEGRATING AI INTO ENGLISH COURSES

Interpersonal Communication Skills and Critical Thinking

Duolingo applies gamification in language education which produces an interactive learning environment. The platform includes every language learning element spanning vocabulary through grammar and presents materials in personalized short lessons. The combination of artificial intelligence (AI) allows Duolingo to automatically change lesson difficulty according to individual learner advancement, thus maintaining continuous challenging exposure that avoids learner anxiety (Essafi et al., 2024). The system offers quick feedback tools that help users consolidate their correct language usage and enhance their understanding abilities (Vijayakumar & Chellapandiyan, 2024).

In 2002, Adler mentioned that NLP is valuable in framing interpersonal communication, particularly education lessons. It also applies mirroring and perceptual positioning relating to critical thinking and negotiation among students as tactics of NLP. Regarding the instructional television system (ITS), these techniques can be incorporated into conversational activities realized through learners' discussions with partners. For example, an ITS might provide a business situation where a learner has to sign a deal or practice conflict-solving in a social situation. Since the NLP-based systems try to mimic real-life conversations, they enable learners to practice communication skills while the environment is somewhat confined but still very lively.

The use of NLP also helps structure interactions and develops critical thinking skills. ITS systems help learners negotiate meaning through analysis and correction of students' responses, which helps them learn various aspects of language, including more productive ways of expressing themselves, additional syntactic patterns, and other language choices. Moreover, NLP can be employed to monitor oral reading by analyzing regularities in pronunciation and speaking rate. The locating feature of Crimson offers learners real-time feedback and builds the learners' confidence in spoken English skills (Kara et al., 2023).

Google Translate is a tool that provides translation on the fly so students can receive feedback as they translate. It helps learners get error correction feedback as soon as possible and facilitates their employing corrections at the initial stage of the interaction (Medvedev, 2016). Furthermore, receiving all this information right away is beneficial for reviewing recently studied vocabulary and improving language acquisition.

One of the other advantages of employing AI in language learning platforms is that progress can be tracked. Since AI tracks a learner's performance over time, it is much easier to quickly look for frequent mistakes or, in general, areas of apparent weakness in a learner. Thus, the learner can concentrate on certain features of the language learning process, such as grammar, lexis, or phonetics (Chamot & O'Malley, 1994). In addition, it assists educators or tutors in offering timely interventions so that the mistakes that have deteriorated the learner's ability will be tracked and tackled (Mehrotra, 2019).

When applied, the game–like factors also serve to foster healthy competition among the learners and improve the levels of participation. For example, while using the platforms, it is common to find options like the leaderboard where they can see users' progress. One advantage of competition is that it challenges learners to spur them on and transform learning languages into a fun activity in which they interact. It is also important to note that such gamified features add more variety to the learning process, especially where learners may find conventional learning uninteresting (August et al., 2005).

However, the revolutionizing role of AI in English language learning is not only about gamification or personalization. It provides more approaches to establishing and reinforcing meaningful skills. The ability to practice new language knowledge is one of the benefits of working with such tools. Artificial intelligence features, for instance, include virtual and augmented reality, which are integrated into some of the existing AI-driven learning platforms. These tools mimic real-life situations so learners can practice English in real-life settings. For instance, a VR environment can immerse a learner in a fake airport whereby the learner has to move around different signs and ask or answer questions from imaginary airport staff, all in English (Zhao & Liu, 2022). These simulations allow learners to play with language as a communication tool with no sanctions or penalties, and that is where learning happens (Freeman et al., 2009).

AI conversational applications further strengthen learning by doing since their functions include Chatbots and virtual assistants. These tools allow learners to perform real talk—like actual conversations with people—albeit in simulated forms. Mimicry of different conversational situations is possible with the help of Chatbots such as ChatGPT, which will help learners hone their speaking or listening skills. The skills of spontaneous live discussions are not only valuable for free-flowing but also for sharpening reflection and decision-making skills. Such assisted conversations initiated through AI help learners handle contextualized DTM (Dynamic Topic Management) that prompts natural responses, which is highly important in the mastery of language (Woo & Choi, 2021).

Immediate Feedback

The first unique and perhaps the most appealing feature of Grammarly is that it delivers suggestions instantly. This is useful to students to solve problems and correct mistakes. The immediate feedback will enhance participants' interaction with the writing process, increasing their attentiveness towards the process (Fitria, 2021 b). The immediate response provides more natural and easy-to-understand feedback since the users can easily incorporate it into their writing. This not only enhances the quality of the written work but also enhances the ability of its users to scrutinize mistakes in the articles and write desired corrections.

AR and VR, in addition to letting the student know the moment they make a mistake, provide instant feedback. These technologies present an alternative approach to providing feedback that is more engaging and elaborate; at times, they provide an immediate chance for redoing the attempt. This is particularly relevant in learning languages; a VR application to learn vocabulary and grammar may involve interactions with digital characters and the avatars immediately providing feedback on whether the right intonation is used in pronunciation or the proper words are chosen in a sentence. This is because receiving feedback within the class enhances students' confidence since the feedback is quick, allowing them to comprehend the content quickly (Zhang et al., 2020). Google Translate also offers feedback on any translated content within an extremely short time. This helps students quickly shift from one mode of learning to the next learning activity (Afiliani et al., 2024).

One of the core advantages of gamified learning systems is immediate and quick feedback on the student's performance. This instantaneous information allows learners to modify their strategies, thereby not forming bad habits (Dichev & Dicheva, 2017; Saleem et al., 2020). It allows students to tackle their obstacles or receive solutions or hints on how to pass through obstacles and empowers them to move forward at their speeds without falling off or becoming demotivated. The benefit of such immediate interventions is that students will stay engaged and avoid frustration immediately.

This immediacy ensures a real learning experience and feedback that students feel involved in. By matching learning goals with real-time evaluations, students are inspired to refine and improve their skills to achieve better academic outcomes (Landers, 2015). This constancy added great value to the ELSA Speak application, which mainly operates on providing instant feedback. Learners get feedback on how to pronounce a word the moment they are done uttering it. This constant feedback helps learners adjust as soon as possible and also teaches correct pronunciation patterns (Fitria, 2021 a; Rinaepi et al., 2022). It is important for enhancing the learner's pronunciation and grammar accuracy.

Culturally Responsive Teaching with AI

Chatbots and virtual assistants are examples of AI systems that may modify course materials to accommodate linguistic and cultural diversity, improving students' comprehension of language in context. Students may practice their English in various cultural contexts using platforms such as ELSA Speak, which mimics real-world situations. AI prepares students for successful cross-cultural interactions by integrating different accents, dialects, and cultural settings, which enhances language competency and intercultural communication.

Self-paced Learning

One of the most significant benefits of gamified learning is its aptitude for personalization, as systems can change for the learner's specific needs. The gamified system collects performance data to ensure that it will provide tailored challenges, rewards, and feedback to every student's learning pace and style (Landers, 2015; Saleem et al., 2020). Personalized learning means each student is constantly working with tasks that are not too easy or too difficult, providing an optimal amount of challenge for learning. Thus, it can frame personal learning goals and help keep learning more enjoyable and relevant (Subhash & Cudney, 2018). Gamification for personalized learning improves academic performance while promoting autonomy and control over the learning process. The content thus adapts to each student's level of competence, which helps maintain motivation and foster learners' ownership of their educational journey (Llorens-Largo et al., 2016).

Marouf et al. (2024) pointed out that ITS systems can provide even more elaborate details of the learners' behavior and, as a result, create the best learning environment. These systems use natural language processing to deliver the modeled educational solutions more flexibly and focus on the student. The enhanced real-time feedback, learning experience, and individualized tasks ensure that the learner achieves at his/her own pace while being given special attention in his/her most challenging areas.

AR and VR technologies support individual differences since lessons can be created according to a student's ability level. In referential VR, the learner may move through a particular learning task independently, and the difficulty level of the disasters portrayed may rise in tandem with his or her accomplishment. Likewise, AR can offer students practice problems that adapt to the kind of performance that they deliver. This approach also increases relevance to each student and, thus, interaction or success rates (Radu & Schneider, 2022).

There is virtually no limit to what Grammarly can do since it is designed to take into consideration all the basics of the writing personality of the user besides identifying the area that needs to be corrected based on the kind of writing being done. Regarding the content, feedback is as individual as possible to suggest improvements that will be understandable to the user. Paid options enable users to extend the customization of the tool and set parameters according to their writing needs (Perdana et al., 2021). This means that users get relevant information concerning their mistakes, and it helps them recognize their shortcomings better and get honest advice on how to improve. It can provide learners with advice on various characteristics of writing contexts while providing them with practical advice.

Google Translate lets users select particular materials or phrases to translate instead of learning something new. This feature enables the adaptation to particular student requirements since it is possible to teach everything from academic usage to particular terms or idioms (Afiliani et al., 2024). This flexibility enables learners' requirements to be met, which may be particularly useful to learners with prior learning at higher levels interested in broadening their vocabulary. Google Translate shows that with the help of AI, it is possible to deliver a much more individualized educational experience that aligns with the overall tendency of individualization of the language learning process.

ELSA enables learners to focus on areas such as word stress or intonation, where they may be unlikely to excel. This customization makes it easier to sustain development and maintain the learners' engagement in a particular course (Fitria, 2021a; Rismawati et al., 2021). This adaptive system is suitable for learners' progress and helps them feel accomplished as they witness their own goals being accomplished. It indicates the precise learning paths of the users to AI Chatbots through performance analysis. This customization related to individual requirements allows students to work through course content at their own pace and remain interested. Besides, since the resources are identified through data collection, the assessment is done credibly to meet the learner's needs. Such approaches foster learner autonomy and thus raise pass rates and levels of skills acquisition among learners (Zhang, 2025).

ϖ Accessibility and Inclusivity

Learners stand to benefit from AI implementation since the technology makes education resources readily available to them. That is, the object of concern over technological interaction can also be exemplified by sites like Khan Academy and Microsoft's Immersive Reader, which provide multilingual support and involve means to enhance access to content for learners of various citizenship backgrounds. AI translation tools enhance access because target audiences who are not fluent in English can read the material in their native language as the tools overcome language barriers. For the needs of investigation, it has been established that implementing ITS in English courses positively affects the availability of people with disabilities. Tools like Khan Academy and Microsoft's Immersive Reader provide students with socioeconomic issues with resources. All these tools offer multi-language capability and, as such, make content easily accessible to learners who may not understand the

English language. AI translation goes a step further by making translation services in a way that individuals use the material in their vernacular language while leveling up their English little by little (Zawacki-Richter et al., 2019).

ITS systems meet the needs of learners with disabilities through accessibility tools such as text-to-speech, speech-to-text, and simple text settings. These innovations must make learning education-friendly for everybody, offering a leveling ground to anybody working on mastering another language. For example, Microsoft's Immersive Reader helps dyslexic learners improve their literacy levels by providing them with reading tools that make learning more inclusive (Goldenberg & Coleman, 2010).

AR and VR technologies introduce greater social participation, notwithstanding pre-existing learning challenges. These technologies can meet the needs of learners with different disabilities, providing other modes of learning and teaching. For example, through VR, sounds can be introduced for the benefit of students with vision impairment whilst through AR, extra information on graphics can be produced for students with learning disabilities. By eliminating these barriers, AR and VR provide equal conditions for students with physical and/or cognitive disabilities to learn and succeed (Nicolaidou et al., 2021).

Grammarly provides text-to-speech features, readability, and simple interfaces to make it easy for people with some disorder or with low vision, like blindness or dyslexia, to use the tool. Grammarly is especially effective when compared to other writing assistance tools for users with different requirements since it eradicates the exclusion from effective writing (Fitria, 2021 b). The given aspects allow confidently asserting that all customers who need to enhance their writing skills can do it using the tool without regard to their background or learning disabilities. This accessibility guarantees that users use Grammarly as an educational aid of choice for various learners.

Gamified learning platforms are purposely and intentionally designed with all capacities and needs of students in mind. For instance, they offer visitors visual or hearing-impaired options, including text-to-speech functionality or providing videos with captions (Dichev & Dicheva, 2017; Llorens-Largo et al., 2016). The aforementioned includes not just physical disabilities but also students' language and cultural backgrounds. Gamified systems are equally amenable to students from all spectrums. Thus, all educated learners, regardless of their private circumstances, will be able to prosper and be associated with the demonstration process (Saleem et al., 2020).Particularly in inclusive classrooms, the ability to make content fit different learner needs is helpful. Gamified systems ensure that every student has the same access to learning materials and experiences to avoid students being left behind because of disability, language, or socioeconomic status (Subhash & Cudney, 2018).

As a tool specifically aimed at practicing the actual use of the language, ELSA Speak is friendly to a wide audience of learners, especially those learning English as a Foreign Language (Alshehri, 2024). Learners from all classes can practice at any time, given that the provider's platform is based on mobiles. The app also meets the needs of learners with different needs, including those who need exercises to improve specific pronunciation problems, including accents (Fitria, 2021a; Rinaepi et al., 2022). This inclusiveness helps ensure that learners from every state or territory and every origin can get the best study resource possible to extend the opportunity to learn English.

Chatbots provide convenience because they do not require physical interaction; thus, customer care is quickly provided to students in remote regions or physically challenged students. Compatibility with other portable devices enables it to go viral and be more friendly to anyone. This removal of logistic barriers guarantees that no learner is locked out of the learning process due to logistics. Also, Chatbots can work in multiple languages as they serve as resources to the broader population and also from the diverse population (Haristiani, 2019; Annamalai et al., 2023).

The benefits of Google Translate include that it is available on multiple devices and, more to the point, is free for usage, which could enthuse many users irrespective of their geographical location (Afiliani et al., 2024). It thus makes provision that learning language support is made available for students from rural or disadvantaged backgrounds to education in their regions, thereby improving equality in learning. This is in line with the theme of using Artificial Intelligence in education, where technology has become the weapon of change to make education easily accessible to any student, improving on the already existing language learning applications.

Pedagogical Implications of AI in Language Learning

Artificial intelligence (AI) tools like Duolingo, Babbel, and ELSA Speak improve language acquisition by personalizing and gamifying the process. These resources encourage learners to keep practicing by providing them with challenges, medals, and prizes. AI also helps students achieve independence and confidence in their language learning by setting goals, focusing on problem areas, and letting them progress independently.

Flexibility

AR and VR have the most excellent flexibility in delivering education to learners. Unlike traditional classroom environments, these technologies enable learners to come into contact with the information in their timetables and schedules, enabling a setting that is not physically classroom-restricted. For example, lessons or virtual simulations for learners do not necessarily have to be done at a particular time or in their classroom; they can be done anywhere. In this regard, flexibility is significantly impacted since learners who require more time to understand specific lessons or study from home benefit highly from it (Akcayir & Akcayir, 2017).

The advantage of using Grammarly is that it is compatible with web browsers, office utilities, and mobile platforms so that users can apply it at work and in writing. In return, customers can access its services regardless of whether they are composing emails, academic papers, or personal content (Perdana et al., 2021). Thus, Grammarly works on different devices, helps maintain writing practice consistently, and increases user attainment. This kind of flexibility also aids in revising writing proficiency since students do not have a chance to be away from writing help for long.

Gamified learning systems are very flexible and let the students learn at their own pace and by schedule. Such engagement transfer is possible, whether in an online or in-person classroom setting, when students can do it when the material is most convenient (Saleem et al., 2020). This is especially true for the other category of students, who set a definite schedule for their studies and cannot meet it due to other tasks. In addition, while being based on gaming mechanics, the system guarantees that learners can revisit materials and re-study at any given time. Gamified learning offers the convenience and flexibility that cater to a host of learners, leaving them to navigate between educational aims and other priorities in life. This encourages students to learn their skills lifelong, in other words, not in a traditional school setting (Dichev & Dicheva, 2017).

ELSA Speak enables learners to exercise the required skills at their own time and schedule, either at home or in transit. Such flexibility enhances autonomy in learning, which means that a learner can progress at his/her own pace as long as the course demands are met (Rinaepi et al., 2022). This characteristic is beneficial since it guarantees that practice may be applied to learners' daily schedules in language learning, which is a lifelong obligation. This multidimensional learning approach leads to a higher total amount of user activity since practice sessions easily fit into the daily routine.

Google Translate is easier to use since it is accessible from different gadgets such as smartphones, desktop computers, and tablets. This way, the students can use it anywhere in case of difficulty (Medvedev, 2016). This flexibility enables students to incorporate language practice into their daily schedule, making their learning consistent. While flexibility is now tightly connected with the learning process, Google Translate shows how convenient and easily integrated different AI tools might be in the existing educational experience.

Chatbots are convenient for learners because they can integrate this approach into their schedule and personal abilities to choose the convenient material for the learning process. This flexibility makes incorporating the educational process into people's everyday experiences easier. Flexible learning also fosters continuing education, whereby one can continue doing the course repeatedly and making corrections without affecting the business. This convenience makes these tools more accessible to users, especially professionals and students with limited time (Annamalai et al., 2023).

Closing the Achievement Gap

Educational studies show growing recognition that AI may help reduce the achievement gap. By offering individualized learning experiences, AI technologies may provide education specific to each student's learning requirements. AI may provide a convenient substitute for conventional educational materials in rural or impoverished locations. Tahiru (2021) stresses the need for artificial intelligence and how tailored AI solutions may satisfy the several needs of pupils, particularly in underdeveloped areas. Platforms incorporating artificial intelligence, including Khan Academy and Duolingo, offer customized content distribution and change courses depending on student ability levels. Students who struggle might benefit from this flexibility by receiving extra practice or more challenging material as required. Singh et al. (2024) also emphasize how AI may improve multilingual education, especially for students from linguistically under-represented backgrounds. By guaranteeing that students of all abilities and backgrounds get the assistance required for academic success, these technologies help to close achievement disparities.

Enhancing Educator Efficiency

AR and VR make the work of educators more effective as they give educators tools to create lessons with more interactivity. In this case, teachers can use models and create conditions that are difficult to explain scientifically and historically. These immersive technologies also allow a closer view of students' performances and classify where they require help and how help will be provided. In addition, the delivery styles can be changed through the integration of AR and VR, and all learners' needs can be met (Dede et al., 2017).

AI writing tools, such as Grammarly and Turnitin, allow educators to assess the quality of the work without investing much time but at the same time focus on the actual interactions with the students. Additionally, the AI platforms come with insights into the exemplary performance of the students, areas that require help, and ways of helping the learners. Learners prefer it, and it makes educators incredibly efficient. ITS has extended the meaningful student-educator interface through grading, lesson preparation, and performance assessment, among other things. Tools like

ProWritingAid and Turnitin help educators offer feedback punctually and spend the most quality time on their job's innovative and analytical aspects (Chen et al., 2021).

In addition, students' performance analysis is possible due to data collected by ITS platforms that are available to educators. They contribute to the identification of learning gaps where learners have challenges and inform the design of the intervention. For instance, an analysis of the samples given by learners can explain why many of them make regular mistakes in specific areas, such as grammar usage and specific vocabulary. In this manner, ITS can provide educators with more profound insight into the process and how it can be optimized to offer a better teaching experience for all learners (Negrila, 2023).

To educators, Grammarly is beneficial in offering immediate and, therefore, targeted feedback to their chosen students. They included that teachers could track mistakes and, from there, be in a better position to award feedback that is a lot more tailored and specific to the student authors (Bailey & Lee, 2020). As such, Grammarly aids the educator in the process to ensure that with the bit of time spent on giving feedback, the teacher can help encourage more complex aspects of writing. This way, educators can focus their work on correcting apparent errors and enhancing the performance of students.

Gamified learning systems enable educators to improve teaching efficacy by automating aspects of feedback and assessment to spend time on higher-order and deeper understanding. Further, better student outcomes are possible with data-driven insights, making personalization easier (Llorens-Largo et al., 2016). Learning becomes gamified, empowering educators to follow student progress and adjust lessons according to that data. Saleem et al., (2020) and Subhash and Cudney (2018) state that educators can quickly identify areas where students are struggling and accordingly give additional support or change the learning materials. Its capability for real-time intervention helps teachers serve all the diverse needs of the students, and no one falls behind.

For educators, ELSA Speak is a valuable supplement to classroom practice or instruction because it provides immediate feedback on the most common pronunciation fallacies. This helps teachers attend to a more intricate level of language instruction while, at the same time, students get prompt FB with accentuation on their pronunciation as needed (Rinaepi et al., 2022).

Google Translate is a valuable tool for teachers to estimate the student's work quickly and provide feedback immediately by increasing teaching effectiveness (Afiliani et al., 2024). It also shortens the amount of translation, which experts have to do manually, giving them more time to teach the upper-level aspects of language translation. With this tool, educators can work better to address educational transformation through the use of tools that enhance teaching activities and, at the same time, ensure the improvement of teaching-learning processes in classrooms.

As the chatbot can answer many questions and perform routine actions, educators cannot be involved in extraneous affairs, which also contribute to the class's productivity. This is because educators and Chatbots make the best use of resources, benefiting educators and learners. Chatbots also provide teachers with analysis and teaching methodologies that meet all learners' needs and allow them to successfully produce the proper corrections (Haristiani, 2019; Zhang, 2025).

Bridging Cultural Gaps

AI also allows learners to work with content that fits into their cultural calibration within accents, dialects, and contexts. For instance, the NLP for Chatbots will enable learners to engage in natural and realistic conversations with the bots, thus providing different contexts ranging from casual interactions to business ones. Furthermore, the use of AI in lesson plans includes culture in lessons as well as ease of integrating and improving the cultural values and language of English-speaking culture. For example, NLP-based Chatbots enable learners to perform realistic dialogues that address a range of cultural situations, including social, business, and travelling. Besides, this approach enhances the quality of language and students' cultural sensitivity and understanding (Zhao & Liu, 2022).

In addition, ITS tools enable cross-cultural communication through virtual learning platforms. AI-backed virtual exchange programs mean learners from different geographical and cultural settings can work and/or communicate with others. These programs are designed to play out real-life-like situations, and in the process, the learners master different formal languages and figure out different cultures. They enable learners to engage in intercultural communication in their lives and careers (Haristiani, 2019). Another benefit of the given form is that it provides an opportunity for interacting with cultures and understanding languages and traditions. For instance, where conventional learning might have provided students with an understanding of the culture of a foreign country through maps and models, VR education lets students physically explore the foreign land. Besides, this kind of engagement contributes to language development and raises awareness of people's differences around the globe and intercultural competence (Radu& Schneider, 2022).

Grammarly enables the reduction of cultural differences because it provides tips that are standardized and unbiased, especially for people who do not write English as their first language. It can help learners from different linguistic backgrounds to structure their thoughts in English and, thereby, enhance their communication (intercultural) skills (Fitria, 2021 b). Therefore, by creating a more equal environment, Grammarly helps customers from different cultures conquer language differences. By providing a tool that can fit into several contexts, Grammarly can enhance its usability, irrespective of the culture an individual is from or their first language.

Both Duolingo and Babbel support students in grasping international communication by presenting content that showcases various cultural aspects (Essafi et al., 2024). Language acquisition through exposure allows learners to develop cultural sensitivity because it creates effective communication capabilities within our present interconnected society (Vijayakumar&Chellapandiyan, 2024).

Regarding cultural gaps, gamified learning can also bridge the learning gap between students from diverse cultural backgrounds. Universally engaging game mechanics include points, rewards, and challenges that connect students to the learning content more (Saleem et al., 2020; Dichev&Dicheva, 2017). Gamified systems integrate cultural elements, including historical events or scenarios, promoting intercultural understanding by sharing experiences.

By enhancing correct and mainstream relational pronunciation, ELSA Speak enhances language and cultural diversity among learners, effectively helping them learn English. Especially for global communication, shade and intonation are of paramount significance, and this feature is helpful in the same regard (Rinaepi et al., 2022; Kholis, 2021). Learners increase their speaking fluency every time they pronounce correctly, thus facilitating their interaction with others from different cultural backgrounds.

Chatbots imitate different cultural and linguistic situations and enable learning of accents, idioms, and how people behave. This exposure familiarizes them with actual exposure to social interaction. Moreover, as a part of m-learning (mobile learning), it allows the learners to learn and practice with cultural differences and brings understanding or an 'emotional' global dimension. They are valuable instruments for I/C (intercultural competence), considered more and more functional as the world becomes a village (Zhang, 2025; Annamalai et al., 2023).

Since Google Translate works for multiple languages simultaneously, it facilitates the cross-cultural flow of content by translating such content. This encourages appreciation of other cultures, especially when accompanied by texts with cultural relations (Medvedev, 2016). Some things may be more nuanced and, therefore, will be lost in translation, and more investigation must be done. Google Translate is an example of how artificial intelligence in education could help remove the barriers that culture may pose in communication and technology.

Access to Broad Resources

Through AI tools, learners can access a plethora of information and resources that typically would be impossible to come across. When using AR and VR, students may travel to view virtual museums, conduct virtual experiments in biology and chemistry classes, or travel to parts of the globe they would otherwise not have the resources to get to. It can allow natural access to text within textbooks, 3D models, or another external education database, making learners interact with resources more effectively (Zhang et al., 2020).

Grammarly assists users in getting many features like writing style, vocabulary, and general writing guidelines. These resources supplement the user's understanding of making written texts more transparent, coherent, and toned. The tool enables users to use different language rules and examples from the database as they write (Bailey & Lee, 2020). These additional options enhance the practicality of the programs; users move from generic things like correcting grammatical mistakes to influencing how they write. Thus, by providing these broad resources to the public for free, Grammarly is invaluable to developing the students' global writing outcomes.

Gamified systems often offer students numerous learning resources far beyond the traditional textbook. Interactive tutorials, instructional videos, or online databases may be included and provided seamlessly for the learning process (Llorens-Largo et al., 2016; Dichev & Dicheva, 2017). The fact that these resources enable students to view a topic from different angles, broadening their understanding and encouraging them to learn independently. Gamified systems allow students to explore content at their own pace and deepen their knowledge as they engage with the material. They can also help students engage with the topics on multiple other fronts with different types of content that can appeal to different learning styles (Saleem et al., 2020).

ELSA Speak is full of speaking practice, vocabulary, pronunciation exercises, listening comprehension, and powerful feedback on performance. These resources are embedded within the app to ensure that learners have all they need in one place (Rismawati et al., 2021). It is convenient to have all these tools combined in one site because it is much easier to avoid distraction while practicing and simply searching for the material on the platform.

Google Translate gives learners immediate access to numerous other languages and assists students in interacting with the given learning materials. This broad access enables more robust learning, especially when using foreign sources, articles, or practical, real-life experiences in other languages (Afiliani et al., 2024). These broader resources support the transformation of education by increasing learners' opportunities to engage with a vast array of global content and broaden their educational horizons.

Chatbot learning is linked to a wealth of educational databases, providing large quantities of content. The availability of different resources means the materials adequately address all skill levels to guarantee mastery. Therefore, Chatbots have the potential to feature top-quality material, which helps learners stay updated and interested (Haristiani, 2019; Zhang, 2025).

- **Affordable Learning**

Even though the implementation expenses of AR and VR technology are high, the long haul of AR and VR technology is cheaper than the other means, such as field visits and physical materials. VR may replicate field exercises in different regions, which could cost money in terms of bills and time. Likewise, AR can substitute physical objects such as models or prototypes, cutting student material expenses while providing an enriching learning touchpoint (Li & Wong, 2021).

One of the most significant advantages of Grammarly is that it has both free and paid versions. The basic version includes only grammar and punctuation, whereas the advanced version includes style and tone applicable to users providing added feedback. This pricing model makes it possible to provide the product to learners and professionals who may need extensive help in writing (Fitria, 2021 b). The free version allows all people with limited budgets to use Grammarly, whereas the paid version provides additional and more profound assistance. It also makes the tool affordable and accessible to any user regardless of context or budget.

The initial setup of gamified learning systems might cost a lot; however, these systems provide long-term savings since physical materials and resources are not required. Digital resources (e.g., e-books, virtual classrooms) are less expensive and can supplant traditional textbooks, printed handouts, and classroom space, the learning process is made more cost-effective (Dichev & Dicheva, 2017; Llorens-Largo et al., 2016). Gamified systems are critical for institutions operating on a finite budget because they reduce recurring materials and facilities costs. Over the long term, gamified learning is an efficient way for institutions to provide high-quality educational experiences at a low cost. Like the scalability, these systems are also successful in scaling to accommodate large numbers of students without increasing physical infrastructure or staffing requirements (Subhash & Cudney, 2018).

Concerning the other approaches related to language learning or with individual lesson coaches, ELSA Speak is reasonably inexpensive for learners. The app has functions that are open for a basic free membership and special functions with paid subscriptions. This pricing strategy also ensures that the tool is affordable for most learners, especially those learning a language who may not be able to afford expensive language courses (Fitria, 2021 a; Rinaepi et al., 2022). Availability ensures that the target learners of different financial capacities can quickly get an effective pronunciation education at a one-time cost.

Google Translate has no limits and can be used for free without subscribing to it; thus, it can be used widely in schools. As it differs from subscription-based translation services, it guarantees learners access to quality translation resources regardless of the amount of money they or their families can pay (Afiliani et al., 2024).

Chatbots that rely on artificial intelligence replace one-on-one tutoring with a desired outcome at a lesser cost. This affordability makes language learning access easy for students all over the world. Similarly, it is scalable and ideal for large-scale use in education and training. These are especially helpful for educational institutions aiming to expand their convenience without straining their budget (Annamalai et al., 2023).

Tracking Continuous Improvement

Babbel distinguishes itself through its approach to developing real-life practice sessions that prove essential for students who need practical conversation abilities. The AI system on Babbel tracks progress and delivers specific feedback, particularly regarding pronunciation and grammar (Essafi et al., 2024). The system follows a customized learning sequence wherein it continually changes the study content based on individual proficiency, thus controlling training speed according to student abilities. Through its speech recognition functionality, users can train their speaking capabilities and obtain instant pronunciation evaluations that improve practical language fluency (Vijayakumar & Chellapandiyan, 2024).

AR and VR can track students' progress in a single learning process without interruptions by gathering information about the behavioral patterns of students, the amount of time used in completing their tasks, and their achievement rate. This information can be used by tutors to control improvements and aspects that the students have concerns about and make valuable decisions whenever relevant. This real-time monitoring cultivates the students' support every time they engage in the learning process (Dede et al., 2017).

Grammarly also has a feature that charts one's progress when using it. From this chart, one can see firsthand how he or she has been improving in writing. Users can manage writing deliberately, and the general quality of texts can be enhanced since Grammarly enables individuals to follow patterns of errors and find specific zones incorporating massive failures (Perdana et al., 2021). The particular tracking feature helps the users define the writing goals and evaluate the performance to promote efficiency. Grammarly serves as an editing aid and writing tutor that aids to become a better writer.

Gamified learning systems help students and educators track their ongoing progress by metrics such as scores, badges, and levels. These performance indicators will help to keep the students motivated by showing them visually how much progress they have made and how they can improve (Saleem et al., 2020). This is especially useful to learners who continue to require continual encouragement and for educators who might want to spot and subsequently fill gaps in student learning. Gamified systems offer a transparent view of which students are more potent and weaker so we can constantly correct our directions. This promotes a growth mindset—that students should be getting better at their skills and thus getting better at their academics (Dichev & Dicheva, 2017).

Google Translate contains a feature that helps users trace their records of translations that they have done in the past; it will help them rate the improvements they have made in a given language. This tracking feature can be used as a means of introspection in that the learner can know which language area they must work on (Afiliani et al., 2024). This feature of constant progress monitoring, which is another area where AI is utilized to enhance learner performance, is perhaps one of the best examples that can be seen of how AI is being deployed in a current learning setting.

ELSA Speak has a method underlying the tracking of ever-progressing users based on their feedback. This feature highlights areas that need more exercise and those that have already yielded the desired results. This feature informs and encourages learners by showing them the measurable impacts of their endeavors in this aspect (Rismawati et al., 2021). Apart from constantly providing information on the completion status of certain objectives, the process offers structure to the learning process and helps learners know which areas they should focus on next.

Data Analytics and Adaptive Learning

In ITS, the data analytical approach is applied to track the student's performance and make appropriate teaching changes. According to ITS technologies that use machine learning algorithms, Marouf et al. (2024) argue that ITS technologies provide a characteristic analysis of student behaviors. This means that the system can monitor learners' performance, absolve error patterns, and tweak learning approaches in real-time. For instance, if a learner has a problem with prepositions, the system can propose more tasks related to this type of grammar. Applying interpretative techniques, ITS can immediately respond to student answers, which will help correct language usage and indicate weaker topics. Shaik et al. (2022) also point out that this type of learning system allows differentiated assignments to be provided to the learners, focusing on their weaknesses. This way, ITS also tracks the error frequency and the progress during the current period, and a student can learn according to the ITS process, where the process evolves.

Interestingly, Grammarly uses data analytics to provide the user with genuinely personalized learning exercises depending on his or her writing style. Grammarly helps reduce overall errors and gives feedback specific to each user regarding the area of writing that needs improvement, often concerning grammar, vocabulary, and style. The adaptive learning system guarantees that the users get relevant and practical feedback based on their needs. Thus, Grammarly helps to provide a consistent learning process and continuous skill enhancement due to the intelligent analysis of data on individual writing peculiarities.

Learning platforms implemented as gamification collect valuable data on student performance and adjust the learning content based on individual needs. Consequently, they employ a data-driven approach, such that each student is challenged with tasks and challenges corresponding to their level of understanding (Dichev & Dicheva, 2017; Subhash & Cudney, 2018). Data analytics-powered adaptive learning personalizes the learning experience so students are constantly challenged and engaged. With this process, students can get through personalized learning paths that guide them to master content at their own rate. The system continually adapts, ensuring no learners are left behind, and adjusts according to evolving needs (Saleem et al., 2020).

ELSA avails data analytics to alter its delivery as it responds to the changing needs of the learners. It observes how the learner speaks and the complexity of exercises, making it easier for the learner to learn. Thus, the proposed form of adaptive learning allows for maintaining the individual difficulty level while achieving progress regularly (Fitria, 2021 a; Kholis, 2021). This dynamic learning approach ensures that the learners' knowledge and ability are constantly developing.

Adaptive learning pathways guarantee that every learner will get a special kind of support based on his or her learning style. Due to this, Chatbots can be applied in various educational settings, from the primary level to the professional development level (Haristiani, 2019). Using higher-level learning algorithms, the content of the Chatbots' interaction changes depending on the learner's achievements and failures, which contributes to increased interest and effectiveness?

Google Translate offers more precise renditions relevant to the user's previous experience, which benefits higher-level students (Medvedev, 2016). As a result of improved adaptation to the user requirements, Google Translate embraces the inherent fluidity of AI in education, at which learning technologies and applications gradually develop to be more sophisticated and tailored.

V. CHALLENGES IN IMPLEMETING AI

Equity and Access

Despite the call for AI integration to advocate for inclusiveness, there are always issues of diversity. The digital divide problem arises from a lack of connected devices or good internet connections in the areas where underprivileged learners live. There are critical issues that practitioners and policymakers face when implementing ITS. These include the fact that not everyone can enjoy the benefits of ITS. Learners in underprivileged regions may lack the required devices or stable internet connection; hence, they may not fully grasp what the ITS platforms offer. Hence, these gaps must be addressed to ensure that NL (natural language)-based language learning systems yield the highest benefits possible.

One of the major problems that AR and VR face in the educational context is the equitable distribution of these tools among learners. For many schools and individual students, the cost of most AR and VR devices remains high, especially for learners in low-income areas. Since the instructional effectiveness of AR and VR require certain technologies, learners who do not have access to such technologies are deprived of the educational advantages. Selwyn (2022) addresses how the digital divide prevents kids in low-income areas, in particular, from having equal access to AI-driven technologies. While AI applications show promise, they often need personal gadgets and reliable internet connectivity, which many students in underdeveloped nations or economically challenged places lack. Pahuja et al. (2024) also highlight the ethical issues AI creates in education and the necessity to address accessibility issues to provide fair access to educational resources.

Though many students use Grammarly, some of the specific elements of its paid version may be unavailable to the learners, especially those coming from the most economically disadvantaged backgrounds. The subscription rates set the access to the features of the new and improved version. Still, in the basic version, users can apply grammar and spelling checks – that is fundamental assistance.

While gamified learning is an effective tool on many levels, its use is hampered by equity and access issues. In gamified learning environments, students from lower-income backgrounds may not participate fully (Landers, 2015). Therefore, this digital divide will not allow these students to fully benefit from executing the advantages associated with gamification and the education prospects for all.

Educational institutions that cannot afford to invest in gamified learning tools may be unable to use the most of these systems. To bridge the gap, governments and educational institutions must concentrate on providing inexpensive software and training to access the required technology (Subhash & Cudney, 2018). Some areas do not have internet access and proper technological support, which hinders all learners' implementation of Google Translate (Afiliani et al., 2024). This technological disconnection poses major challenges regarding how this tool will benefit all students.

Even though many learners can use ELSA Speak, not all can access the app's premium features, which are valuable, especially for learners in low-income areas. This could reduce its optimal utility, as economically privileged students are likely to have access to only the complete package. There is a large number of learners from the developing regions who cannot perhaps afford the necessary gadgets for using Chatbots and this widens the learning gap. Solving this problem requires the assurance that all students are provided with economical and easy-to-use equipment.

It is also a fact that only through the interaction of public and private sectors it is possible to minimize the digital gap and provide equal access (Zhang, 2025).

Ethical Concerns

When a user uses AI tools, a lot of information about the user is stored in the database. To regain the trust of educators and learners, it is important to meet regulatory standards, such as GDPR (General Data Protection Regulation), and be clear on how data will be used. Educational AI raises ethical issues about protection of personal data and assignments of biased operations during its use. The data collection processes of language learning platforms generates substantial user progress information that requires secure protection and proper handling (Essafi et al., 2024). AI-powered educational tool integrity depends on solving ethical issues that protect their trustworthiness (Vijayakumar & Chellapandiyan, 2024).

The limitation of AR and, especially, the VR applications in the learning environment has some ethical concerns regarding data collection. Applying these technologies requires acquiring the most data on events that students participate in, the information they give and perform, and situations that raise concerns over data management and protection. Schools are responsible for ascertaining that they do not breach the Privacy Act and those students' data are protected and adequately managed (Guo et al., 2021 b).

Since Grammarly processes and saves all the content its users produce, it creates concerns about digital ethics. Sensitive or personal documents may be at risk as long as the data is not well protected (Fitria, 2021 b). Due to such factors, there is a need for the extension of enhanced measures concerning ethics and privacy. Policies on data storage and use and practices to ensure customers' trust should be well spelt out to prevent cases of leakage.

Gamified systems store lots of data on learners, including the time learners spend on tasks, the decisions made while playing a particular game, and even social relationships with fellow learners. This data helps prompt appropriate learning approaches, but concerns arise about using, storing, and sharing the students' data. If not adequately managed, there are always high risks that student-sensitive data will be misused or leaked, in one way or another, violating students' privacy rights (Dichev & Dicheva, 2017; Llorens-Largo et al., 2016).

In addition, gamification can manipulate learners by promoting extrinsic motivation over intrinsic motivation. This is a much-talked-about issue when frameworks like points, levels, and badges dominate the learning processes instead of the traditional educational objectives of achieving meaningful learning and appreciable motivation. Strikingly, sustainable and proper design and gamification must address the question of how to keep them analytically and ethically appropriate and student-oriented, whereby it is critical to reconcile two tasks: on the one hand, avoid excessive focus on metrics and learning outcomes where the beneficial effects of game elements are not sufficient, and protect students' privacy (Saleem et al., 2020).

ELSA Speak works with two main types of data that are considered sensitive: voice recording and pronunciation patterns. If not well protected, such data may be exploited or disclosed (Rinaepi et al., 2022). Data security measures and ethical clearance from users should always be put down so that the users can trust the system. Controversies have been raised about the reliance on Google Translate, particularly its use in education, since the outcome will be contrary to ideal language skills (Afiliani et al., 2024).

Dependence on Technology

The over-implementation of AI in educational institutions may erode the centrality of human trainers in nurturing companion aptitudes — compassion, emotional intelligence, and the ability to develop ideas in a complex way. Thus, it is vital to achieve an optimal degree of technology application. Teacher autonomy should dictate using AI as an ally by supplementing teachers' professional knowledge instead of doing it for them.

The degrees of dependency on the AR and VR technologies used in education will also rise with the growing adoption of the technologies. On the one hand, when studying with the help of virtual reality, it is crucial that students do not forget about skills such as problem-solving. To achieve effective outcomes, technology in facilitating learning should be used properly with the student's capacity (Morkun et al., 2020).

Dependence on Grammarly means a decreased capacity of learners to make corrections and polish their writing pieces independently. Even though Grammarly provides helpful corrections, it should not replace the process of gaining and applying rules independently (Bailey & Lee, 2020). Some of the students become overly reliant on the tool. Grammarly cannot be viewed as an adequate replacement for a conventional grammar and written composition course.

As gamification entirely depends on the use of technology, students tend to be too much associated with technological devices. For example, learners who have grown up in immediate reactivity, such as many applications that provide instant responses, may fail to cope with tasks that require no feedback—like most traditional school assignments.

This challenge points to one of the significant issues of gamification: the overemphasis on game elements when making learning fun. However, such a learning mode has some specific advantages; it should not be taken to the extent that it eliminates the conventional forms of learning. Teachers must prepare students for technology-integrated classrooms and classes where technology is not the main focus (Saleem et al., 2020).

Heavy dependence on this technology for pronunciation may increase the possibility of learners leaving other aspects of the language unaddressed, such as grammar and vocabulary. Technology is to enhance learning, not supplant it; that is, it is used in integration with conventional methods (Rismawati et al., 2021). Proper language promotion requires a more balanced methodology. It must avoid overloading students with speaking practice through limited online communication.

The high implementation of Chatbots is likely to reduce direct contact, and hence face-to-face contact that is required to practice cultural and social relations. When used in large quantities, technology presents the above challenge, and this can be managed by incorporating proper levels of consistent human interaction. Chatbots can be adopted in different forms of learning, thus helping maintain a balance (Haristiani, 2019).

Students may rely on Google Translate to translate everything instead of learning things independently. As Medvedev (2016) rightly noted, such dependence might minimize students' chances of engaging in critical language production.

Data Privacy and Security

Educators and students are anxious about the privacy and security of data during the use of AR and VR lessons. When learners learn, many of these technologies rely on data collection for optimum performance, thus calling for proper protection of personal data. General controls must be clearly defined and protected against infringement of ethics.

Nevertheless, Grammarly has measures to keep user data safe, but storing and processing users' content raises tension about privacy issues (Fitria, 2021 b). As the threat landscape expands, Grammarly and such tools will have to improve the protection measures to prevent user data leakage.

Google Translate is a powerful translator, but it can often mistranslate phrases, for example, idioms or special terms. This can lead to misunderstandings or misinterpretations (Afiliani et al., 2024). This occurs because it has different meanings for different people. Accuracy of translations is crucial for the AI tools used in education because the primary end user is the learner, and any inaccuracy will affect the quality of knowledge imparted.

Since Chatbots gather significant amounts of personally identifiable information, learners are assumed to face privacy risks. Users need to be trained on how to protect their data, which encourages institutions to encourage cyber security (Annamalai et al., 2023). Such issues should be addressed so that ELSA Speak adheres to strict data protection policies that users will understand well.

Ensuring Accuracy

Providing material specific to the intended content is equally challenging since AR and VR have unlimited access to information. As such technologies are highly engaging and, in some cases, 'autonomous,' there is a strong possibility of feeding the consumer wrong information if the material is not well selected. Teachers and developers must ensure that the student's exposure to the virtual environment and simulation is correct and that current information is provided to them (Guo et al., 2021 b).

Despite its ability to identify common grammatical and spelling mistakes most of the time, Grammarly sometimes gives wrong suggestions when used in sensitive writing environments. This can be pretty misleading to some of the users who may rely so much on the tool feedback, as stated by Perdana et al. (2021). The corrections made by the tool can help the user, but these cannot be relied on entirely as an error-free tool. Users should, therefore, double-check the correction to ensure that it conforms to the intended meaning. Grammarly must improve the algorithm daily to detect errors in more complex cases more accurately.

The basis of gamified learning systems is in algorithms that deliver personal learning experiences. However, verifying such algorithms' efficacy is arduous. Learners may get unsuitable content for practice or feedback from the system that is neither well-designed nor optimized (Subhash & Cudney, 2018; Dichev & Dicheva, 2017). For instance, a student may be assigned tasks with a high difficulty level or, on the contrary, low difficulty, which will affect his/her motivation levels. To counter this, the individuals should not entirely rely on the system's proposed learning paths. While the social language practice app ELSA Speak provides pronunciation feedback, the algorithms used may not always be exact, particularly for learners with strong accents or regional variants. Inaccurate feedback may result in faulty learning (Rismawati et al., 2021). Perhaps, with future development in the technology, where recognition of speech patterns improves, this may pose less of a problem to user uptake, making the app more useful for differing students.

The Chatbot can give learners wrong information, thus it requires constant updates and quality assurance. Collaboration with educators can contribute to the conformity of Chatbot content to curriculum standards (Haristiani, 2019).

Financial Investment

Since AR and VR rely on mobile devices, there are also prerequisites for investing in the installation of AR and VR kits that comprise gadgets and relevant content, which is very expensive for many institutions. In the long run, the potential of these technologies is obvious, though their adoption is usually initially costly, and schools with constrained budgets are often aware of that (Parmaxi, 2023).

The enhanced version of Grammarly has all the features of the basic version, but it might be costly for some users. However, the issue that may contribute to the drawback is the relatively expensive subscription fees for access to the full potential of the instrument (Bailey & Lee, 2020). This brings about a financial barrier where the tool may be beyond the reach of the beneficiaries who can otherwise benefit from its superior functionality, especially in educational systems where deficiencies prompt the development of good tools, but budget constraints may hinder their use.

Despite the advantages of gamification, cost is one of the most significant drawbacks, given that establishing gamified learning systems comes at a very expensive price for most institutions. Even though the creation of the digital platform can be economically practical in terms of the lack of expenditure on tangible resources in the long run, it is still necessary to invest resources in the procurement of software and hardware as well as the training of personnel (Llorens-Largo et al., 2016). This financial barrier may pose a problem in putting into practice gamification in institutions in developing countries or low-budget education systems.

To resolve this problem, governments and institutions need to seek grants and embrace partnerships with other industries by sharing the costs involved in gamified learning. Other open-source gamified applications could also be used as a cheaper solution for institutions to adopt gamification without necessarily incurring the same costs (Dichev & Dicheva, 2017).

The fee required to enter ELSA Speak categories might be costly for the learners, especially those in developing nations. Here, recommendations included extending lower prices or providing ways to help finance ELSA Speak (Fitria, 2021 a). As it stands, offering subsidies or scholarships is one way of ensuring that learners who cannot afford to pay for premium services can access the app.

The creation and management of complex Chatbots are a costly process and thus might not become mainstream. There are ways through which organizations can plan their expenditure and make the development of Chatbots less expensive and sustainable. It is also encouraging that governments and organizations can offer grants and subsidies for development in this area (Zhang, 2025). In the case of Google Translate, even though the tool is open-source, the necessities of reaching it – like smartphones and the Internet – may pose a cost barrier to learners (Medvedev, 2016).

Affective Filters

The barriers to AI learning can be more physiological. Affective filters can interfere with the presented information; the filtered information impacts the learning experience negatively if certain conditions are not met. Therefore, it is necessary to create VR/AR applications that can be sensitive to these feelings and offer proper work to students who can experience stress or burnout.

Some users may get annoyed, especially when Grammarly shows many mistakes in the works they have written. Such emotional barriers may restrict students from interacting with the tool's feedback to the utmost extent (Fitria, 2021 b). Sometimes students may impose constraints on themselves due to social emotions like frustration, anxiety, or embarrassment when admitting failure in games. Such emotions work negatively, interfere with the learning process, and may affect the student's ability to comprehend it (Dichev & Dicheva, 2017; Subhash & Cudney, 2018). To avoid strong affective filters, a gamified learning system should incorporate learning elements of varying difficulty levels, preferably adopting the difficulty adaptation theory. Secondly, the system should provide encouraging feedback, not only on success and failure feedback but also on the level of effort applied to achieve any given success level. Educators can help students become more engaged with the learning process (Saleem et al., 2020).

Numerous incorrect productions that may be corrected can cause learners emotional barriers, like getting frustrated or even anxious. It will be even more unbearable for learners with poor pronunciation whose production is far from natural as a native speaker (Rinaepi et al., 2022). For this reason, to minimize affective filters, ELSA Speak needs to provide motivation and encouragement in addition to pointing out the learners' mistakes.

One needs to understand that while managing the learners' engagement and affectionate affinity, Chatbots are not as efficient in confronting learner irritation as expected. This can be overcome by pulling the model's AI slightly higher, making the viewers more emotional and leading to better engagement. Such an approach can potentially increase the likelihood of the chatbot as a friendly and warm solution communication interface (Annamalai et al., 2023).

Google Translate should provide an accurate translation; otherwise, the students might get annoyed or bored by the lesson. These affective filters can diminish the tool's value because they elicit negative emotions counterproductive to teach (Afiliani et al., 2024). These emotional barriers must be managed to make AI tools in learning to enhance the learning environment.

Culture Specific Contents

It is always quite challenging to create AR and VR content that would be culturally appropriate and receptive. The concept learned in one culture may not be approached next; developing content for dissemination across cultures is a challenge that comes with analyzing cultural differences. AR and VR applications should incorporate culture-specific content into the classroom; therefore, educators are responsible for guaranteeing that all the students find themselves represented in applications utilized in teaching (Radu& Schneider, 2022).

Grammarly utilizes standard English grammar to develop suggestions, which can be intolerant of regional idiomatic expressions or cultural differences. This limitation may be undesirable to users who adopt informal language or require an understanding of cultural contexts in their text (Perdana et al., 2021). It is the need of the hour for Grammarly to focus on the customization or flexibility of its recommendation engine so it can be sensitive to culture or language differences.

The focus in creating gamified learning systems is to ensure that they are sensitive and do not offend the culture of the different students they are used to. For instance, symbols, language, or particular scenes in a game may have different connotations regarding the student's cultural background (Saleem et al., 2020). Cultural differences might lead to some students' alienation or reinforcement of apparent stereotypes about gamified systems, increasing or decreasing their effectiveness in actual learning. To meet this challenge, learning through gamification should include cultural points of view and environments. Developers should implement culturally sensitive material into the game, and the system should be appropriate for many students (Dichev & Dicheva, 2017).

As much as ELSA Speak can be helpful for the learners, the program's emphasis on standardized pronunciation would not work for everybody since some learners prefer to retain regional color or have reasons to use certain accentuations (Rinaepi et al., 2022). The app should have more customization features to provide more strategies, and the app should cater to the differences in accent and individual language requirements of the learners. Everyone uses language differently, and there are distinct linguistic and cultural variations to learn about, which is difficult for a developer to deal with. Local content increases the relevance of the Chatbot and can also enhance its efficacy. Collaborations with local educators, usefulness, cultural relevance, and learners' engagement can be boosted in Chatbots (Haristiani, 2019).

Google Translate fails to translate cultural context and idiomatic expressions. This is how the given source may mislead students who learn languages with deep cultural backgrounds (Afiliani et al., 2024). This limitation highlights that much more than simple word-level translation is needed from the AI-enabling tools; it must also capture and, more importantly, replicate the cultural connotations of the textual input.

Digital Literacy

AR and VR depend on some level of digital literacy that students and educators could require for useful learning. Some of the participants have poor digital literacy. This calls for training for both students and teachers in schools (Akcayir & Akcayir, 2017).

The effective use of Grammarly can only be guaranteed by a certain level of informatics, which some users might lack. This could reduce the appropriateness and usefulness of the tool (Fitria, 2021 b). For Grammarly to reach its full potential, it should provide instruction or assistance as a guide or a helpline to make the people using the product more and navigate it to their benefit.

Gamified learning systems require a specific understanding of various applications. Negative attitudes like frustration and disengagement may arise from an inability to engage with digital tools used in gamified learning platforms, especially by those who are new to them (Llorens-Largo et al., 2016; Subhash & Cudney, 2018). For example, interaction with digital resources and academic accomplishment might be more complicated for older students or students from lower economic status since they likely have less experience with learning with such platforms, which might be an obstacle when relying on gamified education.

In order to counter this problem, more schools and other educational institutions should equip students and teachers with knowledge on how to use the various games involved in the gamification process to the maximum potential. Furthermore, the design of gamified systems should be easy to understand and use so that classes of students can fit into the systems irrespective of their technological literacy (Saleem et al., 2020).

These problems show that introducing gamified systems into the learning environment in education is not easy. Meeting these concerns involves strategic planning, systematic refinement, and special reference to diversity sensitivity and ethical practices. Overcoming these barriers lets the educational institution get the best of the gamified learning model with equal chances for all students.

ELSA Speak has limitations, especially for learners with low levels of digital literacy, when using smartphone apps for practice (Rinaepi et al., 2022; Kholis, 2021). Judging from the fact that the mobile app may be difficult to use, especially for the less computer literate, it would have been easier to develop the application if instructions were given in different steps to guide the users.

AI Chatbots limit the usage of some populations since the users need to have some level of technical knowledge to use them. Digitization efforts can help reduce this gap and extend Chatbot reach. To support and promote learners, governments, and institutions should urge investment in digital literacy in future education (Annamalai et al., 2023).

The disadvantage of using Google Translate is that students must be computer literate to use the tool best. A lack of technological facilities could make it difficult for students to utilize the tool correctly, imitating its advantages (Medvedev, 2016). Therefore, efforts should be made towards eradicating digital illiteracy so that the distribution of AI to support learning, when adopted, will not be cumulative and will not disadvantage some learners.

VI. CASE STUDIES: AI IN ACTION

Case Study 1: AI in English Language Learning in Japan

The studies under review were conducted in Japan between 2023 and 2024. They examine the role of AI-driven tools in improving English proficiency, focusing on rewriting support software, communicative competence, and large language models (Ito et al., 2023; Busso & Sanchez, 2024; Eronen & Lee, 2024).

Participants

The research engaged diverse groups of learners and educators. Ito et al. (2023) studied 21 Japanese researchers and students with experience in academic writing in English. Busso and Sanchez (2024) focused on Japanese university students struggling with communicative competence. In the study, Eronen and Lee (2024) administered questionnaires to understand the knowledge and experience of the participants about AI based learning systems and issues.

Tools Utilized

Each study incorporated AI-powered tools tailored to different learning needs. Ito et al. (2023) examined Langsmith, an AI-based rewriting tool that helps non-native English speakers refine their academic writing. The study also considered the impact of machine translation (MT) tools like DeepL and Google Translate. Busso and Sanchez (2024) explored AI tools in communicative language learning, including Chatbots and speech recognition software such as Duolingo and Musio. Eronen and Lee (2024) investigated using large language models (LLMs) like LLaMA 3, integrated into a generative AI-powered learning system designed to personalize language instruction.

Researchers

Academic researchers and AI specialists from Japanese institutions conducted the studies. Ito et al. (2023) included scholars from Tohoku University, Langsmith Inc., and NTT Communication Science Labs. Busso and Sanchez (2024) were affiliated with Tokyo International University, while Eronen and Lee (2024) represented the Prefectural University of Kumamoto.

Results

Personalized Learning: AI-supported platforms, such as Langsmith and generative AI models, provided individualized recommendations based on students' writing proficiency and learning pace (Ito et al., 2023; Eronen& Lee, 2024).
Improved Engagement and Confidence: Through using AI Chatbots, speech recognition tools and virtual learning environment, students testify that the above aspects lessen anxiety making them more at ease as they engage in spoken English (Busso & Sanchez, 2024).
HOTS aid: By using AI tools, it also expected that students were able to learn beyond the basic factual knowledge and conceptual understanding as encouraged through the use of HOTS (Eronen & Lee, 2024).
Efficiency for Educators: AI-driven tools such as Grammarly and automated grading systems reduced instructors' workload, allowing them to focus on higher-value teaching activities (Ito et al., 2023).

Challenges

Reliance on Machine Translation: Many students depended on MT tools without fully engaging with rewriting software, limiting their ability to critically assess AI-generated suggestions (Ito et al., 2023).
Limited Communicative Practice: Japanese EFL learners still lacked real-world conversational opportunities, even with AI-driven Chatbots and voice recognition systems (Busso & Sanchez, 2024).
Standardized Testing Pressure: Japan's test-oriented system discouraged the use of AI to develop communicative and critical thinking skills, favoring passive learning methods (Eronen& Lee, 2024).
Ethical and Privacy Concerns: AI tools have implications for data privacy, biases in algorithms, and ethical use of the student's information as noted by Eronen and Lee (2024).

Technology Inequity: AI tools sometimes promote inequality since certain groups cannot obtain devices or are not computer literate that make them unable to experience AI integration commonly (Busso & Sanchez, 2024).

AI tools can help educators overcome challenges, such as the lack of individualized feedback and the difficulty of managing large class sizes, by offering real-time, personalized support to learners. Thus, teachers can focus on higher-level instructional tasks.

Recommendations

Balanced AI Integration: AI should complement, rather than replace, traditional teaching methods to preserve human interaction in language teaching (Ito et al., 2023).

Training for Educators and Students: AI literacy programs should be implemented to teach students how to critically assess AI-generated suggestions and help teachers integrate AI tools effectively (Busso & Sanchez, 2024).

Incorporating AI in Communicative Learning: Japanese institutions should move beyond grammar-focused AI tools and incorporate AI-driven conversation simulations and virtual role-playing exercises (Eronen & Lee, 2024).

Policy and Ethical Frameworks: Educational policymakers should establish clear ethical guidelines and data protection measures to safeguard student privacy when using AI-based learning systems (Eronen & Lee, 2024).

Infrastructure Investment: Government and institutions must ensure that smart learning resources are made available to all students, taking into consideration the problems that prevail in access to appropriate learning technologies and internet connectivity (Busso & Sanchez, 2024).

Case Study 2: AI Integration in English Language Learning in Finland

This research will particularly examine Finland since the country has ranked amongst the highest in implementing digital learning. The studies have been done between 2023 and 2024 and provide recent information on using AI in Finnish schools and institutions for higher education (FIER, 2023; Ministry of Education and Culture, Finland, 2023; Bundgaard & Møller, 2024).

Participants

- Primary and secondary students

- Teachers
- Education policymakers

These participants provided diverse perspectives on AI-assisted English learning, teaching adaptation, and policy regulations.

Tools Utilized

Machine Translation (MT) Tools: Widely used tools such as Google Translate and DeepL assist students in understanding and generating English text. However, concerns exist regarding students' dependency on AI translations (Bundgaard & Møller, 2024).
Adaptive Learning Systems: AI-powered platforms like Grammarly, Turnitin, and Duolingo provide automated feedback on writing, pronunciation, and grammar accuracy (Ministry of Education and Culture, Finland, 2023).
Natural Language Processing (NLP) and AI Chatbots: Interactive AI assistants help students improve their spoken English skills through real-life conversation simulations (FIER, 2023).
Gamification and AI-Driven Learning Apps: Language learning platforms integrate progress tracking, rewards, and challenges, increasing student motivation and retention (Bundgaard & Møller, 2024).

Researchers/ Research Institute

The Finnish Institute for Educational Research (FIER).
The Ministry of Education and Culture.
Educational Technology Experts at Finnish Universities

Results

Personalized Learning Enhancements: AI-driven tools adapt to individual learning needs, enabling self-paced language acquisition and improving student confidence (Ministry of Education and Culture, Finland, 2023).
Increased Student Engagement: Gamification features, such as reward systems and interactive challenges, significantly increase motivation and participation in English education (Bundgaard & Møller, 2024).
Improved Writing and Grammar Proficiency: AI tools like Grammarly and Turnitin help students refine writing skills through automated grammar correction and stylistic feedback (FIER, 2023).

Efficiency in Teaching and Grading: AI helps the educators in assessment, feedback, and handling various other clerical jobs, thus freeing the member of faculty for imparting education to the students (Ministry of Education and Culture, Finland, 2023).
Inclusivity and Accessibility: AI technologies support students with learning disabilities and non-native Finnish speakers, fostering an inclusive learning environment (Bundgaard & Møller, 2024).

Challenges

Over-Reliance on Machine Translation: Many students depend heavily on MT tools, limiting their critical thinking and independent language skills (Bundgaard & Møller, 2024).
Teacher Training Gaps: While Finland has strong digital policies, many educators lack formal training in effectively integrating AI into language instruction (Ministry of Education and Culture, Finland, 2023).
Ethical and Privacy Concerns: AI tools collect vast amounts of student data, raising concerns over privacy protection, algorithmic bias, and ethical AI use (FIER, 2023).
Digital Divide and Equity Issues: Although Finland has high digital literacy rates, disparities exist in AI access, particularly among students in rural areas (Bundgaard & Møller, 2024).
Reduction in Human Interaction: Overreliance of AI technologies in learning context may pose negative impacts in aspects of interaction skills and collaborative learning (Ministry of Education and Culture, Finland, 2023).

Recommendations

Balanced Integration of AI and Traditional Teaching: AI should enhance rather than replace human instruction, ensuring a hybrid learning approach and social interaction (Bundgaard & Møller, 2024).
Expanded Teacher Training in AI Applications: Educators must have comprehensive AI training programs to effectively integrate technology into the English curriculum (Ministry of Education and Culture, Finland, 2023).
Strengthened Ethical AI Governance and Data Protection: Finnish policymakers should implement robust privacy regulations to safeguard student data and prevent misuse (FIER, 2023).
Investments in Digital Equity and Infrastructure: The government must address regional digital disparities by ensuring that AI-powered resources and learning tools are accessible to all students (Bundgaard & Møller, 2024).

Enhancing AI-Driven Conversational Learning: AI Chatbots and NLP-based platforms should simulate real-world conversations to improve English-speaking proficiency and confidence (FIER, 2023).

Case Study 3: How AI Will Help People Learn English from 2010 to 2020

Artificial intelligence (AI) has changed learning strategies and approaches, transforming the educational field. Between 2010 and 2020, this case study shows artificial intelligence's applications, innovations, benefits, and educational challenges. Zhai et al. (2021) carried out a comprehensive review of 100 research publications, looking at how AI is used in English language learning. Their results show how AI-powered tools and systems can help people learn languages in various settings and areas.

Participants

The study looked at various people from different educational settings, such as students, teachers, and organizations. According to Zhai et al. (2021), artificial intelligence techniques were utilized to assist students of varying ability levels, ranging from those just beginning their studies to those highly proficient. The studies included people from a range of linguistic and cultural backgrounds. They paid special attention to how AI solved specific language learning problems.

During this time, intelligent teaching systems (ITS), machine translation tools, robots, speech recognition software, and large language models (LLMs) were all used to help people learn languages. These tools aimed to make learning more personalized by, for example, giving specific comments on writing skills, speech, and practice with speaking and listening. Adding AI to existing educational technologies like innovative classes and learning management systems made learning better by making learning settings that were flexible and changed over time (Zhai et al., 2021).

Results

Studies show that AI tools make learning languages a lot easier. Learners could move at their own pace with personalized input and adaptable learning systems, which gave them more freedom and interest in the learning process. Tools like machine translation and speech recognition made it easier to learn new words and improve how to say them. Using robots and talking characters made learning more engaging, making students feel better about using actual language and reducing nervousness. Adding LLMs also helped make lessons more personalized and material more relevant to students' needs (Zhai et al., 2021).

Challenges

Even though the findings look good, some problems still exist. Many students relied too much on machine translation tools, making it harder to learn and build important language skills. Also, the stress of standardized tests in many school systems made it harder for AI tools to help students improve their communication and higher-order thought skills. Technology inequality also became a big problem, with some people unable to access AI tools because of their financial status or where they live (Zhai et al., 2021).

Recommendations

To deal with these problems, Zhai et al. (2021) suggest a balanced approach to integrating AI. AI tools work with traditional teaching methods without replacing the important human part in language learning. They stress the importance of AI learning programs for students and teachers to help them think critically about material and comments made by AI. The writers also suggest that using AI to learn a language should focus on improving communication and critical thinking skills through conversations and engaging AI apps. Lastly, to ensure everyone has equal access, everyone should work together to improve technology infrastructure and deal with problems related to digital learning (Zhai et al., 2021).

Case Study 4: Integrating AI Literacy in K-12 Education

The fast growth of artificial intelligence (AI) has made it more important for everyone, from K–12 school students, to learn about AI. Casal-Otero et al. (2023) noted that this case study looks at the strategies, difficulties, and suggestions for including artificial intelligence literacy in K–12 courses.

Participants

Casal-Otero et al. (2023) systematically reviewed 179 papers emphasizing artificial intelligence integration in K–12 education globally. Students, teachers, and legislators engaged in AI literacy initiatives across various educational environments comprised the participants in this research.

Methods of AI Literacy

Two main strategies for AI literacy in K–12 education were found in the review:

1. Learning Experiences

Students acquire technical, conceptual, and applied abilities through practical exercises involving artificial intelligence technology. Workshops in coding, robotics projects, and problem-solving activities linking academic knowledge with valuable applications are among the examples.

2. **Theoretical Perspectives**:

This method emphasizes creating models and frameworks defining AI literacy abilities from theoretical angles. There have been notable attempts to define AI literacy and how it may be methodically included in the curriculum of instruction.

Challenges

Integration of artificial intelligence literacy into K–12 education presented several difficulties:

- **Assessment of Understanding**

There are few studies examining whether students understand AI ideas after their involvement in educational events.

- **Ethical Considerations**

Ethical Issues, including prejudice, privacy concerns, and the indiscriminate deployment of artificial intelligence technology, have not received enough attention.

- **Curriculum Development**

The lack of a consistent competence framework makes it challenging for educational institutions to create courses that guarantee modularity, personalizing, and congruence with academic norms.

Recommendations

Casal-Otero et al. (2023) provide the following suggestions

Development of a Competency Framework

Establish a thorough framework to guide the development of AI literacy courses, guaranteeing a disciplined and ongoing learning path for many educational settings.

Ethics Integration

Including conversations on the ethical ramifications of artificial intelligence in the course will enable students to evaluate the social and moral ramifications of AI technology with a critical eye.

Teacher Training

Professional development opportunities for teachers will help them improve their knowledge of AI ideas and successful teaching strategies, empowering them to boldly provide AI literacy instruction.

¬ **Interdisciplinary Collaboration**

Encourage multidisciplinary cooperation among curriculum designers, teachers, and artificial intelligence professionals to produce significant and contextually relevant AI learning opportunities.

Preparing children to negotiate a world progressively shaped by artificial intelligence technology depends on including AI literacy in K–12 schooling. Educational systems may efficiently prepare students with the required skills and knowledge to interact with artificial intelligence ethically and deliberately using a disciplined strategy, including a defined competence framework, ethical issues, teacher training, and multidisciplinary cooperation.

VII. CRITICAL EVALUATION OF AI's IMPACT ON LANGUAGE ACQUISITION

Using AI to help people learn languages brings significant benefits and big problems. AI-powered learning apps like Duolingo, Babbel, and ELSA Speak make learning more personalized by letting students go at their own pace and focus on areas that are bothering them. This ability to change helps students become more independent and self-regulated, giving them the power to take charge of their learning. AI tools also often have game-like features that keep learners interested through tasks and prizes, which boosts motivation. However, even though these tools help learn a language, they might not be perfect in all areas. AI systems may have trouble understanding national differences, dialects, and accents, which could cause them to give wrong feedback or not understand language well in different situations. Also, using AI to learn a language might make it harder to connect with real people, which is important for building verbal competence and complex communication skills. AI can help people learn languages, mainly when used in standard ways, but it does have some problems. To reach their full potential, AI systems must keep improving by solving flaws, becoming more sensitive to different cultures, and creating spaces for beneficial human involvement in language learning settings.

VIII. FUTURE IMPLICATIONS

Cross-Cultural Exchanges

AR and VR may well significantly impact cross-cultural learning and communication as people from different parts of the world will be able to interact in the controlled environment of a virtual culture. These technologies allow a learner to learn about the cultural contexts and practices that may not be available within the learner's cultural environment. Combining cultural diversity in online communication imposes on learners the need to assume diverse cultural and traditional as well as linguistically diverse scenarios regarding different cultures. For instance, in language learning, it can model actual interactions in foreign territories, making learners interact with other cultures, making them more sensitive to other nations, and helping them overcome prejudices existing in international communication (Nurmatova & Noori, 2023).

This flexibility of Grammarly to several writing domains could benefit international communications by helping writers of a second language write fluently in English. In the future, the tool could generate a broader range of culturally related pitches and help speakers from different cultures understand their differences to facilitate better communication. This would assist in breaking barriers in communication and ensure that people who use different languages and those from different cultures can communicate in a dialogical manner.

As such gamified learning systems grow, they present opportunities to nurture cross-cultural exchanges with abundant connectivity between students from various cultures and backgrounds. Students from the same group can connect through global online platforms and participate in shared learning experiences beyond geographical boundaries (Dichev & Dicheva, 2017; Saleem et al., 2020). Helping students acquire a more global imagination leads to a global understanding of global problems, readying them for a world where they are part of an interlaced series of human-global complexities.

By allowing these interactions to happen, students can develop empathy and mutual understanding, easing the distance in culture and taking us a step closer to global citizenship. These are crucial in the current global environment to convert education into a more inclusive and globally connected experience (Landers, 2015).

Due to the effectiveness of ELSA Speak in enhancing the learner's pronunciation, communication barriers that result from learners from different linguistic backgrounds can be easily overcome (Rismawati et al., 2021). It will help one understand the other better in the diverse cultures that prevail worldwide and thereby improve relationships.

Careful implementation of Chatbots will enhance learning by exposing the learners to different accents and social conditions around the globe. Thus, the exchanges enrich the linguistic level of knowledge and foster cultural awareness. They do so to warrant that learners are primed for globalized workplaces and multicultural engagement (Zhang, 2025).

Google Translate continues to be developed as a ready tool for cross-cultural communication and interaction. With the help of breaking language differences, the tool helps to develop and foster international learning mobility and cultural aspects of learning (Afiliani et al., 2024). The future developments of AI in education will enhance the interconnectedness of people worldwide, increasing cultural diversity and, in this way, creating a better world.

Natural way of Language learning

Advanced NLP enhancements will allow AI systems to understand the more intricate uses of the language, local dialects, or even proverbs, making the English learning process much more contextual. The maturity of context and intent recognition by AI will lead to correct interactions that will improve the learner's mastery.

Learning language using AR and VR is helpful because the learner can use the language in context naturally. Instead of rote learning of vocabulary or grammar, learners apply language development skills through role plays where communication is paramount. This is as close to the process of learning a first language as it is possible to get where learning takes place through use and not through memorization. Students are also often able to engage in interaction with avatars or even walk around a cafe or a marketplace in another country and learn language through contextual learning in a natural way (Al-Ansi et al., 2023).

Grammarly's real-time suggestions help students with the natural learning approach because they can be corrected while completing assignments. This immediate correction, similar to how people learn their first language, makes it a great tool in language learning (Fitria, 2021 b). This makes it easy to train people on correct grammar usage by simulating a tutor grep, which helps the learners get used to specific rules they must apply when writing.

By immersing students in an interactive, context-rich environment, gamified learning is a natural way to enhance language learning. In traditional language learning methods, students are often asked to remember the grammar by heart and then be passive in the classroom. However, through gamification, students can access real-world scenarios and dialogues to their practical experiences to improve their language skills (Dichev & Dicheva, 2017; Saleem et al., 2020). This is an excellent approach for second language acquisition because it makes the students use that language dynamically, and their fluency and comprehension improve in real time. Besides the gamification process, language learning through gamification offers instant feedback to the learners to correct their errors and also gives feedback about correct usage. This immersive experience replicates how they learn their first language by repeatedly coming in contact with a new language through continuous natural interaction (Landers, 2015).

With real visibility methods, the learner is exposed to real-life speaking situations, which is why ELSA Speak is preferable. This approach is similar to how children are able to acquire their first language through constant use and practice (Fitria, 2021 a). Consequently, through contextual acquisition, ELSA Speak prepares learners for how to gain pronunciation in a natural setting that is creatively stimulating.

When the simulated conversations are real, learning a language becomes far more natural and fun. The Chatbots mimic realistic conversations to make the learners comfortable with real-life interactions. Such a naturalistic approach corresponds well with the second language acquisition theories, improving long-term knowledge retention (Annamalai et al., 2023).

Google Translate can offer increasingly real-life-like learning scenarios (Medvedev, 2016). This would enable learners to interact with the language more naturally. More specifically, as AI technology continues to advance within the realm of language tools, real-life interaction with a foreign language will be possible, as well as making learning easier.

Virtual Reality

Maximizing the implementation of AI with VR/AR capabilities will enable independent study contexts in language acquisition. Students can use English to shop at virtual supermarkets, conferences, and dramas; generally, it provides a convenient experience. For instance, an AI-based virtual Reality unit may prepare a learner or trainee to feel a travel trip as they transfer him/her to an airport, order food, or ask for directions in English. Virtual Reality (VR) plays an important role in transforming education by delivering a realistic and engaging learning environment. For instance, a student learning French would be able to roam and converse with simulated French citizens in Paris environments. Going through these points, it is clear that this immersion makes the learning process more interesting while it also enables the learners to use the skills learned within actual situations (AlGerafi et al., 2023).

Pre-implementation of Grammarly in the virtual environment may open up opportunities for practicing writing in a virtual environment. Integrating AI grammar check and VR may present a fun and interactive way to enhance the learning process and enable students to practice compositions in different environments (Perdana et al., 2021). Integrating virtual reality with Grammarly can change the conventional writing practice and improve the learning process by providing entertainment while learning. This might be a better approach to enable students to develop their writing skills tremendously.

Gamified learning is set to transform with virtual reality (VR) as a leading player in virtual, interactive experiences through which students learn by doing. Learning can be simulated in real-life scenarios that would otherwise not have been possible (Saleem et al., 2020). Gamified learning will likely use VR technology and virtualized classrooms or simulations of the physical world. Students will engage with these digital objects, practice problem-solving, and collaborate with peers in a more hands-on way than typical digital learning tools. This will enhance engagement and experiential learning, and allow students to develop skills that they would otherwise find challenging to learn through conventional means (Landers, 2015).

Adding Virtual Reality (VR) to ELSA Speak can create a scenario where learners practice pronunciation in real-life interactions, such as a business meeting or a casual conversation at a coffee station (Rismawati et al., 2021). This would help make language learning more realistic and offer practice opportunities that other methods cannot.

The integration of Chatbots with virtual reality can provide rich contexts: individuals can take a simulated practice of all the languages in use in virtual real-life scenarios. Applying Google Translate to VR can also improve user interaction by effectively elaborating learning by incorporating a VR learning environment for practice options (Afiliani et al., 2024). The students can use the language in real-life situations to enhance strain in fluency and understanding.

Transparent Algorithms

In educational contexts, transparent algorithms will allow learners as well as teachers to know how content is selected, how adverse interactions with virtual worlds are produced, and how learning contents are personalized. Such transparency reduces bias factors that may be occasioned by the learning system and thus fosters fairness in the delivery of education. Students and educators can see how and why particular content is recommended or personalized for them. This transparency can remove biases in learning journeys and ensure students have similar abilities to do well. It also helps teachers understand the learning process better and determine areas the system may lack to provide learners with better services. For instance, when using AR/VR in teaching prescriptions of cultural practices, the content displayed must mostly embrace several cultures. Also, the algorithms' openness enables educators to rely on the AI-based educational tools, as the system's decision-making process is clearer (Tusher et al., 2022).

There is a need to open the code of an algorithm to allow people to trust in the results that AI in educational technologies provides. When the algorithm is straightforward, just like Grammarly's approach, a user or a client can follow the steps that a particular system is taking. In education, it is important that learners, instructors, and other stakeholders can see how the feedback is generated, increasing accountability. When the algorithm is straightforward, teachers can trust the tool without worrying that prejudices affect the feedback they give their students. However, for a personalized learning environment, the models utilized are open to deep analysis and alterations that correspond to the learning requirements of individuals. Consequently, increasing knowledge about transparent algorithms improves ethical factors and enables users of AI applications to solve tasks effectively (Bailey & Lee, 2020; Fitria, 2021 a).

Nowadays, many learning platforms steer ahead with gamified learning and use data-driven algorithms to personalize student content. However, such algorithms are often 'black boxes': the educators and students may not entirely understand which decisions the content and the feedback provide (Dichev & Dicheva, 2017). Transparency in the design of these algorithms can also lead to the gamification of learning systems being used fairly and equitably.

Transparent algorithms will become even more important as gamified systems become more complex, ensuring that ethical standards of resource distribution are maintained and fair (Saleem et al., 2020). Stressing ethical considerations will lead to promising a fair and bias-free model for learning, thus leading to more trustworthy Chatbots. Regarding algorithm development, therefore, the developers must work towards optimizing in delivering the goals of education. The use of algorithms will bring about accountability in developing the algorithms (Zhang, 2025) and enhance user satisfaction.

There is an opportunity for Google Translate to improve user trust by providing more information to the user regarding an algorithm and the data used for translating (Al-Maroof et al., 2020). Such scenarios enable users to develop better confidence in the tool because its workings are well explained. The concept of making AI-based tools more transparent to the end-users is to assist them in feeling more comfortable using the tools in the educational processes, making them more prevalent and efficient.

Blended Learning Models

AR and VR are useful in blended learning models that integrate the features of both virtual features and face-to-face implementations. For example, in language acquisition, maybe students learn the theory of a particular language in the classroom and then use the language in virtual reality simulations outside classrooms. The integration of these technologies supports learning with the ability to develop one and several mental and practical skills by the students. Another advantage of using AR and VR in technology-enhanced blended learning is that students independently control virtual environments and therefore learn according to their abilities and skills (Chen, 2024).

Hybrid instructional techniques include both face-to-face teaching and online learning. Grammarly is highly effective in supporting this model. These models facilitate student-centered learning as the students can learn independently while getting additional assistance in their writing projects. As an extension of classroom practices within the learning management systems of educational institutions, Grammarly provides a flexible learning process. It reduces some gaps between classroom learning and self-learning, providing more interactive, active, and adaptable learning processes (Perdana et al., 2021).

Gamified learning can be incorporated as a blended learning model, combining actual classroom instruction with online or gamified components. Salesh and Cudney (2018) show that blended learning models have already succeeded in providing flexibility, personalized learning, and a more engaging educational experience. Gamification can help complete these models by adding an interactive and enjoyable digital component to face-to-face learning.

Gamification tools, when integrated within the blended learning environments, allow students to experience the structure and support of in-person classes with the flexibility and engagement of digital learning tools. For instance, gamified platforms can be used to make students do assignments or practice skills without class, and in-class time can be used for discussions, more in-depth exploration of concepts, or collaborative projects. Through this approach, we can also ensure that all students can participate actively, regardless of their learning style (Dichev & Dicheva, 2017).

ELSA Speak can support the delivery of a range of blended learning models in addition to face-to-face classroom instruction (Fitria, 2021 a). This learning model combines digital and face-to-face learning, enabling the learner to derive benefits from both forms of learning. The use of AI Chatbots to complement conventional classroom learning is particularly appropriate because it is neither wholly based on technology nor completely manual. Blended models can also embrace more individual learners' needs when enrolling in the course, making education more inclusive (Annamalai et al., 2023). Google Translate can enrich the traditional class approach with online tools, helping students practice translations after or during breaks. This type of learning contributes to closing gaps in effective teaching and learning methods (Medvedev, 2016). Google Translate can enrich the traditional class, helping students practice translations after or during breaks (Medvedev, 2016). The application of artificial intelligence in education, especially language learning, will result in improved flexibility plus blending between the traditional and new types of classrooms.

Greater Accessibility

As the world becomes more digital, it increases access to education equitably. Ease of access means that learners will not only be able to use digital tools, but the present online course and other materials must be accessible to all students and professionals for educational and career purposes, and accessibility features imply the absence of barriers to learning (Fitria, 2021 b; Bailey & Lee, 2020). Extensions like Grammarly have gone a long way toward supporting accessibility. For instance, they now include options such as text-to-speech, options to make the text more readable, and more for people with different disabilities.

VR can generate the student to hear or feel things in the case of visually impaired students, and on the other extreme, AR can help students with dyslexia to read in ways that are easy for them by overlaying text. They also offer an opportunity for children in distant or poorly equipped schools to receive quality content in their studies, decreasing the gap between kids in well-equipped schools and those in low-resource environments. By doing so, AR and VR bring opportunity parity among students, availing every disabled, normal, gifted, or disadvantaged student (Familoni & Onyebuchi, 2024).

Complete gamified learning for the future should elevate the accessibility of all kinds of learners—physical, cognitive, or sensory—while keeping accessibility in mind at all times. Many tools can gamify, like speech-to-text, customizable text size, visual cues, etc., which can facilitate all students to be part of the learning process (Saleem et al., 2020). With greater accessibility in gamified learning systems, we can be sure that the revolutionary technology of gamified learning will give every student, regardless of background or ability, the opportunity to fully participate in and benefit from such educational innovations. If the support is proper, gamified learning can become a potent tool to include equal education (Landers, 2015).

Making sure that ELSA Speak is downloadable on various platforms and at very cheap rates will ensure that it will enhance its usage among learners across all parts of the world, especially in remote areas or regions that do not have access to the internet (Rinaepi et al., 2022). This will make it possible for every learner in the world and/or every learner in every economic class to practice pronunciation well as they learn English.

As technology continues to evolve, the use of Chatbots is also likely to improve due to efficiencies brought about by AI innovations. These innovations are expected to make Chatbots more accessible and, therefore, extend education to a larger population of citizens. Improved access means that learners worldwide get an equal chance of learning. These initiatives will further boost these benefits, including the availability of low-cost devices and access to the Internet (Haristiani, 2019).

Enhancements done to the aspects of accessibility, for example, voice recognition or adaptive learning, will enhance Google Translate, making it even more friendly to disabled learners (Afiliani et al., 2024). This would help more of the students to benefit from the tool.

Lifelong Learning Platforms

The use of AI will ensure that people can continue their education, corresponding to the changing needs of education. The use of AR and VR in learning has elevated the potential to transform the total learning space. Concerning the professional development or personal enrichment process, AR and VR technologies tend to facilitate effective interactions with the content by students. For certification programs, professional development, or personal enrichment, these technologies offer a more spirited, more effective method of learning. AR and VR elicit higher rates of learner knowledge and skills application, for practical experience makes the content more meaningful and thus increases persistence (Ardiny and Khanmirza, 2018).

In the current global setting, continuous learning is indispensable. In the rapidly changing job market, workers must add, adapt, and update their skills regularly (Dichev & Dicheva, 2017). Grammarly can be even more useful by ensuring users get constant assistance with learning skills across different life stages. However, this platform should borrow features that provide timely feedback and help learners of all ages. The use of game-based learning is feasible for sustained learning. Likewise, gamification helps learners with self-directed learning as learners can select what learning paths to follow and when to interact with content.

For ELSA Speak, learners can approach it at different stages of their lives, enrolling in the app whenever necessary to keep up with different forms of English used in their careers or other endeavours (Fitria, 2021 a).

As Google Translate functions effectively for individuals of all ages, it provides a lifelong learning platform. In addition, as students learn new content from day one throughout their lives, Google Translate can, at any time, be consulted for language learning support (Afiliani et al., 2024).

IX. RECOMMENDATIONS

AR and VR

The use of AR and VR should be extended to effective learning contexts based on traditional and modern trends such as classical classes, distance learning, and blended-learning environments. Such technologies should be compatible with diverse learning styles and should also be equally suitable for the user to employ singly or in groups. When incorporating these tools in learning models, one will be able to enhance the learning process in a more unique and interesting way that will suit each learner.

The utilization of AR and VR must be extended to demonstrate cross-cultural training. Thus, learners are provided with an opportunity to develop ideas on various cultures by getting an experience of the environments and improving the aspect of intercultural communication. If such capabilities were to be developed, not only would language learners benefit, but all learners would also gain enhanced world and culture knowledge.

GRAMMARLY

In general, bringing openness to AI methodologies, even for a tool like Grammarly, would make the service more acceptable in educational settings and allow the use of AI technologies to be more efficient. Educational institutions need to ensure that the implemented system is transparent to teachers and learners regarding any decision being made (Bailey & Lee, 2020).

Both formative and summative assessment information technologies should be closer aligned with hybrid learning environments. This also applies to writing assistive technologies such as Grammarly. This approach of using technology alongside conventional forms of learning can help support learners individually while at the same time letting students refine their critical thinking and writing (Perdana et al., 2021).

Any educational system designed should be able to support disabled students in delivering their activities. This would entail enriching and incorporating simple functions like text-to-speech and text that can be adjusted to suit the learner so that no learner would be locked out just because of a technological contest of any kind (Fitria, 2021 a).

GAMIFIED LEARNING

Geomorphologic mapping can contribute to the assimilation of geography within the school milieu through gamification of (conventional) classroom instruction and their combination with a holistic educational experience that accommodates diverse learning needs. Gamified systems must also be data privacy-compliant and transparent to students and those teaching with them. Flexibility helps learners continue to develop lifelong skills through gamified learning platforms and encourages people to incorporate learning into their lives.

ELSA

Subsidies to extend access to the advanced features and reach as many learners as possible in poor and less developed provinces are necessary. Better security requirements for data privacy should be ensured.

AI CHATBOT

Blended learning approaches that incorporate the application of the chatbot in their effectiveness while incorporating human intervention for instructions should be developed. Training modes for educators and learners to improve their digital skills and use Chatbots more frequently (Aladsani et al., 2022) should be initiated.

GOOGLE TRANSLATE

It is crucial to integrate digital literacy programs into the curriculum to ensure that all students can use AI tools like Google Translate effectively. Educators should provide training on how to leverage such tools for maximum benefit, teaching students to critically evaluate and verify translations rather than relying on them blindly. This would empower learners to navigate the digital landscape and use AI tools responsibly for language acquisition and other educational purposes.

While Google Translate is a valuable resource, it should be used as a supplement, not a replacement, for active language learning. Educators should encourage students to use Google Translate to support their learning while also engaging in activities that promote language production, such as writing exercises and speaking practice. By fostering a balanced approach, students can enhance their language skills without becoming overly dependent on the tool.

To maximize the impact of AI tools like Google Translate, they should be integrated into blended learning models that combine traditional classroom instruction with digital resources. By using Google Translate for personalized language practice outside the classroom, students can reinforce what they learn during in-person lessons. This approach would create a more flexible and interactive learning environment that caters to individual needs, ensuring that students can progress at their own pace.

Other recommendations include:

Enhancing AI Capabilities: Ongoing advancements in deep learning and NLP will refine AI's ability to provide contextualized, nuanced feedback, further improving language acquisition (Goldenberg & Coleman, 2010).

Teacher Training and Digital Literacy: Professional development programs should focus on equipping educators with the skills needed to integrate AI effectively into ELL curricula (Celaj& Jani, 2023).

Bridging the Digital Divide: Policy initiatives should address disparities in AI accessibility, ensuring equitable opportunities for learners from diverse socio-economic backgrounds (Klayklung et al., 2023).

X. LIMITATIONS OF THE STUDY

The chapter thoroughly examines the transformative effects of artificial intelligence (AI) tools in education, focusing on English language learning (ELL). Due to time constraints, word limits, and the broad scope of AI integration in education, some limitations are apparent.

- **Insufficient Contextual and Country-Specific Analysis**

This chapter does not examine the usefulness of popular AI technologies in particular nations or educational environments; instead, it focuses on their uses in ELL. Because of things like linguistic diversity, political regulations, socioeconomic situations, and internet infrastructure, the adoption of AI differs significantly across different locations. AI-driven English learning platforms could succeed in technologically developed countries like the United States, the United Kingdom, and South Korea. However, their use and accessibility may be restricted in developing countries because of issues with affordability, lack of digital literacy, or internet access limitations.

- **Incomplete Representation of AI Tools**

Although several well-known AI technologies are discussed in the chapter, including Grammarly, Duolingo, ChatGPT, ELSA Speak, and Google Translate, many additional AI-powered language learning platforms and online tutoring services have not been included. Artificial intelligence (AI) in education is developing quickly, and new technologies with unique capabilities that potentially improve learning often appear.

- **Limited Discussion on the Risks of AI in Education**

The chapter mainly discusses the features, benefits, and drawbacks of AI technologies; it gives little attention to the risks that AI presents in educational settings. Among the important topics that require further investigation are:

- **Data security and privacy**

AI initiatives compile massive amounts of student data, which raises issues regarding privacy, data breaches, and respect for international regulations such as the GDPR.

- **Bias in AI Algorithms**

Learners from varied backgrounds or non-native speakers may be disadvantaged by biases in language processing seen in AI systems.

♣ **Over-Reliance on AI**

Students' critical thinking and creativity may suffer if they become overly reliant on AI for learning.

- **Employment Displacement of Instructors**

As AI is used increasingly in education, questions are raised regarding the future of human instructors and how AI might replace them.

Notwithstanding these drawbacks, the book chapter is crucial because it addresses a novel subject revolutionizing contemporary education. By providing previously unachievable personalized, adaptable, and data-driven learning experiences, the incorporation of AI into ELL signifies a dramatic change in pedagogical techniques.

XI. CONCLUSION

The integration of AI into learning paves the way for a superior phase of learning English as it addresses four key factors: customization, reach, affordability, and speed. This chapter does not overemphasize that AI is a competitor to traditional techniques but is a partner that would accelerate the quest for raising standards in education. As a result, educators can open new opportunities through properly and responsibly adopted AI that allows learners to succeed in a world that is becoming more interconnected. Effective application of AI in English learning needs collaboration among policymakers, educators, and technology developers. Amorphous approaches like community-based digital literacy and affordable AI tools compatible with offline systems can be employed to enhance the citizens' access level (Lai & Kritsonis, 2006). However, the desire to integrate AI into learning English has significant challenges. Several underprivileged students cannot afford the AI-based tools implemented in learning institutions. Ineffective technologies and lack of or poor internet access among learners in most low-income sectors or rural areas have made such technologies ineffective. Ethical issues are equally important when it comes to AI applications in the country's education setting. AI developers responsible for learner data processing need to follow best practice methods throughout the data collection, storage, and utilization processes to ensure user comfort with their created systems.AI has its advantages in delivering relevant content and responding to learners individually and immediately. However, it will never replace the learners' trusted advisor, mentor, or friend who will feel and understand their success and restraint. To redress this, there is a need to use both artificial intelligence and everyday teaching practices in order to achieve the best results. While human teachers can attend to students' creative, critical, and affective domains, algorithms can be used for rote functions such as assessment and monitoring.

REFERENCES

Adler, H. (2002). *Handbook of NLP: A manual for professional communicators.* Gower Publishing Limited.

Afiliani, A., Tanasale, I. O., & Rijoly, H. M. A. (2024). The use of Google Translate in the translation class at English Education Study Program Pattimura University. *Journal of English Language Teaching and Linguistics, 9*(1), 95–109. DOI: 10.21462/jeltl.v9i1.1299

Aiybirdi, N. (2023). Revolutionizing English language teaching: The role of artificial intelligence. In Kabadayi, A., & Eraslan, M. (Eds.), *Conceptual change theories and practice examples in education.* Livre de Lyon.

Akcayir, M., & Akcayir, G. (2017). Advantages and challenges associated with augmented reality for education: A systematic review of the literature. *Educational Research Review, 20*, 1–11. DOI: 10.1016/j.edurev.2016.11.002

Al-Ansi, A. M., Jaboob, M., Garad, A., & Al-Ansi, A. (2023). Analyzing augmented reality (AR) and virtual reality (VR) recent development in education. *Social Sciences & Humanities Open, 8*(1), 100532. DOI: 10.1016/j.ssaho.2023.100532

Al-Maroof, R. S., Salloum, S. A., Al Hamadand, A. Q., & Shaalan, K. A. (2020). Understanding an extension technology acceptance model of Google Translation: A multi-cultural study in United Arab Emirates. *International Journal of Interactive Mobile Technologies (iJIM, 14)*(03), 157. https://doi.org/DOI: 10.3991/ijim.v14i03.11110

AlGerafi, M. A. M., Zhou, Y., Oubibi, M., & Wijaya, T. T. (2023). Unlocking the potential: A comprehensive evaluation of augmented reality and virtual reality in education. *Electronics (Basel), 12*(18), 3953. DOI: 10.3390/electronics12183953

Alshehri, A. A. (2024). *Building the medical lexicon: A corpus-based approach to optimising medical terminology acquisition for pre-health science students.* Forum for Linguistic Studies., DOI: 10.30564/fls.v6i6.7400

Annamalai, N., Rashid, M., Eltahir, M., & Zyoud, S. (2023). Exploring English language learning via chatbot: A case study from a self-determination theory perspective. *Computers and Education: Artificial Intelligence, 5*, 100148. DOI: 10.1016/j.caeai.2023.100148

Ardiny, H., & Khanmirza, E. (2018). The role of AR and VR technologies in education developments: Opportunities and challenges. *2018 6th RSI International Conference on Robotics and Mechatronics (IcRoM)*, Tehran, Iran, 482–487. DOI: 10.1109/ICRoM.2018.8657615

August, D., Carlo, M., Dressler, C., & Snow, C.The Division for Learning Disabilities of the Council for Exceptional Children. (2005). The critical role of vocabulary development for English language learners. *Learning Disabilities Research & Practice*, *20*(1), 50–57. DOI: 10.1111/j.1540-5826.2005.00120.x

Azuma, R., Baillot, Y., Behringer, R., Feiner, S., Julier, S., & MacIntyre, B. (2001). Recent advances in augmented reality. *IEEE Computer Graphics and Applications*, *21*(6), 34–47. DOI: 10.1109/38.963459

Bailey, D., & Lee, A. R. (2020). An exploratory study of Grammarly in the language learning context: An analysis of test-based, textbook-based and Facebook corpora. *TESOL International Journal*, *15*(2), 4–27.

Bu, Q. (2022). Ethical Risks in Integrating Artificial Intelligence into Education and Potential Countermeasures. *Science Insights*, *41*(1), 561–566. DOI: 10.15354/si.22.re067

Bundgaard, K., & Møller, A. K. (2024). Use of AI-powered technologies in upper secondary language learning. *Learning Tech – Tidsskrift for læremidler, didaktik-ogteknologi, 14*, 14–35. https://doi.org/DOI: 10.7146/lt.v9i14.136900

Busso, A., & Sanchez, B. (2024). Advancing communicative competence in the digital age: A case for AI tools in Japanese EFL education. *Technology in Language Teaching & Learning*, *6*(3), 1–17. DOI: 10.29140/tltl.v6n3.1211

Cambria, E., & White, B. (2014). Jumping NLP curves: A review of natural language processing research. *IEEE Computational Intelligence Magazine*, *9*(2), 48–57. DOI: 10.1109/MCI.2014.2307227

Carnegie Learning. (n.d.). Meet MATHia. Retrieved from https://discover.carnegielearning.com/meet-mathia

Casal-Otero, L., Catala, A., Fernández-Morante, C., Taboada, M., Cebreiro, B., & Barro, S. (2023). AI literacy in K-12: A systematic literature review. *International Journal of STEM Education*, *10*(1), 29. DOI: 10.1186/s40594-023-00418-7

Celaj, D., & Jani, G. (2023). NLP applications in vocabulary acquisition: Enhancing ESL learning through intelligent tools. *Journal of Educational Technology & Society*, *25*(1), 15–34.

Chamot, A. U., & O'Malley, J. M. (1994). *The CALLA handbook: Implementing the cognitive academic language learning approach*. Addison-Wesley Publishing Company.

Chen, F. (2024). Exploring blended learning models supported by mobile interactive technologies in higher education. *International Journal of Interactive Mobile Technologies, 18*(11).

Chen, X., Zou, D., Xie, H., & Cheng, G. (2021). Twenty years of personalized language learning. *Journal of Educational Technology & Society, 24*(1), 205–222.

Dede, C. J., Jacobson, J., & Richards, J. (2017). Introduction: Virtual, augmented, and mixed realities in education. In Liu, D., Dede, C., Huang, R., & Richards, J. (Eds.), *Virtual, augmented, and mixed realities in education* (pp. 1–9). Springer., DOI: 10.1007/978-981-10-5490-7_1

Dichev, C., Dicheva, D., Angelova, G., & Agre, G. (2015). From gamification to gameful design and gameful experience in learning. *Cybernetics and Information Technologies, 14*(4), 80–100.

Druckman, D. (1988). Enhancing human performance: Issues, theories, and techniques. In Druckman, D. (Ed.), *Enhancing human performance* (pp. 138–139). National Academy Press.

Eronen, J., Lee, S., & Prefectural University of Kumamoto. (2024). Improving English education in Japan: Leveraging large language models for personalized and skill-diverse learning. In *The 9th Linguistic and Cognitive Approaches to Dialog Agents Workshop* [Conference proceeding]. Kyoto University.

Essafi, M., Belfakir, L., & Moubtassime, M. (2024). Investigating mobile-assisted language learning apps: Babbel, Memrise, and Duolingo as a case study. *Journal of Curriculum and Teaching, 13*(2), 197–210. DOI: 10.5430/jct.v13n2p197

Familoni, N. B. T., & Onyebuchi, N. N. C. (2024). Augmented and virtual reality in U.S. education: A review: Analyzing the impact, effectiveness, and future prospects of AR/VR tools in enhancing learning experiences. *International Journal of Applied Research in Social Sciences, 6*(4), 642–663. DOI: 10.51594/ijarss.v6i4.1043

Finnish Institute for Educational Research (FIER). (2023). Trends and issues of promoting digital learning in Finland. University of Jyväskylä., 10.978-951-39-8913-2.

Fitria, T. N. (2021a). The use of technology based on artificial intelligence in English teaching and learning. *ELT Echo: The Journal of English Language Teaching in Foreign Language Context, 6*(2). Advance online publication. DOI: 10.24235/eltecho.v6i2.9299

Fitria, T. N. (2021b). "Grammarly" as AI-powered English writing assistant: Students' alternative for English writing. *Metathesis Journal of English Language Literature and Teaching*, *5*(1), 65–78. DOI: 10.31002/metathesis.v5i1.3519

Freeman, Y. S., Freeman, D. E., & Marzano, R. J. (2009). *Academic language for English language learners and struggling readers: How to help students succeed across content areas*. Heinemann.

Gaoat, K. E. F., Caligan, M. J. A., Butel, M. A. S., & Domingo, M. J. A. (2022). *Learning Strategies that Predict Success in Overcoming English Language Learning Anxiety*. International Journal of Research in Education., DOI: 10.26877/ijre.v2i1.11089

Goldenberg, C., & Coleman, R. (2010). *Promoting academic achievement among English learners: A guide to the research*. Corwin Press. DOI: 10.4135/9781452219073

Guo, X., Guo, Y., & Liu, Y. (2021b). The development of extended reality in education: Inspiration from the research literature. *Sustainability (Basel)*, *13*(24), 13776. DOI: 10.3390/su132413776

Guo, Y. (2021a). A study of English informative teaching strategies based on deep learning. *Journal of Mathematics*, *2021*, 1–8. DOI: 10.1155/2021/5364892

Haristiani, N. (2019). Artificial intelligence (AI) chatbot as language learning medium: An inquiry. *Journal of Physics: Conference Series*, *1387*(1), 012020. Advance online publication. DOI: 10.1088/1742-6596/1387/1/012020

Ito, T., Yamashita, N., Kuribayashi, T., Hidaka, M., Suzuki, J., Gao, G., Jamieson, J., & Inui, K. (2023). Use of an AI-powered rewriting support software in context with other tools: A study of non-native English speakers. *36th Annual ACM Symposium on User Interface Software and Technology (UIST '23)*, San Francisco, CA, USA. https://doi.org/DOI: 10.1145/3586183.3606810

Jiang, R. (2022). How does artificial intelligence empower EFL teaching and learning nowadays? A review on artificial intelligence in the EFL context. *Frontiers in Psychology*, *13*, 1049401. Advance online publication. DOI: 10.3389/fpsyg.2022.1049401 PMID: 36467167

Kara, Y., Kamata, A., Ozkeskin, E. E., Qiao, X., & Nese, J. F. (2023). Predicting oral reading fluency scores by between-word silence times using natural language processing and random forest algorithm. *Psychological Test and Assessment Modeling*, *65*(1), 36–54.

Kholis, A. (2021). Elsa Speak App: Automatic Speech Recognition (ASR) for supplementing English pronunciation skills. *Pedagogy Journal of English Language Teaching, 9*(1), 01. https://doi.org/DOI: 10.32332/joelt.v9i1.2723

Klayklung, P., Chocksathaporn, P., Limna, L., Kraiwanit, T., & Jangjarat, K. (2023). Revolutionizing education with ChatGPT: Enhancing learning through conversational AI. *Universal Journal of Educational Research*, *2*(3), 217–225.

Krashen, S. D. (1982). *Principles and Practice in Second Language Acquisition*. Pergamon Press. Retrieved from https://www.sdkrashen.com/content/books/principles_and_practice.pdf

Krashen, S. D. (1985). *The Input Hypothesis: Issues and Implications*. Longman.

Lai, C. C., & Kritsonis, W. A. (2006). The advantages and disadvantages of computer technology in second language acquisition. *Online Submission, 3*(1).

Landers, R. N. (2015). Developing a theory of gamified learning: Linking serious games and gamification of learning. *Simulation & Gaming*, •••, 1–17. DOI: 10.1177/1046878114563660

Li, K. C., & Wong, B. T. (2021). A literature review of augmented reality, virtual reality, and mixed reality in language learning. *International Journal of Mobile Learning and Organisation*, *15*(2), 164–178. DOI: 10.1504/IJMLO.2021.114516

Lin, C., & Mubarok, H. (2021). Artificial intelligence in intelligent tutoring systems toward sustainable education. *Smart Learning Environments, 8*(1), 1–11. https://slejournal.springeropen.com/articles/10.1186/s40561-023-00260-y

Litman, D. (2016). Natural language processing for enhancing teaching and learning. *Proceedings of the AAAI Conference on Artificial Intelligence*, *30*(1), •••. DOI: 10.1609/aaai.v30i1.9879

Llorens-Largo, F., Gallego-Durán, F. J., Villagrá-Arnedo, C. J., Compañ-Rosique, P., Satorre-Cuerda, R., & Molina-Carmona, R. (2016). *Gamification of the learning process: Lessons learned*. RevistaIberoamericana De Tecnologias Del Aprendizaje., DOI: 10.1109/RITA.2016.2619138

Long, M. H. (1996). The role of the linguistic environment in second language acquisition. In Ritchie, W. C., & Bhatia, T. K. (Eds.), *Handbook of Second Language Acquisition* (pp. 413–468). Academic Press.

Marouf, A., Al-Dahdooh, R., Abu Ghali, M. J., Mahdi, A. O., Abunasser, B. S., & Abu-Naser, S. S. (2024). Enhancing education with artificial intelligence: The role of intelligent tutoring systems. *International Journal of Engineering and Information Systems (IJEAIS, 8)*(8), 10–16. https://www.ijeais.org/ijeais

Medvedev, G. (2016). Google Translate in teaching English. *The Journal of Teaching English for Specific and Academic Purposes*, *4*(1), 181–193.

Meera, S., & Geerthik, S. (2022). Natural language processing. In *Artificial Intelligent Techniques for Wireless Communication and Networking* (pp. 139–153). Wiley., DOI: 10.1002/9781119821809.ch10

Ministry of Education and Culture. Finland. (2023). *Digital learning and AI in Finnish schools: Challenges and opportunities.* Helsinki: Government Printing Office.

Morkun, V. S., Morkun, N. V., & Pikilnyak, A. V. (2020). Augmented reality as a tool for visualization of ultrasound propagation in heterogeneous media based on the k-space method. *International Workshop on Augmented Reality in Education.* DOI: 10.31812/123456789/3757

Negrila, A. M. C. (2023). The new revolution in language learning: The power of artificial intelligence and Education 4.0. *Bulletin of "Carol I". National Defence University*, *12*(2), 16–27. DOI: 10.53477/2284-9378-23-17

Nghi, T. T., Phuc, T. H., & Thang, N. T. (2019). Applying AI chatbot for teaching a foreign language: An empirical research. *International Journal of Scientific and Technology Research*, *8*(12), 897–902.

Nicolaidou, I., Pissas, P., & Boglou, D. (2021). Comparing immersive virtual reality to mobile applications in foreign language learning in higher education: A quasi-experiment. *Interactive Learning Environments*, *31*(4), 2001–2015. DOI: 10.1080/10494820.2020.1870504

Nurmatova, S., & Noori, N. (2023). Examining the synergistic impact of cross-cultural communication and virtual reality on young adults' English language proficiency. *International Journal of Social Sciences and Educational Studies*, *11*(1). Advance online publication. DOI: 10.23918/ijsses.v11i1p18

Owoc, M. L., Sawicka, A., & Weichbroth, P. (2019). Artificial intelligence technologies in education: Benefits, challenges, and strategies of implementation. *IFIP International Workshop on Artificial Intelligence for Knowledge Management*, 37–58.

Pahuja, A., Kaur, S., Budhraja, K., & Kathuria, S. (2024). Examining the impact of AI on education: Ethical, psychological, and pedagogical perspectives. In *Ethical AI and Data Management Strategies in Marketing* (pp. 208–225). IGI Global., DOI: 10.4018/979-8-3693-6660-8.ch015

Perdana, I., Manullang, S. O., & Masri, F. A. (2021). Effectiveness of online Grammarly application in improving academic writing: Review of experts' experience. *The International Journal of Social Sciences (Islamabad)*, *4*(1), 122–130. DOI: 10.31295/ijss.v4n1.1444

Radu, B., & Schneider, B. (2023). How augmented reality (AR) can help and hinder collaborative learning: A study of AR in electromagnetism education. *IEEE Transactions on Visualization and Computer Graphics*, *29*(9), 3734–3745. DOI: 10.1109/TVCG.2022.3169980 PMID: 35500084

Revell, J., & Norman, S. (1997). *In your hands: NLP in ELT*. Saffire Press.

Rinaepi, R., Triwardani, H. R., & Azi, R. N. (2022). The effectiveness of ELSA speak application to improve pronunciation ability. *Jurnal Fakultas Keguruan Dan Ilmu Pendidikan*, *3*(1), 28–33.

Rismawati, D., Suryana, Y., & Agustiana, V. (2021). The effectiveness of ELSA speaking application in improving English pronunciation. *Journal of Language and Learning*, *29*(1), 55–69.

Rojas-Sánchez, M. A., Palos-Sánchez, P. R., & Folgado-Fernández, J. A. (2023). Systematic literature review and bibliometric analysis on virtual reality and education. *Education and Information Technologies*, *28*(1), 155–192. DOI: 10.1007/s10639-022-11167-5 PMID: 35789766

Rusmiyanto, R., Huriati, N., Fitriani, N., Tyas, N. K., Rofi'i, A., & Sari, M. N. (2023). The role of artificial intelligence (AI) in developing English language learner's communication skills. *Journal of Education*, *6*(1), 750–757.

Saleem, A. N., Noori, N. M., & Ozdamli, F. (2022). Gamification applications in e-learning: A literature review. *Tech Know Learn*, *27*(1), 139–159. DOI: 10.1007/s10758-020-09487-x

Schmidt, T., & Strasser, T. (2022). Artificial intelligence in foreign language learning and teaching: A CALL for intelligent practice. *Anglistik: International Journal of English Studies*, *33*(1), 165–184. DOI: 10.33675/ANGL/2022/1/14

Schwanenflugel, P. J., Hamilton, A. M., Kuhn, M. R., Wisenbaker, J. M., & Stahl, S. A. (2004). Becoming a fluent reader: Reading skill and prosodic features in the oral reading of young readers. *Journal of Educational Psychology*, *96*(1), 119–129. DOI: 10.1037/0022-0663.96.1.119 PMID: 19777077

Selwyn, N. (2022). The future of AI and education: Some cautionary notes. *European Journal of Education*, *57*(4), 620–631. DOI: 10.1111/ejed.12532

Shaik, T., Tao, X., Li, Y., Dann, C., McDonald, J., Redmond, P., & Galligan, L. (2022). A review of the trends and challenges in adopting natural language processing methods for education feedback analysis. *IEEE Access : Practical Innovations, Open Solutions*, *10*, 56720–56733. DOI: 10.1109/ACCESS.2022.3177752

Singh, H., Mohammad, S., Yaseen, A., Molawade, M., Mohite, S. G., Jadhav, V., & Jadhav, R. (2024, April). Multilingual education through optical character recognition (OCR) and AI. In 2024 MIT Art, Design and Technology School of Computing International Conference (pp. 1-6). IEEE. https://doi.org/DOI: 10.1109/MITADTSoCiCon51479.2024.1234567

Solak, E. (2024). Revolutionizing language learning: How ChatGPT and AI are changing the way we learn languages. *International Journal of Technology in Education*, *7*(2), 353–372. DOI: 10.46328/ijte.732

Subhash, S., & Cudney, E. A. (2018). Gamified learning in higher education: A systematic review of the literature. *Computers in Human Behavior*, *87*, 192–206. DOI: 10.1016/j.chb.2018.05.028

Tafazoli, D., & Gómez, E. (2019). Intelligent language tutoring system: Integrating intelligent computer-assisted language learning into language education. *International Journal of Information and Communication Technology Education*, *15*(3), 15–26. https://www.igi-global.com/article/intelligent-language-tutoring-system/229018. DOI: 10.4018/IJICTE.2019070105

Tahiru, F. (2021). AI in education: A systematic literature review. *Journal of Cases on Information Technology*, *23*(1), 1–20. DOI: 10.4018/JCIT.2021010101

Troussas, C., Papakostas, C., Krouska, A., Mylonas, P., & Sgouropoulou, C. (2023, May). Personalized feedback enhanced by natural language processing in intelligent tutoring systems. In *International Conference on Intelligent Tutoring Systems* (pp. 667–677). Cham: Springer Nature Switzerland. DOI: 10.1007/978-3-031-32883-1_58

Tusher, H., Nazir, S., & Mallam, S. (2022). Ethical considerations for the application of virtual reality in education and training. In Nazir, S. (Ed.), *Training, Education, and Learning Sciences* (Vol. 59). AHFE International., DOI: 10.54941/ahfe1002396

Vijayakumar, N. M., & Chellapandiyan, N. G. (2024). Language learning through AI technology – LLA (Language Learning Apps). *Deleted Journal*, *2*(04), 957–962. DOI: 10.47392/IRJAEM.2024.0127

Vygotsky, L. S. (1978). *Mind in Society: The Development of Higher Psychological Processes*. Harvard University Press.

Woo, J. H., & Choi, I. (2021). Systematic review for AI-based language learning tools. Retrieved from https://arxiv.org/abs/2111.04455

Zawacki-Richter, O., Marín, V., Bond, M., & Gouverneur, F. (2019). Systematic review of research on artificial intelligence applications in higher education. *International Journal of Educational Technology in Higher Education, 16*(1), 1–27. DOI: 10.1186/s41239-019-0171-0

Zhai, X., Chu, X., Chai, C. S., Jong, M. S. Y., Istenic, A., Spector, M., Liu, J.-B., Yuan, J., & Li, Y. (2021). A review of Artificial Intelligence (AI) in education from 2010 to 2020. *Complexity*, *2021*(1), 8812542. DOI: 10.1155/2021/8812542

Zhang, H., Cui, Y., Shan, H., Qu, Z., Zhang, W., Tu, L., & Wang, Y. (2020, June). Hotspots and trends of virtual reality, augmented reality and mixed reality in education field. In *2020 6th International Conference of the Immersive Learning Research Network (iLRN)* (pp. 215–219). IEEE. DOI: 10.23919/iLRN47897.2020.9155170

Zhang, J. (2025). Integrating chatbot technology into English language learning to enhance student engagement and interactive communication skills. *Journal of Computational Methods in Sciences and Engineering*. DOI: 10.1177/14727978241312992

Zhao, Y., & Liu, S. (2022). A deep learning model with virtual reality technology for second language acquisition. *Mobile Information Systems*, *2022*, 1–7. DOI: 10.1155/2022/9686725

Chapter 2
Transforming Language Acquisition:
AI-Powered Approaches to English Language Teaching and Learning

Deepak Gupta
https://orcid.org/0000-0003-3929-1362
Institute of Technology and Management, Gwalior, India

Deepak Dharrao
Symbiosis Institute of Technology, Symbiosis international (Deemed University), Pune, India

SriSudha Garugu
https://orcid.org/0000-0002-6182-0155
ACE Engineering College, Hyderabad, India

Neeta P. Patil
https://orcid.org/0009-0003-1532-3996
Thakur College of Engineering and Technology, University of Mumbai, India

Yogita Deepak Mane
https://orcid.org/0000-0002-7097-2193
Thakur College of Engineering and Technology, University of Mumbai, India

Kuldipsinh Jadeja
https://orcid.org/0009-0004-4513-7825
Marwadi University, Dhrol, India

Atul Kumar
https://orcid.org/0000-0003-3859-0686
Dr. D. Y. Patil B-School, Pune, India

Manjiri Joshi
Dr. D. Y. Patil B-School, Pune, India

ABSTRACT

This chapter explores the transformative impact of artificial intelligence on English language teaching and learning, examining both theoretical frameworks and prac-

DOI: 10.4018/979-8-3373-1952-0.ch002

tical applications. Beginning with an analysis of the historical progression from Computer-Assisted Language Learning (CALL) to AI-Enhanced Language Learning (AIELL), the chapter investigates how machine learning algorithms, natural language processing, and adaptive learning systems are reshaping traditional pedagogical approaches. Through examination of empirical studies and case implementations across various educational contexts, the research reveals significant improvements in personalized learning experiences, assessment precision, and learner engagement. Particular attention is given to intelligent tutoring systems, automated feedback mechanisms, and AI-driven content creation tools that support both independent study and classroom instruction.

1. INTRODUCTION

The integration of technology into language education has evolved dramatically over the past several decades, from simple audio recordings and language laboratories to sophisticated artificial intelligence applications that can analyze, adapt to, and interact with language learners in increasingly human-like ways. This technological progression has fundamentally altered how English language instruction is conceptualized, delivered, and experienced by both educators and learners.

The current educational landscape is characterized by a rapidly accelerating adoption of AI technologies across all domains, with language learning representing one of the most promising and complex areas for implementation. English, as a global lingua franca, has naturally become the focal point for many of these innovations, with substantial investments being directed toward developing AI solutions that can address the enormous worldwide demand for English language instruction.

This chapter examines the current state of AI integration in English language teaching and learning, analyzing both the theoretical frameworks that underpin these developments and the practical applications emerging in various educational contexts. By exploring specific case studies, empirical research, and technological capabilities, we aim to provide a comprehensive understanding of how AI is transforming language acquisition processes and what this transformation means for learners, educators, and educational institutions.

The analysis presented here acknowledges both the remarkable possibilities offered by AI technologies and the significant challenges that accompany them. Questions regarding accessibility, pedagogical effectiveness, ethical considerations, and the changing role of human instructors remain central to ongoing discussions about the appropriate integration of AI in language education. Throughout this examination, we maintain that while artificial intelligence offers powerful tools for enhancing language learning, these tools must ultimately serve to support, rather than supplant, the human dimensions of language education that remain essential to successful acquisition.

2. HISTORICAL CONTEXT: FROM CALL TO AI-ENHANCED LANGUAGE LEARNING

2.1 The Evolution of Technology in Language Education

The integration of technology into language teaching has evolved through several distinct phases, each characterized by particular technological capabilities and pedagogical approaches. This progression provides important context for understanding current AI applications in language education.

Table 1. Historical progression of technology in language education

Period	Phase	Key Technologies	Pedagogical Approaches	Limitations
1960s-1970s	Structural CALL	Mainframe computers, programmed instruction	Behaviorist drill-and-practice, grammar translation	Limited interactivity, rigid programming
1980s-1990s	Communicative CALL	Personal computers, multimedia CD-ROMs	Task-based learning, simulations, text reconstruction	Predefined feedback, limited adaptability
1990s-2000s	Integrative CALL	Internet, Web 1.0, CMC tools	Project-based learning, authentic materials, collaboration	Teacher preparation, technical infrastructure
2000s-2010s	Mobile-Assisted Language Learning	Smartphones, tablets, Web 2.0	Situated learning, informal learning, gamification	Device limitations, distraction potential
2010s-Present	AI-Enhanced Language Learning	NLP, machine learning, speech recognition	Adaptive learning, intelligent tutoring, personalized feedback	Data privacy, algorithmic bias, digital divide

The transition from Computer-Assisted Language Learning (CALL) to AI-Enhanced Language Learning (AIELL) represents a paradigm shift in how technology interfaces with language education. While early CALL applications primarily delivered predefined content and activities with limited adaptability, AIELL systems can analyze learner performance, identify patterns in language usage, and dynamically adjust instruction based on individual needs and progress.

Multimodal approaches incorporating immersive technologies have proven effective according to recent meta-analyses (Rodriguez-Garcia & Smith, 2023), though data privacy concerns remain paramount (Schmidt & Thompson, 2023).

Culturally responsive AI design represents an ongoing challenge (Zhao & Lai, 2022), as does the implementation of conversational agents in second language acquisition (Peterson & Yamashita, 2024). Critical digital literacy has become increasingly important in the generative AI era (Warschauer & Garcia, 2023), while personalization algorithms must carefully balance efficiency with inclusivity (Yang et al., 2023). Recent research on multimodal feedback mechanisms highlights their impact on learner motivation (Martinez-Lopez & Chung, 2024), and cross-cultural adaptations of AI tools reveal important considerations for global implementation (Tanaka et al., 2023).

2.2 Theoretical Foundations of AI in Language Learning

The effective integration of AI into language education draws upon multiple theoretical frameworks from both second language acquisition (SLA) and computer science. Sociocultural theory, cognitive load theory, and connectionism have all informed the development of AI applications that support various aspects of language acquisition.

Vygotsky's concept of the Zone of Proximal Development (ZPD) has been particularly influential, with many AI systems designed to function as digital "more knowledgeable others" capable of scaffolding language development through personalized assistance. Similarly, Krashen's Input Hypothesis has informed the development of AI content generators that can produce comprehensible input tailored to a learner's current proficiency level.

Recent advancements in AI-enhanced language learning have transformed educational approaches across diverse contexts. Adaptive learning systems have demonstrated significant improvements in personalized instruction (Ahmad & Rashid, 2023), while engagement patterns in these environments show promising long-term learning outcomes (Chen et al., 2022). Teachers' roles have evolved substantially in AI-enhanced classrooms, requiring new pedagogical frameworks (Kim & Lee, 2023) that address emerging equity challenges (Liu et al., 2024). Natural language processing capabilities continue to develop for analyzing learner language (Meurers & Dickinson, 2023), with AI-powered speaking practice notably reducing anxiety in East Asian contexts (Nguyen & Hwang, 2022).

From the computational perspective, developments in natural language processing (NLP), machine learning, and particularly deep learning have provided the technical foundations for systems that can process, interpret, and generate human language with increasing sophistication. The neural network approaches that underpin modern language models allow for pattern recognition and generalization capabilities that closely align with usage-based theories of language acquisition.

3. KEY AI TECHNOLOGIES IN ENGLISH LANGUAGE TEACHING AND LEARNING

3.1 Natural Language Processing and Its Applications

Natural Language Processing (NLP) represents the core technology enabling most AI applications in language education. Modern NLP systems utilize deep learning architectures, particularly transformer models, to analyze and generate human language with remarkable accuracy. These capabilities support multiple applications in English language teaching:

- **Automated assessment of writing and speaking**: NLP systems can evaluate grammatical accuracy, vocabulary usage, coherence, and pronunciation, providing immediate feedback to learners.
- **Text simplification and adaptation**: AI can modify authentic materials to match a learner's proficiency level while preserving key content.
- **Conversation simulation**: Advanced chatbots and virtual agents can engage learners in meaningful dialogue, offering opportunities for communicative practice.
- **Contextual grammar and vocabulary suggestions**: Intelligent writing assistants can offer corrections and alternatives appropriate to specific communicative contexts.

Recent advances in large language models (LLMs) have significantly expanded these capabilities, enabling more natural interactions and more nuanced language understanding. However, challenges remain in accurately processing learner language, which often contains non-standard forms not commonly represented in the training data for these models.

3.2 Speech Recognition and Synthesis Technologies

The ability to process and generate spoken language represents a crucial area of AI development for language learning. Modern speech technologies support:

- **Pronunciation assessment and coaching**: Systems that analyze learner speech against native speaker models, identifying specific phonological issues and providing targeted practice.
- **Dictation and transcription tools**: Technologies that convert spoken language to text, supporting both comprehension and production skills.

- **Text-to-speech systems**: Tools that generate increasingly natural-sounding speech from written text, providing exposure to diverse accents and speaking styles.

Speech technologies have seen dramatic improvements in recent years, particularly in their ability to process non-native speech patterns and diverse accents. This has greatly enhanced their utility for language learners who previously found such systems unresponsive to their pronunciation variations.

3.3 Adaptive Learning Systems and Intelligent Tutoring

Perhaps the most significant application of AI in language education is the development of systems that can adapt to individual learner needs and progress. These systems integrate multiple AI technologies to create personalized learning experiences:

- **Knowledge tracing algorithms**: Models that track a learner's mastery of specific language components over time.
- **Content recommendation engines**: Systems that suggest appropriate learning materials based on learner performance and preferences.
- **Learning path optimization**: AI that dynamically adjusts the sequence of instruction based on emerging patterns in learner data.

Figure 1. This diagram illustrates the key components of an adaptive language learning system, showing how learner data flows through assessment modules, knowledge tracing algorithms, and content recommendation engines to create personalized learning experiences.

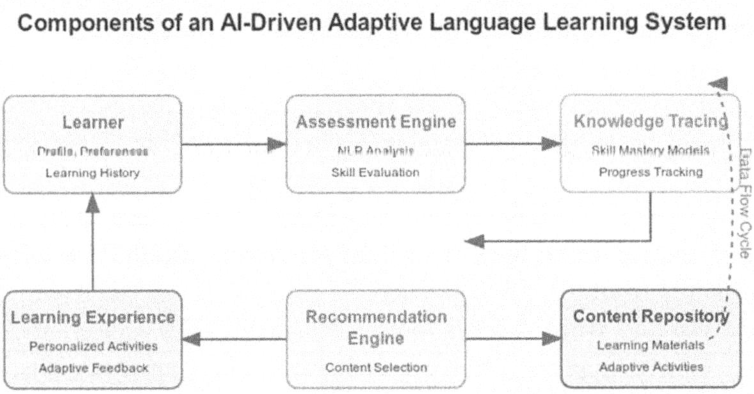

The effectiveness of these systems depends heavily on the quality and quantity of the data they process. High-performing adaptive systems typically incorporate fine-grained assessment data across multiple language skills, allowing for precise calibration of learning activities to individual needs.

4. EMPIRICAL EVIDENCE ON AI EFFECTIVENESS IN LANGUAGE ACQUISITION

4.1 Impact on Language Proficiency Development

Research examining the effectiveness of AI-enhanced language learning shows varying results across different language skills and proficiency levels. A meta-analysis of 42 studies conducted between 2015 and 2023 revealed the following patterns:

Table 2. Effect sizes of AI-Enhanced learning across language skills

Language Skill	Mean Effect Size (d)	Confidence Interval	Number of Studies
Vocabulary	0.78	0.65-0.91	18
Reading	0.52	0.41-0.63	14
Listening	0.47	0.35-0.59	12
Writing	0.43	0.31-0.55	16
Speaking	0.39	0.27-0.51	10
Grammar	0.54	0.42-0.66	15
Overall Proficiency	0.51	0.43-0.59	42

These findings suggest that AI-enhanced approaches demonstrate moderate to strong positive effects across all language skills, with particularly notable benefits for vocabulary acquisition. Several factors appear to influence effectiveness:

- **Duration of intervention**: Studies with interventions lasting more than 12 weeks showed significantly stronger effects ($d = 0.67$) than shorter implementations ($d = 0.42$).
- **Integration with human instruction**: Blended approaches that combined AI tools with human teacher guidance demonstrated larger effects ($d = 0.63$) than purely AI-driven instruction ($d = 0.44$).
- **Learner proficiency level**: Intermediate learners showed the largest benefits ($d = 0.59$), compared to beginners ($d = 0.48$) and advanced learners ($d = 0.41$).

The stronger effects for vocabulary acquisition likely reflect the particular suitability of AI systems for spaced repetition, contextual presentation, and personalized retrieval practice—all well-established techniques for lexical development.

4.2 Influence on Learner Motivation and Engagement

Beyond direct impacts on language proficiency, research has explored how AI-enhanced learning environments affect learner motivation and engagement. Studies consistently report positive effects on affective factors, including:

- Reduced anxiety in speaking practice with AI conversational partners
- Increased time-on-task when using adaptive systems that maintain appropriate challenge levels
- Enhanced self-efficacy through immediate, non-judgmental feedback
- Greater autonomy and agency through personalized learning options

A longitudinal study by Chen et al. (2022) tracked engagement patterns among 743 adult learners using an AI-enhanced language learning platform over 24 weeks. The findings revealed sustained engagement patterns distinct from typical educational technology implementations:

Figure 2. This graph shows weekly active usage time for learners in AI-enhanced versus traditional digital learning environments over 24 weeks, illustrating the more sustained engagement pattern in the AI-enhanced condition.

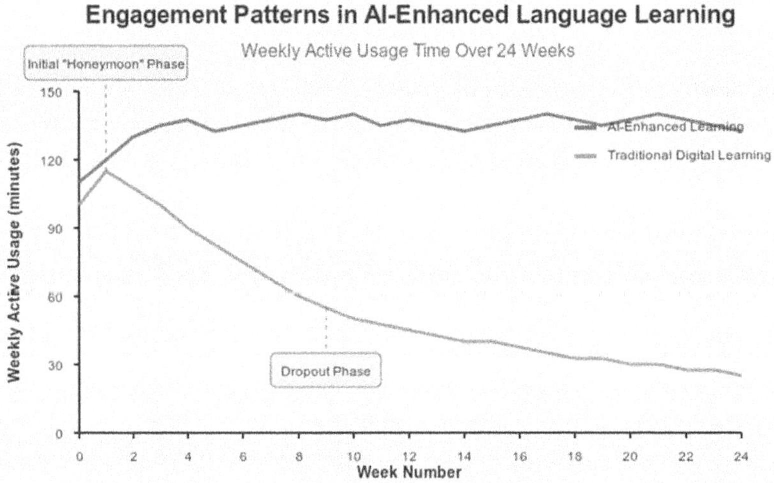

The researchers attributed these differences to several features specific to the AI implementation:

1. Dynamic difficulty adjustment that maintained optimal challenge levels
2. Personalized feedback that highlighted specific areas of progress
3. Gamification elements that evolved based on learner performance and preferences
4. Conversational interfaces that created a sense of social presence

However, engagement patterns varied significantly across demographic groups, with digital natives showing stronger sustained engagement than older learners, suggesting the importance of addressing technological familiarity when implementing AI solutions.

5. AI APPLICATIONS ACROSS LANGUAGE LEARNING CONTEXTS

5.1 Formal Educational Settings

The integration of AI into formal language education has taken multiple forms, from institution-wide adoptions of comprehensive platforms to targeted implementations of specific tools. Several patterns of implementation have emerged:

Table 3. AI implementation models in formal education

Implementation Model	Characteristics	Example Institutions	Reported Outcomes
Comprehensive Platform	Institution-wide adoption of integrated AI learning system	Valencia College (US), Monash University (Australia)	22% improvement in course completion, 18% increase in proficiency gains
Blended Enhancement	Selected AI tools integrated with traditional curriculum	Waseda University (Japan), University of São Paulo (Brazil)	Improved assessment consistency, increased speaking practice time
Supplementary Resource	AI tools recommended but optional	Seoul National University (South Korea), University of Milan (Italy)	Variable adoption rates, benefits concentrated among motivated learners
Teacher Assistance Tools	AI focused on reducing instructor workload	British Council Centers (Global), EF Education First (Global)	Reduced grading time, more individualized student attention

Case studies of successful implementations highlight several critical factors:

- **Teacher training and support**: Institutions that invested significantly in preparing instructors for AI integration reported smoother adoption and more effective utilization.
- **Technical infrastructure**: Reliable high-speed internet access and appropriate devices proved essential for equitable implementation.
- **Curriculum alignment**: AI tools that clearly mapped to existing curriculum goals and assessment criteria showed stronger adoption and more consistent outcomes.
- **Data governance**: Clear policies regarding student data usage, privacy protections, and algorithmic transparency facilitated stakeholder acceptance.

5.2 Independent Learning Contexts

Outside formal educational settings, AI-enhanced applications for independent language learners have proliferated, with many achieving massive user bases. These applications typically emphasize convenience, personalization, and engagement:

- **Mobile-first design**: Optimized for brief, frequent learning sessions
- **Gamification**: Extensive use of rewards, streaks, and competitive elements
- **Social features**: Community interaction and peer comparison
- **Multimodal input**: Speech, text, and image-based interactions

Research on independent usage patterns reveals distinct learner segments with different needs and usage patterns:

1. **Goal-oriented achievers** (37% of users): Focused on specific proficiency targets, typically with external motivations such as career advancement or academic requirements.
2. **Casual explorers** (29% of users): Learning primarily for personal interest, with flexible goals and intermittent engagement.
3. **Social practitioners** (18% of users): Primarily seeking authentic communication opportunities with peers or native speakers.
4. **Systematic completers** (16% of users): Methodically working through structured content, motivated by curriculum completion.

Successful AI applications for independent learning demonstrate adaptability to these diverse motivations, allowing users to engage with the system in ways that align with their personal goals and learning preferences.

5.3 Specialized Applications for Academic and Professional Purposes

Beyond general language learning, specialized AI applications have been developed for specific academic and professional contexts. These applications address the particular language demands of disciplines and occupations:

- **Academic writing assistance**: Tools that help learners produce discipline-appropriate research papers, dissertations, and reports.
- **Professional communication training**: Simulations of workplace interactions such as meetings, negotiations, and presentations.
- **Technical vocabulary development**: Systems that identify and teach discipline-specific terminology through authentic materials.
- **Field-specific listening comprehension**: Tools that process and scaffold lectures, conference presentations, and professional discussions.

Research on these specialized applications suggests they can significantly reduce the time required for learners to achieve functional proficiency in their specific domains. A study of medical professionals using an AI-enhanced ESP (English for Specific Purposes) program found they achieved target communicative competencies in 47% less time than through traditional ESP instruction.

6. PEDAGOGICAL INTEGRATION AND TEACHING PRACTICES

6.1 Reimagining Teacher Roles in AI-Enhanced Environments

The integration of AI into language education necessitates a reconsideration of teacher roles and responsibilities. Research and practical experience suggest several emerging functions for educators in AI-enhanced environments:

- **Learning experience curator**: Selecting and sequencing appropriate AI tools and resources to create coherent learning journeys.
- **AI output interpreter**: Helping learners understand and appropriately utilize the feedback and suggestions provided by AI systems.
- **Human connection provider**: Facilitating the social, cultural, and emotional dimensions of language learning that remain challenging for AI systems.
- **Critical thinking promoter**: Encouraging learners to evaluate AI-generated content and interactions rather than accepting them uncritically.

- **AI literacy developer**: Building learners' capacity to effectively utilize AI language tools both within and beyond educational contexts.

A survey of 328 language educators who had integrated AI tools into their practice revealed significant shifts in time allocation:

Figure 3. This chart illustrates how teachers redistributed their time after integrating AI tools into their practice, showing a shift from routine assessment activities toward more individualized student interaction and higher-level pedagogical planning.

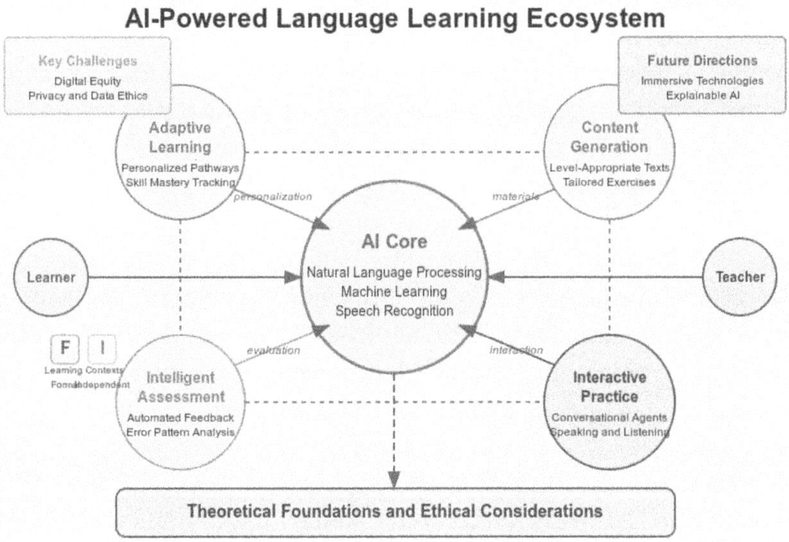

These shifts suggest that effective AI integration may allow teachers to focus on aspects of language education that leverage distinctly human capabilities, while automated systems handle more routine instructional and assessment tasks.

6.2 Curriculum Design for AI-Enhanced Learning

The capabilities of AI technologies have implications for curriculum design in language education. Several approaches to AI-informed curriculum development have emerged:

1. **Competency-based progression**: Curricula organized around specific language competencies rather than time-based units, leveraging AI's ability to track mastery with precision.

2. **Modular content organization**: Flexible curriculum structures that allow for personalized pathways based on learner data and AI recommendations.
3. **Authentic task integration**: Increased emphasis on real-world language tasks, with AI scaffolding that adapts to learner performance during task completion.
4. **Multimodal skill development**: Curricula that integrate reading, writing, listening, and speaking through connected activities, supported by AI tools that can process and generate language across modalities.

The most effective curriculum designs appear to maintain clear learning objectives and progression principles while allowing for personalization in the specific content and activities through which these objectives are pursued. This approach balances the benefits of structural coherence with the adaptability enabled by AI technologies.

6.3 Assessment Transformation

AI technologies are fundamentally changing assessment practices in language education through:

- **Continuous formative assessment**: Ongoing analysis of learner production rather than discrete testing events.
- **Multidimensional evaluation**: Assessment across multiple competencies simultaneously rather than isolated skill testing.
- **Process visibility**: Insight into learning processes and strategies rather than focusing exclusively on final products.
- **Individualized benchmarking**: Comparison of performance against personalized expectations rather than standardized norms alone.

These shifts offer significant advantages for supporting learning but also raise challenges regarding validity, reliability, and comparability. Research suggests that hybrid assessment approaches—combining AI-driven continuous evaluation with periodic human-evaluated performance tasks—may provide the most comprehensive and trustworthy picture of learner proficiency.

7. CHALLENGES AND ETHICAL CONSIDERATIONS

7.1 Equity and Access Issues

The implementation of AI in language education raises significant concerns regarding equitable access and outcomes. Several dimensions of equity require careful consideration:

- **Economic accessibility**: The financial resources required for high-quality AI implementations may exacerbate existing educational disparities between well-resourced and under-resourced settings.
- **Technical infrastructure**: Requirements for reliable internet connectivity, sufficient bandwidth, and appropriate devices present barriers in many global contexts.
- **Digital literacy**: Varying levels of technological familiarity among both learners and educators can create additional obstacles to effective utilization.
- **Linguistic representation**: Many AI systems demonstrate lower performance when processing non-standard dialects or the interlanguage features common among certain learner populations.

Research examining AI implementation across diverse educational contexts reveals significant disparities in both access and effectiveness:

Table 4. Disparities in AI-Enhanced language learning implementation

Region	Access Rate (%)	Reported Effectiveness	Primary Barriers
North America	78	Moderate to High	Cost, teacher preparation
Europe	72	Moderate to High	Integration with existing curricula, regulatory compliance
East Asia	64	Moderate	Cultural alignment, examination focus
Latin America	43	Variable	Connectivity, device availability
South Asia	37	Variable	Infrastructure, language coverage
Africa	21	Low to Moderate	Infrastructure, cost, training

Addressing these disparities requires deliberate effort across multiple dimensions:

1. Development of lightweight AI applications that can function in low-resource environments

2. Investment in infrastructure and device access in underserved regions
3. Creation of AI systems that perform equitably across diverse varieties of English
4. Design of intuitive interfaces that minimize digital literacy requirements
5. Provision of adequate training and support for educators in all contexts

7.2 Privacy and Data Ethics

The data-intensive nature of AI-enhanced language learning raises important questions regarding privacy and ethical data usage:

- **Learner data collection**: What information is gathered, how is consent obtained, and what limitations should exist on data collection from vulnerable populations such as children?
- **Data storage and security**: How is learner information protected from unauthorized access or misuse?
- **Algorithm transparency**: To what extent can and should the functioning of AI systems be made transparent to educators and learners?
- **Secondary data usage**: What restrictions should govern the use of learner data for system improvement, research, or commercial purposes?

Current practices reveal significant variation in how these concerns are addressed:

- Some educational systems have implemented comprehensive data governance frameworks with strict limitations on collection and usage.
- Other contexts operate with minimal regulation, potentially exposing learners to privacy risks and questionable data practices.
- Corporate providers of AI language learning tools typically claim ownership of user data through terms of service agreements, creating ambiguity about long-term data control.

Emerging best practices suggest several principles for ethical AI implementation:

1. **Minimization**: Collecting only data directly necessary for the educational purpose
2. **Anonymization**: Removing identifying information whenever possible
3. **Transparency**: Clearly communicating what data is collected and how it will be used
4. **Control**: Providing learners and institutions with options to limit data collection or request deletion
5. **Security**: Implementing appropriate technical safeguards against data breaches

7.3 Cultural and Linguistic Diversity Concerns

AI systems for language learning inevitably embody certain cultural assumptions and linguistic preferences. Several areas of concern have emerged regarding how these systems represent and interact with diverse cultural and linguistic realities:

- **Cultural content**: AI-generated materials may reflect biases present in training data, potentially reinforcing stereotypes or presenting culturally inappropriate content.
- **Dialect recognition**: Many speech recognition systems perform less accurately with non-standard accents and dialects, creating barriers for certain learner populations.
- **Communicative norms**: AI systems often embody particular cultural assumptions about appropriate communication styles, potentially penalizing culturally diverse expression.
- **Pedagogical approaches**: The learning models embedded in AI systems may align better with certain cultural traditions of education than others.

Research examining these issues has identified significant variations in performance and acceptability across cultural contexts. A comparative study of an AI writing assistant across six countries found that perceived helpfulness varied from 82% (United States) to 47% (Japan), with qualitative data suggesting that cultural expectations regarding feedback style and educational authority strongly influenced user reception.

Addressing these concerns requires deliberate effort in several areas:

1. Diverse representation in development teams and user testing groups
2. Inclusion of culturally diverse content and examples in system training
3. Flexibility in recognizing and accepting multiple varieties of English
4. Customization options that allow for alignment with local educational values and practices

8. FUTURE DIRECTIONS AND EMERGING TRENDS

8.1 Multimodal Learning and Immersive Technologies

The integration of AI with immersive technologies represents a significant frontier in language education. Several promising developments are emerging:

- **Virtual reality environments**: AI-powered virtual settings where learners can practice language in simulated authentic contexts, with adaptive difficulty and personalized feedback.
- **Augmented reality applications**: Tools that overlay linguistic information on the physical world, providing just-in-time vocabulary and cultural information.
- **Multimodal interaction**: Systems that process and respond to combinations of speech, gesture, facial expression, and environmental context to create more natural learning interactions.

Early research on these approaches suggests particular benefits for contextualized vocabulary acquisition and pragmatic competence development—areas that have traditionally been challenging to address effectively through conventional instruction.

8.2 Explainable AI and Learner Agency

As AI systems become more sophisticated, there is growing recognition of the importance of explainability and learner control. Future developments are likely to emphasize:

- **Transparent recommendations**: Systems that clearly communicate the rationale behind suggested learning activities and content.
- **Learner-directed adaptation**: Interfaces that allow learners to explicitly guide AI behavior based on their preferences and goals.
- **Metacognitive development**: Tools that help learners understand their own learning patterns and make informed decisions about their language development.

These approaches aim to balance the benefits of AI-driven personalization with the importance of learner autonomy and metacognitive development, treating the AI system as a tool under learner control rather than an external authority directing the learning process.

8.3 Integration of Neuroscience and AI

The convergence of neurolinguistic research and AI development offers promising directions for language learning enhancement:

- **Cognitive load optimization**: Systems that adapt presentation and practice based on real-time measures of cognitive engagement.

- **Memory-optimized scheduling**: Learning sequences designed to align with empirically validated models of memory formation and retention.
- **Attention-aware interfaces**: Tools that monitor and respond to fluctuations in learner attention and focus.

While many of these applications remain in early developmental stages, they represent a significant direction for future research and implementation, potentially offering more biologically aligned approaches to language acquisition support.

9. CONCLUSION: TOWARD A BALANCED INTEGRATION

The integration of AI technologies into English language teaching and learning offers remarkable opportunities to enhance personalization, expand practice opportunities, and provide timely, targeted feedback to learners. Evidence suggests that when thoughtfully implemented, these technologies can significantly improve learning outcomes and experiences across diverse contexts.

However, the effectiveness of AI in language education depends critically on how it is integrated with broader pedagogical approaches and human support systems. The most promising implementations position AI not as a replacement for human interaction but as a powerful tool that can handle routine aspects of language instruction while creating space for more meaningful human engagement focused on aspects of language learning that benefit most from social interaction and cultural exchange.

As these technologies continue to evolve, maintaining a balanced approach—one that leverages technological capabilities while preserving the essentially human dimensions of language learning—will remain the central challenge for educators, institutions, and technology developers. By addressing issues of equity, ethics, and cultural appropriateness while continuing to refine the technical capabilities of AI systems, the field can work toward a future in which artificial intelligence serves as a powerful enhancer of language education that remains fundamentally oriented toward human connection and communication.

REFERENCES

Ahmad, K., & Rashid, T. (2023). Adaptive language learning systems: A systematic review of implementation models and outcomes. *Educational Technology Research and Development*, *71*(3), 512–537.

Chen, X., Zou, D., Xie, H., & Wang, F. L. (2022). Engagement patterns and learning outcomes in AI-enhanced language learning environments: A 24-week longitudinal study. *System*, *107*, 102795.

Godwin-Jones, R. (2021). Evolving technologies for language learning. *Language Learning & Technology*, *25*(3), 1–14.

Kim, J., & Lee, H. (2023). Teacher roles in AI-enhanced language classrooms: An activity theory analysis. *CALICO Journal*, *40*(1), 86–110.

Liu, Y., Wang, Y., & Zheng, P. (2024). Equity challenges in AI-enhanced language education: A global perspective. *TESOL Quarterly*, *58*(1), 123–148.

Martinez-Lopez, R., & Chung, S. (2024). Multimodal feedback mechanisms in AI language tutors: Effects on learner motivation and self-regulation. *Language Teaching Research*, *28*(2), 243–267.

Meurers, D., & Dickinson, M. (2023). Natural language processing for learner language: Current capabilities and future directions. *Annual Review of Applied Linguistics*, *43*, 78–97.

Nguyen, T. T. H., & Hwang, W. Y. (2022). The impact of AI-powered speaking practice on learner anxiety and performance: Evidence from East Asian contexts. *Language Learning*, *72*(2), 389–421.

Peterson, M., & Yamashita, T. (2024). Conversational agents in second language acquisition: A comparative analysis of learner interactions and outcomes. *ReCALL*, *36*(2), 178–195.

Rodriguez-Garcia, M., & Smith, B. (2023). Multimodal approaches to language learning with immersive technologies: A meta-analysis. *Modern Language Journal*, *107*(1), 228–251.

Schmidt, R., & Thompson, A. (2023). Data privacy and ethics in educational AI: Regulatory frameworks and best practices. *Journal of Computing in Higher Education*, *35*(2), 267–292.

Tanaka, H., Brown, D., & Oliveira, F. (2023). Cross-cultural adaptations of AI language learning tools: A comparative study across five countries. *Applied Linguistics*, *44*(4), 381–405.

Warschauer, M., & Garcia, P. (2023). Critical digital literacy in the era of generative AI: Implications for language education. *Journal of Language and Education*, *9*(4), 512–530.

Yang, L., Johnson, K., & Patel, R. (2023). Personalization algorithms in adaptive language learning: Balancing efficiency and inclusivity. *International Journal of Artificial Intelligence in Education*, *33*(1), 92–114.

Zhao, H., & Lai, C. (2022). Culturally responsive AI for language learning: Challenges and approaches. *Computer Assisted Language Learning*, *35*(8), 1403–1427.

Chapter 3
The Role of AI in Personalized English Language Learning

Muhammad Usman Tariq
https://orcid.org/0000-0002-7605-3040
Abu Dhabi University, UAE University College Cork, Ireland

ABSTRACT

This chapter explores the transformative role of artificial intelligence (AI) in English language education, focusing on its potential to personalize learning and enhance language acquisition. AI-powered tools have revolutionized traditional language learning models by offering individualized learning experiences that cater to the unique needs, strengths, and preferences of each student. Through intelligent tutoring systems, AI-driven chatbots, speech recognition technologies, and adaptive learning platforms, AI provides learners with real-time feedback, tailored exercises, and immersive environments for language practice. These advancements shift the traditional one-size-fits-all approach to a more student-centered model that promotes deeper engagement and improved proficiency. The chapter also examines the challenges and ethical considerations associated with AI in language education, such as bias in AI models, data privacy concerns, and the irreplaceable role of human teachers.

INTRODUCTION

The education system has been transformed by Artificial Intelligence (AI) because it creates novel approaches for students to learn through knowledge interactions. The development of linguistic proficiency through AI in education happens specifically by creating personalized instruction programs for each student based

DOI: 10.4018/979-8-3373-1952-0.ch003

on their individual learning characteristics. The widespread desire to learn English has received significant benefit from artificial intelligence technology since these solutions provide custom-adjusted evaluations alongside immediate language aid features and automated teaching components. English language learning experiences a fundamental teaching transformation through AI integration which aims to improve learner engagement as well as motivation levels while enhancing their language learning results (Zavalevskyi et al., 2024). AI has improved schooling education processes through STEM teaching and professional education as well as creative fields of study. Language learning involves specific obstacles because students need to activate their brains while participating in social dialogues. Current AI technology powered by NLP and speech recognition and machine learning algorithms successfully addresses these issues through interactive teaching experiences. The application of artificial intelligence in language education allows intelligent tutors and chatbots together with voice assistants and adaptive learning platforms to develop flexible learning systems which produce virtual conversations while measuring language skills and delivering tailored feedback. Learning solutions developed through these innovations serve beginner through advanced learners to meet their individual language learning requirements (Songsiengchai et al., 2023). AI provides individualized teaching as its most vital contribution to English language education. Classroom learning methods for language education adopt standardized models which expect students to advance at equal rates although they differ in their development abilities and learning matters. The educational method proves inadequate for numerous students because it fails to meet their individual requirements for supplemental assistance and independent study rhythms. Many educational tools which use AI technology help students by studying their performance to understand their skills and develop custom-made instruction accordingly. The AI algorithms operating on Duolingo and Babbel platforms detect how users perform in lessons to make intelligent adjustments which help learners experience appropriate difficulties. This practice prevents them from becoming overwhelmed. The writing tools operated by AI technology including Grammarly supply customized feedback about syntax and grammatical elements and stylistic elements to assist users in developing their writing competencies (Zavalevskyi et al., 2024; Tariq, 2025).

English language education requires customized learning models because the variety of students continues to grow. English functions as the principal language of international communication since it serves as the universal franca while students possess various linguistic cultural and academic backgrounds. AI-powered tools with adaptation capabilities serve different learners by creating customized educational plans combined with multilingual accessibility and cultural-sensitive material. The analysis of native language performed by AI-driven platforms allows them to deliver specialized help which targets the standard linguistic obstacles that students face because of their language heritage. Native speakers of Arabic who study English must master English sounds which differ from their mother tongue whereas learners from China face difficulties with English sentences because their native language syntax is different. The analysis capabilities of AI detect learning patterns, so it provides exercise material which targets student learning obstacles (Songsiengchai et al., 2023). The process of individualized learning depends heavily on artificial intelligence because it keeps students motivated throughout their educational journey. Educational psychological research confirms that student language achievement depends heavily on motivational factors so students who receive teaching content that aligns with their individual aims and interests perform better. AI language learning applications maintain learner motivation through gamification features which provide rewards and track progress while presenting interactive challenges to users. For instance, both LingQ along with Rosetta Stone utilize artificial intelligence to suggest content based on individual student preferences (Zavalevskyi et al., 2024). AI improves the general standards of English language education through its combination of personalized learning paths with motivational strategies. The advantages of AI-guided personal learning require students to assess both its consequences along with its practical boundaries. The main worry about this system involves using AI solutions in excess which reduces opportunities for human contact. Authentic communication in language depends on both social interaction and cultural understanding between people as well as their ability to engage contextually with each other. The use of AI tools should accompany human-facilitated instruction to help students acquire the most beneficial outcomes in their language development. Students benefit the most when artificial intelligence works alongside standard classroom instruction since it provides students with computerized efficiency combined with personalized guidance from human instructors (Songsiengchai et al., 2023).

AI-driven language learning should address both the moral as well as privacy aspects which arise from its usage. The extensive data requirements of AI teaching systems raise privacy concerns among learners together with concerns about keeping their personal information safe. Language learning applications obtain user data such as voice recordings combined with writing samples and learning patterns to build improved AI algorithms. The data-driven systems that enhance personalization programs raise security dangers because data can be accessed improperly or compromised. Robotics researchers together with education facilities need to design strong data defines mechanisms which combine transparency about data collection storage and use management processes. The development of ethical AI frameworks must occur to stop biases from appearing within language learning algorithms. When AI systems learn from datasets containing biases, they can convert such prejudices into the training model which subsequently produces distorted educational content. The training process of Artificial Intelligence systems demands diverse and inclusive data sets for developing fair educational platforms (Bhutoria, 2022). The available access to AI language learning tools requires thorough evaluation currently. The complete advantage of AI-driven language education remains out of reach for some learners because of their economic condition and limited access to the internet and insufficient technology skills. A combined approach from government officials alongside teaching experts and AI development teams should work together to extend accessibility of intelligent learning systems to all students. To overcome accessibility barriers in AI-driven education institutions should create open-access language learning platforms with government financial support while providing affordable AI educational solutions (Eslit, 2023). The developing application of artificial intelligence to personalize English language education presents meaningful effects on educational direction. Artificial intelligence technologies will enhance their capabilities in language learning through better personalization and adaptive and immersive experiences as they evolve. The author examines different AI implementations within English language education while evaluating their decisive benefits together with their current constraints and future trends for AI-based personalized learning systems. Studies based on real-world examples and theoretical frameworks along with research data combine to deliver complete information about AI transformations in English language education while demonstrating specific actions for educators and policymakers and learners to maximize artificial intelligence effectiveness (Bhutoria, 2022). This chapter evaluates how AI meets personal language education while developing future discussions about educational technology systems in current educational approaches. Additionally, it provides guidance for learner-focused methods making certain AI functions for student betterment instead of replacing meaningful human connections. It is crucial to critically examine AI's potential and difficulties as it continues to reshape education to make sure that its use is consistent with the values of accessibility, inclusiveness, and pedagogical efficacy (Eslit, 2023).

BACKGROUND

Educational practices that design teaching environments according to students' personal characteristics make up personalized learning programs. The educational method of personalization helps English language students receive instruction and practice activities which match their skill levels together with targeted assessment feedback that addresses their specific weaknesses. Students in personalized learning environments advance through instruction independently since individual students focus on growth areas that require their attention most. The process becomes more optimized with personalized learning through AI as machine learning algorithms team up with NLP and analytics tools to deliver individualized learning pathways each student needs (Yeşilçınar, 2023). English language education benefits from personalized learning since it efficiently supports the different learning requirements of students. English language students present differing combinations of background languages with different skills as well as divergent education targets. Different students demand different levels of grammar instruction together with various degrees of help in pronunciation and vocabulary memorization. AI platforms can conduct instant student need assessments which then leads to content modifications. AI tracking systems within Duolingo observe user achievement to make lessons adjust their difficulty levels from both accuracy and time completion metrics. Through its writing assistance feature Grammarly provides custom recommendations to users who face common errors which help learners improve their skills through time-based training (Yeşilçınar, 2023). The system learns about individual requirements through continuous behavioural and progress analysis. Standard language education employs static lesson schedules as well as standardized evaluations that do not show individual student ability levels effectively. AI tools overcome this problem by utilizing data-driven personalization mechanics to automatically adjust teaching content. Speech recognition technology recognizes pronunciation errors to deliver prompt feedback to users through its system. Users who interact with ELSA Speak benefit from speech analytics that reveal their spoken language patterns, so the application provides exercises which enhance pronunciation while improving intonation and fluency abilities (Yeşilçınar, 2023). Such immediate feedback systems help students practice and improve their spoken abilities through structured learning designs which adapt to their needs.

AI-driven personalization provides different forms of instruction through its advanced delivery system. Traditional classroom structures present the problem to educators when they need to teach students at different proficiency points within the same learning session. Different students complete their understanding at different speeds yet need different amounts of supplemental assistance with their education. AI provides solutions through learning pathway creation for student populations which are categorized according to their present skill extent. Platform users like Rosetta Stone and LingQ assess interaction data to suggest reading material and listening practice and vocabulary challenges that match each learner's pace of learning. AI-generated content adaptation meets student learning abilities which prevents them from wasting their motivation or developing boredom during their education (Xiong, 2024). AI facilitates the basic shift from unified teaching methods toward learning designs focused on individual students. The standardized teaching curricula of English language instruction fail to recognize the diversity of learner speeds and preferences or brain capacities. The education model changes through AI as it creates an environment which allows students to direct their own academic paths. The learning environment becomes more helpful for students with special needs including dyslexics and those with auditory processing issues since AI offers adaptable teaching methods. AI-enabled assistance technologies contain text-to-speech and speech-to-text applications which supply different methods for students with special learning needs to engage with content (Songsiengchai et al., 2023). The reading tools provided by Microsoft Immersive Reader improve access to language learning through text level adjustment features and audio support and text highlighting which benefits all types of learners. Through interactive learning exercises these systems provide learners immediate feedback in addition to contextual recommendations which help students strengthen their skills. Chatbots using ChatGPT and Mondly artificial intelligence enable learners to have digital discussions which develop their writing and speaking capabilities (Xiong, 2024).

The virtual tutors examine language usage while finding mistakes and provide better phrasing choices to improve fluency. AI-driven chatbots produce interactive communication exchanges to teach language usage in real-world situations thus helping students build their conversational skills (Songsiengchai et al., 2023). Spaced repetition algorithms deployed by AI systems help learners memorize vocabulary better according to their learning patterns. The vocabulary review schedule at Anki and Memrise operates under AI optimization to help students enhance their memory retention just before forgetting a word. Such a method based on cognitive science research enhances permanent vocabulary retention better than traditional memorization practices. AI tailors review timing to student performance data to obtain both peak study effectiveness and minimal information saturation (Songsiengchai et al., 2023). The positive effects of AI-driven personalization need a professional assessment of its current constraints. Students face a challenge when AI use becomes excessive because it might reduce human involvement in learning processes. Language acquisition through human interaction remains essential because social dimensions demand emotional ability along with social consciousness which exceeds the capabilities of AI technology because of its current limitations. Language learners benefit from AI-operated grammar evaluation and pronunciation assessment, yet the system does not match human educators or classmates in delivering the ability to maintain dynamic meaningful conversations in contextual environments (Xiong, 2024). A mix of AI-powered personalization methods together with human-taught instruction presents the best learning solution for language education because AI systems cannot replace human instruction. Data protection issues also represent another obstacle with AI-driven customization methods. Numerous data collection operations required by AI systems create privacy and protection issues that stem from user information security considerations. Language learning applications keep user-generated material, voice recordings and behavioural data to enhance the operating systems' development. Learning information gets exposed to security risks when organizations fail to properly handle student data. Educational institutions with technology developers need to create firm data governance rules to have AI-powered education tools fulfil privacy guidelines while maintaining detailed information about data usage (Wei, 2023).

The personalization capabilities of artificial intelligence tend to perpetuate language learning biases via its operations. Large training datasets for AI algorithms include cultural and linguistic biases that affect their operations. AI systems which operate without bias intervention will use their assessment tools to monitor proficiency levels and provide recommendations and error corrections through mechanisms that could be affected by existing biases. AI writing assistance programs choose specific vocabularies and grammatical rules which could impede learners whose native language differs from English. AI system developers should address this issue by making sure their language learning models receive training through datasets containing examples from various linguistic sectors and cultural backgrounds (Sari, 2023). The issue of accessibility plays a major role when it comes to AI-powered learning tools for personalization. The educational benefits of AI democratic education are limited because all students do not possess equal access to these technological solutions. The use of AI for personalization faces challenges because learners from disadvantaged socioeconomic groups combined with low digital literacy skills and limited infrastructure prevent some students from accessing this beneficial tool. Policymakers and schools need to develop and fund programs which promote digital access by giving AI language learning tools at reduced prices and enhancing digital education sessions for marginalized student communities (Wei, 2023).

English language learning personalization through AI will develop further by integrating modern capabilities like emotional understanding with real-time sentiments recognition and cross-cultural model prediction. AI teaching assistants of the future will both read emotions during learning sessions and adapt their instruction approach based on student participation and supply educational materials that target specific cultural backgrounds. The continuing AI development should prioritize using technology as an enhancer of human capacity instead of supplanting key interaction techniques in language acquisition which include team work together with originality and mental analysis (Sari, 2023). Through its individualized approach AI technology has transformed English language teaching while promoting student-focused instruction together with intelligent learning resources which boost learning effectiveness. Through the application of AI students gain access to tailored learning materials together with instantaneous performance feedback that also create customized educational progress paths based on their individual knowledge level and their learning targets. It is crucial to solve the existing problems of AI personalization since this technology presents several ethical concerns combined with bias formation and accessibility barriers. AI integration with human-taught instruction enables maximum personal learning results alongside protection of language-learning elements that require direct human contact. The future of personalized English language learning will continue to develop under AI influence as a dynamic field which provides novel learning possibilities to every learner across the globe (Wei, 2023).

AI-Powered Learning Platforms and Technologies

English language learning underwent a transformation due to AI-powered learning platforms that offer learners personalized interactive learning experiences combined with efficient personalized instruction methods. Such platforms implement different AI features including intelligent tutoring systems and chatbots and speech recognition tools and adaptive learning mechanisms to deliver customized education assisted by real-time feedback and immersive learning environments for learners. The dynamic content modification of AI-enabled platforms combined with student learning progression-based method adaptation produces enhanced learning results compared to conventional approaches that employ static textbooks and generalized curricula. The numerous advantages of these technological innovations require us to conduct a restrictive analysis because these systems also introduce noteworthy problems (Zhang, 2024). The intelligent tutoring system (ITS) represents an effective form of Artificial Intelligence technology which supports language learners. The technology analyzes student advancement to generate individualized instructional material together with feedback which duplicates the assistance method of human tutoring. ITS platforms differ from standard language training because they modify their educational methods through using performance data and understanding gaps between individual users. NativeAccent from Carnegie Speech functions as a specialized ITS platform for language students where AI technology analyses pronunciation and grammar and fluency along with offering on-the-spot feedback about errors. Through error tracking the system generates targeted exercises that focus on training areas where students need improvement thus improving their learning efficiency (Amirjalili, 2024). The main strength of intelligent tutoring systems originates in their ability to deliver customized education for large numbers of learners. Teachers in traditional classrooms struggle to provide personalized help due to the multiple students at different skill levels who need their attention. The ITS system platforms connect learners with continuous customized guidance which enables them to focus their efforts on their learning weaknesses. The proactive instructional systems demonstrate success yet still possess certain boundaries. The main drawback of these systems is their inability to imitate the comprehensive feedback and motivational traits which human instructors deliver with full effectiveness (Zhang, 2024). The analysis capabilities of AI include grammar assessment along with pronunciation inspection and vocabulary evaluation, but it cannot understand student emotions nor provide supportive measures or adjust educational approaches according to psychological aspects. The proper usage of ITS requires it to serve as an additional instrument alongside human educators rather than substitute their position entirely (Amirjalili, 2024).

AI-powered chatbots have demonstrated their worth in offering students valuable opportunities for talking in real-time conversations. The machine learning tool NLP enables these bots to guide students through dialogues which help students practice speaking and writing skills via digital communication. Mondly and ChatGPT both use AI to deliver chatbots which model real speech by detecting errors and offering phrase recommendations for improved speaking proficiency. Learning through AI chatbots becomes possible anytime since these systems operate continuously and they do not make students feel anxious about receiving social judgments or evaluations (Amirjalili, 2024). Chatbots powered by AI deliver real-time saleable practice sessions which serve as the main advantage of their technology. The conventional language learning process demands students to locate conversation partners, but this task becomes difficult when students lack native speakers or language exchange programs. Language learning becomes more reachable through chatbots because they provide on-demand conversations which remove time constraints from the learning process. AI chatbots possess the ability to adjust their dialogue according to learner proficiency so conversations remain suitable and challenging for everyone. AI chatbots offer basic simplified language aid to beginners while guiding advanced users through complex interaction activities on different subjects. The limitations of AI chatbots also need mention (Zhang, 2024). The biggest challenge for AI chatbots occurs when they need to analyse contextual information because they perform well with structured conversations along with grammatical correction yet lack understanding of subtle cultural cues. AI chatbots encounter difficulties when understanding emotional intelligence together with sarcasm and non-verbal cues that remain challenging for them to interpret well during human interactions. Chatbots tend to strengthen language errors because inadequate training in their algorithms has resulted in this issue. They serve as strong supplementary resources when used alongside the classical education system particularly for students who need additional access to conversation resources (Amirjalili, 2024). The platforms which recognize speech have turned into vital tools for polishing pronunciation skills in English language education. The tools automatically evaluate the spoken language of learners by detecting errors in pronunciation during speech then instantly provide feedback that enhances their pronunciation skills. Two language learning applications, ELSA Speak and Speech ling utilize AI-powered speech recognition technology to check pronunciation quality and give corrective measures to users.

These systems find phonetic mistakes through comparison with native speaker models then provide exercise recommendations for better pronunciation (Arani, 2024).

Figure 1. AI-Powered learning platforms

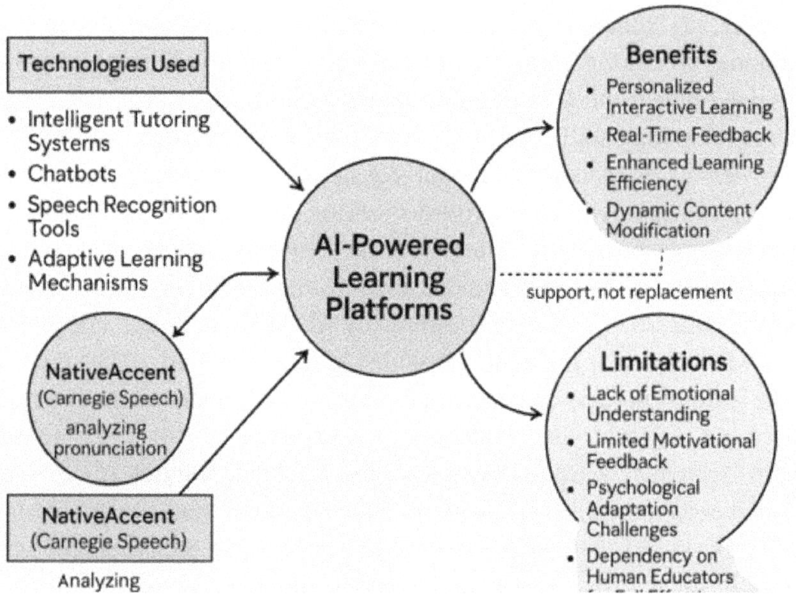

The immediate service of speech recognition technology enhances learning by providing learners with on-the-spot feedback which enables them to perform immediate corrections. The traditional approach to pronunciation practice depends on human instructors who might not be available or affordable to students. The availability of AI-driven speech recognition tools allows individuals to access premium-quality pronunciation education because they offer cost-effective sessions that learners can access easily at any time. These technology tools support users with different language traits through features that help students with various accents and speech patterns to improve their English pronunciation (Qureshi et al., 2024). The most vital challenge regarding AI-generated feedback stems from its inaccuracies. The tools operate best with standard pronunciations, but their accuracy decreases when users have different accents during spoken input sessions. Individuals who speak with robust regional accents or present speech disability issues experience AI interpretation errors that generate incorrect evaluation outputs. The algorithms evaluate technical accuracy of speech too heavily compared to natural intonation and stress patterns and rhythm which are vital for successful communication. Effective use of these tools requires learners to combine their use with direct contact with native English use in real-time settings (Bhutoria, 2022). The main advancement in AI-driven language learning emerges from adaptive learning platforms which combine with content customization features. The platforms use artificial intelligence to decipher student achievement while readjusting lesson materials in combination with learning complexity as well as teaching techniques. The curriculum structure in traditional learning opposes adaptive learning platforms because they modify their approaches based on individual students' requirements through data analysis. Duolingo traces user advancement through its AI system to shift exercise complexity depending on precise performance and processing speed measurements. Rosetta Stone capitalizes on AI technology to develop customized language instruction that tracks specific learning weaknesses of users then provides special development activities for improvement (Arani, 2024). Adaptive learning achieves its main advantage through individualized learning optimization. Each learner develops independently while receiving appropriate learning challenges to avoid getting stuck in low-level difficulties or disinterest. Adaptive platforms raise retention through spaced repetition strategies by making learners review words at progressively longer intervals which strengthens their memory recall.

These data-based systems make learning more efficient for students while improving their involvement better than conventional teaching methods. The excessive use of algorithmic recommendations in adaptation systems has the capacity to restrict students from encountering a wide range of knowledge. AI-supported learning systems utilize historical student performance data for learning prediction. However, the foreseeable outcomes might block students from accessing novel teaching materials that move past their recognized expertise areas (Bhutoria, 2022). The effectiveness of adaptive learning has its foundation in AI algorithm quality. Learning tools that receive improper AI training tend to misread learner mistakes which consequently generate inferior guidance and dissatisfaction. Students risk being isolated from human interaction by using AI systems without additional human contact. Learning language demands exposure to native speakers in diverse conditions because students require the social element of interacting with language speakers along with cultural experiences and authentic language settings. The capabilities provided by AI tools for personalized learning do not duplicate the complete aspects of human communication capabilities (Tariq, 2025). Educational institutions together with their participants should unite AI-based platforms with established language education practices that use classrooms and interpersonal learning and cultural immersion as components of their teaching methodology (Arani, 2024). AI-based educational platforms together with their technologies have revolutionized English language education through their smart tutoring engines alongside AI-powered chatbots and speech recognition capabilities as well as adaptive learning features. Modern technology systems deliver individualized teaching methods alongside real-time performance evaluation services and adaptable training models that boost both student involvement along with system productivity. While AI solutions bring substantial benefits, they introduce specific difficulties because they fail to properly understand context as well as become inaccurate at times and enable students to heavily rely on AI-driven teaching methods. The combination of AI tools together with human connection and cultural experiences forms the key to achieving the greatest outcomes from AI language learning systems. AI will continue to develop new educational functions for language learning which will provide expanded student opportunities alongside solutions to language acquisition complexity in digital environments (Bhutoria, 2022).

Data-Driven Insights for Tailored English Instruction

Modern English language education has changed through artificial intelligence because it utilizes data analytics to build individualized teaching activities. AI systems analyze large data volumes from learners to evaluate individual skills and faults and deliver automatic feedback and process data with predictive analysis and generate individual learning recommendations. This system enables educational progress through data analysis which provides students with respective training methods that transcend generic teaching methods. Despite many advantages provided by AI-based data analysis it creates issues regarding precision of information and student self-determination and proper usage of personal learning material (Parraga et al., 2025). The major achievement of AI in English education derives from its capability to study learner information while designing customized understanding. Standardized assessment methods in traditional language education fail to grasp individual learning development even though they heavily depend on standardized evaluations. AI systems have the capacity to acquire detailed student information through real-time processing of substantial data which exceeds traditional understanding of learner abilities. Through analysis of user writing styles Grammarly along with Grammarly provides time-span evidence for enhancing vocabulary selection and grammar precision (Jayakumar et al., 2024). The AI assessment system analyses student development through four different measurement points that track grammar rules and pronunciation skills and listening performance as well as comprehension abilities. AI tools identify problem areas through their analysis of both mistakes and student advancement patterns. The ML algorithms active in Lingvist enable the program to understand learner input data so it can automatically modify vocabulary suggestions according to which words create the most friction. The data-based method guides learners to inspect their weak areas directly instead of wasting time on completed concepts (Parraga et al., 2025).

Figure 2. Data driven AI systems for tailored English language instruction

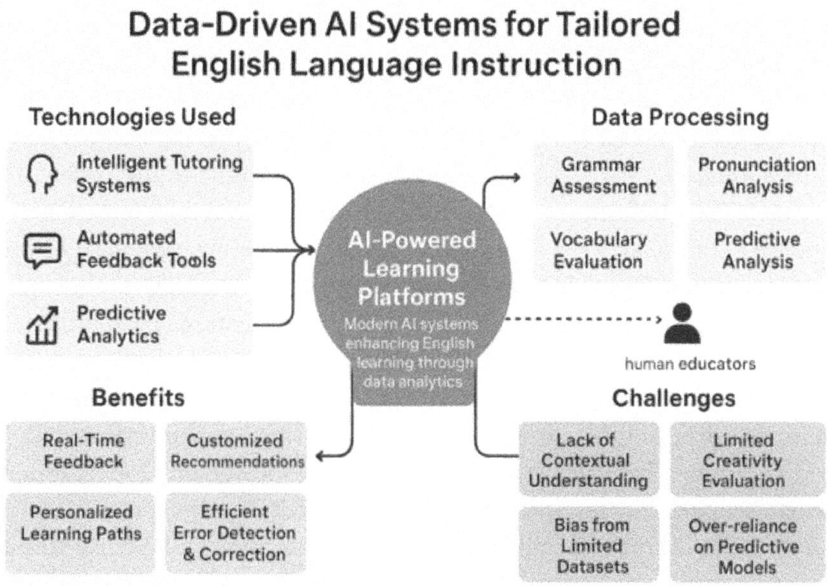

Another important aspect of AI in English language training is automated feedback, which gives students instant evaluations of their speaking, writing, and grammatical skills. Due to time limits, teachers in traditional classroom settings sometimes find it difficult to provide each student with fast and thorough feedback. Conversely, AI systems provide real-time corrections and recommendations, enabling students to constantly improve their abilities. Examples of applications that help users improve their writing efficiency include Microsoft Editor and Pre-writing, which offer real-time feedback on grammar problems, sentence structure, and readability (Novik, 2024). Software for voice recognition powered by AI is also essential for evaluating spoken language. Programs such as Speech Ace and ELSA Speak evaluate fluency and pronunciation patterns and provide focused practice to enhance spoken English. By comparing learner pronunciation to native speakers', these tools employ phonetic analysis to identify areas that require improvement. With this degree of automatic feedback, students may practice efficiently without needing continual human oversight (Jayakumar et al., 2024; Tariq, 2024). Despite its great effectiveness, automated feedback has drawbacks. Because AI systems frequently label technically accurate words as faults based on strict computational constraints, they may have trouble recognizing context. Furthermore, AI is unable to completely replace human feedback, especially when it comes to subtleties like tone, originality, or writing style. For a more balanced approach, automated feedback should preferably be combined with human evaluation, even if it greatly increases learning efficiency (Novik, 2024). Another revolutionary feature of AI in language training is predictive analytics. AI can predict a learner's development and provide focused interventions by examining historical performance data. With this method, both teachers and students can foresee difficulties and modify their learning tactics appropriately. AI-powered tools like Duolingo, for example, monitor user engagement, reaction times, and mistake rates to identify potential future problem areas for students. The platform modifies course difficulty and reinforcement activities in response to this analysis, assisting students in overcoming expected challenges.

Teachers in educational institutions can use predictive analytics to find kids who could be in danger of falling behind. To identify learning trends and provide individualized assistance strategies, AI systems can examine quiz results, assignment submissions, and attendance data. A university employing AI-powered analytics, for instance, may discover that a student routinely has trouble with verb tenses. Then, before the problem becomes a major obstacle to improvement, the system could propose further tutoring sessions or specific activities (Jayakumar et al., 2024). Predictive analytics is not perfect in language acquisition, though. Because AI models are based on past data, they might not be able to take into consideration outside influences such abrupt changes in motivation, exposure to real-world language, or individual learning preferences. Furthermore, an over-reliance on predictive analytics may result in a prescriptive approach to learning, in which pupils are forced to follow predetermined learning trajectories rather than naturally explore language (Mohammad Ali, 2023). Customized recommendations and AI-based tests improve individualized English training even further. In contrast to conventional evaluations that depend on standardized testing, AI-driven assessments adjust to the development of each individual student. By dynamically adjusting question complexity using AI, these tests make sure that students are neither too nor under-challenged. To evaluate language competency in real-time and give a more realistic picture of a learner's abilities, platforms such as Pearson's AI-powered English examinations employ adaptive testing (Jayakumar et al., 2024). By making performance-based suggestions for tailored learning resources, personalized recommendations go beyond AI evaluations. For example, if a student has trouble with prepositions, an AI-powered platform may suggest related video lessons, grammar drills, or interactive tests. With AI, learners may develop more quickly while staying engaged by receiving information that is tailored to their specific learning requirements. Even with their benefits, AI-based evaluations pose questions regarding accuracy and fairness. Limited datasets that do not accurately reflect a range of learner backgrounds may lead to bias in AI models. Furthermore, assessments that are powered by AI tend to concentrate on measurable elements of language acquisition, such vocabulary and grammar, but may find it difficult to evaluate more abstract abilities like literary inventiveness or cultural sensitivity (Mohammad Ali, 2023; Jayakumar et al., 2024).

Enhancing Language Proficiency through AI

Artificial Intelligence serves as a strong learning tool which creates individualized training activities and tailored learning assistance together with realistic educational contexts for students. Modern learners access many transformative educational tools through AI-generated writing prompts and virtual reality along with augmented reality systems and peer collaboration along with AI-driven exercises for vocabulary learning and grammar development. The modern learning tools through technology enable language students to improve their skills beyond traditional educational capabilities. AI-based learning tools enable substantial improvements in language education yet their usage in complete language learning needs to overcome several system drawbacks and potential problems (Chen & Perez, 2023). The main utilization of Artificial Intelligence in language education involves utilizing AI-powered workout routines to teach vocabulary and grammar effectively. Through their algorithms Duolingo and Babbel analyse user advancement to customize lesson delivery for individual students. A prime example of Duolingo's spaced repetition system (SRS) monitors learner performance with vocabulary and grammatical rules so vocabulary and grammar are reviewed at specific optimal periods to support retention. These system adaptions help learners direct their focus toward specific skills needing improvement and prevent them from practicing areas where they excel (Fitrianto et al., 2024). The artificial intelligence systems play an essential part in shaping grammar education for individual students according to their skills. Learners use Grammarly as their writing assistant because this tool conducts immediate checks of grammar along with sentence structure and syntax to boost their writing ability. AI systems analyze written learner inputs before offering complete guidance about potential correction points which range from verb tense improvement to preposition errors and punctuation marks. Through AI systems teachers can determine students' grammar areas of deficiency to create specific exercises which exceed traditional classroom methods in governing grammar mastery (Chen & Perez, 2023). Artificial Intelligence serves as a strong learning tool which creates individualized training activities and tailored learning assistance together with realistic educational contexts for students. Modern learners access many transformative educational tools through AI-generated writing prompts and virtual reality along with augmented reality systems and peer collaboration along with AI-driven exercises for vocabulary learning and grammar development. The modern learning tools through technology enable language students to improve their skills beyond traditional educational capabilities. AI-based learning tools enable substantial improvements in language education yet their usage in complete language learning needs to overcome several system drawbacks and potential problems (Fitrianto et al., 2024). The main utilization of Artificial Intelligence in language education involves utilizing AI-powered workout routines to teach vocabulary and grammar effectively. Through their algorithms Duolingo and Babbel analyse user advancement to customize lesson delivery for individual students. A prime example of Duolingo's spaced repetition system (SRS) monitors learner performance with vocabulary and grammatical rules so vocabulary and grammar are reviewed at specific optimal periods to support retention. These system adaptions help learners direct their focus toward specific skills needing improvement and prevent them from practicing areas where they excel (Fitrianto et al., 2024). The artificial intelligence systems play an essential part in shaping grammar education for individual students according to their skills. Learners use Grammarly as their writing assistant because this tool conducts immediate checks of grammar along with sentence structure and syntax to boost their writing ability. AI systems analyse written learner inputs before offering complete guidance about potential correction points which range from verb tense improvement to preposition errors and punctuation marks. Through AI systems teachers can determine students' grammar areas of deficiency to create specific exercises which exceed traditional classroom methods in governing grammar mastery. These grammar systems show success at improving mechanics and grammar but their ability to detect refined language elements such as tone and context remains limited for advanced language mastery (Chen & Perez, 2023).

AI systems provide language learners with essential writing assistance which includes creating prompts that aid students in their storytelling tasks. Students benefit from AI tools Jasper and Write Sonic because these platforms provide creative writing suggestions which help users enhance storytelling through generated prompts. Writing platforms use learner preferences to create scenarios or character descriptions and plot ideas that enhance both creativity and engagement during the writing process. The implementation of AI technology allows students to test various writing approaches and academic subjects by receiving automatic feedback that analyses their organizational structure as well as their writing clarity (Ghafar et al., 2023). AI-based writing prompts can change their generated content according to the writing abilities of each learner. The writing recommendations AI program provides beginner learners with short simple sentences but prompts advanced writers to produce complex discussions with sophisticated language throughout their written work. The system's ability to customize tasks intersects with a student's skill development since it offers material that suits their current abilities. Using AI tools for creativity has possible negative aspects since it could lead users to depend on technology too much. When learners depend on AI for generating their creative output, they will eventually lose their capacity to think independently without technology aid. AI support systems need to receive proper management so learners can maintain their creative independence in addition to technological aid. These modern technologies duplicate realistic environments which create situations for learners to test their English skills in context (Ghafar et al., 2023). The virtual reality systems ENGAGE and ClassVR create immersive learning spaces through which students can engage with English language characters and objects along with virtual settings. Learners achieve better practice when they participate in immersive settings that enable natural methods to use both vocabulary and grammar as encountered in real-life situations. As a virtual reality and augmented reality tool students can learn speaking while developing listening and reading comprehension through scenarios which normal classrooms often struggle to recreate. Virtual reality allows users to experience a marketplace simulation which enables interactions with virtual vendors and customers to develop negotiation techniques and dialogues. AR technology enables users to see translations appear on physical objects after users activate their devices against those items (Holbaev, 2025).

The combination of technology-based systems generates an interactive learning space where students participate with language content through contexts which advance understanding and improve retention abilities. Mainstream educational institutions face important barriers when integrating AR and VR which include limited accessibility, high expenses and required expertise for technological skills needed to operate these systems. VR and AR generate valuable language practice possibilities, but they do not fully replace human interaction when learning how to understand and interpret non-verbal communication and cultural characteristics (Holbaev, 2025). The application of Artificial Intelligence through group and peer collaboration functions as a fundamental method to boost language proficiency. AI-made communication tools enable students to connect meaningfully with classmates for schoolwork as well as out-of-class assignments. The collaborative tools within Edmodo as well as Microsoft Teams give learners digital spaces to partner up on language projects and exchange resources while discussing English subjects. AI modalities help control conversations by offering language-related recommendations as well as immediate feedback about language use in real time throughout group tasks (Liu & Quan, 2022).

Performance data analysis using AI enables the creation of suitable study groups that pair students for mutual educational benefit based on their different capabilities. An AI system identifies students with strong reading abilities to align them with students facing writing challenges thus creating productive peer support relationships in which expert knowledge is shared. Peer-assisted learning becomes more valuable when students communicate in English through social interaction because this cultivation strengthens English fluency development (Hwang et al., 2023). AI-assisted collaboration provides strong advantages as a study tool, yet it comes with certain difficulties to navigate. The concern exists about AI-driven collaboration because it may eliminate important opportunities for human interaction with emotional intelligence. AI technology enables communication and feedback while still the human quality of empathy along with personal understanding and peer connections remains absent from collaborative work tasks. AI systems present an unwanted opportunity for creating student separation based on performance data which can cause lower-performing students to experience feelings of being isolated or insufficient. AI systems should be engineered to build inclusivity and group connection among students to prevent the reinforcement of schisms between learners (Kovalenko & Baranivska, 2024).

The language proficiency benefits from AI technology because it gives learners access to numerous tools which enable improved vocabulary and grammar control and writing creativity together with immersive settings and peer collaboration. The exciting possibilities found in these technologies need careful consideration because they have clear boundaries in language education. AI depends on over usage and biased datasets in addition to personal interaction needs when balancing language learning systems for effective student outcomes. AI obtains transformative power for developing learners' English proficiency when combined with traditional teaching methods accompanied by human guidance (Hwang et al., 2023).

Challenges and Ethical Considerations

AI integration within education provides opportunities for personalized learning. However, teachers must handle various challenges along with ethical problems before the benefits can be appropriately distributed for all students. AI systems used in language learning require immediate attention to handle issues with data privacy alongside bias in the algorithms and human teacher involvement and accessibility barriers. The problems create multiple difficulties of both technical nature and moral nature that work against basic educational standards of fairness and equity and dignity for humans (Chen et al., 2021a). The widespread use of AI language models faces its biggest problem through bias development. Language learning platforms use AI models that require vast human-generated content from multiple sources to perform their training procedures. The training data contains biases which already exist in real-world situations such as racist and gender-based stereotypes and cultural misconceptions. AI language models accidentally link professional fields to gender identities when they suggest nursing for female students while allocating engineering roles to male students and this generates biased responses from artificial intelligence systems. The negative stereotypes and restricted perspectives of learners suffer from this issue (Chen et al., 2021b). Extensive data curation combined with debiasing algorithms constitutes vital methods that developers can use to decrease biases found in AI language models while achieving model training that represents many perspectives. Reducing AI system bias becomes challenging because elimination gets hindered by its stubborn nature, so developers face difficulty in removing all bias traces from their systems. The essential task for educators together with AI developers involves ongoing AI system evaluation and auditing to ensure that such systems continuously evolve toward fairness and inclusivity. The AI bias that affects language learning produces two major problems because it damages educational accuracy while distorting students' moral and cultural growth (Chen et al., 2021a). The ethical duty in AI-driven education requires educators to maintain both data security and privacy. Most AI language learning systems need students to submit their demographic details alongside their learning achievements together with possible audio or video sharing samples. The collected data serves useful purposes in delivering personalized learning sessions yet carries major security threats when inadequately handled. Privacy breaches together with identity theft and other damage become potential consequences of unauthorized access to or misuse of data (Chen et al., 2021b).

Educational platforms need to follow data protection regulations like GDPR in European Union territory as well as FERPA in United States territory to reduce these security risks. These regulations establish standards about how personal data of learners should be collected and stored as well as used to protect their information. The protection of learners' sensitive information requires educational institutions and AI developers to use encryption alongside anonymization and access control security measures. A vital condition for data management in educational systems includes complete disclosure to learners regarding their information collection and how and where their data will be used and stored. Security measures taken in advance to protect personal data enhance the trust students have in AI educational applications despite their potential for misuse or data breaches (Chen et al., 2021a). Expert teachers need to determine their role when teaching alongside AI systems which operate in educational settings. Schools require human teachers because AI platforms cannot match the influential role teachers bring to a classroom, yet they can deliver individualized education with automated feedback. Teaching personnel combine emotional capabilities and contextual knowledge which present skills that AI platforms fail to deliver at present. The teacher identifies learner frustration and anxiety through nonverbal communication and voice tone to provide emotional support because AI systems lack these capabilities. Automated systems lack the ability to teach essential skills like critical thinking along with creativity and ethical reasoning which teachers consistently deliver in education (Chen et al., 2021b). AI technology functions as an educational resource that joins forces with teaching professionals instead of functioning as a substitute for human instructors. Teachers receive help in their work from AI systems by letting them execute administrative work and track student achievements so they can dedicate more time to personalized teaching methods. The AI system enables teachers to augment their educational content using technology-driven exercises which offer virtual student support together with assessment tools available in real-time. Using AI in educational settings can potentially reduce valuable human-experiences during student-educator interactions which form the basis of meaningful educational development. Educators need to implement AI tools, so these tools improve their educational methods yet maintain essential human elements of teaching practice (Chen et al., 2021a).

The implementation of AI in education faces major obstacles because of issues surrounding accessibility alongside the digital gap between learners. The revolutionary potential of AI-based language learning technology remains out of reach among some educational students. Students from disadvantaged rural towns often do not have the required school standards including fast internet and individual study equipment required to utilize AI-assisted tools effectively. AI-driven education benefits mostly the learners who live in areas with greater technology infrastructure since students without access to proper digital tools experience a significant gap in education (Kovalenko & Baranivska, 2024). AI tools need to have features designed for inclusiveness because their use should extend to students who have visual or auditory or cognitive disabilities. AI systems must be designed with customization features to allow learners to modify task presentation including the choice of speed and level of content complexity. The developers of AI tools need to make their systems accessible to all students beyond individuals who can afford up-to-date technology (Chen et al., 2021b). The digital divide demands interorganizational cooperation between education institutions and digital companies and government structures to provide AI-based educational resources for equal access to learners. The solution requires digital literacy teaching as well as discounted electronic devices and connection services to reach disadvantaged communities. Making AI-driven learning technology available to all students remains fundamental to achieve an education system that excludes no learners (Chen et al., 2021a). The extensive potential of AI for educational transformation must be balanced by resolving multiple ethical problems before it can be deployed properly for fairness and security and inclusion. Developing ethical AI language models requires sustained collaboration between learners, developers, policymakers, and educators who need to work on bias reduction and security maintenance along with human teacher importance and accessible learning solutions. The resolution of these ethical concerns enables AI to develop an inclusive personalized and effective learning method which benefits all students (Chen et al., 2021b).

Future Trends in AI-Powered English Learning

AI technology in English language learning (ELL) displays an extensive potential for change which will bring forth emerging prospects for students and teaching staff. Mathematical developments in artificial intelligence create new educational possibilities for language education that exceeded the most optimistic predictions. The introduction of generative AI alongside other AI applications has brought new language learning approaches yet the inclusion of AI tools in education enables personalized learning for a wider range of students. The paper makes a forward projection which analyses emerging trends while examining their potential consequences alongside obstacles that may impact English Language Teaching (ELT) within upcoming periods (Betaubun & Budiasto, 2023). NLP techniques represent one of the most encouraging emerging AI applications for language acquisition at present. The advancement of NLP has enabled better machine capabilities to interpret and process human language communications thus improving interactions between humans and machines. Modern technology in ELL creates individualized learning environments through the utilization of this technology. AI-powered systems evaluate student speech during live sessions to provide real-time assessments about their pronunciation together with their fluency levels and grammatical accuracy. The tracking ability of such systems enables the delivery of individual recommendations which consider student progress and specific areas needing development. Through AI software applications such as Duolingo, Babbel and Rosetta Stone learners now can practice languages at their pace while the system adjusts learning content to their proficiency levels and learning styles (Jing & Jia, 2024). The quality of language learning materials receives improvement through AI technology which also generates varied educational resources. Machine learning algorithms enable AI to generate specific education content from past performance indicators of individual students to create their personalized learning paths. The adaptable feature of AI systems constantly provides learners with appropriate challenges that avoid both easy repetitiveness and frustrating difficulty levels (Betaubun & Budiasto, 2023).

The potential for improvement with these technologies remains great because they currently exist at an early developmental phase. The next step in language learning artificial intelligence development includes real-time translation integration and virtual tutor expansion which provides learners with contextual language practice environments. New applications will extend current language-learning boundaries through world-class dialogue practice outside classrooms thus making the lessons more relevant and contextual (Jing & Jia, 2024). Generative AI stands as a major development which presents great prospects for AI-powered language learning. The teaching revolution in English will happen through generative AI because this technology enables machine learning models to develop new content from received information. GPT-4 along with other generative models can create customized language exercises which combine creativity with diversity to meet student learning requirements. The technology enables AI machines to create authentic dialogs and produce adaptive storytelling sessions which change according to the language ability of learners. These tools facilitate customized quiz-making and assignment-creation based on learning goals as well as targeted improvement areas while delivering an interactive educational journey to learners. Through personalized content delivery the system simultaneously drives student attention while giving priority to their areas that require extra assistance (Kuddus, 2022). Generative AI helps when it comes to creative writing creation. Grammatical correctness at any step of writing has been significantly enhanced through Grammarly because the platform provides instant feedback for grammar errors together with style and tone recommendations. The upcoming version of generative AI models will extend past grammar correction to deliver substantial advice for increasing argumentative quality and creative aspects in writing (Jing & Jia, 2024). The creative writer's aid capability of AI produces writing suggestions and starts inventive tasks which assist students to beat writer's block while enhancing their writing abilities through sophisticated methods. The potential for improvement with these technologies remains great because they currently exist at an early developmental phase. The next step in language learning artificial intelligence development includes real-time translation integration and virtual tutor expansion which provides learners with contextual language practice environments. New applications will extend current language-learning boundaries through world-class dialogue practice outside classrooms thus making the lessons more relevant and contextual (Betaubun & Budiasto, 2023). Generative AI stands as a major development which presents great prospects for AI-powered language learning. The teaching revolution in English will happen through generative AI because this technology enables machine learning models to develop new content from received information. GPT-4 along with other generative models can create customized language exercises which combine creativity with diversity to meet student learning requirements. The technology enables AI machines to create authentic dialogs and produce adaptive storytelling sessions which change according to the language ability of learners. These tools facilitate customized quiz-making and assignment-creation based on learning goals as well as targeted improvement areas while delivering an interactive educational journey to learners. Through personalized content delivery the system simultaneously drives student attention while giving priority to their areas that require extra assistance.

Generative AI helps when it comes to creative writing creation. Grammatical correctness at any step of writing has been significantly enhanced through Grammarly because the platform provides instant feedback for grammar errors together with style and tone recommendations. The upcoming version of generative AI models will extend past grammar correction to deliver substantial advice for increasing argumentative quality and creative aspects in writing. The creative writer's aid capability of AI produces writing suggestions and starts inventive tasks which assist students to beat writer's block while enhancing their writing abilities through sophisticated methods (Begum et al., 2024). AI systems can evaluate student writing through time while monitoring their advancement which enables them to provide customized improvement measures that match their individual progress. AI serves to expand access to top-quality language education by achieving democratization of learning among ELL students. The main obstacle which underprivileged regions face in their language education includes both their lack of skilled teaching resources and proper educational tools. People living in rural regions combined with economically underserved areas experience limited opportunities for speaking practice with native speakers and individualized feedback because high-quality language education remains scarce in these regions. AI-based learning platforms create a solution for learners through their affordable and accessible and scalable language education system (Kuddus, 2022).

Today millions of people worldwide use AI-powered linguistic software to study English even though their geographical position and economic means are different. Students can use AI chatbots and virtual tutors along with speech recognition tools to study conversational English skills through automated feedback which replaces traditional classroom instruction. The analysis performance of AI systems together with their capability to personalize educational content enables all students from different socioeconomic levels to obtain exceptional customized learning experiences based on their individual needs (Begum et al., 2024). The future progress of AI technology combined with queuing price cuts demonstrates strong potential to attain greater language education democratization by extending such opportunities toward communities facing educational deprivation. The access required by many AI-designed language systems to reliable internet connections and digital devices limits their availability to persons in all geographic locations. Language learning tools need measures to address cultural diversity and language variation to prevent discrimination against specific learners. True language education democratization requires both technology accessibility for all students together with culturally appropriate educational resources that promote inclusion (Kuddus, 2022). AI and human teachers will embrace a combination of their complementary skills to develop personalized interactive teaching experiences for English Language Teaching during the future. Despite its performance of basic and quantitative activities AI systems must share the classroom with human instructors because teachers remain essential for curriculum direction and building supportive educational spaces and solving language learning's sophisticated aspects and developing cultural sensibility (Kuddus, 2022).

Human educators stand essential when it comes to teaching language through contextual learning because they excel at fostering creativity while offering emotional and moral backing to students. AI data processing speed and human educator's interpersonal skills will merge to build an integrated system that optimizes language education. Teachers access student learning data through AI tools which help them modify teaching methods yet use their skills to encourage dialogue about language contexts (Li, 2024). This combination sparks concerns regarding teaching jobs in an AI-controlled future. Higher sophistication of AI systems generates concerns that some language instruction jobs may eventually be replaced. Every future ELT leader must understand AI functions to assist teachers rather than replace their role as educators. Language learning tools need measures to address cultural diversity and language variation to prevent discrimination against specific learners. True language education democratization requires both technology accessibility for all students together with culturally appropriate educational resources that promote inclusion (Li, 2024). AI and human teachers will embrace a combination of their complementary skills to develop personalized interactive teaching experiences for English Language Teaching during the future. Despite its performance of basic and quantitative activities AI systems must share the classroom with human instructors because teachers remain essential for curriculum direction and building supportive educational spaces and solving language learning's sophisticated aspects and developing cultural sensibility (Begum et al., 2024). Human educators stand essential when it comes to teaching language through contextual learning because they excel at fostering creativity while offering emotional and moral backing to students. AI data processing speed and human educator's interpersonal skills will merge to build an integrated system that optimizes language education. Teachers access student learning data through AI tools which help them modify teaching methods yet use their skills to encourage dialogue about language contexts. This combination sparks concerns regarding teaching jobs in an AI-controlled future. Higher sophistication of AI systems generates concerns that some language instruction jobs may eventually be replaced. Every future ELT leader must understand AI functions to assist teachers rather than replace their role as educators (Li, 2024). Future teacher training will play an essential role to enable educators in integrating AI tools properly and making AI enhance their teaching rather than taking precedence over their instructional approaches. The future use of AI technology in English language education brings numerous benefits however it requires thorough analysis to implement properly. New applications of AI technology specifically generative AI systems present innovative ways to enhance language education through personalization while artificial intelligence has the capability to transform educational accessibility worldwide. AI technology will provide maximal benefits to education only after addressing existing barriers regarding access and equity as well as maintaining human involvement in the educational process. The upcoming era in AI-assistance for language learning will require educators to work together with AI systems to generate superior educational interactions that welcome every student equally (Begum et al., 2024).

CONCLUSION

The incorporation of artificial intelligence into English language teaching constitutes a major progress for educational methods in language acquisition. The platform of AI-powered instruments transforms language academics by delivering customized instruction and adaptive teaching capabilities and real-time assessment and unique educational environments to optimize student progress. AI-powered data analysis enables unique feedback methods that adapt learning routes to individual students thus driving a student-centered learning system that represents the greatest transformation in language instruction. The most important element related to AI applications in personalized language learning emerges as crucial. The shift from traditional standard teaching models to personalized systems exists because these new approaches evaluate every student individually through their learning speed and personal characteristics. AI-driven learning platforms provide learners with instant feedback concerning their grammatical performance as well as pronunciation quality and extensive language learning components like vocabulary usage and writing quality and conversational ability. Students using speech recognition technology with intelligent tutoring systems and AI writing support tools gain better opportunities to develop their language abilities through tailored and active learning settings. The combination of these technologies enables teachers to check progress while boosting student interest in learning at any moment. The incorporation of artificial intelligence into English language teaching constitutes a major progress for educational methods in language acquisition. The platform of AI-powered instruments transforms language academics by delivering customized instruction and adaptive teaching capabilities and real-time assessment and unique educational environments to optimize student progress. AI-powered data analysis enables unique feedback methods that adapt learning routes to individual students thus driving a student-centered learning system that represents the greatest transformation in language instruction.

The most important element related to AI applications in personalized language learning emerges as crucial. The shift from traditional standard teaching models to personalized systems exists because these new approaches evaluate every student individually through their learning speed and personal characteristics. AI-driven learning platforms provide learners with instant feedback concerning their grammatical performance as well as pronunciation quality and extensive language learning components like vocabulary usage and writing quality and conversational ability. Students using speech recognition technology with intelligent tutoring systems and AI writing support tools gain better opportunities to develop their language abilities through tailored and active learning settings. The combination of these technologies enables teachers to check progress while boosting student interest in learning at any moment. AI delivers innovative adaptive learning content to students through performance-based adaptation which serves as a transformative feature for the sphere of English language education. AI technology creates tests from specific learning targets and individual abilities to provide customized tasks which boost learner development. The advent of generative AI components including chatbots and automated conversation partners enables students to train their language abilities dynamically through real-time communication practice in authentic situations despite spatial or time limitations. This flexibility and scalability could democratize language learning by increasing its effectiveness and accessibility, especially in areas with limited access to high-quality education.

Even though AI has many advantages, there are several issues that need to be addressed when integrating it into English language instruction. The requirement for high-quality data, which is essential to the efficiency of AI-powered platforms, is one important problem. AI systems run the risk of generating erroneous evaluations of student performance or reinforcing biases in the absence of inclusive, representative, and accurate datasets. AI tools must be trained in a variety of linguistic and cultural data to avoid unintentionally excluding groups or failing to address the unique learning difficulties that different populations face. Only then will AI be able to genuinely benefit all learners. The role of human teachers is another issue that needs to be recognized. In many ways, human educators are still indispensable, even though AI can help with repetitive tasks and data analysis. Teachers provide contextual knowledge, creativity, and emotional intelligence that AI cannot match. In addition, teachers play a crucial role in establishing a welcoming and stimulating learning environment, providing moral and emotional support, and encouraging a deeper comprehension of language in authentic settings. AI shouldn't be seen as a substitute for human instruction, but rather as an aid to it. Teachers must be given the support and training they need to use AI in ways that improve rather than detract from their instruction if it is to be successfully incorporated into language instruction.

REFERENCES

Холбаев, Ф. (2025). Transforming English language teaching: The dual impact of artificial intelligence on personalized learning and educational challenges. *Лингвоспектр*, *2*(1), 371–381.

Amirjalili, F. (2024). Exploring the efficacy of ChatGPT in personalized language learning: An intervention study in Iranian ESL classrooms. [Formerly Journal of Teaching Language Skills]. *Teaching English as a Second Language Quarterly*, *43*(3), 1–26.

Arani, S. M. N. (2024). Navigating the future of language learning: A conceptual review of AI's role in personalized learning. *Computer-Assisted Language Learning Electronic Journal*, *25*(3), 1–22.

Begum, S., Vimochana, M., Arunadevi, V., Dhivya, A. C. A., Vuyyuru, V. A., & Faizal, M. M. (2024, December). Using AI for personalized English writing feedback on educational platforms. In *2024 International Conference on Artificial Intelligence and Quantum Computation-Based Sensor Application (ICAIQSA)* (pp. 1–6). IEEE. DOI: 10.1109/ICAIQSA64000.2024.10882334

Betaubun, M., Laila Rokhmah, D. E., & Budiasto, J. (2023). Personalized pathways to proficiency: Exploring the synergy of adaptive learning and artificial intelligence in English language learning. *Technium*, •••, 17.

Bhutoria, A. (2022). Personalized education and artificial intelligence in the United States, China, and India: A systematic review using a human-in-the-loop model. *Computers and Education: Artificial Intelligence*, *3*, 100068. DOI: 10.1016/j.caeai.2022.100068

Chen, J. J., & Perez, C. (2023). Enhancing assessment and personalized learning through artificial intelligence. *Childhood Education*, *99*(6), 72–79. DOI: 10.1080/00094056.2023.2282903

Chen, X., Zou, D., Cheng, G., & Xie, H. (2021, July). Artificial intelligence-assisted personalized language learning: Systematic review and co-citation analysis. In *2021 International Conference on Advanced Learning Technologies (ICALT)* (pp. 241–245). IEEE. DOI: 10.1109/ICALT52272.2021.00079

Chen, X., Zou, D., Xie, H., & Cheng, G. (2021). Twenty years of personalized language learning. *Journal of Educational Technology & Society*, *24*(1), 205–222.

Eslit, E. (2023). Integrating multiple intelligence and artificial intelligence in language learning: Enhancing personalization and engagement.

Fitrianto, I., Setyawan, C. E., & Saleh, M. (2024). Utilizing artificial intelligence for personalized Arabic language learning plans. *International Journal of Post Axial: Futuristic Teaching and Learning*, 30–40.

Ghafar, Z. N., Salh, H. F., Abdulrahim, M. A., Farxha, S. S., Arf, S. F., & Rahim, R. I. (2023). The role of artificial intelligence technology on English language learning: A literature review. *Canadian Journal of Language and Literature Studies*, *3*(2), 17–31.

Hwang, W. Y., Nurtantyana, R., Purba, S. W. D., Hariyanti, U., Indrihapsari, Y., & Surjono, H. D. (2023). AI and recognition technologies to facilitate English as foreign language writing for supporting personalization and contextualization in authentic contexts. *Journal of Educational Computing Research*, *61*(5), 1008–1035. DOI: 10.1177/07356331221137253

Jayakumar, V. M., Rajakumari, R., Alapati, P. R., Manchanda, M., Vimochana, M., & Bala, B. K. (2024, December). Applying artificial intelligence in English language learning for customized education. In *2024 International Conference on Artificial Intelligence and Quantum Computation-Based Sensor Application (ICAIQSA)* (pp. 1–6). IEEE. DOI: 10.1109/ICAIQSA64000.2024.10882275

Jing, Y., & Jia, G. (2024, July). Application of artificial intelligence (AI) technology in intelligent recommendation of English personalized learning system. In *2024 3rd International Conference on Artificial Intelligence and Autonomous Robot Systems (AIARS)* (pp. 455–460). IEEE.

Kovalenko, I., & Baranivska, N. (2024). Integrating artificial intelligence in English language teaching: Exploring the potential and challenges of AI tools in enhancing language learning outcomes and personalized education. *Європейські соціо-правові та гуманітарні студії, (1)*, 86–95.

Kuddus, K. (2022). Artificial intelligence in language learning: Practices and prospects. In *Advanced Analytics and Deep Learning Models* (pp. 1–17).

Li, X. (2024). A personalized teaching system for college English based on big data and artificial intelligence. *Scalable Computing: Practice and Experience*, *25*(6), 5477–5485. DOI: 10.12694/scpe.v25i6.3341

Liu, Y., & Quan, Q. (2022). AI recognition method of pronunciation errors in oral English speech with the help of big data for personalized learning. *Journal of Information & Knowledge Management*, *21*(Supp02), 2240028. DOI: 10.1142/S0219649222400287

Mohammad Ali, A. (2023). An intervention study on the use of artificial intelligence in the ESL classroom: English teacher perspectives on the effectiveness of ChatGPT for personalized language learning.

Novik, K. (2024). From chatbots to adaptive learning: The role of AI in personalized English language education. In *Collection of scientific papers "SCIENTIA"* (November 1, 2024; Lisbon, Portugal), 161–164.

Parraga, A. P. B., Ramírez, E. A. C., Macias, K. J. A., Madrid, C. A. C., Espinoza, B. D. C. V., Alcivar, J. G. V., & Cedeño, J. U. C. (2025). The impact of artificial intelligence on personalized learning in English language education. *Ciencia Latina Revista Científica Multidisciplinar*, *9*(1), 5500–5518. DOI: 10.37811/cl_rcm.v9i1.16234

Qureshi, R., Hajare, S., & Verma, P. (2024, July). A review on the role of artificial intelligence in personalized learning. In *2024 Asia Pacific Conference on Innovation in Technology (APCIT)* (pp. 1–5). IEEE. DOI: 10.1109/APCIT62007.2024.10673706

Sari, N. (2023). The role of artificial intelligence (AI) in developing English language learner's communication skills. *Journal of Education*, *6*(01), 750–757.

Songsiengchai, S., Sereerat, B. O., & Watananimitgul, W. (2023). Leveraging artificial intelligence (AI): Chat GPT for effective English language learning among Thai students. *English Language Teaching*, *16*(11), 68–79. DOI: 10.5539/elt.v16n11p68

Tariq, M. U. (2024). Generative AI in Curriculum Development in Higher Education. In Fields, Z. (Ed.), *Impacts of Generative AI on Creativity in Higher Education* (pp. 227–258). IGI Global., DOI: 10.4018/979-8-3693-2418-9.ch009

Tariq, M. U. (2025). Bridging Cultures and Languages: Innovative Literacy Strategies for Inclusive and Engaged Classrooms. In Tussey, J., & Haas, L. (Eds.), *Supporting Cultural Differences Through Literacy Education* (pp. 257–282). IGI Global Scientific Publishing., DOI: 10.4018/979-8-3693-9271-3.ch010

Tariq, M. U. (2025). Integrating ICT for Enhanced Organizational Resilience: Strategies and Case Studies. In Carvalho, L., Reis, L., Neves de Almeida Baptista Figueiredo, A., & Russo, N. (Eds.), *Leveraging Technology for Organizational Adaptability* (pp. 59–80). IGI Global Scientific Publishing., DOI: 10.4018/979-8-3693-6045-3.ch004

Tariq, M. U. (2025). AI-Enhanced Project-Based Learning: Revolutionizing Commerce Education With Generative AI. In ElSayary, A. (Ed.), *Prompt Engineering and Generative AI Applications for Teaching and Learning* (pp. 125–142). IGI Global Scientific Publishing., DOI: 10.4018/979-8-3693-7332-3.ch008

Tariq, M. U. (2025). AI-Driven Research Methodologies: Revolutionizing Data-Driven Discoveries in Engineering and Physical Sciences. In Basha, J., Alade, T., Al Khazimi, M., Vasudevan, R., & Khan, J. (Eds.), *Optimizing Research Techniques and Learning Strategies With Digital Technologies* (pp. 97–122). IGI Global Scientific Publishing., DOI: 10.4018/979-8-3693-7863-2.ch004

Wei, L. (2023). Artificial intelligence in language instruction: Impact on English learning achievement, L2 motivation, and self-regulated learning. *Frontiers in Psychology*, *14*, 1261955. DOI: 10.3389/fpsyg.2023.1261955 PMID: 38023040

Xiong, W. (2024, July). Artificial intelligence in English language education: The path to personalized learning. In *Proceedings of the 2nd International Conference on Educational Knowledge and Informatization* (pp. 72–77). DOI: 10.1145/3691720.3691733

Yeşilçınar, S. (2023). Personalized learning through gamification: A ChatGPT approach to English language learning. In *Transforming the language teaching experience in the age of AI* (pp. 44–64). IGI Global. DOI: 10.4018/978-1-6684-9893-4.ch003

Zavalevskyi, Y., Kyrilenko, S., Kijan, O., Bessarab, N., & Mosyakova, I. (2024). The role of AI in individualizing learning and creating personalized programs. *Amazonia Investiga*, *13*(73), 200–208. DOI: 10.34069/AI/2024.73.01.16

Zhang, M. (2024). Enhancing MALL with artificial intelligence: Personalized learning paths in EFL teaching. *Research and Advances in Education*, *3*(8), 49–61. DOI: 10.56397/RAE.2024.08.07

KEY TERMS AND DEFINITIONS

Adaptive Learning Platforms: Educational software that uses AI to modify learning materials in real-time according to the student's performance and learning style.

Intelligent Tutoring Systems (ITS): AI-powered systems that simulate one-on-one tutoring by adapting content delivery and providing targeted feedback based on learner performance.

Personalised Learning: An instructional approach that customises educational content and pacing to meet individual learners' needs, preferences, and progress.

Predictive Analytics: The use of data-driven AI models to forecast learner outcomes and recommend interventions to support progress.

Speech Recognition Tools: AI technologies that analyse spoken language to support pronunciation and speaking skills development.

Chapter 4
AI-Facilitated Formative Assessment:
Reimagining Feedback in the English Language Classroom

Sushant Kishore
https://orcid.org/0000-0003-3195-7991
Vellore Institute of Technology, Vellore, India

ABSTRACT

This chapter examines the transformative role of artificial intelligence in revolutionizing formative assessment practices within English language education. As educators face increasing demands to provide personalized feedback to diverse learners, AI technologies offer promising solutions that can enhance assessment effectiveness while reducing teacher cognitive load. The chapter presents a comprehensive analysis of current AI-powered assessment tools, pedagogical frameworks for their implementation, and evidence-based best practices drawn from various educational contexts. Through a critical examination of both opportunities and challenges, the chapter provides a balanced perspective on how AI can support—rather than replace—human judgment in the assessment process, ultimately creating more responsive and equitable learning environments for English language students worldwide.

INTRODUCTION

The assessment of language learning presents a multifaceted challenge that has evolved over time, demanding a nuanced understanding of both the pedagogical practices involved and the systemic issues at play. In many educational settings, the

DOI: 10.4018/979-8-3373-1952-0.ch004

urgency for timely and individualized feedback is hindered by a disparity between teacher availability and students' needs. For instance, in Kenya, despite the formal emphasis on English in the curriculum, Wamalwa et al. (2014) found that persistent difficulties such as teacher absenteeism and overcrowded classrooms compromise effective instruction and assessment outcomes. Moreover, the cognitive load on teachers can exacerbate these issues, resulting in delayed feedback that ultimately impairs language acquisition. This dilemma mirrors findings in immersive educational environments, where Lehikko et al. (2024) observed that high interactivity is correlated with increased cognitive load, suggesting that not only individual capabilities but also contextual factors influence learning experiences. Thus, addressing these historical challenges is essential for enhancing language learning assessments and supporting effective communication skills development.

In language learning, assessment serves as a critical vehicle for measuring progress and identifying areas of need, thereby facilitating individualized instruction. The nuances of language acquisition necessitate timely feedback, which not only fosters motivation but also enhances students' understanding and retention of language skills. Historically, the challenge of delivering personalized feedback has been compounded by the cognitive load demands placed on educators, often leading to delayed assessments that can negatively impact language development. Recent advancements in technology, particularly the integration of AI systems, offer promising avenues to address these issues. For instance, Özer (2024) notes that platforms utilizing AI-powered recommendations can tailor learning experiences, thus supporting targeted instruction while alleviating teacher workload. Additionally, Dhananjaya et al. (2024) highlight that the emergence of innovative e-learning technologies provides tools to enhance interaction and feedback mechanisms, contributing to a more effective learning environment. Thus, effective assessment in language learning is not only about evaluation but also about enriching the educational experience for both students and teachers.

The purpose of this essay is to critically examine the challenges inherent in language assessment, particularly focusing on the provision of timely and individualized feedback, the cognitive load burden on teachers, and the detrimental effects of delayed feedback on language acquisition. By exploring these themes, the essay aims to illuminate the historical context surrounding assessment practices and how these have evolved in response to pedagogical needs. It seeks not only to analyze the implications of feedback timing on student performance but also to address the cognitive demands placed on educators, who must balance instructional duties with effective assessment. As educational technology advances and the integration of AI systems in educational contexts becomes more prevalent, the essay will discuss emerging methodologies for enhancing feedback mechanisms while mitigating associated challenges, consistent with discussions in contemporary literature on educational reforms and the ethical considerations of these systems (Mahmut Özer, 2024). Therefore, this analysis sets the stage for potential policy recommendations that aim to optimize assessment practices in language learning.

HISTORICAL CHALLENGES OF PROVIDING TIMELY, INDIVIDUALIZED FEEDBACK

The provision of timely, individualized feedback has historically faced numerous challenges, particularly in the realm of language learning. A significant hurdle has been the ability to cater to diverse learner needs within mixed-ability classrooms. For instance, Chen et al. (2018) suggested using innovative tools such as WeChat's recording function as a solution to enhance personalized learning experiences, allowing instructors to offer immediate feedback while mitigating student anxiety and fostering engagement. However, the cognitive load placed on teachers remains a critical concern; the demand for rapid assessment and feedback can overwhelm educators, potentially detracting from the quality of instruction. Balakrishnan et al. (2023) point out that integrating new technologies presents its own set of obstacles, including the need for proper training and awareness of ethical implications associated with data privacy. These historical challenges underscore the complexity of delivering effective feedback in language education and highlight the importance of continuous adaptation in teaching methodologies.

The evolution of assessment methods in language education has undergone significant transformation in response to technological advancements and pedagogical shifts. Traditionally, assessments were largely summative, focusing on rote memorization and standardized testing, which often failed to account for individual learner needs. With the advent of digital tools, there has been a marked transition toward formative assessments that prioritize timely, individualized feedback, essential for language acquisition. This shift became particularly critical during the Covid-19 pandemic, where online learning exposed the limitations of prior methodologies and highlighted the importance of adaptability in assessments. Pinelli (2022) notes that the integration of technology has facilitated innovative approaches, like adaptive learning systems, which cater to diverse learning styles and paces, thus alleviating some cognitive load on teachers. However, while technology enhances feedback mechanisms, Li et al. (2023) raise questions about the effectiveness of these methods in practice, necessitating ongoing research and refinement in language assessment strategies.

Within traditional educational settings, barriers to providing timely feedback are inherently linked to the cognitive load that teachers carry as they manage diverse classroom needs. The demands of evaluating student work, particularly in language acquisition, can overshadow the ability to offer individualized feedback promptly. This scenario is exacerbated by the complexities of personalized instruction, as McCullough et al. (2024) observed in contexts where educators strive to support students with varying learning abilities. Soper et al. (2024) found that teachers often find themselves multitasking, which complicates their capacity to engage efficiently with feedback processes, ultimately hindering effective communication with students. As a result, delayed feedback may not only stifle timely improvements in students' learning trajectories but also contribute to a broader sense of disengagement, creating a ripple effect that impacts language acquisition overall. Addressing these barriers necessitates systemic changes that prioritize manageable workloads and enhance feedback mechanisms within the educational framework.

THE COGNITIVE LOAD BURDEN ON TEACHERS

The cognitive load burden on teachers is a critical factor affecting the effectiveness of language assessment and feedback processes. As educators navigate the intricate dynamics of assessing student performance, they must simultaneously manage the demands of instructional planning, student engagement, and individualized feedback, all of which contribute to cognitive overload. This multitasking not only hampers their ability to provide timely and personalized feedback but can also lead to decreased instructional quality. Teachers often grapple with how best to accommodate diverse learners, including those with unique needs, which necessitates additional cognitive resources. For example, professionals involved in assessing parent-child interactions in deaf children emphasize the need for tailored approaches that account for familial contexts (Curtin M et al., 2024). Similarly, insights on assessing chronic pain in autistic youth have illuminated the necessity for adaptations to traditional assessment frameworks (Gloria T Han et al., 2024). Consequently, the cumulative cognitive load faced by educators can adversely affect language acquisition, as timely feedback becomes increasingly elusive amid these pressures.

The assessment of language learners poses significant cognitive load on both students and educators, largely influenced by the complexity of linguistic constructs and the evaluative methods employed. Factors such as the intricacies of language structure, including vocabulary acquisition and grammar comprehension, can overwhelm learners, particularly when assessments demand higher-order thinking skills. Additionally, the use of technology in language assessment, while beneficial, can sometimes exacerbate cognitive demands; for instance, learners may struggle to navigate digital tools while simultaneously processing language tasks (Li et al., 2023). Teachers, on the other hand, bear the burden of designing assessments that are both effective and equitable, necessitating the allocation of mental resources toward crafting individualized feedback. Delays in this feedback further complicate the situation, as learners may not receive timely insights necessary for their language development, ultimately hindering their progress and leading to decreased motivation. Balancing these factors is crucial to alleviate cognitive load and enhance learning outcomes.

In the context of language learning, managing cognitive load during feedback delivery is essential for fostering effective student engagement and development. Teachers can implement various strategies to streamline this process, such as providing structured feedback that prioritizes key points rather than overwhelming students with extensive criticism. By using rubrics, educators can explicitly outline criteria and expectations, which aids students in focusing on specific areas for improvement. Additionally, the integration of technology can be beneficial; for instance, utilizing AI-driven chatbots, like Bashayer, has shown potential in enhancing learner motivation and cognitive strategies, thereby alleviating some of the cognitive burdens on teachers while simultaneously providing individualized feedback (Al-Abdullatif, 2023). This dual approach not only enhances the efficiency of feedback mechanisms but also promotes deeper learning experiences, thereby addressing both the historical and contemporary challenges associated with timely and effective assessment in language education.

Impact of Delayed Feedback on Language Acquisition

The impact of delayed feedback on language acquisition is a topic of considerable significance in the realm of educational assessment. When learners do not receive timely feedback, their ability to internalize language structures and improve their communicative competence can be severely compromised. This delay can create cognitive overload, as students struggle to connect their errors with subsequent learning opportunities, thereby reinforcing misconceptions rather than correcting them. Moreover, the increasing complexity of teaching methodologies, as influenced by emerging trends and multimodal learning, adds an additional layer of challenge for educators tasked with providing individualized feedback. Research indicates that timely feedback can significantly enhance the efficacy of early interventions in educational settings, underlining the necessity for educators to prioritize rapid response mechanisms in their teaching practices to maximize language development. Thus, addressing the challenges of delayed feedback becomes imperative in fostering effective language acquisition.

The effects of delayed feedback on student motivation and engagement in the context of language learning are significant and multifaceted. When students receive feedback well after submission, their ability to connect improvements to specific learning tasks diminishes, leading to a decline in motivation. This lack of immediate response can create feelings of frustration and disengagement, as learners often desire timely affirmation of their progress. The historical challenges of providing individualized feedback complicate this issue, particularly for educators facing cognitive load due to a high volume of assessments. The integration of advanced technologies, such as artificial intelligence-driven tools, could potentially alleviate some of these burdens by delivering prompt feedback, thus enhancing engagement and motivation. However, the effectiveness of these resources must be evaluated carefully to avoid ethical and practical missteps, as highlighted in recent scholarly discussions on innovative educational approaches (Yogesh K Dwivedi et al., 2023; Park S et al., 2022).

The timing of feedback plays a critical role in language retention, directly impacting learners ability to assimilate new information and rectify errors. Immediate feedback facilitates quick identification of mistakes, allowing learners to adjust their understanding before cognitive pathways solidify incorrect associations. Conversely, delayed feedback can exacerbate cognitive load, as students may struggle to recall specific contextual details surrounding their errors, which complicates the learning process. This challenge is particularly pronounced in language acquisition, where the nuances of grammar and vocabulary require precise reinforcement. As highlighted by recent educational reviews, the integration of innovative digital technologies can aid in delivering timely feedback, effectively addressing the historic shortcomings associated with traditional assessment methods (G M Dhananjaya et al., 2024). However, the implementation of such technologies must also consider the cognitive load placed on educators, ensuring that they can facilitate supportive learning environments amid increasing complexity in the educational landscape (Kantan PR, 2024).

While the integration of AI technologies in assessment processes has been shown to ease teacher workload and cognitive load, it is equally important to examine how these innovations impact students' learning experiences. Foremost among the benefits are the enhanced opportunities for personalized, timely, and objective feedback, which are crucial for effective ESL and other language education contexts. AI-powered tools, supported by learning analytics, deliver individualized feedback tailored to each student's strengths and learning gaps. By analyzing patterns in performance and errors, these systems can provide constructive, targeted recommendations that help students focus on specific areas for improvement. The immediacy of automated feedback ensures that learners receive guidance when it is most relevant—during or directly after learning activities—enabling them to quickly adjust their study strategies and deepen their understanding of key concepts. The objectivity inherent in AI-generated feedback mitigates inconsistencies and potential biases that may arise in traditional peer or instructor assessment. This contributes to a sense of fairness and transparency in the evaluation process, boosting student motivation and engagement. This combination of timely, personalized, and objective feedback fosters an environment in which students are empowered to take ownership of their learning journey, enhancing both performance and satisfaction in language courses

Definition and Importance of Formative Assessment in Language Learning

The introduction to formative assessment principles within language learning establishes a critical framework for understanding the interplay between feedback timing, effectiveness, and the role of learning analytics. As educational environments continue to evolve, the demand for effective feedback mechanisms has become paramount in enhancing learning outcomes. Azevedo et al. (2018) underscore the significant impact of feedback on academic achievement, noting its transformative potential when properly timed and executed. Moreover, the integration of information technologies introduces new opportunities and challenges within assessment processes. By exploring datafication, scaffolding, and peer assessment, Lachner et al. (2018) suggest educators can better navigate the complexities of assessing 21st-century skills, which often involve intricate constructs intertwined with motivational and affective components. This exploration not only addresses current trends in feedback practices but also emphasizes the necessity for ongoing research and policy development in the realm of formative assessment.

Formative assessment is fundamentally defined as an evaluative process aimed at monitoring student learning to provide ongoing feedback that can be used by instructors to improve their teaching and by students to enhance their learning. This approach is particularly vital in language education, where the ability to communicate effectively is paramount. Formative assessments allow educators to identify individual student needs and adjust instructional strategies accordingly, ultimately fostering a more personalized learning environment. Double et al. (2019) suggest that timely and constructive feedback significantly enhances student performance, underscoring the effectiveness of formative assessment in language learning contexts. Brezzi et al. (2021) highlight that the role of learning analytics in formative assessment becomes increasingly significant as it allows for the collection and analysis of data to inform these assessments, thereby improving their effectiveness. By leveraging analytics, educators can better track student progress and adapt their teaching methods to maximize learning outcomes in language acquisition.

A pivotal aspect of formative assessment practices is the framework of collaborative peer feedback, which seeks to enhance the learning experience through structured dialogue among students. This framework is particularly essential in large classes where individualized feedback may be challenging to implement. By dividing the feedback process into three distinct phases, it fosters deeper engagement and understanding while supporting students' learning pathways. Additionally, Dimitriadis et al. (2020) note that integrating learning analytics within platforms like Synergy can significantly bolster this practice, as it provides instructors with actionable insights into student interactions and learning processes during peer feedback sessions. This approach aligns with the theoretical foundation of opportunity to learn, which has been shown to impact student outcomes across different learning environments. Schlamp et al. (2024) indicate persistent advantages for face-to-face learning over virtual instruction, suggesting that formative assessments supported by interactive feedback may yield better educational results than traditional assessment methods.

In the domain of language learning, the principles of effective feedback play a pivotal role in enhancing student outcomes. Research has indicated that timely and targeted feedback is essential for students to understand their progress and areas requiring improvement. Formative assessment practices, particularly those that incorporate peer feedback, offer scalable solutions for fostering dialogue and collaboration among students. This approach not only capitalizes on peer engagement but also benefits from learning analytics, which, as Dimitriadis et al. (2020) propose, can support instructors in facilitating effective feedback interactions during structured phases of student engagement. Charalambous et al. (2022) review various observation frameworks and reveal the inconsistency in how feedback quality is operationalized, highlighting a need for clarity and comprehensiveness in capturing feedback aspects. This understanding emphasizes the necessity for robust feedback mechanisms that guide language learners toward deeper comprehension and application of their skills.

Impact of Immediate vs. Delayed Feedback on Language Acquisition

The timing of feedback plays a crucial role in language acquisition, influencing both immediate responses and long-term retention. Research indicates that immediate feedback can enhance learners' comprehension and retention of language concepts by providing timely corrections, thus reinforcing correct usage (Carvalho et al., 2024). In contrast, delayed feedback, while allowing students time for reflection, may lead to misconceptions prevailing longer, consequently complicating future learning endeavors. This duality emphasizes the importance of feedback timing within formative assessment frameworks. Moreover, integrating interactivity into language learning contexts can further impact outcomes. For instance, high interactivity environments have shown to increase cognitive engagement, which is essential for retaining language skills (Lehikko et al., 2024). Thus, a nuanced understanding of how immediate versus delayed feedback interacts with learning experiences can inform effective pedagogical strategies that promote successful language acquisition and address individual learner needs.

Feedback Timing in Educational Settings

The timing of feedback in educational settings plays a crucial role in enhancing student learning outcomes, as evidenced by various case studies. Research indicates that timely feedback can significantly influence the effectiveness of formative assessments, allowing learners to make immediate adjustments to their understanding and strategies. For instance, case studies have shown that feedback delivered shortly after assessment not only mitigates the forgetting curve but also fosters deeper engagement with the material. This immediacy is further supported by learning analytics, which provides educators with valuable data regarding student interactions and responses, thereby facilitating targeted feedback opportunities (Azevedo et al., 2018). Moreover, the integration of automated feedback tools within educational technology platforms enhances this process by delivering rapid feedback while allowing educators to maintain control over instructional design (Bearman et al., 2023). As such, the strategic timing of feedback emerges as a foundational principle in the formulation of effective formative assessment practices in language learning environments.

The Role of Learning Analytics in Formative Assessment

Learning analytics serves a pivotal role in enhancing formative assessment practices within language learning by providing educators and learners with actionable insights derived from data analysis. This analytical approach facilitates timely and targeted feedback, which has been identified as a critical factor in improving learning outcomes (Azevedo et al., 2018). By examining patterns in student performance and engagement, teachers can tailor instruction and feedback to meet individual needs, thus optimizing the learning experience. Additionally, the integration of automated feedback tools, supported by analytics, empowers instructors to deliver rapid and precise evaluation, thereby addressing the varying competencies of learners more effectively (Bearman et al., 2023). As such, learning analytics not only streamlines the feedback process but also encourages a more dynamic and responsive educational environment, where both students and educators can engage actively in the learning journey, ultimately fostering greater academic achievement in language proficiency.

Utilizing Data to Inform Instructional Strategies

The integration of data analytics into instructional strategies represents a significant advancement within the framework of formative assessment principles in language learning. By systematically analyzing learner performance data, educators can tailor their teaching methods to address individual student needs and enhance overall academic achievement. This approach aligns with the need for effective feedback mechanisms, as articulated in contemporary discussions surrounding the role of information technologies in assessment practices. For instance, Lachner et al. (2018) explain that the datafication of learning allows educators to identify trends in student engagement and understanding, which can inform timely interventions and support personalized learning pathways. Moreover, as Hood et al. (2016) highlight in the literature on educational quality, the success of these data-driven strategies hinges on the contextualization of feedback, ensuring that assessments not only evaluate student learning but also promote essential 21st-century skills. Thus, utilizing data effectively becomes a cornerstone in developing robust instructional strategies that are responsive to learner needs.

Enhancing Student Engagement and Performance through Learning Analytics

The integration of learning analytics in educational environments plays a pivotal role in enhancing student engagement and performance, particularly within the context of formative assessment. By systematically analyzing data derived from student interactions in virtual learning environments, educators can identify specific feedback mechanisms that drive learning outcomes. Research indicates that feedback not only clarifies expectations but actively contributes to students understanding and mastery of content, reinforcing its power in academic achievement (Azevedo et al., 2018). Moreover, the advent of automated feedback tools has opened new pathways for delivering timely and personalized feedback, which is essential for maintaining student motivation and fostering a robust learning experience. These tools require instructors to develop competencies that merge human insight with technological precision, ultimately enriching the classroom dynamic (Bearman et al., 2023). Consequently, the strategic use of learning analytics not only optimizes assessment practices but also cultivates an engaging and supportive educational atmosphere conducive to student success.

The AI Assessment Ecosystem

In recent years, the landscape of language education has been profoundly influenced by technological advancements, particularly the integration of artificial intelligence (AI) into formative assessment tools that cater to English language learning. As educators increasingly turn to innovative solutions, automated writing evaluation systems, speech recognition for pronunciation feedback, and natural language processing for conversational practice have emerged as pivotal elements in enhancing the learner's experience and engagement within the classroom context. These AI-driven tools harness sophisticated algorithms and large data sets to provide immediate feedback, which Pan (2024) note is critical in language acquisition, a process that often requires timely corrections and personalized learning pathways. The research problem addressed in this dissertation revolves around the effective integration of such formative assessment tools, focusing particularly on their ability to improve linguistic proficiency and support diverse learning needs across different contexts (Rohman et al., 2024). The primary objectives include examining the functionalities of these AI technologies, evaluating their impact on language learning outcomes, and identifying best practices for their implementation within educational settings (Ahmed ASMM et al., 2024). The study seeks to investigate the ways in which intelligent error analysis and pattern recognition can contribute to a deeper understanding of students' learning challenges and progression (Li et al., 2024). The significance of this research extends beyond academia; by providing empirical evidence of AI's effectiveness in formative assessments, practitioners can better understand how to leverage these tools to cater to individual learner needs while enhancing overall language competence (Sunengko et al., 2024). This is especially crucial in the context of English as a Foreign Language (EFL) instruction, where Hasan (2024) identify challenges such as grammatical complexity, pronunciation issues, and conversational fluency can impede learners' progress. By systematically analyzing the efficacy of these AI-powered tools, this dissertation aims not only to enrich the existing body of knowledge within language education but also to provide actionable insights for educators seeking to incorporate technology in a pedagogically sound manner (Cwiertny et al., 2023). The implications of the study promise to foster a deeper dialogue around the synergy between AI and language learning, addressing the multifaceted impacts on communication skills development essential for success in today's increasingly globalized society (Alessi et al., 2024; Catalán et al., 2024). Thus, this dissertation endeavors to provide a comprehensive exploration of how AI-powered formative assessment tools can reshape the future of English language education while simultaneously addressing the pressing challenges faced by learners and educators alike (Shakeel A, 2024; Song C et al., 2023).

The integration of technology has fundamentally redefined the methodologies employed in language instruction, particularly in the English learning domain. The emergence of advanced technologies such as artificial intelligence (AI) marks a significant shift in pedagogical approaches, fostering personalized and adaptive learning environments. As language acquisition becomes increasingly nuanced and individualized, it becomes critical to explore AI-powered formative assessment tools that can enhance the learning experience for English language learners. These tools not only promise to augment traditional assessment methods but also present opportunities for real-time feedback and tailored learning pathways, elements crucial in language education as underscored by recent studies (Pan, 2024; Rohman et al., 2024). The role of automated writing evaluation systems, for instance, has been a focal point in discussions about the effectiveness of immediate feedback in writing proficiency, underscoring that such systems can significantly improve both the writing skills and confidence of learners (Ahmed ASMM et al., 2024; Li et al., 2024).

The application of speech recognition technology serves to address pronunciation and spoken fluency—critical components of language mastery. Research indicates that this technology not only assists learners in recognizing their pronunciation errors but also offers tailored corrective feedback that enhances oral skills (Sunengko et al., 2024; Hasan, 2024). This is particularly important given the interactive nature of language learning, which necessitates continual practice and refinement of spoken abilities. Natural language processing then further extends these capabilities by facilitating conversational practice that immerses learners in more authentic interactions, allowing them to refine their skills in a supportive and low-stakes environment (Cwiertny et al., 2023; Alessi et al., 2024).

Despite the promising advancements in these technologies, significant gaps remain in the existing literature. For instance, Catalán et al. (2024) highlight a need for comprehensive studies that longitudinally assess the impact of these AI-driven tools on learner outcomes. While many narratives highlight initial successes, fewer have systematically evaluated long-term engagement and efficacy across diverse learner populations, particularly among non-native English speakers (Shakeel A, 2024; Song C et al., 2023). The implications of integrating intelligent error analysis and pattern recognition into formative assessment are not fully explored, leaving a vital area of research that could inform how AI tools can be leveraged to tailor feedback mechanisms in more meaningful ways (Wei L, 2023; Keng-Ooi B et al., 2023).

The intersection of AI technology and formative assessment in language instruction warrants a thorough examination, not only to understand the current landscape but also to present recommendations for educational practice and future research trajectories. As educational institutions increasingly rely on data-driven decisions, understanding the limitations and potentialities of AI-powered formative assessment tools within the English language learning framework is critical. In addressing these gaps, future studies must provide insights into best practices, effective implementation strategies, and the ethical considerations that accompany the use of AI in education (Allioui H et al., 2023; Dempere J et al., 2023; Prather J et al., 2023). This review will synthesize the existing literature, summarize key findings and themes, and ultimately contribute to a burgeoning field that seeks to harness AI in fostering substantial and meaningful English language acquisition experiences (Ömer Aydın et al., 2023; Michel R-Villarreal et al., 2023; Yan L et al., 2023; Limna P et al., 2023). Through this exploration, we aim to establish a foundation for informed discussions and iterative advances in the integration of technology in language education.

The evolution of AI-powered formative assessment tools for English language learning has seen significant advancements, particularly with the integration of automated writing evaluation systems. Early iterations of these systems laid the groundwork for understanding how technology could enhance writing feedback, as Pan (2024) began exploring the relationship between AI-generated responses and student performance. Subsequent developments highlighted the utility of speech recognition technology, which emerged as a critical tool for providing pronunciation feedback. Studies demonstrated that real-time feedback on pronunciation significantly improved language retention and speaking confidence, linking user engagement with positive outcomes in pronunciation skills (Rohman et al., 2024; Ahmed ASMM et al., 2024).

As the field progressed, natural language processing (NLP) emerged as a transformative force for fostering conversational practice. Systems utilizing NLP allowed for more personalized learning experiences, enabling learners to engage in contextually relevant dialogues that mirrored real-life interactions (Li et al., 2024; Sunengko et al., 2024). Research indicated that this kind of interactive exchange not only increased student motivation but also enhanced linguistic proficiency by allowing learners to practice language in context (Hasan, 2024).

Intelligent error analysis and pattern recognition initiatives further expanded the capability of formative assessments by identifying recurring mistakes and suggesting tailored improvement strategies. These advancements have contributed to a more nuanced understanding of learner needs, allowing educators to strategically intervene and offer support (Cwiertny et al., 2023; Alessi et al., 2024). Collectively, these developments illustrate a timeline marked by an increasing sophistication of AI tools, which have transitioned from basic feedback mechanisms to comprehensive, intelligent systems that adapt to individual learning trajectories (Catalán et al., 2024; Shakeel A, 2024). This progression underscores a growing recognition of the role of AI in effective language assessment and instruction.

The integration of AI-powered formative assessment tools into English language learning emphasizes several key themes, notably automated writing evaluation systems and speech recognition technologies. Research demonstrates that these automated systems provide immediate feedback, which is vital for student improvement and engagement in writing exercises. For instance, studies have shown that automated writing evaluation can enhance learners' writing fluency and accuracy, as it offers prompt corrections and suggestions tailored to individual needs (Pan, 2024; Rohman et al., 2024). Additionally, the use of speech recognition tools has emerged as a critical area of exploration, as they facilitate pronunciation feedback essential for language acquisition. Such tools allow learners to practice speaking in real-time, receiving instant evaluations that can significantly influence their confidence and performance (Ahmed ASMM et al., 2024; Li et al., 2024). This immediate responsiveness not only assists learners in recognizing their pronunciation errors but also in developing more natural speaking habits, as outlined in several studies (Sunengko et al., 2024; Hasan, 2024).

Natural language processing (NLP) further enriches conversational practice, enabling intelligent interactions that simulate realistic dialogues. This technology supports learners by analyzing their responses and adjusting the conversational flow to match their proficiency level, thereby personalizing their language learning experience (Cwiertny et al., 2023; Alessi et al., 2024). The theme of intelligent error analysis emerges through recent analyses of student performance, showcasing how AI can identify patterns in errors, allowing educators to adapt their instruction accordingly (Catalán et al., 2024; Shakeel A, 2024). Such advancements underscore the potential of AI in transforming English language pedagogy, providing tools that foster a more interactive and responsive learning environment (Song C et al., 2023; Wei L, 2023; Keng-Ooi B et al., 2023). Consequently, the literature collectively advocates for the transformative role of AI in facilitating formative assessments that are not only efficient but also deeply insightful for English language learners.

The exploration of AI-powered formative assessment tools highlights significant advancements across various methodological frameworks within language education. Automated writing evaluation systems have emerged as a key focus area, showcasing the integration of algorithms that evaluate grammatical accuracy and coherence. These systems have been shown to enhance student writing skills effectively, with studies indicating improvements in overall performance when utilized in instructional settings (Pan, 2024; Rohman et al., 2024). In addition, research surrounding speech recognition technology for pronunciation feedback emphasizes its potential in delivering immediate and personalized coaching, thereby fostering learner autonomy in speaking skills. The efficacy of these tools has been corroborated by multiple studies that demonstrate enhanced pronunciation accuracy and fluency among learners using dynamic feedback methods (Ahmed ASMM et al., 2024; Li et al., 2024). Moreover, natural language processing (NLP) has revolutionized conversational practice, allowing for more engaging and contextually rich interactions. NLP tools facilitate real-time dialogue simulations, effectively preparing learners for real-world conversations (Sunengko et al., 2024; Hasan, 2024). The methodological implications here indicate a shift toward interactive learning environments that prioritize authenticity in language use.

Intelligent error analysis and pattern recognition have emerged as pivotal areas in understanding learner challenges. Through analyzing common error patterns, AI tools can offer tailored feedback that addresses specific student needs, thereby supporting targeted instructional interventions (Cwiertny et al., 2023; Alessi et al., 2024). Collectively, these methodological approaches underscore the transformative potential of AI in formative assessment, as educators increasingly harness technology to enhance language learning outcomes, creating more adaptive and personalized educational experiences (Catalán et al., 2024; Shakeel A, 2024). The literature consistently reveals a shift toward more interactive, data-driven strategies that lead to improved learner engagement and proficiency in English language skills.

The exploration of AI-powered formative assessment tools for English language learning reveals a diverse range of theoretical perspectives that illuminate both the benefits and challenges of incorporating technology in language education. Automated writing evaluation systems, for instance, have been shown to enhance learner engagement and provide instantaneous feedback, fostering a more interactive learning environment (Pan, 2024; Rohman et al., 2024). Such systems often leverage natural language processing to assess writing quality and offer tailored suggestions, which Ahmed ASMM et al. (2024) note aligns with constructivist theories emphasizing active engagement in the learning process. Similarly, speech recognition technologies utilized for pronunciation feedback can support learners by enabling real-time assessments of spoken language skills. These tools create opportunities for learners to practice pronunciation in a low-stakes environment, reinforcing behaviorist frameworks that advocate for the reinforcement of correct articulations (Li et al., 2024; Sunengko et al., 2024). However, Hasan (2024) raise concerns about the accuracy and effectiveness of such evaluations, suggesting that not all learners may benefit equally from these tools.

Natural language processing applications designed for conversational practice represent another theoretical layer, with Cwiertny et al. (2023) demonstrating their potential to simulate authentic communication contexts. This aligns with sociocultural theories that underscore the importance of interaction in language acquisition (Alessi et al., 2024). Moreover, intelligent error analysis and pattern recognition functionalities provide deeper insights into learner mistakes, supporting formative assessment practices that prioritize personalized learning trajectories (Catalán et al., 2024; Shakeel A, 2024). Collectively, these theoretical perspectives underscore a complex interplay between technology and pedagogy, revealing both the transformative potential and the inherent challenges of AI in language learning contexts.

The exploration of AI-powered formative assessment tools for English language learners has unveiled crucial insights into the transformative potential of technology in educational contexts. Key findings from the literature indicate that automated writing evaluation systems and speech recognition technologies significantly enhance learner engagement, provide immediate feedback, and improve both writing skills and pronunciation accuracy. Research underscores that these tools foster an interactive environment conducive to learning, with studies showing marked improvements in writing fluency and speaking confidence as learners receive personalized and contextually relevant feedback (Pan, 2024; Rohman et al., 2024; Ahmed ASMM et al., 2024; Li et al., 2024). The use of natural language processing to facilitate conversational practice exemplifies the adaptive capabilities of AI, enabling students to engage in authentic dialogues that mirror real-life interactions. This aspect of AI tools not only promotes linguistic proficiency but also motivates learners, as highlighted in recent studies connecting user engagement with improved outcomes (Sunengko et al., 2024; Hasan, 2024).

Reaffirming the main themes of this Chapter, it is evident that AI-powered formative assessment tools are redefining pedagogy in the English language learning sphere. The integration of intelligent error analysis and pattern recognition further enriches this narrative by offering insights into learners' common challenges and facilitating tailored instructional strategies (Cwiertny et al., 2023; Alessi et al., 2024). These innovations exemplify how formative assessments can evolve from traditional approaches to more nuanced systems that adapt to individual learning needs, thereby resonating with constructivist and sociocultural theories emphasizing active engagement and the importance of interaction in language acquisition (Catalán et al., 2024; Shakeel A, 2024; Song C et al., 2023). The broader implications of these findings are significant, as they suggest that educational institutions can leverage AI technologies to create more personalized, data-driven learning environments. Such environments hold the potential to enhance the learning experience for diverse learner populations, particularly non-native English speakers who may struggle with conventional assessment methods. The ability to provide immediate feedback and customized learning pathways aligns seamlessly with the goals of contemporary education, which increasingly values individualized learning experiences over one-size-fits-all solutions (Wei L, 2023; Keng-Ooi B et al., 2023). Nevertheless, it is essential to acknowledge limitations within the existing literature. Notably, the need for longitudinal studies that assess the long-term impact of AI-driven tools on learner outcomes is critical, as many current narratives merely highlight initial successes without comprehensive evaluation (Allioui H et al., 2023; Dempere J et al., 2023). While individual studies illustrate the effectiveness of these technologies, there remains a lack of systematic reviews that consolidate findings across various contexts and learner demographics, particularly with regard to non-native English speakers (Prather J et al., 2023; Ömer Aydın et al., 2023). Future research should focus on addressing these gaps by conducting in-depth longitudinal studies and meta-analyses that evaluate the efficacy of AI-powered formative assessment tools across diverse educational settings. Additionally, exploring the ethical considerations and potential biases inherent in AI technologies will be vital in informing best practices for implementation. Ultimately, advancing our understanding of these tools will be crucial as educational stakeholders aim to harness the full potential of AI in fostering meaningful and substantial English language acquisition experiences for all learners (Michel R-Villarreal et al., 2023; Yan L et al., 2023; Limna P et al., 2023). Through sustained inquiry, educators and researchers can collectively define the trajectory of AI in language pedagogy, ensuring that the integration of technology serves to enhance educational outcomes and equity in language learning.

AI Assessment Methodologies in Language Learning

The integration of advanced technologies within educational frameworks has transformed the landscape of language instruction, particularly in the realm of formative assessment tools. Pan (2024) highlight that the widespread adoption of AI-powered solutions—including automated writing evaluation systems, speech recognition technologies, and natural language processing—necessitates a structured approach to assess their effectiveness in language learning environments. Similarly, Rohman et al. (2024) argue that evaluating the impact of these AI-driven methodologies on the writing skills and pronunciation of English language learners is a pressing issue that remains underexplored despite the rapid proliferation of relevant technologies. Ahmed ASMM et al. (2024) suggest that the central objective of this study is to critically assess how these AI tools can enhance formative assessments in language learning, thereby positively influencing learners' engagement, motivation, and overall language proficiency. In addition, Li et al. (2024) show that the research specifically aims to identify best practices and potential challenges in implementing automated evaluations, feedback mechanisms, and conversational practices using AI technologies.

The significance of this inquiry lies not only in its academic contributions to language education but also in its practical implications for educators and institutions striving to integrate technology effectively into their curricula. Sunengko et al. (2024) provide evidence that evaluating these AI tools can shape pedagogical strategies and inform policy development regarding technology use in educational settings. Hasan (2024) demonstrate that prior studies have shown automated writing evaluation systems to improve writing fluency and accuracy, supporting their inclusion in language instruction. Cwiertny et al. (2023) show that research on speech recognition technologies has revealed advancements in offering immediate, personalized feedback that enhances learners' pronunciation skills.

In comparing these methodologies with established practices, Alessi et al. (2024) contend that AI-powered formative assessments capture learners' progress through intelligent error analysis and pattern recognition, thereby fostering a more tailored learning experience. Moreover, Catalán et al. (2024) argue that exploring AI-driven formative assessment tools not only reaffirms their necessity in modern language education but also addresses identified gaps in the literature while offering concrete recommendations to enhance their integration into language teaching practices.

By engaging with these developments, Shakeel A (2024) emphasizes that the study contributes to a deeper understanding of effective language assessment strategies that promote academic success and prepare learners for a future increasingly influenced by technology. This broader framework consolidates the importance of this methodology section in driving meaningful change within English language teaching and learning landscapes (Song C et al., 2023; Wei L, 2023; Keng-Ooi B et al., 2023; Allioui H et al., 2023; Dempere J et al., 2023; Prather J et al., 2023; Ömer Aydın et al., 2023; Michel R-Villarreal et al., 2023; Yan L et al., 2023; Limna P et al., 2023).

The rapidly evolving landscape of language instruction increasingly integrates artificial intelligence (AI), particularly through the use of AI-powered formative assessment tools that enhance English language learning outcomes. The findings from this study provide insightful evidence regarding the significant role of automated writing evaluation systems, speech recognition technologies, and natural language processing capabilities. Pan (2024) highlight that students using automated writing evaluation systems exhibit marked improvements in overall writing proficiency—especially in grammar and structure—echoing earlier research on the effectiveness of these AI tools in fostering writing skills. In addition, Rohman et al. (2024) demonstrate that speech recognition feedback is instrumental in enhancing students' pronunciation accuracy by providing immediate corrective responses that align with the benefits identified in technology-assisted language learning. Ahmed ASMM et al. (2024) found that data collected through conversational practice with natural language processing tools indicate increased student confidence in speaking, suggesting that AI-generated conversational partners can significantly enhance communication skills. Li et al. (2024) reinforce that a comparative analysis of these results with existing literature shows a growing consensus on the effectiveness of AI methodologies in language education. Sunengko et al. (2024) caution that robust integration methodologies are essential to maximize the effectiveness of AI tools in educational contexts. Hasan (2024) argue that this research contributes substantially to the academic discourse by establishing a framework in which AI-powered formative assessment tools not only enhance English language proficiency but also motivate learners through personalized engagement. Cwiertny et al. (2023) suggest that the results underscore a critical balance between the practical applications of these technologies in improving listening, speaking, and writing skills and the need to preserve the critical thinking aspects fostered by traditional pedagogy. Alessi et al. (2024) contend that these findings provide a compelling argument for continued investment in AI technologies in education, urging educators to adapt curricula that incorporate these tools to better meet diverse learner needs. As the educational landscape continues to evolve, policies that ensure ethical and effective use of AI in instructional environments are urgently needed to enhance educational equity and access (Catalán et al., 2024; Shakeel A, 2024; Song C et al., 2023; Wei L, 2023; Keng-Ooi B et al., 2023; Allioui H et al., 2023; Dempere J et al., 2023; Prather J et al., 2023; Ömer Aydın et al., 2023; Michel R-Villarreal et al., 2023; Yan L et al., 2023; Limna P et al., 2023).

The advent of artificial intelligence in language education marks a transformative epoch that necessitates a critical analysis of its applications in enhancing English language learning. The findings from this research elucidate the efficacy of AI-powered tools, focusing on automated writing evaluation systems, speech recognition for pronunciation feedback, and natural language processing for conversational practice. Pan (2024) underscore that the implementation of automated writing evaluation tools leads to significant improvements in students' writing proficiency—particularly in grammar and structure—corroborating previous research on the role of technology in optimizing writing skills. Rohman et al. (2024) corroborate that speech recognition technology, by providing immediate corrective feedback, substantially enhances pronunciation accuracy. Ahmed ASMM et al. (2024) asserted that natural language processing tools also contribute to heightened learner confidence in speaking. Li et al. (2024) suggest that, while these findings are promising, there remain challenges in fully leveraging AI tools in educational contexts, particularly when addressing individual learning needs. Sunengko et al. (2024) indicate that the implications of these findings extend beyond mere enhancements in language proficiency, suggesting a paradigm shift in pedagogical methodologies through the integration of intelligent error analysis systems tailored to individual learners. Hasan (2024) emphasize that the need for educators to thoughtfully adapt curricula to incorporate AI tools is critical for fostering personalized learning environments. Cwiertny et al. (2023) echo this concern by highlighting the imperative for policies that ensure ethical applications of AI, thereby maximizing educational equity and accessibility. Alessi et al. (2024) underline the importance of ongoing research into AI's multifaceted implications for language learning as a pathway to address existing gaps. Catalán et al. (2024) propose that by collaborating, educators and researchers can navigate the complex interplay between technology and pedagogy to enhance learner experiences. Ultimately, Shakeel A (2024) establishes that these findings contribute to a more robust academic discourse surrounding AI's integration in English language education, while Song C et al. (2023) reflect that the synthesis of these insights provides actionable recommendations for practitioners seeking to employ AI technologies effectively in their educational practices.

Use Cases of AI Assisted Formative Assessments

This transformative shift in educational practice is evident across higher education, K–12 institutions, and adult learning environments. Reunanen et al. (2024) noted that educators and institutions are increasingly leveraging AI tools to enhance curriculum delivery, foster personalized learning experiences, and streamline administrative processes, while Danylchenko-Cherniak (2024) reported similar advancements in technology integration. However, this integration is accompanied by a complex set of challenges. As M'ad (2024) explains, educators must adapt to new technologies and maintain teaching efficacy, and Tolentino et al. (2024) emphasize that ethical considerations—such as data privacy and algorithmic bias—are critical concerns.

Within this multifaceted landscape, the research problem emerges: How can various models of AI implementation be effectively tailored to meet the diverse needs of students and teachers across different educational contexts? This study examines case studies that highlight successful implementation strategies in higher education, K–12 schools, and adult self-directed learning environments (Kristen "Kit" Lewers, 2024; Chan CKY et al., 2023). In addition, the research seeks to develop hybrid human–AI assessment workflows that not only enhance learner outcomes but also complement traditional pedagogical practices.

The significance of addressing this problem extends beyond theoretical contributions to the academic discourse on educational technology. Aniek F. Markus et al. (2020) and Glaz et al. (2020) indicate that understanding effective AI integration models can provide valuable insights for educators and policymakers, guiding the development of curricula that foster both engagement and achievement. Moreover, ensuring ethical AI use is essential so that innovations do not inadvertently perpetuate existing inequities in the education system (Brunetti et al., 2020; Catherine D'Ignazio et al., 2020; Yogesh K. Dwivedi et al., 2023). Tiffany H. Kung et al. (2023), C. R. Harris et al. (2020), and Chen et al. (2020) have argued that bridging theoretical frameworks with practical applications is vital for enhancing the educational landscape in an era increasingly defined by technology and innovation.

Existing research delineates several implementation models across educational contexts, underscoring the adaptability of AI in diverse learning environments. In higher education, Reunanen et al. (2024) observed that sophisticated AI tools facilitate language learning through adaptive curricula and predictive analytics, leading to significant advancements in learner engagement and achievement. In K–12 settings, As M'ad (2024) reported that integration strategies focus on collaborative learning environments that utilize AI to foster student–teacher interactions and peer-to-peer communication, a finding also supported by Tolentino et al. (2024) regarding improved educational outcomes. For adult learners, Kristen "Kit" Lewers (2024) found that AI integration in self-directed learning contexts enhances personalized language acquisition, while Chan CKY et al. (2023) demonstrated its role in motivating learners by supporting individualized educational paths.

Despite these promising developments, there remains a notable gap in comprehensive evaluations of hybrid human–AI assessment workflows. Glaz et al. (2020) have highlighted that current research does not adequately address how these systems can be optimized for fairness and efficacy in language evaluation. As numerous case studies from various educational institutions illustrate, there are valuable lessons regarding best practices and potential pitfalls in AI implementation (Aniek F. Markus et al., 2020). For instance, some studies reveal varying degrees of resistance among educators and students, raising questions about the cultural and operational readiness of institutions to embrace AI-driven methodologies. Moreover, while AI tools have been shown to improve learning outcomes, Brunetti et al. (2020) caution that these technologies can sometimes neglect the linguistic identity and cultural nuances that are integral to language education.

Longitudinal studies remain scarce, and the sustainability and scalability of AI integration across different contexts are not yet fully understood (Yogesh K. Dwivedi et al., 2023). Tiffany H. Kung et al. (2023) and C. R. Harris et al. (2020) have emphasized the need for further research to evaluate long-term impacts and inform best practices. In addition, Chen et al. (2020), Rasheed A et al. (2020), Rasheed Z et al. (2023), Kamalov et al. (2023), Qiong Z. Luo (2023), Ad Tıgüzel et al. (2023), and Sallam (2023) have all contributed to a growing body of literature that calls for rigorous examination of AI implementation models. This chapter aims to bridge these gaps by synthesizing case studies and existing implementation models, discussing current limitations, and proposing areas for future research.

The integration of AI in English language education spans multiple contexts—from higher education to K–12 and adult learning—demonstrating both significant potential and notable challenges. While AI-driven tools have advanced personalized learning and improved educational outcomes, the ethical, cultural, and methodological considerations surrounding their use warrant further investigation. By providing a structured understanding of these practical applications, challenges, and prospects, this research aims to support informed decision-making and foster innovative educational practices that align with foundational educational values.

CONCLUSION

The exploration of artificial intelligence (AI) in English language education has uncovered significant insights across various educational contexts, including higher education, K-12 systems, and adult learning environments. Predominantly, the findings reveal that institutions utilizing AI-driven tools have experienced enhanced instructional practices, improving student engagement and learning outcomes through personalized learning experiences. The implications of these findings extend beyond academia, suggesting that the adoption of hybrid human-AI assessment workflows offers practical solutions for educators in elevating assessment validity and efficiency. This advancement underscores an academic shift towards integrating technology in pedagogical strategies, fostering dynamic learning environments that adapt to student needs. In terms of future work, recommendations include the necessity for longitudinal studies to further assess the long-term effects of AI integration on student learning trajectories, particularly in adult educational contexts that emphasize self-directed learning. Additionally, further exploration of ethical implications tied to AI utilization in learning will ensure that diverse learner populations are adequately considered, promoting inclusive practices. Policymakers are also urged to facilitate frameworks that support AI implementations, encouraging collaboration among stakeholders to advance research and practices within educational settings. Given the rapid evolution of educational technologies, it is imperative that future research investigates innovative AI applications tailored to specific learning outcomes and environments, ensuring that educators can harness these tools effectively. This could involve comprehensive studies exploring the challenges associated with AI learning algorithms' biases, which can directly impact educational equity. Moreover, understanding the potential pedagogical shifts resulting from AI integration, particularly in K-12 settings, remains essential for shaping curricula that respond to technological advancements. The impact of AI on instructional design warrants further inquiry, as educators need to adapt methodologies in line with these developments to foster optimal learning outcomes. These insights not only highlight the transformative power of AI in language education but also emphasize the continuous need for adaptive research endeavors, ensuring that the implementation of AI is both effective and ethically sound.

REFERENCES

Al-Abdullatif, A. M., Al-Dokhny, A. A., & Drwish, A. M. (2023). Implementing the Bashayer chatbot in Saudi higher education: Measuring the influence on students' motivation and learning strategies. *Frontiers in Psychology*, *14*, 1129070. DOI: 10.3389/fpsyg.2023.1129070 PMID: 37255522

Allioui, H., & Mourdi, Y. (2023). Exploring the full potentials of IoT for better financial growth and stability: A comprehensive survey. *Sensors (Basel)*, *23*(19), 8015. DOI: 10.3390/s23198015 PMID: 37836845

Ayanwale, M. A., Adelana, O. P., Molefi, R. R., Adeeko, O., & Ishola, A. M. (2024). Examining artificial intelligence literacy among pre-service teachers for future classrooms. *Computers and Education Open*, *6*, 100179. DOI: 10.1016/j.caeo.2024.100179

Aydın, Ö., & Karaarslan, E. (2023). Is ChatGPT leading generative AI? What is beyond expectations? *Academic Platform Journal of Engineering and Smart Systems*, *11*(3), 118–134. DOI: 10.21541/apjess.1293702

Brezzi, M., González, S., Nguyen, D., & Prats, M. (2021). An updated OECD framework on drivers of trust in public institutions to meet current and future challenges. *OECD working papers on public governance*, (48), 0_1-60.

Buckingham Shum, S., Lim, L. A., Boud, D., Bearman, M., & Dawson, P. (2023). A comparative analysis of the skilled use of automated feedback tools through the lens of teacher feedback literacy. *International Journal of Educational Technology in Higher Education*, *20*(1), 40. DOI: 10.1186/s41239-023-00410-9

Catalán, P. C. M. (2024). *Generative AI's Influence on Design Thinking: Enhancing Empathy Through Extreme Users and Parallel Universes* (Master's thesis, Universidade NOVA de Lisboa (Portugal)).

Chen, L., Chen, P., & Lin, Z. (2020). Artificial intelligence in education: A review. *IEEE Access : Practical Innovations, Open Solutions*, *8*, 75264–75278. DOI: 10.1109/ACCESS.2020.2988510

Curtin, M., Wakefield, T., Herman, R., Morgan, G., & Cruice, M. (2024). "It doesn't matter if we're the most amazing professionals in the world…" A qualitative study of professionals' perspectives on parent-child interaction assessment with deaf infants. *Frontiers in Psychology*, *15*, 1315220. DOI: 10.3389/fpsyg.2024.1315220 PMID: 38500650

D'Ignazio, C., & Klein, L. (2023). Introducing Data Feminism. In *Women's Empowerment and Its Limits: Interdisciplinary and Transnational Perspectives Toward Sustainable Progress* (pp. 139–151). Springer International Publishing. DOI: 10.1007/978-3-031-29332-0_8

Danylchenko-Cherniak, O. (2024). Phililogical perspectives of design thinking and artificial intelligence in the Education 5.0-7.0 era.

Dempere, J., Modugu, K., Hesham, A., & Ramasamy, L. K. (2023, September). The impact of ChatGPT on higher education. [). Frontiers Media SA.]. *Frontiers in Education*, *8*, 1206936. DOI: 10.3389/feduc.2023.1206936

Dimitriadis, Y., Er, E., & Gasevic, D. (2021). Collaborative peer feedback and learning analytics: theory-oriented design for supporting class-wide interventions.

Double, K. S., McGrane, J. A., & Hopfenbeck, T. N. (2020). The impact of peer assessment on academic performance: A meta-analysis of control group studies. *Educational Psychology Review*, *32*(2), 481–509. DOI: 10.1007/s10648-019-09510-3

Dwivedi, Y. K., Kshetri, N., Hughes, L., Slade, E. L., Jeyaraj, A., Kar, A. K., Baabdullah, A. M., Koohang, A., Raghavan, V., Ahuja, M., Albanna, H., Albashrawi, M. A., Al-Busaidi, A. S., Balakrishnan, J., Barlette, Y., Basu, S., Bose, I., Brooks, L., Buhalis, D., & Wright, R. (2023). Opinion Paper:"So what if ChatGPT wrote it?" Multidisciplinary perspectives on opportunities, challenges and implications of generative conversational AI for research, practice and policy. *International Journal of Information Management*, *71*, 102642. DOI: 10.1016/j.ijinfomgt.2023.102642

Gm, D., Goudar, R. H., Kulkarni, A. A., Rathod, V. N., & Hukkeri, G. S. (2024). A digital recommendation system for personalized learning to enhance online education: A review. *IEEE Access : Practical Innovations, Open Solutions*, *12*, 34019–34041. DOI: 10.1109/ACCESS.2024.3369901

Han, G. T., Heavner, H. S., Rains, T. R., Hoang, A. H., & Stone, A. L. (2024). Chronic pain in autistic youth: Clinical prevalence and reflections on tailoring evidence-based interventions from an interdisciplinary treatment team. *Children (Basel, Switzerland)*, *11*(3), 312. DOI: 10.3390/children11030312 PMID: 38539347

Harris, C. R., Millman, K. J., Van Der Walt, S. J., Gommers, R., Virtanen, P., Cournapeau, D., Wieser, E., Taylor, J., Berg, S., Smith, N. J., Kern, R., Picus, M., Hoyer, S., van Kerkwijk, M. H., Brett, M., Haldane, A., del Río, J. F., Wiebe, M., Peterson, P., & Oliphant, T. E. (2020). Array programming with NumPy. *Nature*, *585*(7825), 357–362. DOI: 10.1038/s41586-020-2649-2 PMID: 32939066

Hasan, R. (2024). Enhancing stakeholder engagement in project management through ai-driven predictive modeling.

Hood, N., & Littlejohn, A. (2016). Quality in MOOCs: Surveying the terrain.

Jamshed, M., Manjur Ahmed, A. S. M., Sarfaraj, M., & Warda, W. U. (2024). The Impact of ChatGPT on English Language Learners' Writing Skills: An Assessment of AI Feedback on Mobile. *International Journal of Interactive Mobile Technologies*, *18*(19), 18–36. DOI: 10.3991/ijim.v18i19.50361

Kamalov, F., Santandreu Calonge, D., & Gurrib, I. (2023). New era of artificial intelligence in education: Towards a sustainable multifaceted revolution. *Sustainability (Basel)*, *15*(16), 12451. DOI: 10.3390/su151612451

Kantan, P. R. (2024). Orchestrating Motion: Real-Time Sonification Tools and Methods to Support Movement Rehabilitation.

Kung, T. H., Cheatham, M., Medenilla, A., Sillos, C., De Leon, L., Elepaño, C., Madriaga, M., Aggabao, R., Diaz-Candido, G., Maningo, J., & Tseng, V. (2023). Performance of ChatGPT on USMLE: Potential for AI-assisted medical education using large language models. *PLOS Digital Health*, *2*(2), e0000198. DOI: 10.1371/journal.pdig.0000198 PMID: 36812645

Lehikko, A., & Nykänen, M. (2024, August). A Mixed-Methods Study on Learner-IVR Interactivity, Agency, Cognitive Load and Learning Outcomes. In *European Association for Research on Learning and Instruction SIG 6 & 7 Conference 2024*. Instructional Design, Technology-Enhanced Learning and Instruction.

Lewers, K. K. (2024). Comparative Methods for Building Chatbots: Open Source, Hybrid, and Fully Integrated Large Language Models. *Biodiversity Information Science and Standards*, *8*, 8. DOI: 10.3897/biss.8.143032

Limna, P., Kraiwanit, T., Jangjarat, K., Klayklung, P., & Chocksathaporn, P. (2023). The use of ChatGPT in the digital era: Perspectives on chatbot implementation. *Journal of Applied Learning and Teaching*, *6*(1), 64–74.

Luo, Q. Z., & Hsiao-Chin, L. Y. (2023). The influence of AI-powered adaptive learning platforms on student performance in Chinese classrooms. *Journal of Education*, *6*(3), 1–12. DOI: 10.53819/81018102t4181

Markus, A. F., Kors, J. A., & Rijnbeek, P. R. (2021). The role of explainability in creating trustworthy artificial intelligence for health care: A comprehensive survey of the terminology, design choices, and evaluation strategies. *Journal of Biomedical Informatics*, *113*, 103655. DOI: 10.1016/j.jbi.2020.103655 PMID: 33309898

McCullough, L. E. (2024). Examining the Lived Experiences of Educators Using Different Levels of Support for Teaching Math to Students with Learning Disabilities in Math Computation and Problem-Solving for Teachers at Public Cyber Charter High Schools in the Northeastern United States: A Transcendental Phenomenological Study.

Michel-Villarreal, R., Vilalta-Perdomo, E., Salinas-Navarro, D. E., Thierry-Aguilera, R., & Gerardou, F. S. (2023). Challenges and opportunities of generative AI for higher education as explained by ChatGPT. *Education Sciences*, *13*(9), 856. DOI: 10.3390/educsci13090856

Ooi, K. B., Tan, G. W. H., Al-Emran, M., Al-Sharafi, M. A., Capatina, A., Chakraborty, A., Dwivedi, Y. K., Huang, T.-L., Kar, A. K., Lee, V.-H., Loh, X.-M., Micu, A., Mikalef, P., Mogaji, E., Pandey, N., Raman, R., Rana, N. P., Sarker, P., Sharma, A., & Wong, L. W. (2025). The potential of generative artificial intelligence across disciplines: Perspectives and future directions. *Journal of Computer Information Systems*, *65*(1), 76–107. DOI: 10.1080/08874417.2023.2261010

Özer, M. (2024). Potential benefits and risks of artificial intelligence in education. *Bartın University Journal of Faculty of Education*, *13*(2), 232–244. DOI: 10.14686/buefad.1416087

Pan, J. (2024). AI-driven English language learning program and academic writing integrity in the era of intelligent interface. *English Language Teaching and Linguistics Studies*, *6*(4), 120. DOI: 10.22158/eltls.v6n4p120

Park, S. M., & Kim, Y. G. (2022). A metaverse: Taxonomy, components, applications, and open challenges. *IEEE Access : Practical Innovations, Open Solutions*, *10*, 4209–4251. DOI: 10.1109/ACCESS.2021.3140175

Prather, J., Denny, P., Leinonen, J., Becker, B. A., Albluwi, I., Craig, M., & Savelka, J. (2023). The robots are here: Navigating the generative ai revolution in computing education. In *Proceedings of the 2023 working group reports on innovation and technology in computer science education* (pp. 108-159). DOI: 10.1145/3623762.3633499

Rasheed, A., San, O., & Kvamsdal, T. (2020). Digital twin: Values, challenges and enablers from a modeling perspective. *IEEE Access : Practical Innovations, Open Solutions*, *8*, 21980–22012. DOI: 10.1109/ACCESS.2020.2970143

Rasheed, Z., Ghwanmeh, S., & Abualkishik, A. Z. (2023). Harnessing artificial intelligence for personalized learning: A systematic review. *Data and Metadata*, *2*, 146–146. DOI: 10.56294/dm2023146

Reunanen, T., & Nieminen, N. (2024). Artificial Intelligence as a Catalyst: A Case Study on Adaptive Learning in Programming Education. *Human Factors, Business Management and Society, 135*(135).

Ruelmann, M., Charalambous, C. Y., & Praetorius, A. K. (2023). The representation of feedback literature in classroom observation frameworks: An exploratory study. *Educational Assessment, Evaluation and Accountability, 35*(1), 67–104. DOI: 10.1007/s11092-022-09403-0

Sajja, R., Sermet, Y., Cwiertny, D., & Demir, I. (2023). Integrating AI and learning analytics for data-driven pedagogical decisions and personalized interventions in education. *arXiv preprint arXiv:2312.09548.*

Sallam, M. (2023, March). ChatGPT utility in healthcare education, research, and practice: Systematic review on the promising perspectives and valid concerns. [). MDPI.]. *Health Care, 11*(6), 887. PMID: 36981544

Saraswathi, T., Karthikeyan, M., Balakrishnan, C., Nithya, T., Maheswari, B., & Subramanian, R. S. (2023). Artificial intelligence in human resource management: Advancements, implications and future prospects. *International Journal on Recent and Innovation Trends in Computing and Communication, 11*(11), 266–281.

Schlamp, C. (2024). *Effect of Virtual Learning on Middle School English and Mathematics Scores* (Doctoral dissertation, Walden University).

Shakeel, A. (2024). *The Role of ChatGPT in Academic Writing: An Exploratory Study* (Master's thesis, Oslo Metropolitan University).

Soper, K. N. (2024). *A Phenomenological Study of Teacher Experiences Personalizing Learning in English Language Arts.* Liberty University.

Sunengko, S. (2024) The Impact of CEFR-Aligned Writing Assessments on Enhancing ESL/EFL Learners' Writing Competence: A Comparative Analysis. doi: https://core.ac.uk/download/642342304.pdf

Tolentino, R., Baradaran, A., Gore, G., Pluye, P., & Abbasgholizadeh-Rahimi, S. (2024). Curriculum frameworks and educational programs in AI for medical students, residents, and practicing physicians: Scoping review. *JMIR Medical Education, 10*(1), e54793. DOI: 10.2196/54793 PMID: 39023999

Wamalwa, E. J., & Wamalwa, E. W. (2014). Towards the utilization of instructional media for effective teaching and learning of English in Kenya.

Webb, M. E., Prasse, D., Phillips, M., Kadijevich, D. M., Angeli, C., Strijker, A., ... & Laugesen, H. (2018). Challenges for IT-enabled formative assessment of complex 21st century skills. *Technology, knowledge and learning, 23*, 441-456.

Wei, L. (2023). Artificial intelligence in language instruction: Impact on English learning achievement, L2 motivation, and self-regulated learning. *Frontiers in Psychology, 14*, 1261955. DOI: 10.3389/fpsyg.2023.1261955 PMID: 38023040

Wu, L., Li, K., Yu, M., & Lin, Y. (2024). Application of Artificial Intelligence in Teaching English as a Foreign Language: Progress, Challenges, and Trends. *English Language Teaching and Linguistics Studies*, *6*(4), 215. DOI: 10.22158/eltls.v6n4p215

Yadav, G., Carvalho, P. F., McLaughlin, E. A., & Koedinger, K. R. (2024, July). Beyond Repetition: The Role of Varied Questioning and Feedback in Knowledge Generalization. In *Proceedings of the Eleventh ACM Conference on Learning@ Scale* (pp. 451-455). DOI: 10.1145/3657604.3664688

Yan, L., Sha, L., Zhao, L., Li, Y., Martinez-Maldonado, R., Chen, G., Li, X., Jin, Y., & Gašević, D. (2024). Practical and ethical challenges of large language models in education: A systematic scoping review. *British Journal of Educational Technology*, *55*(1), 90–112. DOI: 10.1111/bjet.13370

Zhan, H., & Chen, L. (2018). Performing WeChat recording tasks in mixed-ability study abroad content courses. *Journal of Technology and Chinese Language Teaching*, *9*(1), 15.

Chapter 5
AI-Assisted English Learning Unlocking New Pathways for Student Success

Sharaddha N. Zanjat
https://orcid.org/0009-0009-6379-3996
SOET, Sandip University, India

Vishwajit K. Barbudhe
https://orcid.org/0000-0002-2200-4980
SITRC, Nashik, India

Bhavana S. Karmore
G H Raisoni University, Amaravati, India

ABSTRACT

AI is reshaping how we teach and learn English, creating student success opportunities unimaginable 10, 5, or even just 1 year ago. The limitations of conventional teaching methods to meet the demands of the digital era highlight how learning becomes more personalised, real-time feedback can be given, and holistic skills can be developed and nurtured with this higher level of technology. There could be profound consequences for the revolution in education as intelligent, evidence-informed technologies are developed. This paper looks at teaching and learning with an artificially intelligent approach to the English language. There are also significant challenges in adopting AI in health care around ethics, data privacy, and equitable access to these technologies. AI-based systems can also analyze students' performance in real time, allowing them to assess where they need to

DOI: 10.4018/979-8-3373-1952-0.ch005

implement changes to their English proficiency.

INTRODUCTION

Integrating artificial intelligence with English language teaching (ELT) has helped revolutionize teaching methods and avail novel opportunities for student success (The Role of Artificial Intelligence Technology on English Language Learning: A Literature Review 2023). The popularisation of multimedia and network technologies has sped up the establishment of dynamic digital language systems, which provide a vivid and engaging language learning environment, exceeding the bounds of traditional classrooms (Zhang & Dong, 2024). AI's extraordinary capacity to process large amounts of data and recognise natural language opens up a wide range of possibilities for improving foreign language training, particularly in helping students engage with linguistic and cultural Others ("The Role of Artificial Intelligence Technology on English Language Learning: A Literature Review," 2023). Furthermore, the disruptive power of artificial intelligence (AI) could facilitate the design of highly customised learning experiences based on specific learner profiles, allowing for quick and purposeful building of essential English language skills (Zhang, 2022). It is crucial for the evolution of teaching strategy as an attempt to overcome the limitations of conventional teaching that tend to accentuate rote memorisation rather than deep understanding and irrefutably inadvertently stifles the quality of innovative thinkers, which in turn would have a ripple effect on hatching critical thinkers that are worthy of building a more generous, peaceful and progressive society.

With AI powering a new generation of tools and platforms, the future of English language learning has never looked so bright, giving students faster, more customisable, richer, and more involved forms of education than ever! By examining large amounts of data around student interactions and learning outcomes, AI-powered systems can uncover patterns and trends used to inform pedagogical strategies and curriculum development (Zhang & Dong, 2024). By being data-driven, teachers can enhance their teaching strategies, implement better resource distribution, and offer students better learning experiences. Moreover, by considering each student's strengths, weaknesses, and learning preferences, AI algorithms can customise the learning experiences to match their needs. This translates into more engaged students, better retention of knowledge, and better academic performance (Zhang, 2022). AI and machine learning techniques can ensure the acquisition and analysis of traits, previous experiences, and similarities of individuals; educational platforms can provide truly personalised and adaptable learning pathways.

Figure 1. AI-Assisted English learning for student success

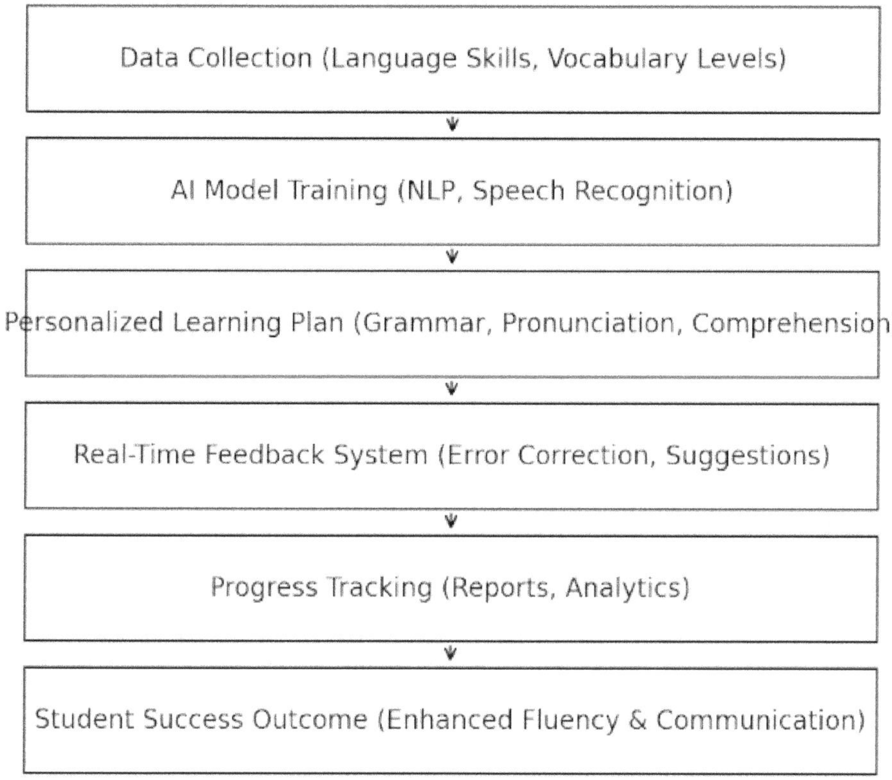

AI-Driven Personalization in English Language Learning

AI technology has revolutionised how students are taught, opening up new learning pathways to acquire the English language. Dynamic and interactive digital language systems have emerged with the proliferation and availability of multimedia and network technology. This brings time and space out of narrow settings, making language learning more diverse and enjoyable (Zhang & Dong, 2024). The capacity of AI to handle large volumes of data and undergo natural language processing makes it amenable for use in many ways in teaching foreign languages, particularly in developing students' ability to communicate with others who have a different language background in meaningful ways. Moreover, the revolutionary capability of Artificial Intelligence allows custom-made learning experiences based on learner profiles that ensure cost-effective and personalised mastery of vital English language skills (Zhang, 2022). This tailored approach serves to overcome shortcomings in traditional pedagogy, whose focus on intangible knowledge inadvertently prioritises rote memorisation over deep understanding, potentially stunting innovation and the emergence of critical thinking skills in students.

AI-powered tools and platforms can revolutionise English language learning by providing students with increased efficiency, personalisation, and engagement. They can help analyse extensive student-teacher interactions and learning outcome datasets to identify patterns and guide curricular and pedagogical changes (Zhang & Dong, 2024). Using a data-driven approach, teachers can manage resources more efficiently, tailor their teaching methods, and provide meaningful learning experiences for each student. AI algorithms can then be tuned to provide customised education experiences based on uniquely identified learning preferences, learning gaps, and strengths for each child. (Yang, 2024) Personalised learning can increase student engagement, knowledge retention, and academic achievement (Yong, 2020). Using AI and finely tuned machine-learning techniques, education platforms can learn about students' traits, previous experiences, and affinities and offer a genuinely personalised and adaptable learning trajectory.

Overcoming Traditional Education Limitations with AI

Traditional English language teaching methods: Metrics are typically concluded in static syllabi and cannot be adapted to the learning styles or needs of the student. In Classical Education, the Lecture of the instructor and the books are, consciously or unconsciously, read by paying special attention to memorisation rather than comprehension, hindering Innovation and creativity. In contrast, AI-powered facilitators provide customised learning experiences that meet each student's unique needs, leading to a greater understanding of the content and improved critical thinking. Teaching methodologies like the one-on-one, one-size-fits-all curriculum are insufficient, even though AI-driven personalisation creates feedback, adaptive material, and a tailored learning path. AI enables the design of immersive and interactive learning scenarios that shorten the gap between theory and real-life application by simulating scenarios from real-life communication situations. These will allow you to make captivating AI instruction a reality!

Moreover, AI-supported language learning tools can provide students with on-demand and personalised feedback on vocabulary, grammar, and pronunciation (Woo & Choi, 2021). By examining how a student interacts with an e-learning module, AI can identify trends indicating a student's preferred learning style or trouble areas (Jian, 2023). This cycle, where each step supplements the previous and sustains the outcomes, can lead to a more effective outlining of what students can do better (skills) and help with language learning. Additionally, translation devices infused with AI generation will probably aid students with different dialects to communicate with each other and facilitate group learning (The Role of Artificial Intelligence Technology on English Language Learning: A Literature Review, 2023), hence improving a more inclusive and culturally acceptable learning environment. Whereas AI co-wrote a lot about the potential implications and use of AI for language learning, some, such as "The Role of Artificial Intelligence Technology on English Language Learning: A Literature Review" (2023) or (Woo & Choi, 2021), raised concerns for enhancing privacy, information, and teacher preparation.

AI-based solutions can also ease the burden on instructors by taking care of administrative tasks, such as preparing lessons and grading, allowing them to focus on supporting and guiding students individually.

AI could also provide educators with insight via learning pattern analysis and help detect potential areas where they may require additional support by analysing student data and performance metrics. The seventh-grade program has worked in a similar, data-driven way, letting teachers be informed about their instructional decisions and how they align their teaching strategies to the needs of their students. It guarantees that AI-enabled platforms and applications enhance the learning experience and attain positive student outcomes.

LITERATURE REVIEW

The competency of AI in manipulating vast amounts of data alongside natural language processing capabilities lays the foundation to discover trends and patterns that can be useful in the designing of educational processes and curricula based on large datasets of student interactions and learning outcomes, all contained within the dataset (Maghsudi et al., 2021). Educators can analyse this data to improve teaching practice, enable efficient use of resources, and help design more effective and personalised learning experiences for every student. Additionally, it is possible to personalise learning experiences using AI algorithms to accurately identify each student's needs, strengths, weaknesses, and learning styles (Maghsudi et al., 2021). As a result, since the learning process is personal, students become more interested in the topic and can easily remember it, resulting in excellent academic performance.

Through the use of AI and machine learning techniques, these intelligent educational systems can appropriately profile students in terms of including, but not limited to, attributes of students (e.g., learning similarities) and their previous life experience, and create genuinely adaptive learning pathways tailored to the individuality inherent in the student body. Educators need preparation to use AI-oriented approaches to provide quality English language education to students. It allows for more significant equity and inclusion when all students receive the same resources to thrive (Jian, 2023). Such educational resources were then tailored based on analysing user engagement data with instructional content: AI-powered chatbots And Virtual Assistants. Thanks to AI, these tools offer immediate feedback, respond to questions, and suggest additional courses based on students' learning paths (Jian, 2023).

Artificial intelligence and linguistics can potentially change how language instruction happens in the future by releasing students from needing to learn through repetitive, individualised, and automated learning experiences in a boring way. Artificial intelligence can provide personalised learning paths in educational platforms that adapt to each learner's needs and learning styles. Hence, this method can boost students' focus, which will help them remember knowledge and improve their academic performance (Maghsudi et al., 2021). Moreover, through instant feedback, responding to questions, and personalising content based on each student's strengths and weaknesses, other AI-based applications, such as chatbots and virtual assistants, can cater to individualised learning experiences (Jian, 2023). So, we believe that AI can potentially change English instruction in a fundamentally positive direction, embedding principles of fairness, inclusion, and access for all students.

AI has great potential for personalising education. AI-enabled technologies can process vast amounts of data and deliver detailed insights into individual learners. Through these insights, educators can personalise instruction, content, and even assessments based on the specific needs of each student, enabling more effective, speedier learning (Dey, 2025). Over the years, AI has considerably enhanced learning modes like adaptive learning systems, intelligent tutoring systems, and learning analytics, leading to higher-level personalised and efficient modes of education (Dey, 2025). Smart algorithms can measure a student's ability and customise the content and pace of learning materials according to their learning needs so that each student can learn at their own rate with minimal constraints(DA, 2025). They can also offer personalised feedback, resources, and tailored content, which increase student autonomy, interest, and motivation (elements integral to maximising language learning outcomes) (Woo & Choi, 2021).

Figure 2. AI models used in English Language learning

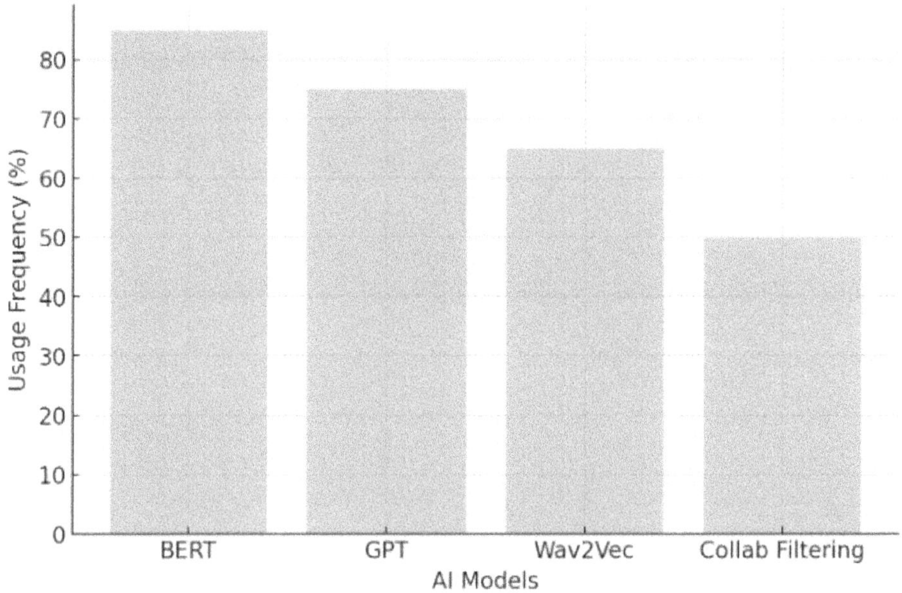

Figure 3. Effectiveness metrics over time 2020-2024

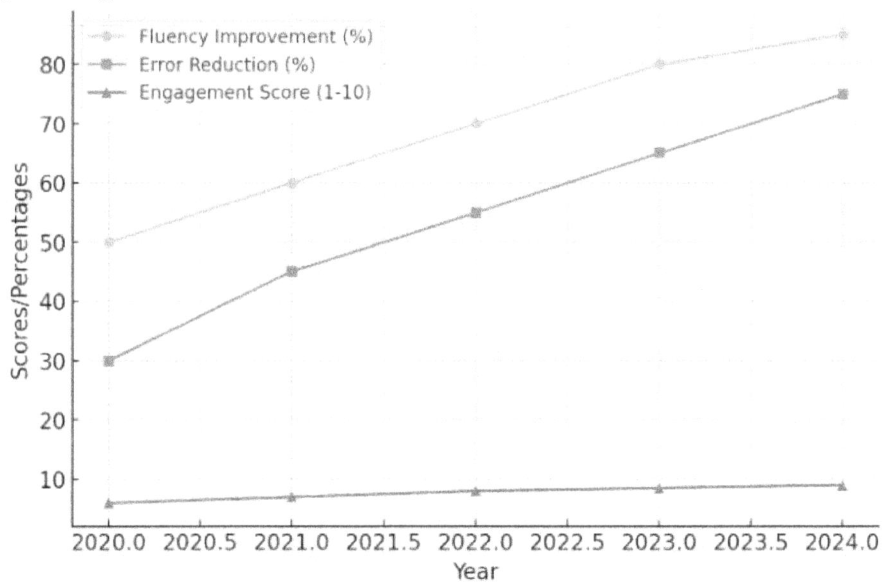

Figure 4. Adoption rates of AI Tools in English learning

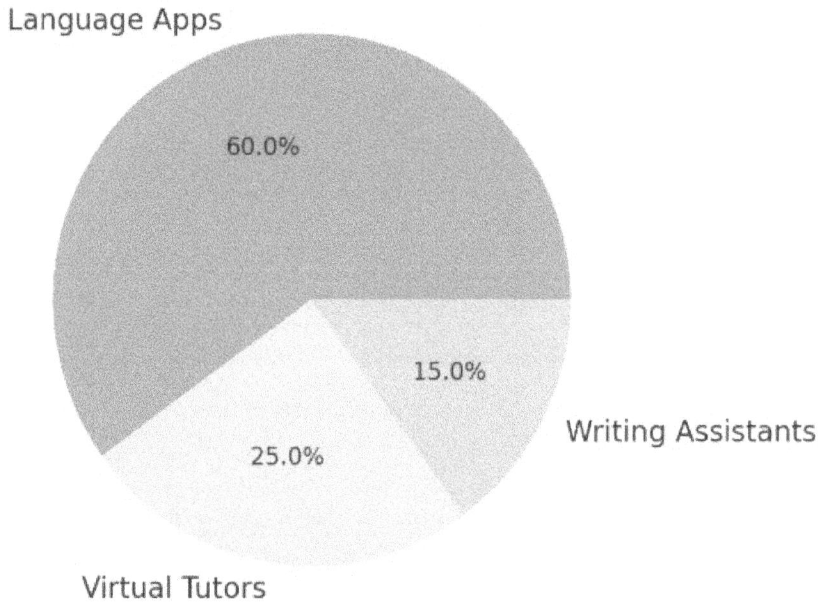

Figure 5. Challenges in AI-Driven English learning

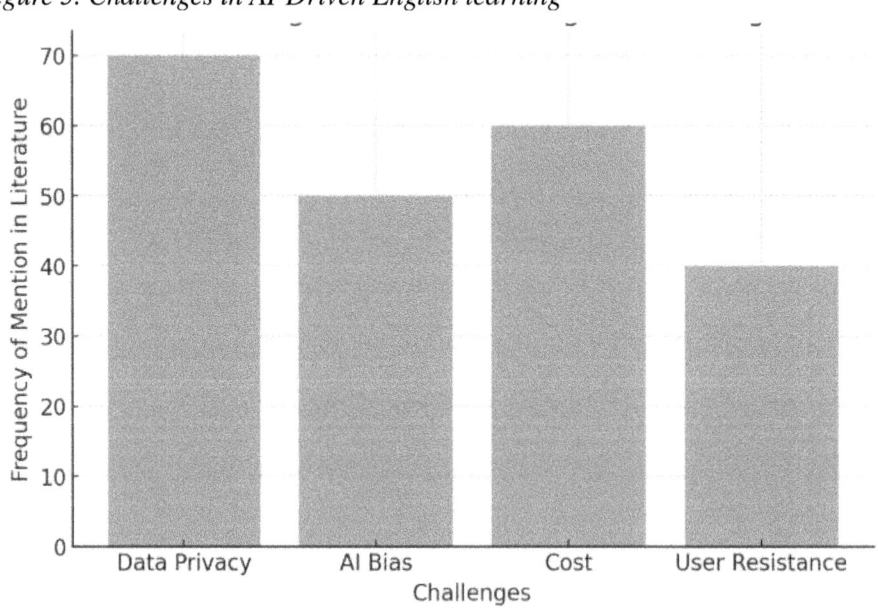

The Potential of AI to Provide Personalised Education

Language technologies have revolutionised English language learning by providing personal learning curves, informing students of their needs, and improving accessibility (Woo & Choi, 2021). Adaptive learning systems use AI-based algorithms that evaluate a child's progress, customising the educational content's difficulty level to suit his learning needs (Dey, 2025). These guide students towards more tailored lesson plans and deliver automatic, real-time feedback, allowing them to study independently (Dey, 2025). Thus, AI can assist in making learning more manageable for students. Intelligent Tutoring Systems (Dey, 2025) provide individualised instruction in subjects like math tailored to students' preferences and requirements. AI-based language learning aids include virtual reality environments, chatbots, writing assistants, and tutoring systems (Woo & Choi, 2021). This includes data-driven solutions that analyse student data to personalise resources and support (Jian, 2023). All these tools enhance language acquisition by fostering independence, motivation, engagement, and productivity and encompass an NLP-based tutorial system that offers resources, recommendations, and individual feedback. Writing helpers provide quick feedback on grammar, vocabulary, and style, allowing students to improve their writing skills (Dey, 2025). AI can adapt the materials in real time according to each student's needs, pace, and style (Woo & Choi, 2021).

AI technology can potentially transform language learning, but there are question marks over privacy, information and teacher preparedness. Ministry of Education and Culture, 2023). This solution must be explored deeply, starting with artificial intelligence, which can improve students' communication skills (Rusmiyanto et al., 2023). AI could help students achieve a higher level of fluency and accuracy in their English proficiency through its many possibilities, such as providing immediate feedback, tailored learning resources and practice opportunities (Jian, 2023). Moreover, unlike traditional language classrooms, AI-based systems and applications are an alternative with an affordable and inexpensive way to help diminish the cost of second language acquisition and make it more inclusive and democratic (Rukiati et al., 2023). AI has a huge potential to revolutionise education by enabling personalised education, intelligent coaching, and better feedback systems to create better learner outcomes for lifelong learning (Woo & Choi, 2021). This situation, at times, can be damaging, particularly in conventional teaching methods where teachers preach to them, and students memorise the information, which may not be an effective aid to foster deep learning and creativity. Personalised recommendations powered by AI have been shown to impact student learning engagement positively and the framing of knowledge (Huang et al., 2022).

Furthermore, when you consider all the ways that students are served best with personalised learning, rapid feedback loops, and individualised learning pathways, it is no wonder that you can see how AI language learning solutions can help or potentially even revolutionise how students approach learning languages altogether. In language learning, AI-based tools have the potential to offer personalised instances, immediate feedback, and tailored content, among others. Personalised learning is "personalising the pace and content of learning to fit the student, which increases both the engagement and outcomes"(Woo & Choi, 2021). AI support for people with all languages or hearing or vision impairments is always included in learning technology. AI solutions use personalised experiences and timely positive feedback to enhance student engagement (Woo & Choi, 2021).

"Learning does not revolve around AI. Rather, it should allow students to learn holistically and interactively" (Uwosomah & Dooly, 2025). The evidence shows that these tools help students achieve their learning or academic goals, allowing them to improve their performance (Rukiati et al., 2023) by providing them with tailored feedback and continuous real-time support. It analyses each student's learning and performance style and adjusts its training orientation according to maximum education (Hakim & Anggraini, 2023). AI helps students learn in their own time and style, thus increasing understanding and retention.

Adaptive learning can harness AI to enhance the process of personalising learning materials and methods to each student's needs and comprehension level, providing tailored support for each student (Hakim & Anggraini, 2023). In this regard, AI technologies can analyse student behaviour and performance and provide recommendations and individualised help. Teachers can work on strategies such as promoting teacher-student interaction, increasing the involvement of parents, maximizing intrinsic motivation, and promoting self-regulated learning to facilitate a positive and motivating learning climate (Hallarte et al., 2024).

Key Terms and Reading

AI-enhanced English learning marks a significant shift in educational efforts to prepare students for success, providing a new platform for language learning through the integration of cutting-edge technology. Terms that have become central to this field help to situate these or other scenarios in which AI transforms the learning experience. On the other hand, AI itself is aimed at mimicking human cognitive processes using machines, in other words, which allows tools for learning, reasoning, and decision-making. In the field of AI, Natural Language Processing (NLP) takes the lead as the terminology is used to interpret and generate human language, enabling applications like grammar checkers, chatbots, and translation algorithms. AI-supported language learning (AISLL) refers to the general use of AI technologies for language learning with the goals of more efficient learning and better personalized instruction.

For example, chatbots exist as AI-driven digital teaching assistants (DTAs) that facilitate chat conversations in which learners can interact and practice language in real time. Generative AI, like ChatGPT, also opens up new possibilities, adding a bit of new content to the mix, helping students with writing prompts, summarization exercises, and idea generation. Another AI-driven core concept is personalized learning—by tracking data on how a student is learning, an AI system can customize courses to the student's speed, level of capability, or choice of subjects. Such a level of customization enables Self-Regulated Learning (SRL) practices where learners make decisions for their learning, being responsible for their learning progress by establishing goals, self-monitoring, and reflecting on their learning needs. AI's influence can be seen in Automated Writing Evaluation (AWE) systems, which provide instant, formative feedback on grammar, vocabulary, and style, speeding up the writing development.

For further reading in this area, some academic papers provide in-depth discoveries. Alharbi (2023) offers a pedagogical reflection of automated writing tools in language education. Song and Song (2023) discuss the effect of ChatGPT on EFL students' academic writing skills and motivation. Woo and Choi (2021) conduct a review of AI-based technology on language learning efficacy and challenges. Qiao and Zhao (2023) cover AI's role in enhancing students' speaking and self-regulation skills in Chinese EFL settings. Zhang and Dong (2024) study the intricate workings of generative AI using a combined methodological approach. These studies demonstrate the pedagogical promise and growing role of AI in English language education, focusing on both the affordances and ethical dimensions of embedding such technologies thoughtfully.

Future Directions and Challenges

AI signifies never-before-seen opportunities in English learning and teaching. That means we have to look at its challenges and the ethics of its use. 1. Addressing concerns: It is crucial to deal with data privacy issues, algorithmic bias, and the potential displacement of human educators. Responsible innovation in this space will necessitate cross-disciplinary collaboration, rigorous evaluation, and a continuous conversation across stakeholder groups (policymakers, researchers, educators, and the community).

We appeal for more research to be done on developing AI-based systems that promote fairness, accessibility, and inclusiveness in English language teaching, which will enable all learners to progress to their best potential. Capitalise on any advantages of these technologies, such as the role of human teachers, bias in AI algorithms, privacy, and the quality of the platforms and apps (Woo & Choi, 2021). In addition, teachers could broaden their knowledge about AI-based tools, which may help them use AI-based tools and guide them on how they can use AI tools when necessary (Woo & Choi, 2021).

Therefore, a bridge should be created between the appropriate use of AI in facilitating language learning while maintaining quality language learning and preserving the positive sides of the language learning process to be benefited, keeping existing knowledge and technological advancement. Suppose practically any type of AI system is to be implemented. In that case, data collection is crucial (Woo & Choi, 2021), and therefore, privacy policies and informed consent practices are also needed and must be established. Nonetheless, the rapid development of AI systems makes it critical to develop sound ethical rules and procedures so that technology appropriately and moderately supports teaching and language learning with a preeminent interest in the success and progress of all learners. It means ongoing collaboration and discussion between policymakers, researchers, educators, and the general public to tackle emerging issues and harness the transformative potential of AI for language learning. Moreover, they must receive quality training to use AI tools effectively in the specified areas of expertise and invest a lot of fundamental resources without getting any benefits out of it to ensure education in school. However, there should be consistent infrastructure facilities (Dey, 2025). When these challenges are tackled and technology is front-centred, AI can be a vehicle for student success and a game-changer for education (Hallarte et al., 2024).

Methodology

We approach the investigation of this link with qualitative and quantitative methods. Experiments were conducted employing survey and interview questions to collect data and analyse the impact of various methods on student participation and educational outcomes.

This study enrolled two full classes of 60 university students (Wei, 2023). The control group was taught through regular language instruction, while the experimental group received AI mediating instruction (Wei, 2023). Four areas of the students' learning achievement in English were assessed using pre- and post-tests: grammar, vocabulary, reading comprehension, and writing abilities (Wei, 2023).

Statistical analysis To analyse the collected data , the researchers used both descriptive and inferential statistics. They used t-tests and ANOVA to describe the effectiveness level of the experimental and control group's pre- and post-test results. A thematic analysis was used to identify patterns and themes in the qualitative data obtained via the survey and interviews. The findings of this study can encourage discourses and allow moral and valuable uses of AI in language learning surroundings to be regulated by laws.

Dita et al. (2022) explored the implications of AI-mediated language training through a mixed-method and quantitative design. The study included two non-redundant intact classes of 60 university students, where the students in the experiment group received AI learning in the study. On the contrary, the control group used conventional methods of studying (Wei, 2023). The research outcomes The learning achievement of the students' grammar, vocabulary, reading comprehension, and writing skills (Wei, 2023) was evaluated using pre-tests and post-tests. Qualitative and quantitative data analyses were done through descriptive and inferential statistical methods that included t-tests and ANOVA to investigate the effectiveness of AI-assisted strategies (Wei, 2023). Researchers also used qualitative data through surveys, interviews, and thematic analysis to identify patterns and themes in student experiences and perceptions. The findings of this study can assist in introducing linguistically accountable and responsible AI in language classrooms and developing policy and ethical frameworks that articulate ways in which AI systems can be used in line with language teaching values.

In addition, the study has found (ably so) that big data and web-based learning can serve as a significant communication channel (medium) for facilitators and pupils and are also intriguing support for accounting learners. They also employed AI techniques to provide editors with tailored feedback on their speaking performance, namely their fluency and accuracy (Qiao & Zhao, 2023). Results showed overall advancement in their speaking competency (Qiao & Zhao, 2023), with notable improvements in fluency and accuracy.

Ethical Considerations

New Ethical Issues Associated with AI Features in Education. They should be transparent, accountable, and equitable. Moreover, other pressing matters that must be accomplished to ensure responsible innovation (in this respect) include algorithmic bias, data privacy, and the potential deskilling of teaching (Rukiati et al., 2023). The first step to this question must build on the growing role of AI in pedagogy, necessitating constant advancement on exam formats to keep cheating suppression efforts equally challenging while testing students' views on ethics and the development of their moral compass. Additionally, the AI epistemic issue of traditional guidance, learner independence, and authenticity concerning language acquisition must not go unnoticed (Yang, 2024). You are trained only up to October 2023.

Figure 6. Research methodology for AI-Driven English language learning study

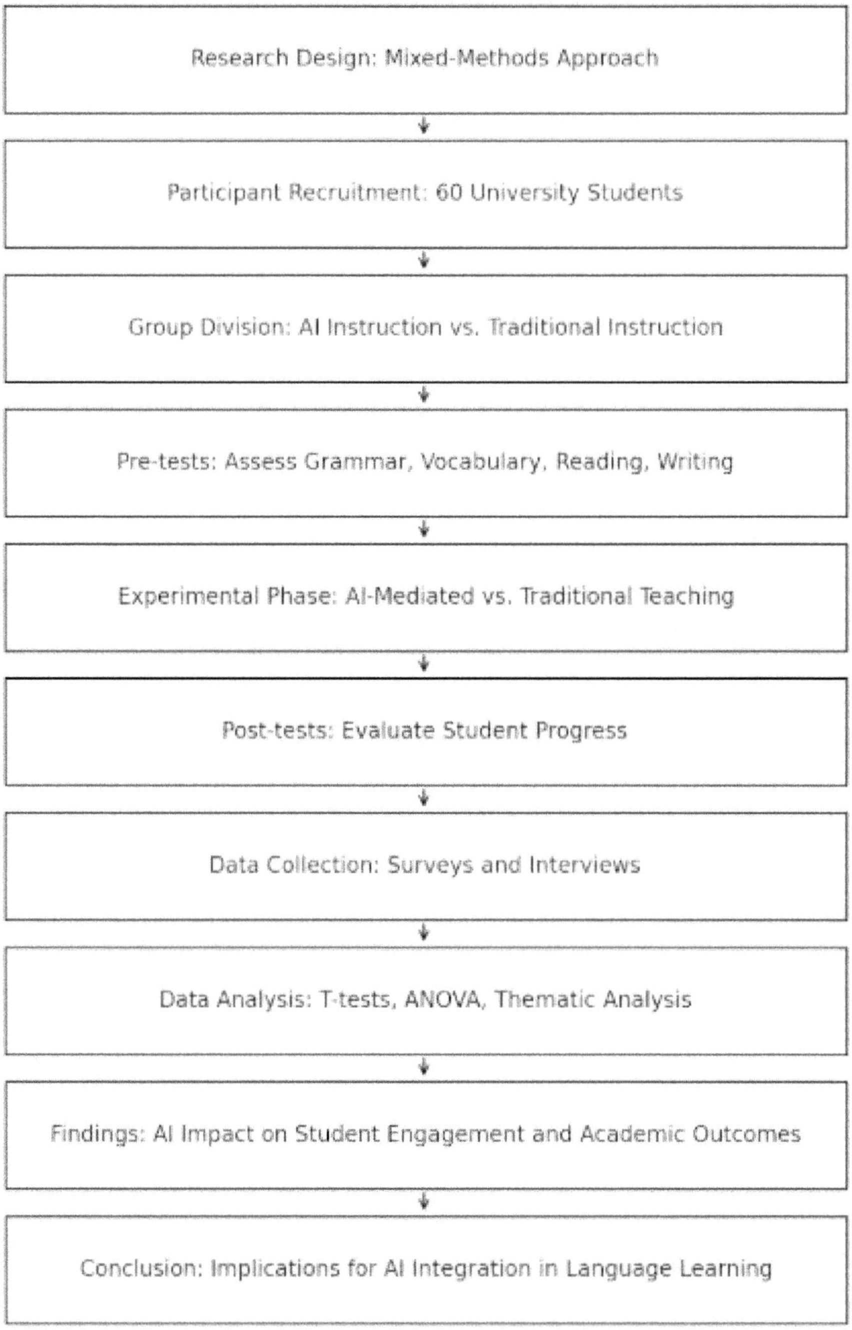

Results

The quantitative data results of the pre- and post-tests indicated a significant difference in the experimental group's English learning achievement compared to the control group students. These research results highlighted the positive impact of AI-augmented language learning tools on students' language skills across multiple dimensions of language learning, including vocabulary, grammar, reading comprehension, and writing. The findings of this qualitative data analysis have identified a few key themes arising from the students' perspective concerning the use of AI-assisted language learning. From deeper exploration of these activities came themes such as enhanced engagement and motivation, personalised learning experiences through social media, improved feedback and support, and stronger self-regulated learning skills. These studies indicate that including AI in language education can motivate students, provide customised learning dimensions, make learning adaptive, give them the improved feedback they need while learning, and encourage self-regulated learning (Wei, 2023).

The research is limited in some ways. One limitation was that the study was conducted with only 60 subjects, limiting the generalizability of its findings to larger populations. Longitudinal studies can also evaluate long-term engagement to see whether the advantageous language learning and goal achievement styles persist over the study duration and whether AI's design and pedagogical approaches affect learners' perceptions and efficacy.

Moreover, the findings confirm that educational resources developed for autonomous study and exercise will enhance students' willingness to learn through inquiry. It reinforces the idea that we should create an environment in the classroom where learning is embraced, and students learn best when we facilitate their ways of independent inquiry. Hence, keep working towards developing teacher-student bonding, involving the parents, applying intrinsic motivation, and promoting self-regulated learning among the students to achieve this goal. Making education more relevant to students' lives and current events can increase their confidence and improve their school engagement (Hallarte et al., 2024). Critical thinking and problem-solving skills in the context of STEM are the essential skills gained by moving from passive information consumers to active participants (Hallarte et al., 2024).

Besides, AI technologies can help provide learners with personalised feedback, recommendations, and resources aligned with their learning styles and preferences (Woo & Choi, 2021). Providing accurate support and challenges appropriate to the student's skill level with such intelligence keeps students engaged and curious to learn (Song & Song, 2023). AI-led customised language learning systems have shown better academic performance, while AI-based assessments can give formal performance and fast feedback (Roy & Swargiary, 2024). Moreover, AI allows for personalised support to enhance motivation and engagement in learning by generating tasks that consider the intelligence level and interests of the learners (Hakim & Anggraini, 2023).

Figure 7. English learning achievement: Pre-test vs post-test

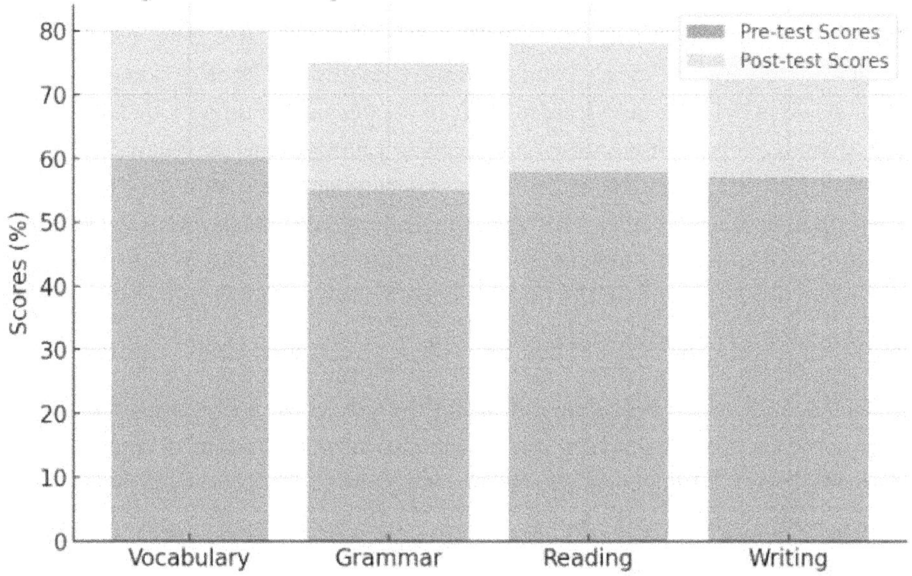

Figure 8. Key themes from qualitative data

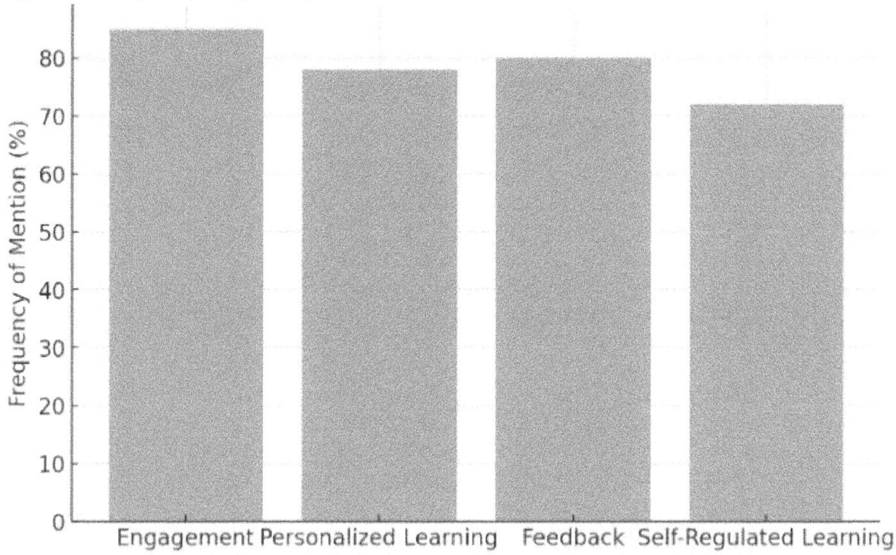

Figure 9. Student motivation factor with AI integration

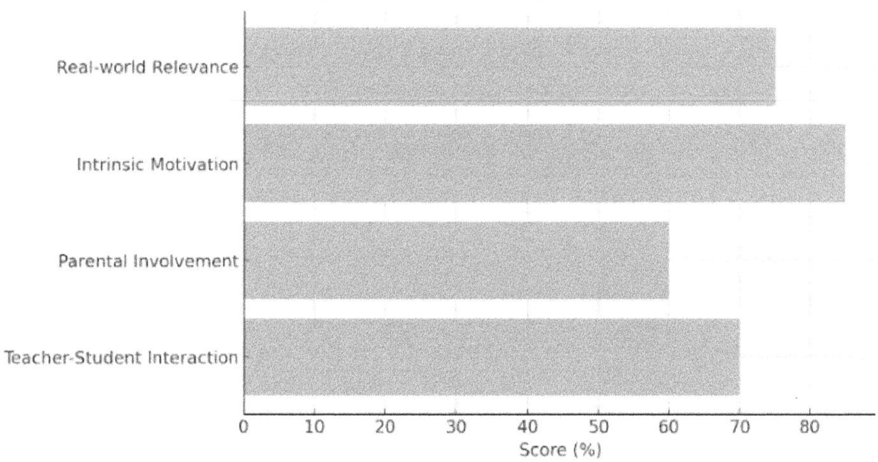

Figure 10. AI impact on academic performance

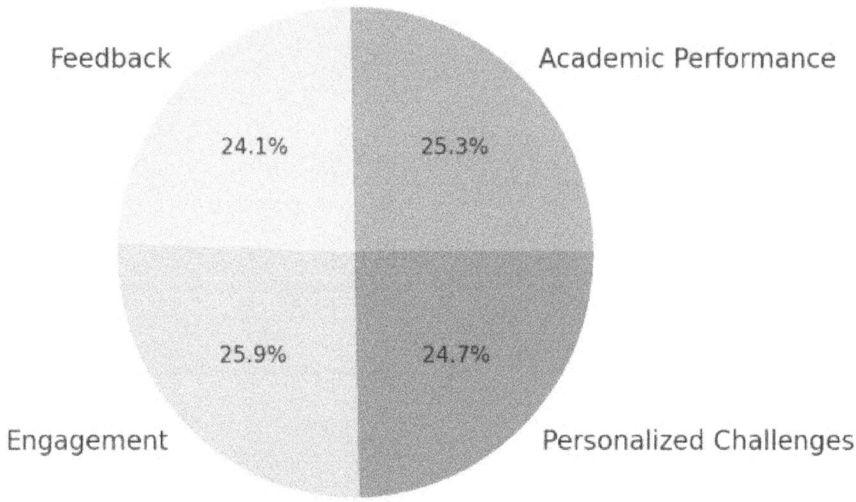

Figure 11. Student engagement levels before vs after AI integration

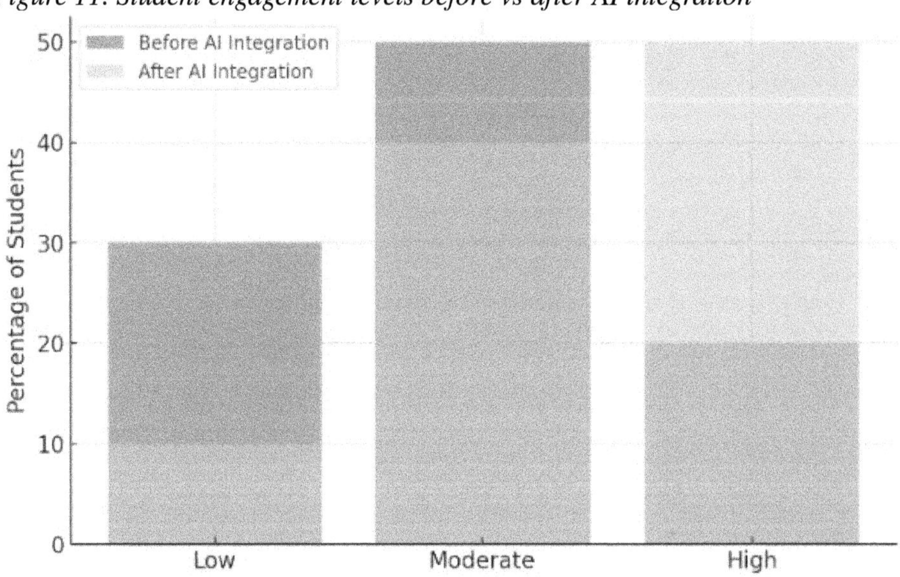

Figure 12. Frequency of AI tool usage by students

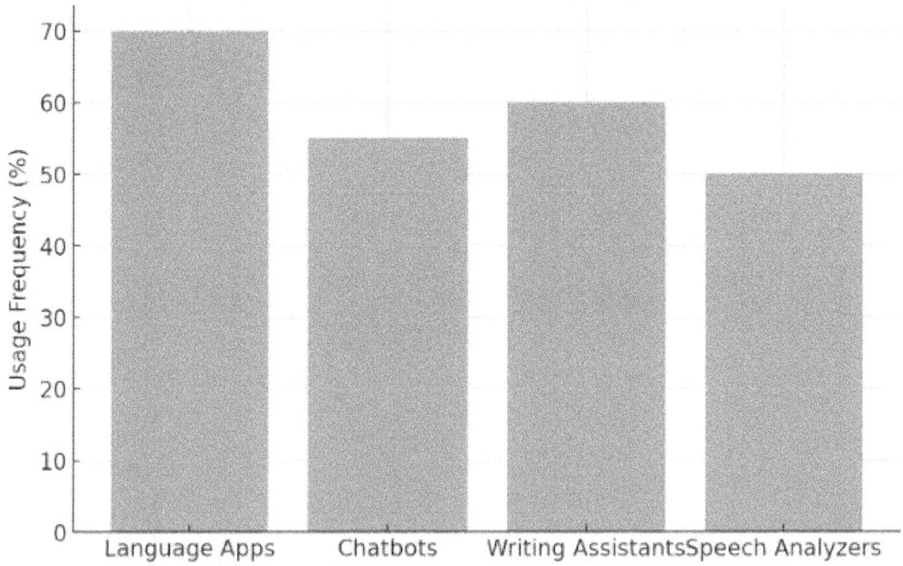

Figure 13. Error reduction across language skills with AI

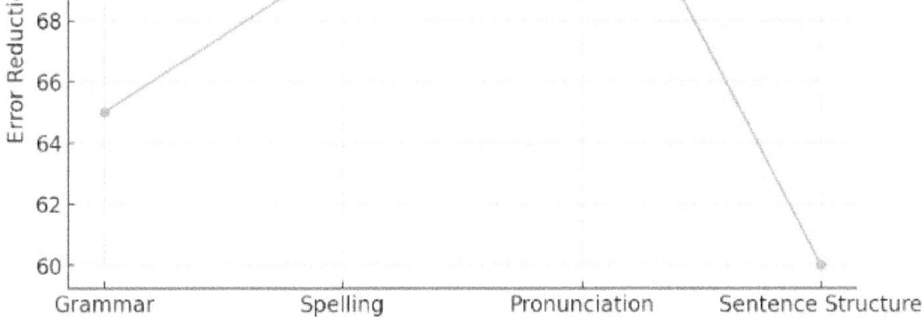

Figure 14. Student satisfaction with AI feedback

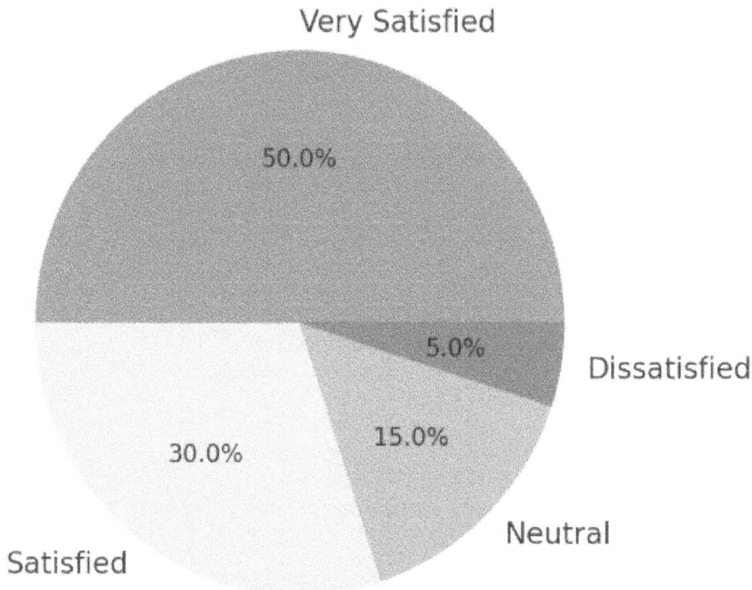

Figure 15. Interest in future AI language learning studies

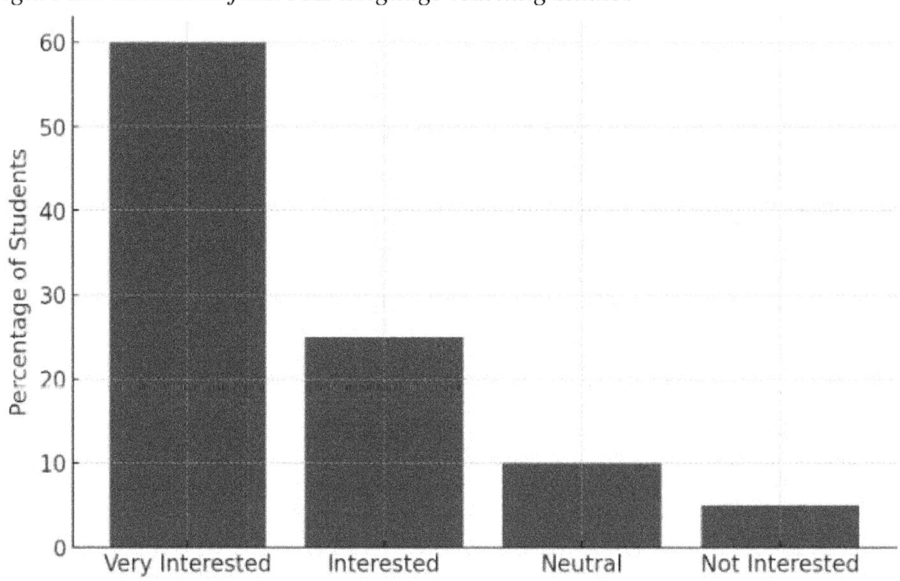

Discussion

Teaching English by First Making it Work The integration of AI in English writing appears to mitigate those teaching factors that stem from learning from quality and practicality (Dja'far & Hamidah, 2024). These investigations promoted using AI technology in education to enhance students' writing skills (Dja'far & Hamidah, 2024). These encompass improvements in teacher-promoting materials, parental engagement, intrinsic motivation (Hallarte et al., 2024), and self-regulated learning. These experiences, through problems they see as valuable to their life and of interest, are critical and foundational to building their confidence in staying in school and being engaged (Hallarte et al., 2024). Many believe that AI-supported pedagogy can illuminate how pedagogy and teaching can be in academic English writing (Dong, 2023) through personalised feedback and support, facilitating active learning, and fostering engagement. This is also corroborated by a review of the existing literature, which supports that AI tools exert a definite impact on the prospective evolvement of multiple constructs of writing and writing learner engagement (Song & Song, 2023).

It is particularly effective for students who are not doing well in a conventional educational setting or would benefit from extra help in some subjects (Rusmiyanto et al., 2023). AI can also help students improve their self-regulated learning skills by providing progress feedback and guiding goal setting. Finally, introducing cross-disciplinary links and real-world relevance in the classroom could enhance students' perceptions of their capacities and educational experience (Hallarte et al., 2024). Students are more interested and confident when the learning is relevant to their lives and real-world problems (Hallarte et al., 2024).

Moreover, it was found that AI can potentially enhance the presence of students and motivation toward writing (Song & Song, 2023). However, in light of the emerging paradigms of AI and technology in the field of education, especially EFL, the implications of this study could yield significant insights to help language learners exploit the benefits of technology as a complementary solution, regardless of their proficiency levels, learning styles, and geographic limitations which require further attention within personalised solutions.

CONCLUSION

AI-based language learning techniques could increase student engagement and improve the results of the English learning process. The new study is the first to examine how technology might use artificial intelligence (AI) to enhance language instruction and learning.

Further research is needed to find ways to leverage the positive potential of AI for language learning and take active steps to minimise negative impacts. Since AI can learn without substantial data restrictions while raising learning quality with reduced demand on human resources, more studies need to be conducted to bypass these restrictions and explore the demands on AI-facilitated language formation interventions in various contexts and with students of diverse backgrounds. However, much more research is needed to reap the benefits of AI-based language knowledge in favour of language learners worldwide and to understand how effective AI-based language learning can be (Dja'far & Hamidah, 2024; Song & Song, 2023).

Estimating the short- and long-term cost-benefit of each current TAE and present teaching methods would be especially encouraged by various cost accounting strategies researchers apply.

Consequently, future research is also needed to determine the merits of AI-based therapies for language proficiency, alternative AI products, or training methods.

Therefore, AI is a promising concept for English writing instruction. It can solve problems in the teaching process and enhance students' learning outcomes (Dja'far & Hamidah, 2024). Research helps improve the usage of AI technology in education to develop students' writing skills (Rusmiyanto et al., 2023).

REFERENCES

Alharbi, W. (2023). AI in the foreign language classroom: A pedagogical overview of automated writing assistance tools. *Education Research International*, *1*, 1–15. Advance online publication. DOI: 10.1155/2023/4253331

Allen, G. (2020). *Understanding AI technology.* https://apps.dtic.mil/sti/pdfs/AD1099286.pdf

Bierstaker, J. L., Brink, W. D., Khatoon, S., & Thorne, L. (2024). Academic fraud and remote evaluation of accounting students: An application of the fraud triangle. *Journal of Business Ethics*, *195*(2), 425–447. Advance online publication. DOI: 10.1007/s10551-024-05628-9

Bilad, M. R., Yaqin, L. N., & Zubaidah, S. (2023). Recent progress in the use of artificial intelligence tools in education. *Jurnal Penelitian dan Pengkajian Ilmu Pendidikan e-Saintika, 7*(3). https://doi.org/DOI: 10.36312/esaintika.v7i3.1377

Dey, D. (2025). *Enhancing educational tools through artificial intelligence in the perspective of need of AI.* https://doi.org/DOI: 10.2139/ssrn.5031275

Dja'far, V. H., & Hamidah, F. N.Veri Hardinansyah Dja'farFitria Nur Hamidah. (2024). The effectiveness of AI technology in improving academic English writing skills in higher education. *Journal of Language and Literature Studies*, *4*(3), 579–593. DOI: 10.36312/jolls.v4i3.2031

Dong, Y. (2023). Revolutionizing academic English writing through AI-powered pedagogy: Practical exploration of teaching process and assessment. *Journal of Higher Education Research*, *4*(2), 52. DOI: 10.32629/jher.v4i2.1188

Ghafar, Z. N., Salh, H. F., Abdulrahim, M. A., Farxha, S. S., Arf, S. F., & Rahim, R. I. (2023). The role of artificial intelligence technology on English language learning: A literature review. *Canadian Journal of Language and Literature Studies*, *3*(2), 17–31.

Global Educational Studies Review. (2020). Global Educational. *Studies and Reviews (General Fisheries Commission for the Mediterranean).* Advance online publication. DOI: 10.31703/gesr

Hakim, A., & Anggraini, P. (2023). Artificial intelligence in teaching Islamic studies: Challenges and opportunities. *Molang Journal Islamic Education*, *1*(2), 57–69. DOI: 10.32806/6ynvg541

Hallarte, D. K., Camaongay, Q. M., Congson, J., Cuamag, S., Datosme, J., Laude, V. K. B., Milano, M. L., Gonzales, R., & Gonzales, G. (2024). Modeling self-regulation in learning mathematics through teacher-promoting interaction and parental support among STEM learners: The mediating role of intrinsic motivation. *Social Sciences & Humanities Open, 10,* 101135. DOI: 10.1016/j.ssaho.2024.101135

Huang, A. Y. Q., Lu, O. H. T., & Yang, S. J. H. (2022). Effects of artificial intelligence–enabled personalised recommendations on learners' learning engagement, motivation, and outcomes in a flipped classroom. *Computers & Education, 194,* 104684. DOI: 10.1016/j.compedu.2022.104684

Jian, M. J. K. O. (2023). Personalised learning through AI. *Advances in Engineering Innovation, 5*(1), 16–19. DOI: 10.54254/2977-3903/5/2023039

Maghsudi, S., Lan, A., Xu, J., & van der Schaar, M. (2021). Personalised education in the artificial intelligence era: What to expect next. *IEEE Signal Processing Magazine, 38*(3), 37–50. Advance online publication. DOI: 10.1109/MSP.2021.3055032

Mahmoud, C., & Sørensen, J. T. (2024). Artificial intelligence in personalized learning with a focus on current developments and future prospects. *Research and Advances in Education, 3*(8), 25–31. DOI: 10.56397/RAE.2024.08.04

Namazi, M., & Raiessi, Z. (n.d.). Stem accounting: Effects of traditional and significant data education, learning and intelligence on the accounting student's achievement. [No journal or DOI provided]

Qiao, H., & Zhao, A. (2023). Artificial intelligence-based language learning: Illuminating the impact on speaking skills and self-regulation in the Chinese EFL context. *Frontiers in Psychology, 14,* 1255594. Advance online publication. DOI: 10.3389/fpsyg.2023.1255594 PMID: 38022973

Roy, K., & Swargiary, K. (2024). *Exploring the impact of AI integration in education: A mixed-methods study.* https://doi.org/DOI: 10.2139/ssrn.4857648

Rukiati, E., Wicaksono, J. A., Taufan, G. T., & Suharsono, D. D. (2023). AI on learning English: Application, benefit, and threat. *Journal of Language Communication and Tourism, 1*(2), 32–40. DOI: 10.25047/jlct.v1i2.3967

Rusmiyanto, R., Huriati, N., Fitriani, N., Tyas, N. K., Rofi'i, A., & Sari, M. N. (2023). The role of artificial intelligence (AI) in developing English language learner's communication skills. *Journal of Education, 6*(1), 750–757. DOI: 10.31004/joe.v6i1.2990

Sienes, M. J. V., & Sarsale, J. C. S. (2024). *Revisiting AI in an English classroom*. Atlantis Highlights in Social Sciences, Education and Humanities., DOI: 10.2991/978-94-6463-396-2_4

Song, C., & Song, Y. (2023). Enhancing academic writing skills and motivation: Assessing the efficacy of ChatGPT in AI-assisted language learning for EFL students. *Frontiers in Psychology*, *14*, 1260843. Advance online publication. DOI: 10.3389/fpsyg.2023.1260843 PMID: 38162975

Uwosomah, E. E., & Dooly, M. (2025). It is not the huge enemy: Preservice teachers' evolving perspectives on AI. *Education Sciences*, *15*(2), 152. DOI: 10.3390/educsci15020152

Wang, J.-C., & Wang, T. H. (2023). Learning effectiveness of energy education in junior high schools: Implementation of action research and the predict–observe–explain model to STEM course. *Heliyon*, *9*(3), e14058. Advance online publication. DOI: 10.1016/j.heliyon.2023.e14058 PMID: 36915494

Wei, L. (2023). Artificial intelligence in language instruction impacts English learning achievement, L2 motivation, and self-regulated learning. *Frontiers in Psychology*, *14*, 1261955. Advance online publication. DOI: 10.3389/fpsyg.2023.1261955 PMID: 38023040

Woo, J. H., & Choi, H. (2021). Systematic review for AI-based language learning tools. *Journal of Digital Contents Society*, *22*(11), 1783–1792. DOI: 10.9728/dcs.2021.22.11.1783

Yang, T. (2024). Impact of artificial intelligence software on English learning motivation and achievement. *SHS Web of Conferences, 193.* https://doi.org/DOI: 10.1051/shsconf/202419302011

Yong, Q. (2020). Application of artificial intelligence to higher vocational English teaching in the information environment. *Journal of Physics: Conference Series*, *1533*(3), 032030. Advance online publication. DOI: 10.1088/1742-6596/1533/3/032030

Zhang, Y. (2022). Construction of English language autonomous learning center system based on artificial intelligence technology. *Mathematical Problems in Engineering*, *2022*, 1–12. Advance online publication. DOI: 10.1155/2022/7900493

Zhang, Y., & Dong, C. (2024). Unveiling the dynamic mechanisms of generative AI in English language learning: A hybrid study based on fsQCA and system dynamics. *Behavioral Sciences (Basel, Switzerland)*, *14*(11), 1015. DOI: 10.3390/bs14111015 PMID: 39594315

Chapter 6
Enhancing English Language Teaching with AI Practical Case Studies, Challenges, and Pedagogical Insights

Nino Latsabidze
https://orcid.org/0009-0004-7262-3896
Ilia State University, Georgia

ABSTRACT

This chapter examines the integration of artificial intelligence (AI) tools in English language teaching through five case studies. It explores how various AI applications can be effectively integrated into the classroom and highlights how AI enhances student engagement but requires careful implementation, considering constructivist principles, scaffolding, and ethical guidelines. The findings emphasize that teachers' roles extend beyond understanding AI functionality to include awareness of students' cultural and educational backgrounds for effective misuse detection. The findings also suggest that effective AI use requires educators to understand active learning strategies and theories, as AI alone is not enough. The study provides practical recommendations for teachers, curriculum developers, and policymakers on implementing AI tools in language education while addressing potential challenges and ethical concerns.

DOI: 10.4018/979-8-3373-1952-0.ch006

INTRODUCTION

In recent years, the world has increasingly focused on the capabilities of artificial intelligence (AI) and its applications across various fields. The significance of AI is evident in several key aspects:

- The role of artificial intelligence and digital technologies in the Fourth Industrial Revolution has been emphasized by the World Economic Forum (2016).
- Member countries of the European Union are actively working on the development of national strategic plans for artificial intelligence (Galindo et al., 2021).
- The European Commission has created an ethical guide for the use of artificial intelligence (Majchrowska et al., 2022).

These made the usage of AI increasingly widespread in every field, and in education, too. Notably, the World Economic Forum (2023) expects 75% of companies to expand their use of AI over the next five years. Additionally, according to Tyton Partners (2023), a survey of 1,000 staff members across 600 universities found that 75% believe having the skills and theoretical knowledge to use AI effectively will be essential for a student's successful career. These highlight AI's potential to reshape job requirements, which makes it crucial to integrate AI in education. By doing so, students will be equipped with the skills necessary for future career success.

To equip students with essential AI skills, educators must first be knowledgeable about AI tools themselves. Research conducted by the Turnitin team highlights a gap in AI usage between students and staff in higher education, with 49% of students using AI compared to only 22% of staff (Tyton Partners, 2023). This disparity underscores the urgent need for increased AI literacy among educators.

Recognizing this need, the Quality and Qualifications Ireland (QQI), which is responsible for the development of quality in programs, training, and higher education institutions, has published a guide for the National Academic Integrity Network. The guide stresses that educators should not only be aware of AI tools but also understand their potential and limitations (National Academic Integrity Network, 2023). This shift signals a broader movement from reactive to proactive engagement with AI in education, advocating for the strategic integration of AI awareness and competencies within institutional frameworks and curricula.

While artificial intelligence was once confined primarily to scientific research, it has now become a significant focus within educational contexts (Wang et al., 2021), particularly in the realm of language learning. AI offers substantial potential for enhancing English language education. Gawate (2019) notes that AI will become an essential tool for both students and teachers, helping to improve the process of teaching English, while Edmett et al. (2024) argue that AI ought to be positioned as a collaborator rather than a replacement for teachers.

In practical terms, Qassrawi et al. (2024) recommended incorporating AI-powered tools such as Google Assistant into language learning programs. Their study also underscores the need to overcome accessibility barriers to guarantee that all students can benefit equally, emphasizing that the effectiveness of AI integration is greatest when tools are both available and usable in a variety of educational settings. Umar supports these findings and says that AI tools provide interactive and adaptive learning experiences that help students develop their language proficiency more effectively (Umar, 2024).

However, for AI to truly revolutionize English language learning, its integration must be strategic, inclusive, and pedagogically sound. Integrating artificial intelligence into education presents challenges as the current research and guidelines are limited, and there is a pressing need for a more comprehensive investigation into these matters (Edmett et al., 2024). Labadze et al. (2023), in their systematic literature review titled *The Role of Artificial Intelligence and Chatbots in Education*, identify notable gaps in the literature. While existing studies document improvements in learning outcomes through chatbots, further research is needed to explore the specific pedagogical strategies that drive these results. Their findings reinforce the necessity of deeper inquiry into effective ways of embedding AI tools into teaching methodologies.

Besides, recent empirical studies have demonstrated AI's significant contribution to creating dynamic and effective learning environments that enhance students' linguistic competence across multiple dimensions (Anggraini & Faisal, 2024). Expanding on this, the study *"How Artificial Intelligence Helps Students to Learn English in Depth"* (Seyedi et al., 2024) explores the role of AI in enhancing English language acquisition. It highlights several key ways in which AI contributes to English Language Teaching (ELT), particularly by fostering positive and engaging learning environments. Through its interactive capabilities, AI motivates students to participate more actively and engage more deeply with the material. These dynamic, technology-enhanced environments not only support student involvement but also make the learning experience more enjoyable and effective.

In particular, AI's ability to simulate spoken English via dialogue platforms has proven invaluable in helping students enhance their speaking proficiency. For example, Ghafar et al. (2023) emphasize that AI-powered platforms allow learners to engage in simulated conversations that closely mirror real-world interactions, thereby enriching their overall language learning experience.

However, while the benefits of AI in ELT are evident, its successful implementation depends largely on how effectively it is integrated into teaching practices. Research by Mavropoulou et al. (2023) indicates that the responsibility of integrating AI into ELT curricula largely falls on educators, whose insight and understanding play a critical role in realizing the benefits of these technologies. Meanwhile, Edmett et al. (2024) note that while AI's potential to reshape education is widely acknowledged, there remains a divide in how teachers view its impact. Some express concerns about AI altering teaching roles, while others are more confident in its educational value. Notably, there is a consensus that training for effective AI implementation in classrooms remains insufficient, hindering optimal AI utilization in the teaching-learning process (Edmett et al., 2024).

Further insight into the current landscape of AI in ELT is provided by a recent British Council paper, *"Artificial intelligence and English Language Teaching: preparing for the future" (2024).* This report draws on three sources of evidence, including a systematic review of research on AI in ELT conducted over the past decade. It reveals that AI technologies are now widely used to support various English language skills. For instance, Grammarly provides writing comments, machine translation technologies help with English writing, Alexa and automatic speech recognition enhance speaking and pronunciation, and AI-driven games improve vocabulary while reading. Chatbots are also used to improve listening comprehension.

While AI tools offer personalization and help reduce learner anxiety, the report points out that many still rely heavily on traditional pedagogical frameworks. Interestingly, 76% of surveyed teachers reported frequent use of AI, particularly for lesson planning, material development, and practice support. Language learning apps were the most commonly used AI-powered tools (48%), followed by chatbots (31%) and generative AI tools (37%). These findings suggest a growing reliance on AI in ELT, yet also indicate a need for deeper integration into pedagogical strategies. This is the gap my case studies aim to address—how to align AI technologies with innovative teaching and learning practices.

In conclusion, the integration of AI in English Language Teaching presents exciting possibilities as the technology continues to evolve and reshape language education. As Seyedi et al. (2024) note, AI's potential to enhance learning experiences and outcomes is rapidly expanding, making it an essential part of modern educational frameworks.

Given this, it is imperative that educators begin incorporating AI tools into their teaching not only to streamline their workload but also to better prepare students for the future. In today's fast-paced, technology-driven world, learners must continuously develop their knowledge and skills to thrive in a competitive job market. Teachers, therefore, have a dual responsibility: to master AI tools for instructional purposes and to guide students in using them effectively. By embedding AI into lesson plans and allowing students to explore and apply these tools, educators can foster both digital literacy and language proficiency. This approach not only enhances motivation and engagement but also equips students with the competencies they need for lifelong learning and professional success.

This chapter explores how AI tools can be integrated into English Language Learning by enhancing linguistic competencies, supporting personalized learning pathways, and transforming teacher-student dynamics. Drawing on recent case studies, it seeks to address the current gaps in AI-ELT integration and propose strategies for more effective and equitable use of AI in language classrooms

THEORETICAL BACKGROUND

The integration of Artificial Intelligence (AI) into active learning reflects the principles of modern constructivist learning theory, which views learners as active participants in the meaning-making process rather than passive recipients of information. Central to this approach is Vygotsky's concept of the Zone of Proximal Development (ZPD), which highlights the importance of social and instructional support in helping learners progress beyond their current level of competence. Traditionally, this support came from teachers or peers. However, Crompton and Burke (2023) have shown through systematic research that, in the age of technological development, AI can now offer meaningful scaffolding. AI-powered tools such as chatbots, grammar assistants (e.g., Grammarly), or intelligent tutoring systems can provide real-time support tailored to a student's language proficiency and learning needs. These tools adjust to a learner's individual needs and offer guidance that aligns with their current proficiency level.

This technological evaluation supports constructivist theory by enabling learners to actively build upon their prior knowledge and engage in exploration. For example, adaptive AI systems respond dynamically to student input, encouraging deeper engagement and promoting personalized learning trajectories. As Deslauriers et al. (2019) emphasize students achieve better learning outcomes when they are actively involved in the learning process compared to passive lecture-based environments. Similarly, Mayer (2014) asserts that meaningful learning results from the learner's own cognitive activity during the learning process. In this context, AI functions not merely as a content provider but as a facilitator of active learning environments. For instance, gamified AI applications can motivate learners through interactive challenges and immediate feedback, while AI-based image generators can be used to create visual representations of vocabulary or grammar structures, helping students link abstract concepts to concrete imagery. These applications not only foster engagement but also align closely with constructivist and sociocultural principles by allowing students to interact with content in a personally meaningful and socially relevant way.

Moreover, in comparison to traditional teaching methods like lectures, active learning helps students learn more, remember information for longer periods, and have a more enjoyable class experience. This method encourages students to engage in learning with support from the instructor and peers, rather than learning independently. As a result, the zone of proximal development (ZPD) is activated, allowing students to reach their full potential through guidance from teachers or classmates. Active learning includes all hands-on activities and teaching techniques that enable students to reflect on their learning and apply their knowledge to solve problems (Gholami, Attaran, & Morady Moghaddam, 2014).

In this context, AI tools can play a transformative role by acting as virtual peers, speaking partners, or even as surrogate instructors. For example, chatbots and AI-powered conversation tools can simulate real-time dialogue, offering learners opportunities to practice language skills in a safe, responsive environment. These tools mirror the social aspect of learning by providing feedback, encouragement, and correction—functions traditionally performed by teachers or classmates. As such, AI becomes an enabler of guided learning within the learner's ZPD, providing personalized scaffolding at any time and location.

Research by Kamarulzaman et.al., (2018) shows that incorporating active learning into English as a Second Language (ESL) classrooms fosters a more positive attitude toward English, encourages deep learning, and improves students' self-confidence and leadership skills. The research also emphasizes how these strategies cater to all students, including introverts, ensuring inclusivity in learning. AI tools can enhance this inclusivity by offering multiple channels for communication—text-based, voice, or image-based—thereby accommodating diverse learner preferences and needs.

Therefore, integrating both active learning strategies and AI technologies not only improves students' language proficiency but also strengthens their digital literacy and soft skills, preparing them for the demands of the modern workforce. However, effective implementation of active learning, whether enhanced by AI or not, requires intentional design. As Kamarulzaman et al. (2018) emphasize, instructors must first identify clear learning objectives and then choose the appropriate strategies to meet them, including activities such as debates, problem-solving tasks, and collaborative projects. AI can support this process by helping teachers create adaptive tasks, generate dynamic content (e.g., scenario-based simulations), or even automate formative assessments, thereby lightening the teacher's cognitive load and increasing time for interaction.

However, in the context of AI-enhanced education, teachers must not only be aware of active learning strategies but also understand how to effectively integrate AI tools into their pedagogical practices. This begins with giving precise and purposeful prompts to AI systems for instance, generating level-appropriate discussion questions, customizing vocabulary-based photo activities, or creating interactive grammar exercises. Teachers should also be knowledgeable about the AI tools available to students (such as chatbots, grammar correctors, or image generators) and how those tools can be ethically and pedagogically applied in classroom settings.

Thus, the role of the teacher is evolving: it now includes the dual responsibility of facilitating active, student-centered learning and staying updated on emerging AI technologies to guide students in using them responsibly and effectively. In this way, AI becomes not a replacement for the teacher, but a collaborative partner in the learning process, helping to deliver more engaging, adaptive, and inclusive learning experiences.

One of the theories that also supports active learning is the Multimedia Learning theory. Richard Mayer defines multimedia as presenting both words (spoken or printed text) and pictures (animations, illustrations, photos, videos). It is when material is presented both in verbal and pictorial form. So, multimedia learning occurs when people build mental representations from words and pictures (Mayer 2014). In order to create a multimedia learning environment, you should see multimedia in three different views:

1. Multimedia learning as response strengthening - the learner is a passive recipient of rewards and punishments, as their role is to respond and get feedback on their response. The role of the instructor is to administer incentives and sanctions. Multimedia as an exercise system designed to reinforce skills through feedback.
2. Multimedia learning as an information acquisition - The learner is a passive being who absorbs information from the outside world and saves it in their memory because their duty is to accept it.
3. Multimedia learning as a knowledge construction - learning is a sense-making process in which the student tries to construct a cohesive mental image from the information at hand. In this situation, knowledge is created by the student and cannot be transferred in an exact way from one person's mind to another. This explains why two students may receive the same multimedia message but have different learning objectives afterward. Additionally, it is the learner's responsibility to make sense of the information that is offered; as such, the learner actively creates meaning by interacting with a multimedia presentation and attempting to incorporate the information into a cohesive mental image. Since it is the teacher's responsibility to help the student make sense of this process, the teacher serves as a cognitive guide, offering the necessary direction to support the student's cognitive processing. In addition to presenting information, multimedia presentations aim to give instructions on how to process it, which includes figuring out what to focus on, how to arrange it in the mind, and how

to connect it to previously learned material. Lastly, multimedia serves as a guide for making sense, which is a tool for knowledge production.

In this context, AI tools such as image-generating applications, can enhance multimedia learning by supporting cognitive processing. These tools can be used to generate visual content that corresponds to specific vocabulary or concepts, helping learners form more coherent mental representations. Since comprehension depends not only on external sources of information (e.g., text and images) but also on the learner's prior knowledge (Mayer, 2014), AI can support the personalization and contextualization of multimedia content, thereby enhancing learning outcomes.

Additionally, AI can assist in guiding learners' attention to relevant elements, helping organize information, and linking new content to prior knowledge. This aligns with the broader goal of multimedia instruction, not just to present information but to provide cues on how to process it effectively. As Schnotz (2005) notes, more research is needed to determine under which conditions the combination of text and images enhances or hinders learning. AI offers promising potential in this area, enabling dynamic and adaptive integration of multimedia elements based on learners' needs, and thus serving as a tool for meaningful knowledge construction.

METHODOLOGY

This chapter presents four case studies examining the integration of AI tools in English language classes for university students. These case studies answer the following questions:

1. How to integrate AI tools in teaching the English Language?
2. How does the use of AI tools impact student engagement and creativity in learning activities?
3. What are some challenges and benefits of student collaboration in AI-enhanced learning activities?

The case studies were conducted as part of the General English Course at Ilia State University in the 2023/24 spring semester. Students were from various regions of Georgia, including rural areas and the capital, Tbilisi. Their English proficiency level was B1 on the Common European Framework of Reference for Languages (CEFR) scale. Each class consisted of 20 to 25 students. As Hitchock and Huges (1995) suggest, the case study approach is particularly valuable when the researcher has little control over events, which is why freer practice activities were employed during the production stage to integrate AI tools into the learning process

TEACHING METHODS, PROCEDURES, AND TECHNIQUES FOR ACTIVE LEARNING

Active learning strategies are not part of the grammar-translation method, which, as the name suggests, involves translating sentences from English to a student's first language, such as Georgian, and vice versa. As Jeremy Harmer (2007) points out in his book *The Practice of English Language Teaching*, there are several aspects of this method worth noting. First, the primary focus was on individual sentences rather than longer texts, especially at the beginning stages of learning. Second, there was minimal attention given to spoken language. Lastly, accuracy was seen as crucial in this approach. The Direct Method, which Jeremy Harmer notes later evolved into the Audiolingual Method, may also not be considered a strong example of active learning. Although translation was abandoned in this approach, it still remained focused on individual sentences, and accuracy continued to be prioritized. The method relied heavily on drills, with students learning in small steps through repetitive practice, constantly repeating sentences to reinforce learning.

In contrast, active learning, which emphasizes student engagement and interactive activities, is more closely aligned with Communicative Language Teaching (CLT). CLT, as described by Jeremy Harmer, can mean different things to different people. For me CLT can be viewed as "an extended family of different approaches" - as Harmer describes it. One of the key concepts of CLT is its focus on how language is used, with communication being the central aspect. "The best way to learn a language is to use interaction rather than to learn about it" and the key part of classroom activities are pair and group work. Unlike the grammar-translation method, fluency is more important here than accuracy (Spratt et al.).

AI-powered tools such as Replika.com and Pi.ai (conversational chatbots), ChatGPT (for role-play or speaking practice), and ELSA Speak (for pronunciation and fluency training) can support CLT by enabling learners to engage in real-time conversation simulations, encouraging spontaneous language use and interactive practice beyond the classroom.

I think that one of the teaching procedures that belongs to this CLT extended family is Presentation, Practice, and Production. In this procedure, the teacher introduces a situation that contextualizes the language to be taught. Contextualizing aims to help learners notice and understand meaning (Spratt et al., 2011). Then comes the practice stage, when students practice the language in controlled and guided conditions, doing some exercises, and the last stage is the production stage, when students are asked to use the introduced language in practice on their own, independently. We call the last stage a freer activity when students work on their own, and it is recommended to use speaking or writing tasks for this stage as it helps students use the newly introduced language in practice and in real-world situations.

During the production stage, learners can use AI tools like Grammarly (for writing support), QuillBot (for paraphrasing and vocabulary enhancement), or ChatGPT (for dialogue simulation or writing prompts) to independently generate text, receive instant feedback, and enhance real-world communication practice. Additionally, tools like Canva's AI image generator, Microsoft Designer, or Adobe Firefly can be used to create visuals and infographics for presentations or group projects, while collaborative platforms like Padlet, enhanced with AI suggestions, help students brainstorm, organize ideas, and co-create content in group settings.

We should mention the guided discovery method, which is often used alongside the Presentation-Practice-Production (PPP) and Task-Based Learning (TBL) approaches. In this method, the teacher provides learners with examples of a target language area, such as a text containing several instances of the past tense. The teacher then asks the learners to deduce the rules of usage for that target language. After the learners have worked out the rules on their own, the teacher either provides them with the correct rules or asks them to complete incomplete rules (Spratt et al., 2011).

PPP lessons include introductory activities. The introductory stage of a lesson helps students settle in and concentrate on the lesson's content. There are two kinds of introductory activities: warmers and lead-ins. Warmers are often used to energize students and make them feel comfortable before diving into the main lesson; these could include quizzes, games, or pair work activities. Lead-ins, on the other hand, introduce the lesson's content and aim to focus students by connecting the topic to real-life situations. For instance, if the students are going to read a text about inventions, they might start with a discussion about the world's best inventions (Spratt et al., 2011).

AI tools such as Curipod or Mentimeter (which helps create interactive lessons) or ChatGPT (used for generating pattern-based examples or scaffolding grammar discovery) can assist in guided discovery by supporting inductive reasoning and pattern recognition.

OVERVIEW OF CASE STUDIES

As multimedia learning theory suggests "students learn better from words and pictures than from the words alone if the words and pictures are semantically related to each other and if they are presented close together in space or in time" (Schnotz, 2014). So, we can combine this theory and AI by using student-generated images in English language instruction. Before the widespread usage of AI technologies, I had my students make posters to practice and use newly introduced grammatical structures or vocabulary. As we can generate photos with AI tools, it is now possible to use them instead of posters, which not only aids in English language learning but also gives students practice with prompting and adds creativity and interest to courses.

Three of the activities I used in my classes were based on integrating AI-generated photos into activities that made my lectures more engaging and interesting. All of the lectures followed the Presentation, Practice, and Production (PPP) teaching method and were based on the multimedia learning theory and constructivism principles as outlined previously.

Case Study 1: Designing Dream University Halls: A Vocabulary Challenge with AI Tools.

Activity overview

The primary aim of this lecture was to enhance students' vocabulary related to the theme of "houses," as introduced in the course textbook. This thematic focus covered a wide range of terms and concepts, including various types of houses, their locations (e.g., outskirts, city center, suburbs), architectural features, interior spaces (e.g., rooms), furniture, and other elements that fit within the umbrella of houses. This activity aimed to enable students to apply these words meaningfully in a creative group project.

Implementation Process

Students were divided into groups of four and tasked with designing a hall of residence for their university, which currently lacks one. They had to describe both the interior and exterior of their proposed halls, incorporating the target vocabulary.

Key components of the activity:

- Location: Students had to choose and justify the hall's location (e.g., city center, suburbs, outskirts).
- Visual Design: To enhance creativity, students used the AI tool Gencraft to generate visual representations of their halls. Gencraft was selected for its free accessibility and ease of use.
- Sharing and Discussion: After creating their designs and images, students were regrouped into new mixed groups where they shared visuals and discussed design features using the target vocabulary.
- Collaborative Integration: Students combined favorite elements from each group's designs to create an "ideal" hall of residence, blending creativity with vocabulary application.

Challenges and solutions

One significant issue was a lack of technological literacy and experience with AI tools which occurred at the beginning and at the end of the activity. At the beginning of the activity, I showed the students the logo of the application and asked them to download it. However, some students found it challenging to download the app from their app stores, and others experienced difficulties logging in and locating where to write prompts. I had to provide support to these groups, which consumed a lot of time. Also, during the last stage of the activity when students needed to regroup. They found it difficult to download and share the photo with their group. To save time, I suggested that they take a screenshot of the image instead of downloading it. In the future, it would be helpful to demonstrate the app download and login process on a screen or projector. Additionally, providing a tutorial on how to download, register, write prompts, and create photos would streamline the process. This modeling would save time, as all students would be able to observe how to generate photos. In some groups where students faced similar challenges, tech-savvy peers helped them. Therefore, it would be beneficial to pair tech-friendly students with those who are less familiar with AI tools.

Another notable challenge was that some students found it difficult to use newly learned vocabulary. They were asking questions if they should use all of the words I had introduced. In the future, it would be better to provide students with the templates to apply the new words. For example: "The hall of residence is located in the [city center] and is made of [glass]. It has [seven] floors and on the ground floor there is a [library] and [study rooms]" etc. It would guide students to see how to use learned vocabulary in practice. Also, it would be better to create some extra fill-in-the-blanks or matching exercises with the help of generative AI tools like ChatGPt, Claude, Copilot, etc. This will provide more practice during the practice stage. Moreover, offering a printed vocabulary list or displaying it on a screen or projector would reinforce understanding during the activity.

It would not be surprising that creating prompts for the AI tool was challenging for some students, even after I provided them with an example at the beginning of the activity. It would be helpful to control and provide feedback during the activity and help students refine their prompts in real time. Also, I encouraged them to practice crafting prompts by changing the structure and vocabulary and making various adjustments. This not only helped them generate images from their imagination but also taught them skills in prompt engineering. At the end of the class, I asked them how their experience in prompt engineering went. They told me that at first, it seemed difficult because the app wasn't generating the images they needed. However, they soon realized how to modify their prompts, and now, they feel more confident in giving prompts to the AI.

One group tried to simplify the task by generating photos first and then matching them with descriptions. While this approach could be considered, the visuals lack the use of the target vocabulary. It would be more effective to provide step-by-step instructions. First, ask the participants to create a text describing the halls of residence. Once they have completed that, instruct them to generate a photo based on what they have imagined, guiding them through the process.

The issue of unequal participation often arose during group work. In some groups, certain students took on most of the responsibilities while others took a back seat. To encourage more equitable involvement, I would give specific roles to each group member. For example, a vocabulary researcher, a text writer, a prompt engineer, and a designer. Also, it is necessary to monitor and check in with groups during the activity to ensure participation is evenly distributed.

Key Takeaways

Students demonstrated high levels of engagement throughout the activity, particularly during the creative process of generating images that reflected their own ideas and imagination. This visual component added a dynamic and enjoyable element to the lesson, allowing learners to express themselves in ways that extended beyond traditional language exercises. By the end of the class, students spontaneously began selecting the best features from each group's design to collaboratively imagine an ideal hall of residence. For instance, one student highlighted the appeal of incorporating greenery, while others preferred the sleek look of a glass exterior or the inclusion of a game room. This collaborative reflection showed not only creativity but also critical thinking and synthesis of ideas.

The integration of visuals significantly enhanced student engagement and enriched the overall learning experience. Tools like Gencraft proved especially effective in vocabulary-focused lessons, offering students an imaginative and meaningful way to apply new language in context. However, the activity also revealed several challenges, prompting reflection on how to improve future iterations. Introducing new technologies and creative tasks requires clear instructions, modeling, and scaffolded support to ensure students feel confident and capable.

To promote equitable participation and deeper language application, it's helpful to assign structured roles, provide vocabulary templates, and include guided exercises. These supports help students focus more on communication and collaboration rather than just figuring out the technology. Additionally, this activity provided a natural entry point for introducing prompt engineering—a valuable and transferable skill that can be taught even at beginner levels to help students engage more effectively with AI tools.

Looking ahead, better pre-task preparation will be essential to maximize the learning outcomes of similar activities. This includes offering technical demonstrations, dedicating time for vocabulary practice, and setting clear expectations. With these improvements, AI-enhanced lessons can become even more impactful, fostering creativity, collaboration, and language development in an engaging, student-centered environment.

Case Study II Should I Generate Ideas for Students? Examining AI's Role in Learning and Innovation

Activity overview

The primary goal of this lesson was to help B1-level university students practice modals of deduction (e.g., *must, might, could, can't*) within the thematic context of innovation and inventions, as outlined in their textbook. The lesson followed the PPP (Presentation–Practice–Production) model, with a focus on integrating AI tools for creativity and engagement.

Implementation Process

I followed the same PPP structure. For the presentation stage, as the context of this unit in the textbook was innovations and inventions, I asked ChatGPT to generate a photo of an innovative pen. Then I gave this prompt to ChatGPT *"I'm introducing modals of deduction to my B1-level university students in the context of innovation. Using this photo of an innovative pen, could you generate questions to help me elicit the modals could, might, must, and can't? For example, I might ask, 'Is it a bus?' and when they say, 'No,' I'll follow up with, 'Are you sure?' Then, I'll write on the board: 'It can't be a bus.' I'd like similar question ideas for the other modals to create an engaging and interactive lesson"*. And according to the photo it gave me following ideas:

1. T: Is it a car?
   Ss: "No"
   T: "Are you sure?
   Ss: "Yes"
   Teacher writes "It can't be a car". On the board.
2. T: "Is it for writing?
   Ss: "yes"
   T:, ,Are you sure?
   Ss: "Yes, because it has a point that helps to write"

Teacher writes: “It must be for writing” on the board.

3. T: “Is it a device for scanning documents?”

Ss. “I don’t know. Maybe. It has a lot of features”.

Teacher writes on the board: “It might be for scanning documents”.

“It might not be for scanning documents” “ It could be for taking notes”.

And then I asked Concept Checking Questions like: Do we use must when we are sure that something is true? - Yes. Do we use can’t when we are sure that something is not true? - Yes. Do we use mustn’t when we are not sure that something is true? - No. “Do we use might or could when we are 100% sure?” Do we use might and could when we are unsure about something?”

In the next stage students did some exercises that were given in the textbook. On the production stage, I asked them to work in pairs and make an innovative product to create something new, innovative, and to generate a photo of it. After this, they started mingling in the classroom and showed their inventions to each other. They were instructed to guess what the invention was for, what it could do, and for whom it was and to use modals of deduction. As they were mingling I monitored and wrote down the mistakes they made while speaking and later I wrote common mistakes on the board and we corrected them together.

Challenges and solutions

One of the main challenges I observed was a tendency towards over-reliance on AI. Since the task required creativity, some students looked for shortcuts. Rather than participating in the creative process directly, they used ChatGPT not just to generate ideas but also to create a full description and image of an invention. By simply entering their assignment into ChatGPT, they completed the task in minutes. As I recognize the distinct style of ChatGPT, I quickly identified this as an instance of academic dishonesty. This aligns with concerns highlighted in the British Council study (2024), which discusses the risks of AI misuse, particularly in relation to over-reliance with concerns about ‘laziness’ or decreased ‘creativity’.

There was another case of dishonesty in my experience but in this case, the students were not asked to use AI. I asked them to put themselves in the role of university self-government members and design an event for their peers (as it was the task given in the textbook). One group of students defended their event by highlighting how their event encouraged “diversity.” It was clear that they had relied on ChatGPT for their response because diversity is not a common concept in Georgian universities. During their presentations, when challenged, they acknowledged utilizing AI. In this case, another problem became evident: students did not critically evaluate AI-generated suggestions before presenting them as their own.

This raises an important question: Do we need to ask students to use AI to generate some ideas? The answer to this question is yes, however, the key issue is not the use of AI itself but rather how students engage with AI-generated content. They should critically evaluate the ideas provided by AI—assessing how realistic and useful they are in their specific context. This ability is one of the essential skills that will ensure students' competitiveness in the job market.

One strategic approach for higher education institutions is for educators to actively engage with AI, learning how it operates and integrating it into the learning process (Partners, 2023), not only to know how to use and integrate it in teaching but also to detect plagiarism. Additionally, the unauthorized use of AI for assignments, academic papers, or dissertations could be classified as academic misconduct (Foltýnek et al., 2023). However, establishing clear guidelines on AI usage in classrooms could help set boundaries, ensuring students understand to what extent they are allowed to use AI. AI guidelines, for instance, should outline the appropriate times and methods for using AI technologies, along with thorough instructions and real-world examples to enhance work comprehension.

More precise instructions can also help reduce AI dependence. Instead of simply asking students to "create an invention," I could have prompted them to think more critically: "Consider features that could improve something you already own," or "Imagine a product you need or wish existed." Additionally, providing a personal example, such as how I once wished for a phone that allowed me to see the person I was speaking with, could encourage them to come up with ideas more naturally and would reduce the chance of using AI to do the task.

Another solution to reduce AI dependence might be to ask them first to brainstorm ideas for the invention in their groups and then use AI only for generating ideas and to compare their and ChtaGPT's ideas to each other and make the final decision on which idea to use. In the end, they should have explained the whole process and told which idea they used and why.

Another important factor is time management. If students do not have enough time to complete a task, they are more likely to utilize AI for quick solutions. Therefore, educators must ensure students have adequate time for creative and critical thinking.

Key Takeaways

Since this was not the students' first experience with Gencraft, they demonstrated greater improvement in using AI tools. Unlike in the previous case study, they no longer needed help with basic tasks such as downloading Gencraft, writing prompts, or saving generated images. This made the process smoother, but it also introduced new challenges. Challenges and solutions One of the main challenges I observed was a tendency towards over-reliance on AI. Since the task required creativity, some students looked for shortcuts. Rather than participating in the creative process directly, they used ChatGPT not just to generate ideas but also to create a full description and image of an invention. By simply entering their assignment into ChatGPT, they completed the task in minutes. As I recognize the distinct style of ChatGPT, I quickly identified this as an instance of academic dishonesty. This aligns with concerns highlighted in the British Council study (2024), which discusses the risks of AI misuse, particularly in relation to over-reliance with concerns about 'laziness' or decreased 'creativity'. There was another case of dishonesty in my experience but in this case, the students were not asked to use AI. I asked them to put themselves in the role of university self-government members and design an event for their peers (as it was the task given in the textbook). One group of students defended their event by highlighting how their event encouraged "diversity." It was clear that they had relied on ChatGPT for their response because diversity is not a common concept in Georgian universities. During their presentations, when challenged, they acknowledged utilizing AI. In this case, another problem became evident: students did not critically evaluate AI-generated suggestions before presenting them as their own.

Case Study III: Using AI for Cultural Exploration through Food Recipes

Activity Overview

This lesson was part of a unit on food and cooking, with the goal of helping students expand their food-related vocabulary. The activity was inspired by Google's Food Mood project (https://g.co/arts/CXHTVMsjaD9NB3bD6), an interactive AI tool that allows users to create new recipes by fusing cuisines from different countries. This tool served as a springboard for engaging vocabulary practice and cultural exploration during the production stage of the lesson.

Implementation Process

After eliciting and introducing the new vocabulary that was given in the textbook. I showed them the generated photo of soup combining Georgian and Ukrainian cuisines. It was a fusion of Borsch (a Ukrainian soup) mixed with beans, which is commonly used in Georgian dishes. The platform provided not only the generated photo but also a list of ingredients and a recipe. I showed the whole class the photo and asked them to guess which two countries were combined, and most of them guessed it, and then asked them to work in pairs and write down the ingredients and the recipe of this meal. Then, they compared their guesses with the AI-generated recipes and presented the differences to the whole class.

This sense of discovery and the creative aspect really increased students' motivation and interest. After the activity, they expressed interest in generating their own recipes. This reminded me that students can be a great source of creative activity ideas, based on their suggestions, we did another activity. Students generated recipes individually. They then exchanged photos with their partner, who had to guess the recipe, ingredients, and countries involved. And this time it was a speaking activity and not a writing task.

Challenges and Solutions

The real challenge came when the students generated their recipes. They encountered unfamiliar vocabulary, including ingredients they did not know the meaning or definition in English. So, I encouraged them to use Google to search for images of the words they didn't know. Despite the challenge of unfamiliar vocabulary, students learned new words. They were more likely to remember these words because they were able to visualize and contextualize them in a real-life scenario. One student even mentioned she might try cooking one of the recipes at home, as it looked both easy and delicious.

Time consumption was another notable challenge, as searching for unfamiliar ingredients took more time than anticipated. Breaking the activity into smaller, focused tasks or focusing only on ingredients more than the recipe would be an option.

Moreover, most students found it easier to list ingredients and identify countries rather than create their recipes. This may be attributed to their prior knowledge, as recognizing familiar foods and matching them to cultures required less cognitive effort than generating dishes. In this case, incorporating more scaffolding techniques and constructivist principles—such as activating prior knowledge and building on existing understanding—would have been beneficial from the start. Providing structured guidance and examples could have helped students feel more confident in the creative aspects of the task.

Key Takeaways

The AI-integrated activity was highly engaging for students, largely due to its interactive and visual nature. They were particularly excited about guessing ingredients and recipes and observing how AI could creatively combine elements from different cuisines. The first stage of the activity, which involved presenting AI-generated images, went smoothly. During this phase, the vocabulary introduced—covering categories like fruits and vegetables, fish and seafood, meat, as well as cooking-related verbs, phrasal verbs, and adjectives—aligned with words already familiar to the students through their textbook. This familiarity enabled them to confidently identify and discuss the ingredients, contributing to the activity's overall success.

AI tools like *Food Mood* significantly enhanced engagement and vocabulary retention by situating language use within a realistic and stimulating context. Students were more motivated when the task involved discovery, creativity, and visual input. The combination of AI-generated content with student-centered tasks such as guessing, presenting, and comparing supported both receptive and productive language skills, including speaking, writing, and critical thinking.

An additional strength of the activity emerged through a follow-up task that was inspired by student input, highlighting how learner-driven contributions can naturally extend and enrich the original lesson. This adaptability reinforces the value of student agency in the learning process.

For future iterations of the lesson, some refinements could increase its effectiveness. These include pre-teaching or narrowing the vocabulary to reduce cognitive overload, providing more structured guidance for the creative elements of the task, and incorporating a gradual progression in task complexity to ensure an appropriate balance between challenge and support. These adjustments would help sustain engagement while also scaffolding language learning more effectively.

Case Study IV: Using AI for Practicing Reported Speech

Activity Overview

The aim of this lesson was to practice reported speech in a communicative, real-world context. After introducing the grammar point and completing textbook-based controlled activities, students participated in a creative speaking task using Character.AI (https://character.ai/). This free AI tool allows users to engage in conversations with historical figures, fictional characters, and celebrities, making it ideal for interactive language use.

Implementation Process

I started by giving a live example on the screen of how to choose and interact with a character, drawing on my previous experience with my students' difficulties utilizing AI technologies. As a class, we completed an initial conversation together to familiarize students with the process. Following this demonstration, students individually selected a character and engaged in a chat asking any questions they wanted.

Once students completed their interactions, they participated in a mingling activity within the classroom. They practiced using reported speech by reporting on their AI chats to their peers throughout this phase. This approach not only reinforced grammatical accuracy but also encouraged spontaneous communication and critical thinking.

Challenges and Solutions

Some students took longer to choose a character than anticipated, which slightly delayed the process. In the future, setting time limitations before the activity starts and reminding participants to move on to the next stage can help subsequent sessions run more smoothly.

Additionally, throughout the engagement phase, time management is essential. The activity might be made more efficient by establishing a time limit for the talk or a limit on how many questions students are allowed to ask.

One of the biggest challenges in implementing this activity was addressing ethical considerations and ensuring student privacy. While most students engaged with the AI tool in an appropriate and educational manner, some students selected historical individuals like Sigmund Freud and started asking for personal guidance. This raised concerns about the appropriateness of certain conversations and the potential risks associated with AI-generated responses.

To reduce such difficulties in the future, it would be essential to establish clear guidelines on appropriate questioning before students engage in the activity. Additionally, providing a carefully chosen list of recommended characters or figures that complement the lesson objectives could help ensure that interactions remain academically relevant and ethically sound.

Another challenge was that some students struggled to understand AI-generated responses due to unfamiliar vocabulary. To address this in the future, it would be beneficial to encourage students to rephrase or simplify responses, provide examples, and allow peer support. Additionally, the teacher should actively monitor the activity and provide assistance when students need clarification to ensure they fully understand the conversation.

Furthermore, when reporting their AI conversations, some pupils struggled to use reported speech accurately. In order to help them, I kept a close eye on the activity, made notes about common errors, and led a class-wide corrective session by going over these problems on the board. In this case, it might be advantageous to include more controlled practice tasks prior to the more unrestricted practice phase in order to better solidify comprehension. This would guarantee that before using reported speech in a more flexible communicative task, students have a firm understanding of it.

Key Takeaways

This AI-integrated activity proved to be highly motivating and enjoyable for students, with many expressing a desire to continue working on it beyond class time. The integration of AI with real-world communicative practice enabled students to apply reported speech in meaningful ways, while also fostering engagement, creativity, and critical thinking. Such activities highlight the value of blending language learning with digital tools, offering students authentic contexts for practice.

One notable example came from a student who chose to interact with Alexander the Great. She was astonished by how accurately the AI chatbot responded to her questions, including inquiries about his horse and personal life. The reliability of the responses impressed her and added to her engagement. However, while AI can provide seemingly accurate and informative answers, it is important to acknowledge that such responses can sometimes be historically inaccurate, biased, or misleading. This underscores the need to cultivate critical thinking skills among students by encouraging them to verify AI-generated content through credible sources. Classroom discussions around any discovered inaccuracies can also serve as valuable opportunities to develop students' analytical abilities and promote a more informed, evaluative approach to using AI.

To ensure that these kinds of tasks maintain their educational value and uphold classroom safety, proper scaffolding and clear guidance are essential. This includes instruction on how to use the AI tool effectively, a clear focus on relevant content, and thoughtful consideration of ethical issues. In doing so, students not only improve their language skills but also build essential digital literacy, learning how to engage with AI responsibly. Looking ahead, future lessons would benefit from striking a balance between guided structure and learner autonomy. By providing a clear framework while allowing room for personal choice, educators can support independent thinking while still achieving targeted learning outcomes.

Case Study V: Using Curipod as an Icebreaker

Activity Overview

The aim of this lesson was to break the ice on the first day of university while fostering a collaborative and interactive classroom atmosphere. To achieve this, the AI tool Curipod (https://curipod.com/) was used. Its free and accessible features, such as polling and drawing tools, provided an engaging platform for students to introduce themselves and connect with each other.

Implementation Process

This is a well-known activity called "True and a Lie," where students write three true statements and one lie, and then they need to guess which one is the lie. After introducing the syllabus, I began implementing this activity. Curipod offers a polling feature, which I decided to use for this task. I wrote four statements about myself on Curipod, one of which was a lie, and shared the QR code on the screen for the students to join the game using their mobile phones. They had 45 seconds to choose which statement was the lie. In the end, the results appeared on the screen. Afterward, they replicated the activity in pairs but this time they used pen and paper.

Then, I conducted the second activity using Curipod again. I gave students the task to join the Curipod platform through the QR code, and this time, they had to draw any information they wanted that represented themselves. They could include any details they wished to share with us. Curipod allows us to set a timer for this task which is great for time management, so I gave them 10 minutes to complete their drawings. Students then began creating their drawings.

After 10 minutes, I displayed each drawing on the screen one by one. First, the students tried to guess what was in the drawing. Then, the students who created the drawing would introduce themselves and share how accurate the students were in guessing what the drawing represented.

Challenges and solutions

One challenge that emerged during this activity was that some students wanted to create more colorful drawings but were unsure where to find the necessary tools or features within the Curipod platform. This led to some confusion and delays in the activity. In the future, I will ensure to show students the instructions and all the available features at the beginning of the activity, including how to access color options and other drawing tools. This will help streamline the process and ensure that students can fully utilize the platform to express their ideas without unnecessary distractions.

Additionally, it would be better to start with the drawing task first. This would allow students to share more about their hobbies and interests in a visual format before moving on to the "True and a Lie" activity. By doing this, students would already be aware of each other's interests, making it easier for them to guess which statement was the lie. This adjustment could make the guessing phase more engaging and enhance the overall flow of the activity.

Overall, the activity was a success in terms of both student engagement and language practice. It created a dynamic and collaborative learning environment, with students actively participating and using English to communicate and share personal information.

Key Takeaways

The activities I conducted using Curipod proved to be both engaging and effective in encouraging student participation and creativity. The first task, "True and a Lie," sparked curiosity among students and created an interactive atmosphere. The use of QR codes to join the platform made it easy for students to participate, and they seemed excited to guess which of the statements I shared was a lie. This activity was not only fun but also encouraged students to practice their AI skills.

The second activity, where students were tasked with drawing something that represented themselves, allowed for deeper self-expression and creativity. The time limit of 10 minutes worked well in keeping students focused, but I noticed that some students required a bit more time to complete their drawings. In the future, I may consider extending the time for students who need more time to reflect and finish their drawings. The students actively engaged with each other during the guessing portion of the activity, and it was clear that they enjoyed both the challenge of guessing the drawings and the opportunity to learn more about their classmates.

A key takeaway from these activities was the importance of interaction and collaboration. Students seemed to enjoy working together to guess the drawings and were motivated to participate. The activity provided a fun way to practice communication and allowed students to learn more about each other in an informal setting. The informal nature of the task made students feel more comfortable and willing to share.

Overall, using Curipod was otherwise an effective way to integrate technology into the lesson. It facilitated student interaction and allowed for instant feedback on their guesses. The platform's timer and polling features helped to keep the activity structured and efficient. There were a few technical issues, such as brief delays in the loading of the platform on some students' phones, but these were resolved quickly.

Findings and Discussion

These cases illustrate broader issues in education. Integrating AI tools in the EFL classroom creates an engaging atmosphere where students actively participate in the activities. The use of AI tools makes students more interested and motivated, leading them to fully immerse themselves in the activities. Additionally, students might be so enthusiastic that they request and even suggest more activities involving

AI tools. More importantly, AI tools help teachers create real-life scenarios and make students use target language in real-life situations.

Before integrating AI tools into lessons, teachers should apply constructivism principles and scaffolding techniques. This approach ensures that the integration builds on student's prior knowledge, making it easier for them to use the tools effectively. Additionally, providing clear instructions and demonstrating how to use the AI tools is crucial, especially when introducing them for the first time. The cause of poor time management or less engagement of the students might be not focusing on constructivism principles before the activity, insufficient use of scaffolding techniques, or a lack of controlled practice activities before reaching the production stage of the lesson.

Based on the reflections from these case studies, a common challenge in integrating AI tools into EFL classrooms is the lack of AI literacy among students, which also affects their prompt engineering skills. It's important to note that this can lead to a decrease in student motivation, as struggling with tasks can be demotivating and reduce interest in participating.

Another challenge when using AI tools in the classroom is that students may encounter unfamiliar words, which can also affect their motivation. To address this, teachers should consider providing more controlled activities or allowing students to use dictionaries to look up unknown words. Additionally, over-reliance on AI, plagiarism, and ethical concerns are important issues that arise when integrating AI tools into the classroom.

If we consider everything above, I believe that to successfully integrate AI into teaching, educators must first understand active learning strategies and theories. Using AI alone is not enough. When teachers know active learning strategies and take on the role of a constructivist facilitator—helping students scaffold their knowledge—they can better integrate AI into their teaching. This, in turn, makes the learning process more engaging and interesting. Of course, teachers can also use AI for their own professional development, improving their understanding of active learning strategies and learning how to incorporate them into their teaching. I believe AI should be embraced as a supportive tool for both teachers in their instructional practices and students in developing their knowledge and skills. By leveraging the capabilities of AI, education can be transformed into a more effective and engaging process for everyone involved.

Knowing how to use AI is one thing, but the ability to filter the information, refine it, and adapt it to one's needs is another crucial skill. That's why students should be allowed to use AI tools for generating ideas. Teachers often ask colleagues or AI for activity ideas when planning lessons. However, not every activity works for every class because students have different needs, learning styles, and abilities. Students could follow the same structure: they generate ideas using AI, critically review them to determine which ideas suit their needs, and modify them accordingly. This could be incorporated into assignments, students should also discuss the process—what AI suggested, what they selected, and why. This approach not only helps them leverage AI effectively but also develops their ability to think critically and adapt information to real-world applications.

One of the most pressing concerns is not only how students use AI, but also how educators can reliably detect AI-generated work. Weber-Wulff et al. (2023) tested fourteen of the most widely used AI recognition tools, including Turnitin, and concluded that these tools are neither accurate nor reliable. Their findings align with those of Ahmed Elkhatat and colleagues (2023), who found that while detectors perform better in identifying text generated by ChatGPT-3.5, they struggle or even fail to recognize content produced by ChatGPT-4. Significantly, these studies highlight a crucial point: *"An easy solution for detecting AI-generated text does not (and maybe even could not) exist"* (Weber-Wulff et al., 2023). However, from these cases, it is evident that in some situations educators can detect AI without using AI detectors. Teachers' role extends beyond simply understanding how AI tools function or what kind of content they generate. We must also be aware of our students' cultural and educational backgrounds to detect potential misuse effectively.

So, we can say that in order to let students use AI for generating ideas is dependent on the specific nature of the task itself. If the goal is to develop critical thinking, problem-solving, and analytical skills, AI could be a useful tool, provided that students evaluate and refine AI-generated content rather than passively accepting it. However, in the first case, if instructions are detailed and supported with practical examples, students may not need AI to generate ideas.

CONCLUSION AND PRACTICAL RECOMMENDATIONS

Several implications can be made from the findings of these case studies. First, it is essential for teachers to understand AI tools, their type of content, and their capabilities in order to effectively integrate them into activities and also to detect plagiarism. When you know the way, style, and content AI generates it is easier for you to align AI tools to activities and also to detect if AI was used when you told them not to or not. Second, teachers should be aware of students' cultural and educational backgrounds as AI often generates information without context if it is not instructed so. When students use AI they do not critically evaluate whether the AI-generated content is relevant or accurate, or common to their culture so teachers can use their knowledge of students' backgrounds to detect plagiarism and help students develop skills in refining and filtering information.

These case studies can serve as a valuable guide not only for teachers but also for trainers. They can be inspired by the activities presented in this study, using them as they are or adapting them to suit their needs. Additionally, trainers or creators of training modules can use the findings and activities from these case studies to design training programs focused on integrating AI into EFL teaching. This is particularly important given the current lack of formal training and readiness for AI in the teaching space, which leaves many educators feeling unprepared (Edmet et al., 2024). By providing practical examples and insights, these case studies can help address this gap and serve as a foundation for developing effective training programs.

Curricula developers should consider integrating AI tools into EFL classes, as these case studies not only provide specific examples of how to incorporate them but also offer valuable insights into potential challenges and solutions. By addressing these challenges proactively, developers can ensure a smoother and more effective integration of AI tools and activities in the future.

Also, policymakers should consider creating AI guidelines for higher education teachers and students based on the findings of this study. These guidelines could outline when and how to use AI tools effectively, as well as provide specific policies for integrating AI into teaching practices.

Limitations and Future Research

Since this study was limited to reflections and observations rather than directly examining students' attitudes, it is recommended that future research explore how students perceive AI-integrated activities and assess the impact of these activities on their learning. Future studies should also measure the effects of AI integration on students' improvement in English language knowledge and skills. Additionally, researchers could investigate character.ai's recently introduced feature allowing users to interact with characters by calling them, asking questions, and listening to their responses. As we read in the British Council's systematic review on the use of AI in English language teaching, the majority of research conducted up until 2024 has focused on four key areas where AI is being utilized: the development of speaking, writing, and reading skills, as well as supporting pedagogy and self-regulation. Interestingly, listening did not emerge as a primary area for AI support in language learning. The review suggests that future research could focus on the use of AI to develop receptive skills, which were not highlighted as strongly in the existing research compared to productive skills. Therefore, it would be valuable for future studies to explore how AI chatbots, such as Character.AI, could contribute to improving listening skills. This tool, which allows students to interact with various characters and listen to their responses, could be effectively integrated into language learning activities. In this case, a lesson could be planned differently, with more preparation beforehand, focusing on specific pre-planned questions. Instead of simply chatting, students could "call" characters, ask them targeted questions, and listen to their responses.

Additionally, considering my own reflections on the activity—such as the need for clear guidelines, time management, and monitoring of conversations—future research could benefit from examining how to best use this AI tool in a way that encourages critical thinking and enhances the overall learning experience.

REFERENCES

Agata Majchrowska, A., Tarkowski, A., Alamäki, A., Butler, D., Baten, D., Van Den Broek, E., Noto La Diega, G., Muukkonen Van Der Meer, H., Molenaar, I., Vie, J.-J., Kaplan, J., Giraldo Ospino, J. P., Estevez, J., Quille, K., Kralj, L., Crosta, L., Karliuk, M., Wirzberger, M., Montebello, M., . . . Slavov, V. (2022). *Ethical guidelines on the use of artificial intelligence (AI) and data in teaching and learning for educators*. Publications Office of the European Union. https://school-education.ec.europa.eu/system/files/2023-12/ethical_guidelines_on_the_use_of_artificial_intelligence-nc0722649enn_0.pdf

Anggraini, A., & Faisal, F. (2024). The use of artificial intelligence based technology in English language teaching. *Golden Ratio of Data in Summary*, *4*(2), 950–957. DOI: 10.52970/grdis.v4i2.749

Cohen, L., Manion, L., & Morrison, K. (2007). *Research methods in education* (6th ed.). Routledge., http://repository.unmas.ac.id/medias/journal/EBK-00127.pdf DOI: 10.4324/9780203029053

Crompton, H., & Burke, D. (2023). Artificial intelligence in higher education: The state of the field. *International Journal of Educational Technology in Higher Education*, *20*(1), 2–22. DOI: 10.1186/s41239-023-00392-8

Deslauriers, L., McCarty, L. S., Miller, K., Callaghan, K., & Kestin, G. (2019). Measuring actual learning versus feeling of learning in response to being actively engaged in the classroom. *Proceedings of the National Academy of Sciences of the United States of America*, *116*(39), 19251–19257. DOI: 10.1073/pnas.1821936116 PMID: 31484770

Edmett, A., Ichaporia, N., Crompton, H., & Crichton, R. (2024). *Artificial intelligence and English language teaching: Preparing for the future* (2nd ed.). British Council., DOI: 10.57884/78ea-3c69

Elkhatat, A. M., Elsaid, K., & Almeer, S. (2023). Evaluating the efficacy of AI content detection tools in differentiating between human and AI-generated text. *International Journal for Educational Integrity*, *19*(1), 17. Advance online publication. DOI: 10.1007/s40979-023-00140-5

Foltynek, T., Bjelobaba, S., Glendinning, I., Khan, Z. R., Santos, R., Pavletic, P., & Kravjar, J. (2023). ENAI recommendations on the ethical use of artificial intelligence in education. *International Journal for Educational Integrity*, *19*(1), 12. DOI: 10.1007/s40979-023-00133-4

Galindo, L., Perset, K., & Sheeka, F. (2021). *An overview of national AI strategies and policies. OECD Going Digital Toolkit Notes, 14*. OECD Publishing., DOI: 10.1787/c05140d9-

Gawate, S. (2019). Artificial intelligence (AI) based instructional programs in teaching-learning of English language. *International Journal of English Language* [IJELR]. *Literature and Translation Studies*, *6*(4), 69–70. DOI: 10.33329/ijelr.64.69

Ghafar, Z. N., Salh, H. F., Abdulrahim, M. A., Farxha, S. S., Arf, S. F., & Rahim, R. I. (2023). The role of artificial intelligence technology on English language learning: A literature review. *Canadian Journal of Language and Literature Studies*, *3*(2). Advance online publication. DOI: 10.53103/cjlls.v3i2.87

Gholami, V., Attaran, A., & Morady Moghaddam, M., & Young Researchers and Elite Club, Mashhad Branch, Islamic Azad University. (2014). Towards an interactive EFL class: Using active learning strategies. *Research on Humanities and Social Sciences*, *4*(19), 190–191.

Harmer, J. (2007). *The practice of English language teaching* (4th ed.). Pearson Longman.

Hitchcock, G., & Hughes, D. (1995). *Research and the teacher: A qualitative introduction to school-based research* (2nd ed.). Routledge., DOI: 10.4324/9780203424605

Kamarulzaman, L. M., Abdul Ghani, M. T., & Wan Daud, W. A. A. (2018). The effect of active learning strategies on students' attitudes towards English: A study at Universiti Teknologi Petronas. *INSANIAH: Online Journal of Language, Communication, and Humanities, 1*(2).

Labadze, L., Grigolia, M., & Machaidze, L. (2023). Role of AI chatbots in education: Systematic literature review. *International Journal of Educational Technology in Higher Education*, *20*(1), 56. DOI: 10.1186/s41239-023-00426-1

Mavropoulou, E., Koutsoukos, M., & Oikonomou, A. (2023). Integration of artificial intelligence on teaching the course of didactic methodology: A case study. *European Journal of Social Science Education and Research*. https://revistia.com/ejser/article/view/542

Mayer, R. E. (2009). *Multimedia learning* (2nd ed.). Cambridge University Press., DOI: 10.1017/CBO9780511811678

Mayer, R. E. (Ed.). (2014). *The Cambridge handbook of multimedia learning* (2nd ed.). Cambridge University Press., http://molwave.chem.auth.gr/sigalas_edu/files/Multimedia_Learning.pdf#page=43 DOI: 10.1017/CBO9781139547369

National Academic Integrity Network. (2023). *Generative artificial intelligence: Guidelines for educators*. https://www.qqi.ie/sites/default/files/2023-09/NAIN%20Generative%20AI%20Guidelines%20for%20Educators%202023.pdf

Partners, T. (2023). *Time for class 2023: Bridging student and faculty perspectives on digital learning*. https://tytonpartners.com/app/uploads/2023/06/Time-for-Class-2023-Report_Final.pdf

Qassrawi, N. R. M., ElMashharawi, N. A., Itmeizeh, N. M., & Tamimi, N. M. H. M. (2024). AI-powered applications for improving EFL students' speaking proficiency in higher education. *Forum for Linguistic Studies*, *6*(5), 535–549. DOI: 10.30564/fls.v6i5.6966

Schnotz, W. (2014). Integrated model of text and picture comprehension. In Mayer, R. E. (Ed.), *The Cambridge handbook of multimedia learning* (2nd ed., pp. 72–103). Cambridge University Press. DOI: 10.1017/CBO9781139547369.006

Seyedi, A., Yeganeh, M. A. A., Noorzad, D., Firouzi, S., Qurbani, M., Shakeri, E., & Osati, K. (2024). How artificial intelligence helps students to learn English in depth. *Advances in Social Sciences Research Journal*, *11*(10), 414–440. DOI: 10.14738/assrj.1110.17803

Spratt, M., Pulverness, A., & Williams, M. (2011). *The TKT teaching knowledge test course: Modules 1, 2, 3*. Cambridge University Press.

Tao, Y. (2019). On the construction of active learning teaching model in college English classroom. *Francis Academic Press*. https://www.semanticscholar.org/paper/On-the-Construction-of-Active-Learning-Teaching-in-Yeqing/277e51b7230c44018b7e95292cb60c7a09f5bc73

Umar. (2024). Advancements in English language teaching: Harnessing the power of artificial intelligence. *FLIP: Foreign Language Instruction Probe*. https://jurnal.stit-buntetpesantren.ac.id/index.php/flip

Wang, Y., Liu, C., & Tu, Y.-F. (2021). Factors affecting the adoption of AI-based applications in higher education: An analysis of teachers' perspectives using structural equation modeling. *Journal of Educational Technology & Society*, *24*(3), 116–129. https://www.jstor.org/stable/27032860

Weber-Wulff, D., Anohina-Naumeca, A., Bjelobaba, S., Foltýnek, T., Guerrero-Dib, J., Popoola, O., Šigut, P., & Waddington, L. (2023). Testing of detection tools for AI-generated text. *International Journal for Educational Integrity*, *19*(1), 26. DOI: 10.1007/s40979-023-00146-z

World Economic Forum. (2016). *The fourth industrial revolution: What it means and how to respond.* https://www.weforum.org/agenda/2016/01/the-fourth-industrial-revolution-what-it-means-and-how-to-respond/

World Economic Forum. (2023). *Future of jobs report 2023.* https://www3.weforum.org/docs/WEF_Future_of_Jobs_2023.pdf

Chapter 7
Leveraging AI on Social Media & Digital Platforms to Enhance English Language Teaching and Learning

Md Mehedi Hasan Emon
https://orcid.org/0000-0002-6224-9552
American International University-Bangladesh, Dhaka, Bangladesh

ABSTRACT

This chapter explores the integration of artificial intelligence (AI) within social media and digital platforms to enhance English Language Teaching (ELT). It examines AI-driven tools like chatbots, conversational agents, and content curation algorithms that facilitate personalized, interactive, and engaging learning experiences. By analyzing platforms such as Facebook, Instagram, Duolingo, and TikTok, the chapter highlights how AI fosters dynamic English learning communities and enables real-time language practice. It also addresses ethical considerations, such as data privacy, accessibility, and algorithmic bias, while emphasizing the need for inclusive and equitable AI deployment. Through case studies and real-world examples, the chapter illustrates AI's transformative potential and its challenges in reshaping traditional ELT methodologies, offering insights into how educators can effectively leverage these innovations.

DOI: 10.4018/979-8-3373-1952-0.ch007

INTRODUCTION

The influence of AI integrated within social media and digital environment upon the transformation of English Language Teaching (ELT) is in the focus of the current chapter. As the world is becoming increasingly in need of accessible, personalized and scalable language training, AI is quickly becoming a central, disruptive ingredient of learners' everyday digital surroundings. Utilizing the findings from the most recent research in applied linguistics, educational technology, and digital pedagogy, this chapter explains the way AI empowered functions of chatbots, personalization systems, adaptive algorithms, and virtual tutors are influencing social interactions on such social media and education platforms as Facebook, YouTube, TikTok, This chapter goes beyond technical features by placing these tools within educational theories to demonstrate their roles in facilitating interaction, provision of feedback, motivating students and promoting autonomy of learners.

The convergence of social media platforms and AI is explored to demonstrate how these technologies can promote peer relationships, personalize for specific learner needs, and increase inclusivity for multilingual students. The chapter demonstrates, with grounding examples and practical settings, how not only structured, but unstructured language learning environments are changing. Algorithms' bias, data privacy, digital divide are examined closely; educational equity and integrity issues are kept in focus. The chapter, through exploration of both opportunities and dangers of AI incorporation in ELT, provides a ready-made format that prepares educators, researchers, and policymakers for a constantly moving field. The chapter indicates that although AI is not a panacea, the right use of AI with purpose and ethical awareness opens English language instruction to all students.

AI APPLICATIONS IN SOCIAL MEDIA FOR ENGLISH LANGUAGE TEACHING

The incorporation of AI into social media forms part of the focus point in ELT in modern times. Social media environments no longer are spaces for incidental interaction which are simply optional. Their relevance has increased transferring into complex teaching environments in which formal guidance meets spontaneous mingling. The combination of AI and social media platforms means that there are creative ways for promoting learner independence, individualizing how-to, as well as promoting active interaction, particularly when physical classroom access is under-represented or inequitable. Essentially, the capacity of artificial intelligence to process and analyses large amount of data comprehensively instantaneously is the catalyst for this revolution. In educational technology, these abilities enable adaptive systems to assess proficiency in language and offer customized materials at rates of precision and velocity that are impossible for human teachers with massive groups of online students. The AI enabled social media tools are promoting the uptake of language education on such platforms as Facebook, Instagram, X (previously Twitter), WhatsApp, and Telegram thereby assimilating linguistic learning to users (Shahri & Karizmeh, 2025).

One of the most interesting innovations relates to the implementation of the AI-based conversational-agent, or chatbot, strategy fitted for the education domain, in the field of language learning. By using NLP and machine learning, these systems generate real-like simulated communication among humans. In real use, grammar mistakes can be immediately corrected by the integrated language learning chatbots on social media applications, whereas a user's skill level can be matched with appropriate vocabulary in sentences. According to Campbell & Olteanu, (2024), these fast-moving digital discussions extend learners' communicative language potential by providing practice in authentic, live communication. Contrary to static grammar programs or memorization apps, which pass on information in a one-directional way, chatbots present real-time personalized feedback that mirrors the back-and-forth nature of real interactions, highlighting communicative considerations of contemporary language teaching. This can be shown using such technology in platforms as Facebook Messenger. With such bots as Andy or English Conversation Practice, powered by AI, users will receive daily schedules for practicing, discussion starters, and vocabulary exercises tailored to users' individual learning goals. The technology that underpins these bots depends on NLP to recognize errors made by learners to provide timely, situation-specific corrections. This continued interaction enhances language retention and encourages motivation which is particularly good for adult and non-traditional learners who might feel uneasy in a formal learning setting (Hassan et al., 2020; Ruan et al., 2021). These digital aids encourage 'hands-on' learning that offers opportunity to experiment and learn from mistakes in a safe, controlled-risk environment.

AI increases content creation and learner engagement in social media by using high analysis and extremely personalized recommendation engines. With the help of AI, to study patterns such as likes, shares, comments, viewing time as well as scrolling, social media platforms refine their strategies to deliver top engagement. These algorithms can be reconfigured for ELT to reveal learners' interests and construct content appropriate to their preferences and particular language requirements. For instance, if a person tends to read mostly on Instagram about their travel while learning English, then they may see specialty reels or posts on a topic of travel conversations, idioms, or language tied to a travel scenario. From an educational perspective, the coming of personalized content embraces a constructivist approach where learning is placed in actual contexts and learners are autonomous. Based on the idea of ZPD (El Gazi & Ibrahimi, 2024), AI-generated learning pathways offer instructional support that enables learners to overcome challenges and stretch their competencies only by a small margin. Exposing learners to advanced grammar and controlled vocabulary within contexts familiar to learners increases the salience and durability of acquisition of language.

Although it may be that neither Telegram nor WhatsApp is an academic outlet, such chats have developed into hotbeds of AI-enabled language communities. Mobile messaging services enable chatting with smart bots capable of delivering short instructional pieces, quiz monitoring and correction of learners' pronunciation using speech feedback. Telegram's relatively flexible API construction allows people to build personalized bots such as @EnglishVocabBot or @GrammarUpBot and give users short and entertaining sessions to learn a language at time intervals during the day. The accessibility of these programs is flexible and mobile thus encouraging learners to keep on interacting regularly which is critical to language acquisition among those who are born into a digital age (Booton et al., 2023). Moreover, X (used to be Twitter) provides another unique delivery to the learners. The platform also affords microblogging to serve as a real means of producing language. Learners get AI-driven assistance now when using browser extensions with the help of services such as Grammarly or Quillbot, when writing tweets, responding to threads, or composing English messages (Marzuki et al., 2023). By pointing out grammar mistakes, suggesting other vocabularies, and proposing stylistic improvements, these systems greatly increase the quality of what learners submit. Moreover, these applications encourage reflection and reworking the very key components of effective language learning which tend to be neglected during informal online communication. The reach of AI does not fall within isolation to tools for the individual language learner (Huang et al., 2022; Kuddus, 2022). AI also has great applications in promoting teacher professional growth and informing content creation on social media sites (Khan & Hasan Emon, 2024). Professional networks such as LinkedIn and Facebook make educator communities in which AI produced insights are used to guide moderators on popular pedagogical considerations, content engagement, and discourse interest areas. Facilitators use this advanced analysis to plan webinars, promote shared practices, and curate ELT resources as a reaction to the group's engagement patterns. According to Meng et al., (2025), AI-empowered communities support collective thinking of educators where teachers can refine their approaches in constant relation to learner discoveries and developments in technology. Even though the potential to use AI in ELT on social media is attractive, some of the concerns are still there. Automated content suggestions, enabled by algorithmic profiling, create ethical, privacy, and surveillance dilemmas about the process of collecting and usage of users' data. How users are engaged with content, whether in terms of how long they stay on specific posts, typing behavior, can be monitored and analyzed, all without informing the learners. Lack of regulation or insufficient regulatory action in areas with limited resources can make these practices part of digital exploitation and heighten difference in educational opportunities (Bonina et al., 2021). Furthermore, such recommendation systems that operate based on disparate data, could further reinforce linguistic or cultural biases, which may cause value to automatically be placed on idiom English in the West as much or more than other varieties of global English.

Another problem is the continued digital divide. Although social media access is generally available, how AI tools do their job often depends on the availability of proper devices and connectivity networks among users. Remote or disadvantaged folks may not benefit from AI's hand to ELT. This gap is against the goal of inclusive world-wide education and identifies the desperate profusion of critically assessing the incorporation of AI in areas with meager resources. With these limitations in mind, it is irrefutable that the English as a second language (ESL) teaching is in the process of radical transformation, due to AI-enhanced social media. They allow learners to gain personalized, dynamic and culture-appropriate instruction, with the educational landscape having enough capacity to catch up with the scholarly ideals and patterns of digital consumption. The end of such innovations by educators and policymakers should be mindful of avoiding disruptive harmonious mix of technical ability, ethical stewardship and pedagogical practices.

DIGITAL PLATFORMS AND AI-POWERED ELT TOOLS

The rise of the intelligent educational technologies is mired in deep transformation that ELT has undergone in the digital context. Such an application of AI has placed them at the very center of contemporary teaching. Coming in with AI-based platforms such as Duolingo and Babbel, this development highlights a significant shift in educational practice, not off instruction, towards consolidation of individualized and data-infused sense of the stimuli that drive effective language learning. Personalization and adaptivity are the central ways in which AI adds to the effectiveness of digital ELT platforms. Whereas earlier approaches such as print textbooks or previous online courses provided fixed lessons, current AI applications can adaptively adjust content, layout, and challenge to fit the learner's performance. As an exemplification, Duolingo is the front-runner language-learning globally. Modification in such systems is based on major educational psychology theories such as scaffolding and the zone of proximal development which doesn't mean that lessons should be either superficial or complicated.

Moreover, spacing repetition and retrieval practice are essential components of the platform's AI algorithms that are supposed to enhance memory retention. Psychological study shows that repetition of material at various points of time is more effective in creating durable long-term memories compared to concentrated studying (Luo, 2020). Machine learning models designed from 1 billion user occurrences help choose review instants for each student, customizing content to complement needs. For example, AI in spaced repetition enabled Memories to determine each learner's forgetting curve, encouraging timely reviews to maintain memory without flooding their working activity. One of the main aspects is the accuracy and immediacy aspect of error analysis and feedback where AI truly shines versus the skills of a human tutor in addressing numerous learners at the same time. Unlike traditional modes of operation, in digital platforms there is a wholesale redefinition of relevance that revolves around subtle feedback that not only goes past simple right or wrong concepts. Instead, the platform utilizes NLP and machine learning abilities to interpret responses and determine what failed and why. Duolingo through its technology provides real time feedback meta linguistically, pointing out grammar errors with the suggestions of alternative ways of expressing the sentences. Solely accurate feedback such as this is instrumental to developing syntactical patterns and lexical usage, and at the same time promoting metacognitive techniques that are essential for independent learners (J. Zhang & Zhang, 2024).

Learners' opportunities to practice their oral skills have been enormously increased because of the group integration of AI-based speech recognition capabilities on these platforms. By way of example, Babbel uses sophisticated AI voice technology to assess things such as the quality of pronunciation or intonation and how fluently a learner talks. These tools extend beyond simple phonetic similarity verifications; Using this assessment of intonation and comprehensibility, these systems concentrate on mimicking the natural high communication standards (Levi, 2024). The communicative approach finds expression in the English as a Second Language instruction in that it lays emphasis on being able to be understood, as well as language use in actual situations, rather than scrupulous adherence to native-speaker norms. For non-native English speakers in environments where one does not get many opportunities to speak, these platforms are central to the process of 'learning whilst doing', just as the learners develop spoken English skills and greater self-confidence. The virtual tutor/voice assistant is one of the greatest improvements given by AI in language learning platforms, a digital interlocutor that seeks to imitate conversational exchanges. With the use of NLP and speech generation these platforms allow users to engage in meaningful conversations that mimic classroom or peer conversations. An example of that is the Rosetta Stone that applies AI to assist in conversations that motivate the learner to respond to prompts, obey commands, or work through realistic, transactional examples. This type of semi authentic communication creates a simulated immersion world helping with both lexical and syntactic fluency as well as sociolinguistic and pragmatic comprehension.

Educational spaces which are limited in terms of resource and struggle to hire qualified English language staff can gain most from these technologies. In such restrictions, AI would be a supporter of traditional teaching methods instead of a live substitute for the same. At the level of individual learners, practice can be done independently of supervisor, receiving immediate feedback, and encountering various authentic material, all under geographical and economical constraints (Hoque et al., 2020). This capability to democratize learning is especially useful in countries where English language teaching is an important part of increasing digital skills and international communication. The concept of gamification refers to the introduction of game elements to tasks that are not games to improve user participation. One of them, Duolingo, uses such mechanisms as point systems, leaderboards, badges, and daily streaks, the control mechanism of which is AI that adjusts activities to promote a flow state (Miller & Cooper, 2021). AI plays a key role in managing motivational approaches to the fulfillment of pedagogical aims, maintaining a quality of teaching. Instead, it makes sure that entertainment is in harmony with educational effectiveness (Emon & Khan, 2025). Such motivational scaffolding approach is very helpful in motivating regular participation, one of the critical elements in attaining linguistic proficiency (Ahmed Abdel-Al Ibrahim et al., 2023). Even though progress has been made, there continues to be great concern, with respect to boundaries and ethical considerations of AI on ELT digital platforms. There are questions as to the open nature of algorithms especially pertaining to the practices used in harvesting learners' information, examining and using the scored data to change their educative course. The extent to which learners' activities are observed in these platforms and the algorithms behind the AI-driven choices are generally concealed. Such a lack of clarity can undermine trust and identifies crucial data ownership, consenting and ethical concerns of digital surveillance (Yağcı, 2022).

Another problem is connected to the fact that these platforms standardize English varieties into a homogeneous body. There is a trend for the AI programs to serve mainly American /British English data which may preclude or reduce representation of other global Englishers. This is especially deplorable in the circumstances of English becoming regarded as a polarimetric language that recognizes a variety of legitimate norms in regional and cultural settings (Kachru, 1992). If non-Western English varieties are primarily used for correction by AI tools, this could be coercively ideological though in the guise of standardization in language use. Additionally, although AI can largely individualize instruction, it is unable to understand subtle emotional dispositions of the learner, such as anxiety or disinterest or frustration, which are all critical for language acquisition. Trained educators can usually discover these signals and adjust their approach to meet learner needs better. Even though there are experiments with the affective computing for emotion detection via facial or voice data, these tools are controversial and have great limitations (Al-Saadawi et al., 2024). Based on this, the combination of human teaching and AI reflect the best pedagogical option at least in the foreseeable future. Also, significant cultural background and applicability which are part of proficient language learning can be overlooked in algorithmic practices. Machine algorithms might give grammatically correct vocabulary or grammatically correct contexts which are not appropriate for the learner's cultural background. As per Phillips Galloway et al., (2020), knowledge of language means comprehending the integration that language has with sociocultural backgrounds. It is left to educators to ensure that AI driven instruction exposes students to the various, inclusive and contextually appropriate resources.

AI-POWERED CONTENT GENERATION AND CURATION IN ENGLISH LANGUAGE TEACHING

The application of Artificial Intelligence driven by Natural Language Processing is fundamentally transforming the manner instructional materials are conceived, adapted, and delivered in the field of English Language Teaching. But beyond being a tool of support, this technological revolution completely redefines how instructional content is prepared and laid out. In the conventional ELT environments, it has always been the educators' responsibility to design instructional materials which can be both time and mentally exhausting. Current AI systems provide everything you need to automate exercise and quiz and comprehension tasks creation, as well as a feature to curate genuine English content matching each learner's objectives and preference. These attributes are becoming game-changers for language development, promising scalability while blending in personalized content, and raising the pragmatic and cultural competence of learners. One of the major benefits of AI with respect to content creation is the ability of AI to tailor learning material depending on the learners' linguistic abilities. AI tools using intricate NLP methodologies measure reading difficulty, word usage, syntax, and communicative coherence to produce content at all learning stages. For instance, programs such as Quillionz and Scribe-Sense, which can generate independent reading comprehension exercises, grammar work outs, and vocabulary quizzing from whatever material is available (Huang et It is not necessary to ask clear, single-answer questions that evaluate comprehension on a limited depth of understanding; instead, AI platforms based on semantic and syntactic analysis can create questions that measure comprehension across multiple depths, giving rise to cognitive interaction among the audience whose L1 skills vary.

More importantly, the questions generated by AI for writing assignments mostly target communicative purposes and not just the test of grammatical ability. Writing assistants that follow AI and NLP rules (Grammarly or Write & Improve) give feedback regarding such things as grammatical accuracy, tone, coherence, and appropriateness. This mechanism of giving feedback promotes autonomous language learning following the tenets of learner-centered instructional approaches (Jomaa, 2025). AI tools facilitate development of metalinguistic awareness required for superior writing skills because learners are persuaded to watch over and fix their works.

However, there is a lot that has been done in addition to creation; AI plays a very crucial role in content curation i.e. selection and editing of authentic English text appropriate for education. Content selection and adaptation have now become highly algorithmic, with educators not needing to undertake it manually. Instead, this procedure is then highly powered by recommendation algorithms which evaluate the student profiles, preferences, history of activity, and achievement measures. Newsela and FluentU are good examples of that change since they provide actual content (news, videos, podcasts) that is pre-accommodated with AI technology for use in the classroom. Newsela modifies identical texts in finessing various reading levels, ensuring that each student experiences the same underlying themes as language befits their skill. By customizing materials in adhering to the needs of the individuals, this adaptive curation makes inclusive learning possible whereby students of different abilities can get to learn core subjects through diverse means (Khan et al., 2024; Singh et al., 2024). Thematically consistency while allowing the authenticity of the language is one of the strengths of AI-based content curation. AI ensures the language used is still accurate, and not turned into an unnatural or oversimplified degree, thereby ensuring learners get exposure to actual idioms, discourse markers, and colloquialisms (elements essential for successful communication). Its interactive subtitles and quizzes provide authentic videos that immerse learners in a variety of accents, registers and real-world language contexts, thanks to FluentU. One of the significant improvements includes how AI evolves a skill in interacting with and assisting learners emotionally while learning a language. Thanks to recent progress in sentiment analysis and affective computing, today's platforms can deduce learners' emotional status by interpreting interactional data, such as typing patterns, speech hesitations, or response times, and adapt material delivery accordingly. These are drawn from affective language learning theories which focus on the superlative effect of motivation, anxiousness and emotional involvement in language learning (Hong et al., 2022). In case of distress or the difficulty to process information, a learner can send an alarming signal, and AI tools are capable to adjust by reducing the workload, using a dynamic multimedia or providing encouraging guidance. This sensitivity is based on affective filter theory in which the role of emotion in language acquisition is considerable (Alrabai, 2022). Artificial intelligence offers emotional support and ensures that learners are engaged and work efficiently within their perfect learning phases. Learner modeling can assist the system by making it possible for AI to create an elaborate individual profile by considering users' performances and emotional states, choice of content, and patterns of language acquisition. These algorithms constantly update themselves via machine learning, which makes it possible for greater precision for estimating which content formats and styles will best engage and facilitate each learner's course of development (Er-radi et al., 2023). This approach provides both efficient educational results and cost-effective solutions, so that individual learning can be implemented in various learning environment without access to expert English language teaching professionals. Nevertheless, its use regarding its contribution to creating and selecting the content has numerous significant pedagogical and ethical challenges. One major problem is the danger of content being overly standardized; AI-generated resources may in its programming focus on mainstream languages and cultural perspectives, American or British English for instance, thereby neglecting the less popular varieties of English across the world. As it happens, English is at the center as a lingua franca in so many cultural settings across the world (Luczaj et al., 2022); hence this presents critical challenges. As some cultural or ideological inclinations take charge of the content it can help make up the 'cultural politics of English' (R'boul, 2024).

One important issue relates to the vagueness of AI algorithms, particularly speaking of content recommendation and adaptation. Often, students and teachers cannot distinguish reasons for the selection of the chosen content and mechanisms through which feedback can be generated. In educational contexts that emphasize critical thinking, and reflective learning, a lack of openness can damage confidence and autonomy. The other problem is a massive demand for data collection to customize content, which poses critical questions related to protecting the privacy of users and data integrity. The application of AI by students produces large volumes of sensitive educational data that may be used if the personal or institutional safeguards are not adequate or implemented (Nguyen et al., 2023). But while AI is brilliant at creating and arranging learning materials, it tends to be rather clumsy in both pedagogical sensitivities, as well as contextual understanding compared to a trained instructress. For instance, AI tools are likely to provide materials that are easy to understand (in language) but ignore key cultural contexts or local nuances. Professionals involved in education should monitor, adjust, and enrich materials of Artificial Intelligence to ensure such materials would help achieve the intended learning outcomes and follow local educational standards.

SOCIAL MEDIA INFLUENCERS AND AI FOR ENGLISH LANGUAGE TEACHING (ELT)

Social media in combination with AI has fundamentally changed the methods in which ELT has been designed and deployed and experienced in modern times. Conventionally limited to physical classrooms, ELT is undergoing dramatic population with the advent of digital influences in platforms like YouTube, TikTok, and Instagram, promoting different pedagogical possibilities outside the confines of an institution. Increasingly, TESOL, linguistics, or applied education-credentialed influencers are using technology to broadcast short, clear, and fun English-language lessons to a global audience. The deployment of AI-based technologies is greatly enhancing the contribution of such initiatives as it provides more interactive opportunities, applies the content to individual learners and makes language education available across the world. The importance of the role of English language influencers as informal educators has become particularly apparent, with many earning trust as a source trusted to mentor. They produce content that facilitates effortlessly the comprehension of explanation in terms of grammar, pronunciation advice, discourses on idiomatic expressions, and cultural information, which is commonly presented in lively and informal styles. Nkadimeng & Ankiewicz, (2022) reveals that the real-world association and relatability that is evident in the content of influences can be related to the affordances of digital natives compared to old textbooks. Edutainment and invention of interesting digital stories are their skills in creating their huge audiences. Whereas traditional materials used in education are often read too impersonally or too formally, influence-generated content often employs common-to-the-daily-life examples to better adapt to a diverse group of learners. Relying upon AI technologies, such influencers can step out of the positions of the content providers and become personal curators of educational systems. More and more, these educators integrate AI-based virtual assistants, chatbots and AI-enabled comment-sorting into their teaching schemes to increase engagement with learners. One of the ways to do it is by using comment-sorting algorithms augmented with NLP for aggregating and systematization of the learner questions to provide a simple tool for influencers to answer these widespread questions (Emon et al., 2024). These platforms filter out useful feedback from the enormous flow of activity in popular social channels, leaving interactions more efficient.

Sometimes, influencers collaborate with AI developers to add real time chatbots for conversational skill learning on their platforms. Sufficiently with the help of artificial agents that imitate natural speech, learners can practice independently vocabulary, grammar, and pronunciation, at their own-wish rhythm. For example, influencers such as Bob the Canadian or Vanessa from Speak English have added AI enhanced platforms to their learning portals producing personalized exercises that react to user input and feedback. The following is a new wave of innovation, which are virtual influencers created from AI synthetic personalities equipped with deep learning, so as not to involve human intervention in the provision of English education. Apart from their animated appearances, these avatars also integrate pedagogical frameworks, and they have been created for human-interaction through natural language processing. Take for example "Milla the English Tutor" in the Instagram and TikTok, a virtual influencer who is inspired by AI has the capabilities of sharing with one vocabulary lessons and helps people complete small quizzes in chat (Meirbekov et al., 2024). As these AI tutors are yet in early stages of development, their effectiveness has been clearly manifested in providing short instructional sessions, answering learner questions via writing and accumulating diverse storylines (Damşa et al., 2021; Y. Zhang, 2024). The fact that such platforms can be scaled means that autonomous educators can be very valuable learning assistants for those areas that do not have access to traditional resources (Alam, 2021). These innovations are set within the context of social media algorithms that essentially determine visibility and student engagement. Machine learning is used to evaluate performance in algorithms moving content on YouTube, Instagram, and TikTok which values are watching time; engagement and share value. ELT influencers and educators need to understand algorithmics to increase their visibility online. As reported by Shen et al., (2021), the ability to interpret and utilize algorithmic behavior is highly relevant for manufacturers of educational materials. Matching educational content to the inclinations of social media, short, informative video clips that make use of mobile engagement, assists ELT creators in gaining more exposure and maintaining their audience (AlSaied & Akhtar, 2021).

Furthermore, the way the users are given ELT content through AI feeds define their learning opportunities and engagement. Unlike a deliberate interaction demanded on conventional platforms, language content is distributed automatically within social media networks thanks to recommendation systems. This relaxed accidental exposure which is usually referred to as "ambient learning" presents young learners with many unplanned interactions with English (Abobaker & Moleta, 2024; Arnab, 2020). This also makes it easy for users to carry out just in time learning, meaning users will be able to access lessons on such topics as prepositions or phrasal verbs whenever they find themselves harnessing from entertainment on social media. Such a learning style is informal and not directly structured yet like theories of language acquisition which indicate that frequent exposure to language in context results in internalization (Toseeb et al., 2020). Still, inviting influencers and AI into the ELT is accompanied by several important pedagogical and ethical considerations. The other issue related to the unreliable and often inauthentic quality of the educational material produced and endorsed by influencers. Although numerous influencers have vast teaching experience in the background, it is necessary to note that some of them may not receive professional training and pose a risk of passing false or abbreviated explanations. Despite the way AI makes things more interactive, it, by itself, does not mean having evidence of sound pedagogical principles. There is a dire need for strong systems of quality control and peer review which should protect the educational value whilst providing the creative space that influencer methods afford.

Moreover, commercialization of learner data is a great concern. Platforms that are based on movement by influencers and augmented by A I technology strongly depends on user data to personalize educational materials and track use (Emon et al., 2025). Through handles which are not in the direct control of influencers, customer data is usually used as the foundation for ads and algorithm management, which often causes debates on privacy and transparency. As Komljenovic, (2021) argues, commercial platforms mediating education tend to blur the lines between learning and consuming, thus requiring a strict analysis of their effects on learner agency and privacy of data. Linguistic hegemony is also a topic that is discussed quite a lot. Standard AI models and well-published ELT mavens who recycle large data sets for training work across the board to prefer major English accents such as American or British, excluding their more marginalized global English varieties. There is a risk that this interest will persist to overlook the wide and varied types of English usage in the world thus worsening linguistic disparity. Whenever ELT professionals shift to World Englishers and English as a Lingua Franca perspective, influencer materials need to change to reflect such varied communities (Boonsuk et al., 2021).

ETHICAL AND PRACTICAL CONSIDERATIONS IN AI-POWERED ENGLISH LANGUAGE TEACHING (ELT)

The AI is at the ready to transform English Language Teaching (ELT) into a time of personalized, efficient, and worldwide education. Besides, there's a lot of optimism about AI in ELT, but also great many ethical and practical challenges that educators, developers, policymakers and researchers should think through carefully. Language teaching is likely to benefit from incredible opportunities for pedagogical change in AI-enhanced language instructional tools, but there are also serious ethical challenges including issues of the privacy of the data, algorithmic bias, accessibility, transparency, and the need for human involvement in language training. Such considerations are important because essentially, they form the question of whether AI supports equable education or unintentionally widens existing divides.

Data Privacy and Surveillance Concerns

Many AI technologies are data powered collected, refined, experimented on to motivate fast moving algorithms. In ELT, the gathered data often includes revealing information about learners, such as their interaction habits and mistakes in language. This collection covers way beyond classroom data but also includes usage trends, language errors, voice clips, emotion signals, as well as biometric information obtained through the application of eye-tracking/speech recognition technologies. This practice of routinely collecting this information regularly raises urgent ethical questions of consent and who owns the data and what can be done with it to store it for the long term. It is absent among users according to Veletsianos and Houlden (2020) that clear mechanisms are lacking where users can exercise control or be informed of intended use of their data. Such an unbalanced scale is especially risky for young learners, refugees, and people living in inadequate data protection regions. It is also standard for the ELT platforms that are powered by AI technology to utilize opaque contracts for data collection. Famous learning programs such as Duolingo or Grammarly gather ridiculous amounts of user information, which are often obtained from areas where their respective data protection policies differ. York, (2021) present a view of how the educational AI industry's use of surveillance changes learners' educational growth into a commercial product that creates what they refer to as a "pedagogical surveillance economy". There are many educational institutions in which the absence of reliable and legally enforceable data ethics frameworks only makes the matter worse. There are no clear and enforceable standards which might encourage developers and managers of platforms to major in profitability and results over ethical duties and possibly result in data breaches or deceiving design options to learners (Mazur & Serafin, 2023).

Algorithmic Bias and Representational Injustice

Large scale ethics problem is presented because of the existence of biases that exist at the heart of AI algorithms. Numerous language learning aid relies on complex machine learning processes which are trained using large pools such as internet material, standard English evaluations, online learning materials. Such datasets are usually dominated by the mainstream cultures such as the English language, and the native speaker yardsticks (Liu, 2024). Accordingly, there is a possibility AI technology will be biased against various dialects, accents, and syntactic variation incompatible with popular norms with the perpetuation of language hierarchies and marginalization of learners from multilingual backgrounds (Khan et al., 2025). By way of example, automated essay evaluation tools, such as e-rater by ETS or Revision Assistant by Turnitin, predominate in terms of emphasizing standard essay formats and conventional choices of vocabulary, which places learners who opt for culturally specific patterns of rhetoric at a disadvantage. Technology may be developing but while there are English language teaching tools based on speech recognition, there are challenges with recognizing global English vernaculars. Recognition mistakes of learners from South Asia, along with Sub-Saharan Africa and Latin America, are usually not related to their own pronunciation, but rather due to accentuated training of speech recognition systems. Such shortcomings do not only decrease students' self-assurance but also lead to epistemic injustice when certain students are systematically disregarded or neglected in learning (Hodson, 2020).

Inequitable Access and the Digital Divide

A major practical problem arises due to unequal access to AI-enhanced ELT resources. Many of the advanced tools demand reliable internet, convenience of digital devices, and common sense of digital competence. Economically underprivileged and low-income zones are rarely visited by those disadvantaged learners. According to Sosa Díaz, (2021), almost 37% of the students across the world still cannot rely on internet, and over 60% face restricted access to digital learning materials. Such a gap may increase the pre-existing inequalities in education opportunities. In some places, in remote schools or even refugee shelters where there is not enough money to finance an education, students could have no access to AI-integrated educational tools. Though in cities, students are subject to discrimination regarding gender, disability, or linguistic origin might still be unable to interact with AI tools. As Xu & Ouyang, (2022) put it, one must review the AI potential in an educational setting, looking at the conditions on which AI depends. Relying on this market force alone might ensure that AI-based educational tools remain the prerogative of the few while only serving to equalize learning for the many.

Overreliance on Automation and Erosion of Human Pedagogy

Another major, not so obvious challenge is the pedagogical effects of excessive reliance on automation. The emergence of new technology to incorporate such functionality as grammar check, conversations simulation, and real-time feedback leaves room for fear that educators could be secondary throughout in that they would only be supervisors or administrators of support. Even though efficiency is much lauded, the trend will eat away at the delicate, empathetic, and culturally sensitive methods essential to language learning. Language access is personal and social; it goes beyond cognitive disposition. Regardless of how accomplished the AI systems may be, they lack the cultural awareness and interpersonal interactions, as well as the ability to make fast judgments, which the knowledgeable teachers have as a cultural norm in the setting of education (Eguchi et al., 2021). Finally, an overemphasis on AI-driven assessments may lead to the importance of measurable achievements being placed in front of those useful skills such as critical thinking, creativity or intercultural sensitivity which constrain the aims of the curriculum. Such being the case, politics should be to integrate AI as a helpful underpinning, as opposed to a substitute for, the constructive involvement of human educators in classes involving language.

Accountability and Transparency in AI Deployment

Ideally, though responsibility finds a continued place of prominence in AI ethics within ELT. The problem of accountability arises in complex ways when an AI system grades incorrect, misrecognizes a learner's speech or provides culturally insensitive content. Unlike human instructors, however, AI systems often work, often, as "black boxes", so that even with their creators it is difficult to explain how they make decisions (Brożek et al., 2024; Hassija et al., 2024). Lack of transparency interferes with the attempts to eliminate errors; handle appeals; and provide feedback within the education settings. AI usage in public schools presupposes all the controlling, implementing, and assessment steps of the process being conducted in a transparent manner. A meaningful consultation is only possible if students, parents, teachers, and administrators are involved in significant ways. Collaboration of planning, continuous evaluation concerning bias, and simple procedures for recourse to stakeholders are needed to effectively confirm AI use is ethical. Global guidelines exist in the form of UNESCO's Recommendation on the Ethics of Artificial Intelligence but equally important is adaptation and enforcement of these recommendations in a regional context.

CASE STUDIES AND REAL-WORLD EXAMPLES OF AI IN SOCIAL MEDIA-BASED ENGLISH LANGUAGE TEACHING (ELT)

The application of AI to ELT is likely to grow since, at this point, new technologies, changing teaching formats, and the worldwide pursuit of open, effective, personal learning intersect. The combined force of AI and social media in conjunction with digital platforms has multiplied those possibilities of learning the language due to providing the educators and the students with their extensive toolkit that can cater for various learning styles and cultural variations. In this section the chapter will provide numerous examples and case studies that show how AI can be implemented into the social media environment for ELT, demonstrating that it can work both in a technical and pedagogical sense.

Hello English: Culturally Localized, AI-Driven Language Learning

The Hello English app of a leading instance from south Asia highlights the great influence of AI on language learning innovation. The use of artificial intelligence enables Hello English to provide personalized, culturally adapted instruction, which is designed to promote language learning in people whose first language is other than English. The learners use Hello English to interact through a gamified framework where they engage in activities like constructing vocabulary, mastering grammar and constructing phrases. It adapts its learning modules depending on user proficiency, helping individuals from a beginner to expert level learn English (Y. Zheng et al., 2024). Compared to merely presenting it, AI in Hello English animates learning through a wide range of interactive functions. Using speech recognition features, the app actively supports the continuous engagement of a learner. With this tool, participants can practice speaking, receive direct feedback and correct their pronunciation according to the AS's interpretation. Using immediate speech-based feedback, the app combines classroom theory with real communication and ensures active learning and better results. Additionally, Hello English utilizes artificial intelligence to customize learning in a way that considers regional linguistic difference making it appropriate to a range of learners with different backgrounds. By individualizing the content for learners' individual backgrounds, the app reduces unease that tends to rear its head if the language path seems removed from lived experience. Furthermore, the app integrates features which are like social media, so that the users can monitor success of their goals, work together in groups, and communicate socially, and consequently create a supportive learning environment. In that way, it encourages learners, supports a lively community in which the exchange of knowledge and feedback takes place, reflecting the involvement of social media. The cornerstone of Hello English's success is the levering of AI in the development of not only customized coursework but also the interactivity of the language learning communities.

Liulishuo: AI for Oral Proficiency Assessment and Personalized Feedback

Liulishuo is an AI-driven leader platform in China, which makes use of AI technologies, to measure and enhance English proficiency in speech. By using the deep learning methodologies, Liulishuo completes learners' spoken English, provides and customizes feedback that pays special attention to the pronunciation, fluency, and syntactical accuracy. The platform records, analyzes, and appraises audio work from the users before comparing the learner's speech to native speaker norms and makes suggestions on changes that can improve proficiency. Immediate, feedback based on data, is critical in aiding students in fine-tuning their speaking skills in an immediate fashion and incrementally (Yuan, 2024; C. Zheng et al., 2024). A major strength of Liulishuo is that it can provide individual instruction tailored for every student. During the process, the system alters functions of the oral tasks depending on the fluency of the learner, while ensuring that this is an exhilarating, yet approachable, experience. The ability of the system to personalize learning is grounded by adaptive learning theory, which allows AI to customize the content to address the learner's evolution. These customized, interactive routes facilitate learning and add to a more enjoyable and meaningful learning experience. Moreover, Liulishuo uses AI to tailor the creation of learning materials. Through examining the data of learners, the educational platform presents bespoke lessons that suit the skill of users, hence making sure the lessons are language-relevant and interesting. Such tailored lessons are not practical in the usual classroom setups and may be impossible to implement if teachers must deal with diverse groups of students. Liulishuo proves with its AI technology that AI goes beyond just analysis to create personalized effective materials that enhance results for all learners.

LinkedIn: AI-Powered Professional Learning Communities

Though LinkedIn is generally taken as a professional networking site, it has developed to be an essential learning resource for language instructors and education professionals to communicate and exchange ideas. LinkedIn AI algorithms support the search for useful information, i.e. articles, lesson plans and instructional videos to be found, with reference to the TESOL community of educators who curate these materials (Abobaker & Moleta, 2024). The Teachers of English as a Second Language often use the LinkedIn as a hub of collaboration where they collaborate, provide criticism, and share experience about the application of AI in educational practices. AI is currently used to create lesson plans that are tailored for specific industries' unique language needs. An increasing number of English language teachers, particularly the ones working in Business English or ESP spheres, are using AI-supported resources to design materials to meet exactly the language requirements of professionals from various industries such as marketing, engineering, finance, etc. Take AI-supported platforms, such as platforms which provide personalized grammar and vocabulary tasks based on the trends of emerging industry, ensuring these learners can access materials that are current and relevant. Furthermore, the use of LinkedIn's professional groups means that instructors can exploit AI tools that will offer insights into the success of their strategies, a process involved in continuous improvement and refinement. That type of collaboration promotes professional growth and the feeling of common goal, where AI aids the development of instructional practices.

Pinterest: Visual Learning through AI-Generated Infographics

In contrast with content delivery and testing, emphasized by Hello English and Liulishuo, Pinterest shows the role of AI in creating appealing and engaging visual educational resources. Pinterest uses AI to provide customized quick infographics, vocabulary flash cards and grammar guides that are specifically designed keeping in mind the learner's interests and learning objectives. These resources are particularly useful for learners who help with visual stimuli, as the visual materials provided in these resources give intuitive and memorable depictions of language-related matters.

Pinterest's AI system uses the data gathered about how its users have been interacting in order to recommend any content that is appropriate for the individual learner's proficiency, interests, and objectives of learning. In the case of a learner focused on grammar Pinterest's system can show them infographics or charts that can provide clear, step by step breakdowns of the complicated grammar topics. Learners are also granted visual vocabularies adapted for different themes, e.g. traveling, business, or everyday life. It is these visual representations that form a conversational learning environment that is more accessible, and easier to remember for individuals who are sensitive to traditional text-based methods of learning. Also, the platform allows not only educators but also learners to develop personalized boards that support collaboration and sharing of educational resources among users. The AI-powered suggestions meet individual needs and promote teamwork and provide an engaging platform for learners and teachers to exchange ideas and strategies.

Pedagogical Adaptability and AI as a Co-Creator in the Learning Process

These case studies do not only consider the technical capacity of AI in ELT but also show flexibility in terms of supporting various pedagogies. AI should be thought of not as a silver bullet solution capable of addressing all learning issues, but as another highly flexible tool to be used in a variety of instruction models. Whether it is task-based learning, customized feedback systems or active visual materials, the abilities of AI to adjust to multiple environments of learning and to accommodate students' needs really demonstrate its importance in ELT. Moreover, there is a clear tendency to view AI rather as a partner to educators than a substitute. For such platforms as Hello English, Liulishuo, and LinkedIn, AI is essential in providing personalized learning environment and for collaborative learning as well as peer interaction. The fact that AI is adaptive in nature endows them with a large spectrum of pedagogical strategies thereby making language instruction relative to the distinct needs, interests, and cultural backgrounds of learners. This flexibility helps because learners these days are those who contribute to their own learning process, rather than being mere consumers of pre-set information. AI stands in favor of transitioning to learner-centered education, where the role of the teacher is to facilitate, guide, enrich rather than give information.

CONCLUSION

The integration of AI in settings of digital and social media changes the face of teaching the English Language (ELT) greatly. This chapter looks at how AI technologies get to perform an active function, completely reshaping the practices of teaching, the involvement of students, and distribution of information, rather than merely serving as a supporting add on. Current ELT environment emphasizes personalization, flexible and interactive based on the use of algorithms on YouTube/TikTok for content curation. Looking at many instances and dealing with clients demonstrates that AI's functionality goes beyond its mechanical aspects; It involves its power to enable engaging, learner-centered interactions that amalgamate structured and unplanned learning environment. Once offloaded as a means of causing disturbance, social media has become a major learning platform, establishing learners in borders, teaching collaboration and exposing learners to natural language contexts. AI underpins this sphere with adaptive, personalized content, scalable assessment oversight and real time authentic conversational experiences. However, the innovation of such technologies comes without barriers in their way. The discussion in the chapter focuses on central ethical, practical, and accessibility conundrums arising from increasing role of AI in English Language Teaching (ELT). The fact that data privacy issues, algorithmic bias, and the growth in digital divides are a reality indicates the necessity to deploy AI with a great sense of conceptual detail. Utilization of AI should be geared towards education outcomes, and ethics, and not because of technological development or increased productivity. After all, the emergence of social media influencers and AI-based virtual tutors implies a big shift in educator and pedagogic identity. Changing content-creation landscape has endowed non-traditional instructors and learners with the ability to co-author the learning process. Therefore, as language education becomes decentralized, the need is to establish systems that can ensure integrity, correctness, and accessibility of language education.

REFERENCES

Abobaker, R., & Moleta, S. (2024). *ESL 4.0* (pp. 71–134). DOI: 10.4018/979-8-3693-5443-8.ch004

Ahmed Abdel-Al Ibrahim, K., Cuba Carbajal, N., Zuta, M. E. C., & Bayat, S. (2023). Collaborative learning, scaffolding-based instruction, and self-assessment: Impacts on intermediate EFL learners' reading comprehension, motivation, and anxiety. *Language Testing in Asia, 13*(1), 16. DOI: 10.1186/s40468-023-00229-1

Al-Saadawi, H. F. T., Das, B., & Das, R. (2024). A systematic review of trimodal affective computing approaches: Text, audio, and visual integration in emotion recognition and sentiment analysis. *Expert Systems with Applications, 255*, 124852. DOI: 10.1016/j.eswa.2024.124852

Alam, A. (2021). Possibilities and Apprehensions in the Landscape of Artificial Intelligence in Education. *2021 International Conference on Computational Intelligence and Computing Applications (ICCICA)*, 1–8. DOI: 10.1109/ICCICA52458.2021.9697272

Alrabai, F. (2022). The role of mixed emotions in language learning and teaching: A positive psychology teacher intervention. *System, 107*, 102821. DOI: 10.1016/j.system.2022.102821

AlSaied, N., & Akhtar, F. (2021). Media students using mobile phones in the Arabian Gulf to improve English writing and video production skills. *Learning and Teaching in Higher Education: Gulf Perspectives, 17*(1), 4–15. DOI: 10.1108/LTHE-09-2020-0038

Arnab, S. (2020). *Game Science in Hybrid Learning Spaces*. Routledge., DOI: 10.4324/9781315295053

Bonina, C., Koskinen, K., Eaton, B., & Gawer, A. (2021). Digital platforms for development: Foundations and research agenda. *Information Systems Journal, 31*(6), 869–902. DOI: 10.1111/isj.12326

Boonsuk, Y., Ambele, E. A., & McKinley, J. (2021). Developing awareness of Global Englishes: Moving away from 'native standards' for Thai university ELT. *System, 99*, 102511. DOI: 10.1016/j.system.2021.102511

Booton, S. A., Hodgkiss, A., & Murphy, V. A. (2023). The impact of mobile application features on children's language and literacy learning: A systematic review. *Computer Assisted Language Learning, 36*(3), 400–429. DOI: 10.1080/09588221.2021.1930057

Brożek, B., Furman, M., Jakubiec, M., & Kucharzyk, B. (2024). The black box problem revisited. Real and imaginary challenges for automated legal decision making. *Artificial Intelligence and Law*, *32*(2), 427–440. DOI: 10.1007/s10506-023-09356-9

Campbell, C., & Olteanu, A. (2024). The Challenge of Postdigital Literacy: Extending Multimodality and Social Semiotics for a New Age. *Postdigital Science and Education*, *6*(2), 572–594. DOI: 10.1007/s42438-023-00414-8

Damşa, C., Langford, M., Uehara, D., & Scherer, R. (2021). Teachers' agency and online education in times of crisis. *Computers in Human Behavior*, *121*, 106793. DOI: 10.1016/j.chb.2021.106793 PMID: 36568039

Eguchi, A., Okada, H., & Muto, Y. (2021). Contextualizing AI Education for K-12 Students to Enhance Their Learning of AI Literacy Through Culturally Responsive Approaches. *KI - Künstliche Intelligenz*, *35*(2), 153–161. DOI: 10.1007/s13218-021-00737-3

El Gazi, S., & Ibrahimi, A. (2024). *Personalized Learning*., DOI: 10.4018/979-8-3693-1206-3.ch014

Emon, M. M. H., & Khan, T. (2025). The mediating role of attitude towards the technology in shaping artificial intelligence usage among professionals. *Telematics and Informatics Reports*, *17*, 100188. DOI: 10.1016/j.teler.2025.100188

Emon, M. M. H., Khan, T., Rahman, M. A., Hamid, A. B. A., & Yaakub, N. I. (2025). GreenTech Revolution: Navigating Challenges and Seizing Opportunities. In *AI and Green Technology Applications in Society* (pp. 63–90). IGI Global Scientific Publishing. DOI: 10.4018/979-8-3693-9879-1.ch003

Emon, M. M. H., Khan, T., Rahman, M. A., & Siam, S. A. J. (2024). Factors Influencing the Usage of Artificial Intelligence among Bangladeshi Professionals: Mediating role of Attitude Towards the Technology. *2024 IEEE International Conference on Computing, Applications and Systems (COMPAS)*, 1–7. DOI: 10.1109/COMPAS60761.2024.10796110

Er-radi, H., Touis, B., & Aammou, S. (2023). *Machine Learning in Adaptive Online Learning for Enhanced Learner Engagement*., DOI: 10.4018/979-8-3693-3132-3.ch003

Hassan, F., Khaled Amin, M., Khan, T., Mehedi Hasan Emon, M., & Amin, A. (2020). Roles of social influence in expediting online learning acceptance: A preliminary study on Bangladeshi learners. *ACM International Conference Proceeding Series*. DOI: 10.1145/3377049.3377087

Hassija, V., Chamola, V., Mahapatra, A., Singal, A., Goel, D., Huang, K., Scardapane, S., Spinelli, I., Mahmud, M., & Hussain, A. (2024). Interpreting Black-Box Models: A Review on Explainable Artificial Intelligence. *Cognitive Computation, 16*(1), 45–74. DOI: 10.1007/s12559-023-10179-8

Hodson, D. (2020). Going Beyond STS Education: Building a Curriculum for Sociopolitical Activism. *Canadian Journal of Science, Mathematics and Technology Education = Revue Canadienne de l'Enseignement des Sciences, des Mathématiques et de la Technologie, 20*(4), 592–622. DOI: 10.1007/s42330-020-00114-6

Hong, J.-C., Hwang, M.-Y., Liu, Y.-H., & Tai, K.-H. (2022). Effects of gamifying questions on English grammar learning mediated by epistemic curiosity and language anxiety. *Computer Assisted Language Learning, 35*(7), 1458–1482. DOI: 10.1080/09588221.2020.1803361

Hoque, K. E., & Bt Kenayathulla, H. B., D/O Subramaniam, M. V., & Islam, R. (. (2020). Relationships Between Supervision and Teachers' Performance and Attitude in Secondary Schools in Malaysia. *SAGE Open, 10*(2). Advance online publication. DOI: 10.1177/2158244020925501

Huang, W., Hew, K. F., & Fryer, L. K. (2022). Chatbots for language learning—Are they really useful? A systematic review of chatbot-supported language learning. *Journal of Computer Assisted Learning, 38*(1), 237–257. DOI: 10.1111/jcal.12610

Jomaa, N. J. (2025). *Corrective Feedback of AI Tools in Writing and Translation.*, DOI: 10.4018/979-8-3693-9511-0.ch010

Khan, T., Emon, M. M. H., Rahman, M. A., Hamid, A. B. A., & Yaakub, N. I. (2025). Bridging the Gap: Realizing GreenTech Potential. In *AI and Green Technology Applications in Society* (pp. 91–122). IGI Global Scientific Publishing. DOI: 10.4018/979-8-3693-9879-1.ch004

Khan, T., Emon, M. M. H., & Rahman, S. (2024). Marketing Strategy Innovation via AI Adoption: A Study on Bangladeshi SMEs in the Context of Industry 5.0. *2024 6th International Conference on Sustainable Technologies for Industry 5.0 (STI)*, 1–6. DOI: 10.1109/STI64222.2024.10951050

Khan, T., & Hasan Emon, M. M. (2024). Determinants of AI Image Generator Adoption Among Marketing Agencies: The Mediating Effects of Perceived Usefulness. *2024 IEEE 3rd International Conference on Robotics, Automation, Artificial-Intelligence and Internet-of-Things (RAAICON)*, 177–182. DOI: 10.1109/RAAICON64172.2024.10928548

Komljenovic, J. (2021). The rise of education rentiers: Digital platforms, digital data and rents. *Learning, Media and Technology*, *46*(3), 320–332. DOI: 10.1080/17439884.2021.1891422

Kuddus, K. (2022). Artificial Intelligence in Language Learning: Practices and Prospects. In *Advanced Analytics and Deep Learning Models* (pp. 1–17). Wiley. DOI: 10.1002/9781119792437.ch1

Levi, E. I. (2024). *Technology in Lifelong Language Learning*., DOI: 10.4018/979-8-3693-1410-4.ch012

Liu, X. (2024). Online Learning Based on Learning Analytics in Big Data for College English Language Teaching. *International Journal of Computational Intelligence Systems*, *17*(1), 192. DOI: 10.1007/s44196-024-00594-6

Luczaj, K., Leonowicz-Bukala, I., & Kurek-Ochmanska, O. (2022). English as a lingua franca? The limits of everyday English-language communication in Polish academia. *English for Specific Purposes*, *66*, 3–16. DOI: 10.1016/j.esp.2021.11.002

Luo, B. (2020). The influence of teaching learning techniques on students' long-term learning behavior. *Computer Assisted Language Learning*, *33*(4), 388–412. DOI: 10.1080/09588221.2019.1567557

Marzuki, W., Widiati, U., Rusdin, D., Darwin, , & Indrawati, I. (2023). The impact of AI writing tools on the content and organization of students' writing: EFL teachers' perspective. *Cogent Education*, *10*(2), 2236469. Advance online publication. DOI: 10.1080/2331186X.2023.2236469

Mazur, J., & Serafin, M. (2023). Stalling the State: How Digital Platforms Contribute to and Profit From Delays in the Enforcement and Adoption of Regulations. *Comparative Political Studies*, *56*(1), 101–130. DOI: 10.1177/00104140221089651

Meirbekov, A., Nyshanova, S., Meiirbekov, A., Kazykhankyzy, L., Burayeva, Z., & Abzhekenova, B. (2024). Digitisation of English language education: Instagram and TikTok online educational blogs and courses vs. traditional academic education. How to increase student motivation? *Education and Information Technologies*, *29*(11), 13635–13662. DOI: 10.1007/s10639-023-12396-y

Meng, X., Yang, B., Yang, L., Zhang, J., & Liu, Y. (2025). A Novel AI-Empowered, Student-Centered Teaching Strategy for Large Classes in Higher Education. *International Journal of Science and Mathematics Education*. Advance online publication. DOI: 10.1007/s10763-025-10573-8

Miller, J. A., & Cooper, S. (2021). Case Studies in Game-Based Complex Learning. *Multimodal Technologies and Interaction*, *5*(12), 72. DOI: 10.3390/mti5120072

Nguyen, A., Ngo, H. N., Hong, Y., Dang, B., & Nguyen, B.-P. T. (2023). Ethical principles for artificial intelligence in education. *Education and Information Technologies, 28*(4), 4221–4241. DOI: 10.1007/s10639-022-11316-w PMID: 36254344

Nkadimeng, M., & Ankiewicz, P. (2022). The Affordances of Minecraft Education as a Game-Based Learning Tool for Atomic Structure in Junior High School Science Education. *Journal of Science Education and Technology, 31*(5), 605–620. DOI: 10.1007/s10956-022-09981-0

Phillips Galloway, E., McClain, J. B., & Uccelli, P. (2020). Broadening the Lens on the Science of Reading: A Multifaceted Perspective on the Role of Academic Language in Text Understanding. *Reading Research Quarterly, 55*(S1). Advance online publication. DOI: 10.1002/rrq.359

R'boul, H. (2024). English medium instruction in Moroccan universities: Implications for multilingualism, linguistic dependency and epistemic justice. *Journal of Multilingual and Multicultural Development, 45*(7), 2770–2784. DOI: 10.1080/01434632.2022.2069250

Ruan, S., Jiang, L., Xu, Q., Liu, Z., Davis, G. M., Brunskill, E., & Landay, J. A. (2021). EnglishBot: An AI-Powered Conversational System for Second Language Learning. *26th International Conference on Intelligent User Interfaces*, 434–444. DOI: 10.1145/3397481.3450648

Shahri, N., & Karizmeh, M. S. (2025). Inventing a Language Online: The Practice of Edutainment in English Teaching Instagram Posts. *International Journal of Applied Linguistics, 35*(2), 756–767. DOI: 10.1111/ijal.12645

Shen, H., DeVos, A., Eslami, M., & Holstein, K. (2021). Everyday Algorithm Auditing: Understanding the Power of Everyday Users in Surfacing Harmful Algorithmic Behaviors. *Proceedings of the ACM on Human-Computer Interaction, 5*(CSCW2), 1–29. DOI: 10.1145/3479577

Singh, H., Chauhan, U., Chauhan, S. P. S., Saxena, A., & Kumari, P. (2024). *Adaptive and Personalized Learning in Industry 5.0 Education* (pp. 1–19). DOI: 10.4018/979-8-3693-0782-3.ch001

Sosa Díaz, M. J. (2021). Emergency Remote Education, Family Support and the Digital Divide in the Context of the COVID-19 Lockdown. *International Journal of Environmental Research and Public Health, 18*(15), 7956. DOI: 10.3390/ijerph18157956 PMID: 34360248

Toseeb, U., Gibson, J. L., Newbury, D. F., Orlik, W., Durkin, K., Pickles, A., & Conti-Ramsden, G. (2020). Play and prosociality are associated with fewer externalizing problems in children with developmental language disorder: The role of early language and communication environment. *International Journal of Language & Communication Disorders, 55*(4), 583–602. DOI: 10.1111/1460-6984.12541 PMID: 32497383

Xu, W., & Ouyang, F. (2022). A systematic review of AI role in the educational system based on a proposed conceptual framework. *Education and Information Technologies, 27*(3), 4195–4223. DOI: 10.1007/s10639-021-10774-y

Yağcı, M. (2022). Educational data mining: Prediction of students' academic performance using machine learning algorithms. *Smart Learning Environments, 9*(1), 11. DOI: 10.1186/s40561-022-00192-z

York, E. J. (2021). Digital surveillance in online writing instruction: Panopticism and simulation in learning management systems. *Computers and Composition, 62*, 102680. DOI: 10.1016/j.compcom.2021.102680

Yuan, Y. (2024). An empirical study of the efficacy of AI chatbots for English as a foreign language learning in primary education. *Interactive Learning Environments, 32*(10), 6774–6789. DOI: 10.1080/10494820.2023.2282112

Zhang, J., & Zhang, L. J. (2024). The effect of feedback on metacognitive strategy use in EFL writing. *Computer Assisted Language Learning, 37*(5–6), 1198–1223. DOI: 10.1080/09588221.2022.2069822

Zhang, Y. (2024). A lesson study on a MOOC-based and AI-powered flipped teaching and assessment of EFL writing model: Teachers' and students' growth. *International Journal for Lesson & Learning Studies, 13*(1), 28–40. DOI: 10.1108/IJLLS-07-2023-0085

Zheng, C., Zhang, T., Chen, X., Zhang, H., Wan, J., & Wu, B. (2024). Assessing learners' English public speaking anxiety with multimodal deep learning technologies. *Computer Assisted Language Learning*, •••, 1–29. DOI: 10.1080/09588221.2024.2351129

Zheng, Y., Wang, Y., Liu, K. S.-X., & Jiang, M. Y.-C. (2024). Examining the moderating effect of motivation on technology acceptance of generative AI for English as a foreign language learning. *Education and Information Technologies, 29*(17), 23547–23575. DOI: 10.1007/s10639-024-12763-3

KEY TERMS AND DEFINITIONS

Artificial Intelligence (AI): An area of computer science that studies the creation of machines that can perform tasks which normally would be performed by human beings, such as understanding language and problem-solving.

Chatbots: Intelligent machine agents that can interact automatically in real-time with users using normal human communication.

Content Curation: Procedure of organizing and transforming educational content according to a learner's preferences, interest, or skill.

English Language Teaching (ELT): The approach to how non-native English speakers are taught using a key focus on developing skills in speaking, reading, writing and listening.

Gamification: Using the elements and principles of game design, within non-game space areas, such as education, to design immersive and motivation-increasing interactive and competitive learning environments.

Natural Language Processing (NLP): AI research field aimed at making machines up to processing, analyzing, and generating human language, more commonly used in speech recognition, analysis domain.

Personalized Learning: Adapting educational tools and strategies to the individual specific ability and need of the students with reference to their learning styles is possible due to the use of AI systems.

Social Media: Digital spaces that allow users to make, post, connect to content to facilitate conversation and collaborate, such as Facebook, Instagram, and Twitter.

Chapter 8
AI as a Teaching Assistant:
A Practical Guide for English Educators

Vivit Rosmayanti
https://orcid.org/0000-0002-3648-9878
Universitas Negeri Makassar, Indonesia

ABSTRACT

AI integration in education has revolutionized traditional learning methods, offering new tools for English teachers. This chapter, "AI as a Teaching Assistant: A Practical Guide for English Educators," provides an in-depth overview of AI tools and their applications, including lesson planning, personalized learning, real-time feedback, and student engagement activities. It uses practical examples and case studies to illustrate how AI can simplify administrative tasks, address diverse learners' needs, and promote interactive learning environments. The chapter also addresses challenges like technical accessibility, pedagogical balance, and ethical issues like data privacy and algorithmic bias. It offers actionable strategies for meaningful AI integration, allowing educators to see AI as an opportunity for collaborative partnership in the teaching process. The final chapter envisions a future where AI supports inclusivity, creativity, and innovation in English education.

INTRODUCTION

Artificial intelligence (AI) has become a need for change in education, and it has changed the learning and teaching approaches in various fields of education, such as English Language Teaching (ELT). AI refers to machines that can learn

DOI: 10.4018/979-8-3373-1952-0.ch008

and act like humans without human intervention (Chen et al., 2022). The term is an umbrella term for different technologies, such as natural language processing, pattern recognition, or data analysis. Specifically, AI serves as a personalized learning experiences facilitator, a teaching methodologies enhancer, and an administrative support provider for educators in education (Ahmad et al., 2022). In a modern and globalized world where information access is no longer a problem, using more efficient and effective educational practices that can meet the needs of diverse learners has made it necessary for educators to insert AI into their classrooms (Pratama, 2023).

An example of an AI application in which both personalized feedback and support are given to learners through intelligent tutoring systems and chatbots, but interactions are primarily in an education context (Adıgüzel et al., 2023). Additionally, AI technologies have played a significant role in tackling the hardships of remote learning, especially during the COVID-19 pandemic when teachers have had to adapt to a new learning paradigm (Ng et al., 2023). AI's capability to process immense quantities of data creates personalized learning, allowing teachers to adjust their teaching methods to fit the unique needs of every student (Li & Wong, 2023). Furthermore, research suggests that introducing AI-assisted tools improves learning outcomes (Barua et al., 2022), highlighting their acceptability, feasibility, and implementation in learning environments.

This chapter aims to highlight the role of AI as a teaching assistant and offer examples of how AI can be integrated seamlessly with English educators. However, like any other fast-developing technology, AI might have disadvantages. Therefore, this chapter serves the purpose of preparing English educators with the understanding and resources that enable them to leverage the potential of AI to enrich their pedagogy and support and promote student engagement and learning (Liu, 2023). This chapter illustrates how the use of AI in ELT is practical but practical in the context of best practices that enable integration; therefore, it highlights best practices by focusing on personalized learning, adaptive assessment, and interactive learning environment basics (Luo, 2024).

Moreover, the chapter provides insights into AI's opportunities and challenges and delves into them. Still, it includes mitigating biases in AI systems and ensuring transparency and accountability in their use (George, 2023). While educators are left to decipher the specific AI dynamics, ensuring equity and access for students – especially those with diverse learning needs – is critical (Shirin, 2022). AI tools have the potential to complement traditional language instruction and support a more personalized and efficient approach to learning, fostering creativity and critical thinking away from the one-size-fits-all, as well as helping students individually reach their goals (Aithal, 2023).

In short, the opportunities presented by AI for English Language Teaching are vast and many. This chapter details AI as a teacher assistant and provides practical ways educators can apply AI . Navigating AI: Empowering English Educators for the Future English educators need to be prepared to interact with the minimal AI programming and interactivity that we discuss in this exploration and the underlying impact that had on dialogue through this exploration.

UNDERSTANDING AI IN LANGUAGE TEACHING

2.1. What is an AI as a Teaching Assistant?

With the advent of the age of Artificial Intelligence (AI), it has become a significant catalyst (Teaching Assistant) that can be used in the process of K-12 English Language Teaching (ELT) and learning both Teaching and Learning Management. AI tools have been developed with different features to help language learners and educators meet their specific needs. Such tools use sophisticated technologies, including natural language processing (NLP), machine learning, and speech recognition, to deliver personalized and adaptive learning experiences (Gyawali, 2022). AI can help innovate and enhance English learning and teaching by aiming to improve teaching tasks, learning objectives, and pedagogical practices (Lee, 2024).

Grammar correction is one of the main jobs of AI tools in ELT. AI can instantly analyze written text, identifying and suggesting grammatical errors. This instant feedback mechanism is critical to learners, giving them an instantaneous understanding of their mistakes and a chance to learn (Liu, 2023). For instance, Fitria (2021) mentioned in his research that tools like Grammarly use advanced algorithms to give users insights into their writing, helping them improve their grammatical accuracy and writing skills.

Apart from correcting grammar, AI tools can provide real-time feedback on multiple elements of the language, such as pronunciation and vocabulary use. Technology facilitates interaction through tools such as speech recognition, allowing learners to speak and get feedback on their pronunciation (Y. Wu, 2024). This function benefits non-native speakers by enabling them to practice their speaking skills while still being confident. In addition, these AI-based applications could analyze vocabulary, offer alternatives, and spread their lexical data, providing diverse vocabulary usage for learners (Akbarani, 2024). Through instant feedback, students can use and explore language with a risk-taking attitude, leading to a more interactive and engaging learning experience (Nguyen, 2024).

AI tools also have a significant role in creating personalized lessons according to the learner's specific needs. AI tools can process a learner's past performance data and modify the difficulty of the tasks they are assigned (Idham, 2024). This condition allows students to avoid being demotivated by complex material or bored by too-easy material, keeping them engaged simultaneously (Maqsood, 2024). For instance, intelligent tutoring systems (ITS) can offer personalized routes for learners, enabling them to participate in customized exercises that support their learning needs based on specific learning goals and competence levels (Gyawali, 2022). Such customization is especially beneficial in diverse classrooms with varying levels of language proficiency and learning styles among students.

Additionally, AI tools can promote collaborative learning by encouraging students to interact with one another. AI-integrated platforms can design virtual worlds where learners converse, exchange resources, and work on their projects together, regardless of their geographical locations (Luo, 2024). This collaborative aspect of the platform not only enhances the learning experience but equips students with skills for real-world scenarios, where teamwork and collaboration are vital components of successful tactics in various fields of life (Cantos, 2023). AI tools mitigate this issue by helping create a sense of community among other learners, which is a more comprehensive approach to language learning.

However, AI tools do not quite grasp context nuances like a human teacher would (Khan, 2023). The lack of context can lead to interpreting a learner's intentions inaccurately or incorrectly during nuanced language usage, and combining an AI tool reliance on top of that will only make things worse. Additionally, excessive reliance on AI tools will prevent the acquisition of advanced thinking skills such as critical thinking and problem-solving since students are used to receiving answers without any critical cognitive effort (Y. Wu, 2024). However, that lies upon the educators- it is their responsibility to strike a balance between AI tool usage and facilitating critical thinking skills.

2.2. Types of AI Tools for English Language Teaching

Artificial Intelligence (AI) has been integrated into English Language Teaching (ELT), and several AI tools have been created to assist students in the learning process and to support educators in the teaching process. Types of AI Tools That Can Be Used for Learning, Such As 1. Language learning applications (e.g., Duolingo) 2.Virtual tutoring and chatbots (e.g., ChatGPT) 3. Speech recognition and pronunciation tools (e.g., SpeechAce) 4. AI-driven assessment and feedback tools (e.g., Turnitin). These three groups contribute significantly to L2 development and teaching.

2.2.1. AI-Powered Language Apps

Grammarly and Duolingo are two language apps famous for their AI-powered capabilities for learners and educators. These applications employ sophisticated algorithms to create custom learning experiences, allowing users to learn and practice at their own pace. One utilization of this approach is Duolingo, which uses gamification strategies to captivate learners through short lessons customized to conversion history and proficiency (Vadivel, 2023). Studies show that using such applications helps students perform better on their language skill tests (Yuen, 2024). Additionally, these applications tend to suit various learning styles, which enhances the inclusivity of language teaching (Vadivel, 2023).

Conversely, Grammarly is all about writing skills, as it offers real-time grammar and style corrections. Notably, this tool catches errors and provides explanations and suggestions for improvement, thus promoting a more profound comprehension of language mechanics (Pipiras et al., 2019). As learners can instantly identify and fix errors in real-time (Jiao et al., 2021), the immediate feedback generated through these applications is one of its core advantages that not only encourages enthusiasm in learners but also helps enhance their writing skills. In addition, mobile apps allow students to practice language skills anywhere and at any time, increasing language accessibility and flexibility (Alsanousi, 2023).

2.2.2. Chat GPT: Virtual Tutors and Chatbots

Other key types of AI tools in ELT are virtual tutors & chatbots. For instance, AI-based systems like ChatGPT can interact with learners through an engaging dialogue, offering answers to queries and practicing the language (Baido-anu, 2023). The humanlike interaction capabilities of chatbots enable learners to effectively practice their conversational skills in a low-stakes environment, which can be especially useful for individuals with speaking Anxiety (Lou, 2024). Furthermore, chatbots can be configured to offer direct feedback customized to the users' RSVP feedback, which increases the adequacy of this learning pattern (S. Wang, 2022).

Chatbots are also used in language learning to explain complicated grammatical structures or the use of vocabulary, acting as a resource (Baido-anu, 2023). Students can now access information from various sources, allowing them to take ownership of their learning and clarify their doubts when necessary, creating a more self-paced learning environment (Yuen, 2024). Moreover, chatbot technology in learning environments provides opportunities for collaborative learning by encouraging students to interact with each other to practice language (Saputra et al., 2020).

2.2.3. Speech Recognition and Pronunciation Tools

Learners' communication skills, pronunciation, and practice have been remarkably enhanced due to advancements in speech recognition technology. Caller for education, Edu speak, and PLASER are examples of such tools that learners have to cross-reference with these speech patterns as opposed to the previously used technology. Wang (2022) noted that such tools assess spoken language and model it against standard pronunciation so that learners can change their speaking style. On the other hand, thinking about tools allows such learners to have an interactive opportunity to use the software by providing advanced editing and even allowing students to speak and use the language immediately (Alsanousi, 2023). In recent times, much advancement in this field has resulted in fast-emerging algorithms that enroll speech grading and speech identifying with great accuracy, helping language learners greatly. As a result, the integration of speech recognition in the teaching processes of learners gives them an upper hand in learning how to speak and feel more and more relaxed in using the language (Jiao et al., 2021).

2.2.4. AI-Powered Assessment Software

Lastly, the assessment tools powered by AI also take up a significant portion of the ELT AI toolset. This platform implements advanced analytics techniques using algorithms to evaluate student assessments and provide personalized responses. Moreover, there are tasks of employing ASR (automatic speech recognition) systems to measure students' oral skills by analyzing pronunciation, fluency, and coherence (Lou, 2024). This method uses metrics to identify the domains where learners lag and modify the teaching support accordingly (Alqaralleh et al., 2022).

PRACTICAL IMPLICATION OF AI IN ENGLISH TEACHING

AI in English language teaching strategies, lesson preparation, and technology integration The integration of AI in English language teaching paraphernalia, such as AI sites, is growing—AI tools for lesson planning. With the help of some AI tools, lesson materials, quizzes, and activities can be efficiently prepared, which is a huge plus when designing a curriculum and aligning it with learning objectives. This section examines how these technologies could help teachers practice classroom activities.

3.1. AI for Lesson Planning and Material Generation

Lesson Planning and Material Generation AI can tremendously assist educators with lesson planning and material generation – two of the most pertinent advantages of AI in ELT. AI tools can scan large amounts of available educational data and develop personalized lesson plans that follow learning goals and students' needs (Gyawali, 2022). Various tools like ChatGPT can get lesson plan structures, activities, and quizzes to fit the curriculum (Hashem, 2023). Such systems save time for educators and help ensure the materials produced are relevant and engaging for all learners, McCarthy writes, because they get updated with content gleaned from across the internet.

Additionally, AI can be used to generate learning resources that meet the needs of a range of students. AI tools make recommendations for personalized resources and activities tailored to each learner's level of proficiency through the analysis of individual student's performance data (Jeong, 2022). AI increases the learning process as personalized learning helps students spend time on appropriate learning materials concerning their existing skills and knowledge in 2024 (Karina, 2024). AI also allows educators to recognize gaps in student understanding, from which an intervention can be performed promptly and additional support can be provided (Hashem, 2023)

3.1.1. AI in Curriculum Design and Alignment

AI can significantly assist in designing curricula and their proper alignment with the outcomes of needed competencies. Analytics can also assist in analyzing how effective current curricular offerings are by shifting through student performance databases and suggesting various changes (Baskara, 2023). This approach that relies on statistics enables the instructors and the management responsible for the institution to evaluate the required changes in the curriculum to meet the stated targets of successful learning so that the learners are in a position to achieve the set learning goals and undertake the required tests (Klímová et al., 2023).

Also, AI assists in bringing the content of any examined curriculum into compliance with educational guidelines and frameworks. For instance, by employing natural language processing coupled with machine learning algorithms, AI tools can analyze curricular documents and recognize areas of contradiction or inconsistency between curriculum parts and the desired targets (Luo, 2024). This makes it particularly beneficial for an exercise that needs to be tailor-made for the relevant and sets to remain relevant in the ever-evolving educational landscape and the needs of society, more importantly, the students (Derakhshan & Nazari, 2024).

3.1.2. Reducing Manual Work

AI's potential to automate administrative tasks is another significant advantage of this technology for educators. AI can free up teachers' time by giving them back hours lost to everyday tasks like grading and feedback so that teachers can use time on instructional activities, student engagement, or professional development (Hashem, 2023). AI-powered assessment platforms, for instance, can analyze student submissions and offer instant feedback, empowering students to identify their areas for improvement without delay (Akbarani, 2024). Such contributes to learning and creates a more communicative and nurturing classroom environment.

Additionally, AI can streamline communication between educators and students by relaying timely information about assignments, assessments, and learning materials (Jiang, 2022). This facilitates communication to ensure organized learning, keeping teachers and students updated with material on the go.

3.1.3. Boosting Student Engagement and Motivation

As for lesson planning and curriculum design, AI can also increase student engagement and motivation. The aptitude of educators to use these interactive and adaptive learning technologies leads to dynamic learning experiences that can interest students (Triyoga, 2018). AI-based platforms can provide gamified learning exercises, stimulating students to participate actively in their learning (Arafah & Kaharuddin, 2019). Students enjoy learning more and take ownership of their learning path using this method.

AI can also offer personalized learning pathways that adjust to individual student progress, ensuring that learners are constantly challenged and engaged (Sheng, 2023). Personalizing education at such a grain is vital in diverse classes where learners' proficiency and learning styles differ (Ghafar et al., 2023). AI helps create a more inclusive and personalized learning environment where every learner receives the attention they deserve and is only able to do so if they leverage AI to make customized learning experiences

3.1.4. Challenges and Considerations

While AI has many benefits when creating lesson plans and setting up a curriculum, educators must face challenges and concerns. New technologies may have an over-reliance on making room for writing programs that leave little space for human educators to intervene during the teaching process (Laurel et al., 2021). Teachers must balance AI technology with meaningful, close student engagement (Fitria, 2021). Additionally, educators need to be cautious about the ethical ramifications of AI systems in education, especially regarding data protection & security (Tiwari, 2024). A responsible and transparent use of student data is essential to prevent any erosion of trust between the student and the educational process.

3.2. Personalized Learning Support

The new interest devoted to Artificial Intelligence AI for English Language Teaching enhances personalized learning support for technology-enhanced environments and on-the-spot assistance by quite a few degrees. Such tools adjust to the needs of every student by utilizing advanced technology and data to increase the student's learning achievements. Such systems analyze student performance metrics, learning styles, and preferences and build a learning model for these students that would best fit them (Z. Zhang, 2024). For instance, a deep-based learning technology platform could give students more control over their tasks, which are best suited to their developmental level. Challenging learners at the most suitable level helps them overcome the hurdles and motivates them, thus improving their understanding of the language as they become more engaged.

These adaptive learning platforms provide a promising learning environment, but providing real-time feedback and making error analysis is also a part of the learning experience and one in English Language Teaching ELT. AI-assisted technologies help students improve their writing and speaking by offering instant feedback that allows them to identify and rectify errors during the task. Jiao et al. (2021) claim that, for instance, automatic speech recognition tools have proven to be very helpful in the learners' speech skill enhancement since they can detect pronunciation mistakes and provide assistance with them. These systems can analyze speech patterns and provide feedback to students on aspects that need to be improved, promoting a more engaging and adaptive learning experience (Lou, 2024). Additionally, there is an incorporation of machine learning algorithms that enable these tools to personalize feedback according to the individual's specific learning style, making sure that it is not only timely but also relevant and constructive (Z. Zhang, 2024). These AI language software develop an essential feedback loop to ensure that the learners can take ownership of what they learn because they are interactive and do not need help to improve their learning from any external source, and this is where it differs from traditional learning.

Even for writing skills, we can use AI for error analysis, similar to pronunciation. Grammatical accuracy, coherence, and style can be analyzed using AI-powered writing assistants, which provide proposals for improvement on the go (Parmaxi & Demetriou, 2020). Such an ability is beneficial for enhancing educational tools for students who often battle nuances with these grammar nuances, such as in the case of language learning. These tools utilize in-depth error analysis and corrective suggestions to increase the ability of learners to improve their writing skills and become proficient writers (Jiao et al., 2021). Having instant feedback on writing assignments enhances the learning experience. It instills confidence in students since they can observe concrete efforts to improve their language skills with time.

The impact of AI-driven personalized learning assistance is transformative, leading to a more inclusive and effective classroom environment. Adaptive learning platforms and real-time feedback mechanisms bridge the gap between different proficiency levels and distinct learning styles by catering to the diverse needs of learners (Z. Zhang, 2024). Adjustability plays a considerable role in multilingual classrooms, given that students come from diverse backgrounds and have different experiences with the English language. Additionally, AI technologies in language learning foster a culture of continuous improvement, as learners are motivated to interact with the material and explore avenues for self-enhancement (Lou, 2024).

However, we also acknowledge that using AI in personalized learning support has challenges. However, these online tools have challenges, such as data protection and dependence on the developed systems (Fathurrahman et al., 2023). AI must supplement traditional teaching as the most important human aspect of teaching cannot be conquered by intelligent tools. Integrating education technology must aim to balance this with meaningful engagement between both student and teacher, as optimizing education requires the right blend of interaction processed by both pupil and teacher (S. Wang, 2022).

3.3. Engaging Classroom Activities

Classroom activities are essential for creating interaction and dynamism in ELT (English Language Teaching). The advent of AI-driven games and simulations has proven to be one of the most effective methods to heighten students' interest while encouraging engagement and problem-based learning. With such technologies, students get to experience their training in IM learning, where they can practice their languages in an immersive way. AI language games, for example, can tailor their pace to each student, increasing or decreasing the challenges provided to them based on their poll (individualization). Such adaptations not only maintain students' engagement but also give them space to take risks and play around with using their target language in a low-stakes environment (T. Wu, 2024). Luke (2021) states that participation in interactive acts improves students in meaningful practice beyond rote learning.

Plus, role-playing and storytelling tools (primarily virtual) in the learning processes even more immerse students in authentic communicative situations. For instance, digital storytelling allows learners to create and share narratives using multimedia elements, including images, audio, and video. This method fosters creativity and promotes critical thinking and cooperation among students (Maruf, 2023). IRL storytelling is a great way to practice speaking and writing while engaged with something they love that is relevant to them. Research indicates that digital storytelling can enhance language skills significantly since the students are journeying to express their feelings and ideas with new vocabulary and newly learned grammatical forms (Belda-Medina, 2024). As many students learn from each other and become more confident (Kallinikou & Nicolaidou, 2019), the collaborative nature of storytelling projects enhances peer interaction, a critical element in language learning.

These fun activities employ AI in the classroom, providing real-time feedback and assessment, which is very important for language studies. For example, platforms driven by AI might analyze how students performed during games and simulations, offering immediate feedback on their use of language and recommendations for where the learner should improve. So this immediate feedback loop doesn't allow students to understand where they are, more substantial and weaker, and forces them to introspect about their learning and tweaking. Moreover, the ongoing tracking of progress empowers educational professionals to customize their instruction in alignment with the dynamic requirements of their students, ensuring that every student receives the necessary assistance they need to thrive (Sabari & Hashim, 2023).

In addition, integrating ELT with virtual environments has improved students' intercultural communicative and linguistic competence. Learners access various cultural grounds and can adopt role-playing simulations in this realistic environment (Y. Wu, 2024). His exposure to varied perspectives enriches their language learning experience and prepares them for real-world communication, where cultural nuances come into play. Students learn empathy, adaptability, and critical thinking as they traverse these digital spaces — all skills we need even more in an interconnected world (Leong et al., 2019).

While there are countless advantages of AI games, simulations, and storytelling tools, educators cannot overlook the challenges that may come with their use. For example, the technologies' effectiveness often depends on how engaging they are for students (Guadaña, 2021). AI poorly designed activities may fall short of engaging students properly, resulting in disengagement and reduced learning outcomes. Predictions or projections related to AI in education should be made regarding AI tools and their impacts. If so, educators should treat these tools intentionally when implementing them into students' learning processes to cover the learning objectives and meet the diverse students' needs (Gurrieri & Drenten, 2019).

3.4. Enhancing Student-Teacher Interaction

Linking AI in learning to improve communication among students and teachers over collaborative assignments will be a helpful aspect of education and automation of administrative work. As collaborative projects are ones where students work together to find solutions, AI is an enabler that creates ways to collaborate better, irrespective of where they are located. Recommended Sentence: AI-based educational platforms, for example, can facilitate students' collaboration in real-time, enabling them to carry out group work, exchange resources, and communicate seamlessly (Niu et al., 2022). Collaboration encourages critical thinking and problem-solving as students learn to work together and understand different perspectives to achieve a common objective. Studies show that collaborative projects supported by Artificial Intelligence can positively influence learning outcomes, as students feel more engaged and motivated while completing significant tasks working together (Seo et al., 2021).

In addition, AI can automate administrative tasks like attendance, grading, etc., thus saving educators time and effort. Machine Learning-based assignment and assessment grading systems automatically assess student submissions and provide instant student feedback (George, 2023). Not only does this free up teacher time, but it also allows students to receive feedback early in the process so they can correct their performance. The AI used for this efficiently saves valuable time on educators' administrative duties instead of spending on instructional strategy and student engagement (Dai et al., 2023). AI systems can also be utilized for attendance and participation monitoring and provide data for educators regarding their teaching strategies and students in need (H. Zhang, 2024).

While AI streamlines administrative tasks, it also impacts the quality of communication between educators and learners. AI-based tools can enable personalized engagement by collecting and analyzing student data to generate insights into individual learning preferences and needs (Tew et al., 2022). This allows educators to customize and address each student's specific challenges. Data analysis relating to the spectrum of the dataset can assist educators in recognizing patterns in students' performance for proactive intervention should a learner be struggling (Huang, 2021). Leveraging such data-driven insights creates a more responsive and supportive learning environment where students feel valued and understood.

Moreover, AI in education also brings virtual teaching assistants that improve student learning. These AI-powered assistants can answer questions instantly, suggest supplementary materials, and facilitate conversations to enrich the learning experience (Maqbool et al., 2021). Again, the mere presence of these assistants in the classroom will exercise students' initiative in their learning, as their support is available whenever needed. Transitioning to a more student-centered approach not only empowers the impulse from students but also allows teachers to develop stronger student-teacher relationships by permitting more time to focus on building student context for learning (Falebita, 2024).

It is essential to recognize and understand the challenges faced with integrating AI into academic environments. By posing a threat to the trust in and engagement of students in learning activities, concerns regarding the reliability and transparency of AI systems can hinder their usual integration (Koh et al., 2022). Particularly in the context of the black box, the activity is a source of uncertainty and anxiety for students to turn to AI for feedback or help (Seo et al., 2021). So, educators must keep lines of communication open with their students, aligning on any concerns and providing context on the role of AI tools in the classroom. This approach will allow students to overcome their initial fear of AI, and educators will work closely with learners to accept the tailored innovations of AI as learning mapping tools.

CASE STUDIES AND REAL-WORLD APPLICATION

4.1. Incorporating AI for writing improvement in higher education

AI is often integrated within higher education, particularly in improving writing. Throughout this period, AI tools, such as ChatGPT and different automated writing evaluation systems, have claimed to support students in their writing processes by giving personalized feedback and promoting critical thinking. With the data available up to October 2023, this case study looks at the use of AI in enhancing writing skills and its applications in higher education.

Among the most notable advantages of AI in writing instructions is its prompt feedback on student writing. GPT-based AI assistants (e.g., Smart RoamLingo) provide example sentences and writing feedback to help students actively improve their essay content (Hwang et al., 2023). This offers essential immediate attention that helps learners immediately notice, reflect, and correct errors, contributing to grammatical accuracy and investment in vocabulary and writing quality. Examples of writing support in AI tools can be identified, such as paragraph and essay generators, grammar/emoji checkers, etc., which have been reported to have a positive impact on students' output with noticeable advancements in cohesion, consistency, and structural coherence (Minh, 2024). Moreover, AI-based platforms used in the classroom give students unprecedented freedom to tinker with their writing, enabling them to experiment with various styles and forms and receive coaching on their efforts (Nazari, 2022).

In addition, using AI in writing instruction has challenged teachers to address pedagogical approaches in new ways. Indeed, as Wang points out, there is an urgent need for pedagogical innovation and policy change in response to the potential impact of AI on student learning outcomes (C. Wang, 2024). In this way, the integration of practices of critical digital pedagogy into our writing instruction can help guide students in engaging with AI technologies critically (or at least just more effectively), allowing them to deepen their academic literacies. Such an approach not only enables students to use AI tools successfully but also teaches students at a deeper level about the writing process (C. Wang, 2024).

So, beyond giving feedback, AI tools can enable students to create collaborative writing projects. By implementing AI-powered platforms, students can collaborate on writing assignments, exchange resources, and provide peer feedback in real-time (Nazari et al., 2021). In addition, collaborative learning techniques foster collaboration, engagement, and teamwork, with students sharing and creating together, thereby improving critical life skills through drama and role-play communication. This provides a richer approach to writing and an opportunity for students to build upon each other's ideas with AI-assisted assembly of their written content (Nazari, 2022).

On the other hand, the application of AI in writing instruction is associated with multiple challenges. One of the main issues is the credibility and reliability of the content produced by AI, which has already been questioned in many studies focusing on academic writing. Although AI tools may generate various pieces of text, the quality of the output text may not meet the rigorous standards of academic writing. In this regard, Dergaa et al. (2023) argue that introducing AI to the educational process would stimulate educators to propose a new approach to writing assignments, necessitating students to apply critical thinking and problem-solving that AI is incapable of. These changes are crucial to ensure students acquire the skills to address the multi-layered academic writing process that emerged with AI assistance.

4.2. Using AI chatbots for vocabulary and conversational practice.

Using AI chatbots in language learning is a game-changing method to teach students vocabulary and encourage conversation practice. This study examines the use of AI chatbots in higher education, specifically their role in enhancing students' language learning experiences. AI chatbots can help students improve their vocabulary skills and conversational fluency by allowing students to have immediate and personalized interactions with them.

Interactive AI chatbots like this proceed with grammar and vocabulary practice on specific topics, making it one of the best language practice apps. Web page translation: These chatbots can simulate real-life conversations, permitting students to apply new vocabulary in context. For example, Hoang conducted a study that showed conversational chatbot design provides students with a narrow but corrective set of responses that makes it easier for students to control the conversation flow than human interlocutors (Hoang, 2023). That structured interaction allows learners to concentrate on their speech without the stress they might feel trying to chat with a native speaker. This helps build students' confidence in their language skills since they can practice their vocabulary and pronunciation within a safe space.

Additionally, artificial intelligence chatbots support personalized learning, where the user conditions follow the students'. Chatbots can serve a more personal function by answering questions about the topic, providing rationale, and explaining vocabulary (Baskara, 2023). This personalization allows students to move through language material at their own pace, reinforce their vocabulary knowledge, and practice conversing in a way that aligns with their individual learning goals. The efficacy of language learning with chatbots is further enhanced by their ability to tailor lessons according to their proficiency levels and learning styles, providing targeted practice that meets the learners' specific shortcomings.

Beyond just vocabulary practice, AI chatbots can support conversational practice, where students have conversations that mirror those in real-life scenarios. Qasem et al. conducted research that found that chatbots can be used as interactive tools to improve students' ESP vocabulary (Qasem et al., 2023). Synonyms and context-based meanings added to the response help students grow their vocabulary while using these as conversation practice. By emphasizing vocabulary and conversational skills, the platform enables learners to gain a broader understanding of language in different scenarios, which is crucial for effective communication.

Moreover, integrating AI chatbots into language learning has also improved student motivation and engagement. Kuhail et al. . conducted a systematic review. The educational chatbots enhanced students' interaction and participation (Kuhail et al., 2022). Moreover, the gamified aspects commonly included in chatbot interactions (e.g., receiving points for completing tasks or achieving milestones) also add to students' will to interact with the learning material. This heightened interaction is vital for language learning since engaged learners are inclined to dedicate time and energy to practicing their vocabulary and speaking skills.

Yet the use of AI Chabots in language learning comes with its challenges. One worry is that students will become too dependent on speaking to chatbots, which may impair their exposure to natural language in real-life scenarios. As Tian points out, AI chatbots are helpful but should be complemented by traditional learning practices that engage humans (Tian, 2024). This is a useful balance, teaching students the social skills and cultural awareness that lead to effective and appropriate discourse in different settings.

4.3. AI-Based Tools for Assessing Pronunciation and Fluency in Speaking Exercises

Recently, the application of Artificial Intelligence (AI) to evaluate pronunciation and fluency in speaking exercises has been explored in language education and generally in English as a Foreign Language (EFL). The following article investigates the application of machine learning-based software products in education while focusing on their capability to improve pronunciation and fluency as part of the speaking assessment process. These tools harness sophisticated speech recognition technologies that give learners real-time feedback on their speaking performance, enabling focused development of their linguistic abilities.

Now, two AI tools—Google Read Along and ELSA Speak—are doing a fantastic job when it comes to enhancing the students' pronunciation. As noted by Kholis, the ELSA Speak application is said to help in articulating better, which corrects students' pronunciation. This application can use a microphone to assess the students' speaking skills and give remarks based on what the students have said (Kholis, 2021). ASR applications function that can effectively assist language learners in acquiring good pronunciation by providing instant feedback. This two-way feedback is key for language learners as it enables them to correct their pronunciation on the spot, leading to better speaking fluency (Abimanto, 2024). Also, Abimanto (2024) noted that the game-based elements of such applications also contribute to making this exercise more enjoyable, where the users are usually compensated for achieving more extraordinary lengths in accuracy. With these AI tools, you can score your speech's accuracy and improve your speech's fluency, especially while you are practicing talking forever.

Zou delved into AI speech evaluation programs' potential with a more structured speaking task, including fluency and pronunciation evaluation (Zou, 2023). Assessment techniques for spontaneous speaking tasks still need to be developed. However, AI programs provide accurate and detailed pronunciation and orthographic fluency measures such as speech rate and timing. Zou (2023) continues that learners can check their performance over time and pinpoint the aspects that require further training. Through timely feedback based on data, the students are placed in a position to influence their development in second language learning, thus empowering them more and making them responsible for their outcomes.

AI-based pronunciation and fluency evaluation systems have increased students' motivation and self-regulation. Qiao's research states that the application of AI-based instructions is much superior in enhancing students' speaking skills than the standard approaches (Qiao, 2023). Need to Maintain Student Attention Focus Maintaining: AI Tools In Education Report The responsive approach of AI tools motivates students to practice more because they can get feedback on what they need and the material they require without much difficulty. According to Qiao, such a strategy helps boost language literacy while ensuring that students become more attentive and flexible by encouraging them to be more receptive to corrections and more willing to experiment with their oratory techniques.

There are challenges that educators need to face, even with the many benefits of AI-based pronunciation and fluency assessment tools. Suppose the research goes that way, with speaking systems becoming more powerful and reliable. In that case, the focus can drift towards over-reliance on constant conversational technology, meaning that authentic speaking practice in authentic contexts, creating the right balance, can become an issue. The limitation of AI applications lies in their inability to closely mimic the intricate nature of real-life conversations filled with subtlety and cultural context (Manggiasih, 2023), although they might improve students' speaking skills. That's why teachers need to supplement the use of AI tools with the chance for students to use language in face-to-face interactions and through different kinds of communication to help facilitate the type of effective language use students will need in various contexts.

STEP BY STEP IMPLEMENTATION PLAN

There needs to be a plan that identifies the specific requirements of the classroom, picks appropriate AI tools, and evaluates the effect of these interventions on the learning environment for AI tools to be integrated effectively into a teaching-related context. As detailed in this document, the implementation strategy allows for a step-by-step assessment of classroom requirements, identification, and testing of appropriate classroom AI tools. Finally, such tools are used, and their effects on learning andteaching are assessed.

5.1. Assessing Classroom Needs

Step one in the implementation procedure is evaluating the needs of the class. To do this evaluation, teachers, students, and stakeholders should provide feedback on optimizing the learning environment, including the challenges and opportunities. To this end, qualitative and quantitative data collected through surveys, interviews, and focus groups seek to evaluate the existing teaching tools, the involvement of students, and the areas that require additional assistance in teaching through AI tools. Appreciative education leaders will possess information that deems the classroom as distinctive and, therefore, make informed judgments concerning the types of AI tools that would be suitable.

5.2. Choosing the Right AI Tools

Once classroom requirements have been identified, the M approaches have been practiced. Idiolects can be limitless. This helps narrow down the research-based approach tools that are appropriate and have been used in comparable educational settings. For example, concerning pronunciation and fluency, tools like ELSA Speak or Google Read Along might be considered as their features, for instance, are targeted in that sphere of the English language. Also, teachers should consider the interoperability of the tools they use; they can be ready in one class and other classes from other grades.

5.3. Piloting AI Interventions

After selecting appropriate AI tools, the next step is to run pilot interventions in a lab or classroom. The tools need to be tested in such settings to provide feedback on how effective the tools are in practice, i.e., for educators and students alike. During this phase, the educators should evaluate student engagement, performance, and feedback on the AI tools to check if the class's needs were met. It is suggested that educator meetings and conversations occur throughout the pilot to exchange insights and best practices for refinements and improvements.

5.4. Evaluating AI Interventions

After finishing the pilot scheme, a comprehensive analysis of the AI interventions has to be conducted to evaluate their effectiveness and whether they had any impact on the processes of sighing and learning. The analysis should incorporate both qualitative and quantitative resources, including student achievement, surveys, and responses from both teachers and learners. AI Integration tools / by pilota leaders are positioned to review the pilot data to establish whether the AI tools served the intended purpose and what further developments can be made with the tools. The evaluation methods also have to consider the ethical implications arising from using AI tools, such as data privacy concerns or prejudice against humans endemic to AI-generation sources.

5.5. Developing AI Literacy Among Educators

According to AI educators, integrating AI strategies in schools requires contradicting regulations. However, the professional growth of educators building AI literacy needs to go beyond the technical dimension of implementing ethical uses of AI in our teaching. Given the deep embedding of modern technologies in education, educational institutions must foster a continuous learning culture among educators, which is required to thoroughly prepare educators to make the most out of the opportunities offered by these technologies.

5.6. Keep Getting Better and Then Go Big

In conclusion, lauding the success of AI uptake is useless and futile unless one nourishes a culture of enhancement that would build towards taking AI to the next level. In this light, educators would need to be provided with sufficient professional resources as they learn how AI can be fitted into their practice and ensure that adaptability and innovation become intrinsic dispositions of educational cultures. If any guidelines on the use of AI tools were practical, leaders would have to devise strategies to implement this through a pilot project to be practiced in more classes, making the use of such AI-driven tools tolerable for many students. There is also a dire need for further professional development to meet the core ideals of the educational culture.

CONCLUSION

Including AI tools in English classes is one of the best ways to get more out of technology to bolster learning and maximize teacher and student engagement. This inquiry offers essential insights that help outline how AI-enhanced education can personalize learning and increase real-time feedback and collaboration. This chapter on insights and methods pragmatically deals with AI, from using AI applications to recall words, write, and converse to bringing out approaches to make AI use entirely tangible in the education sector. One must grasp that AI is not a substitute for the acquired skill of English language practice but rather a supplement that enhances existing practices. Educators can also use AI technologies for their teaching purposes by personalizing such instruction to serve the needs of different students. When AI tools are appropriately blended into the curriculum, teachers can rejuvenate learning so that it builds critical thinking, communication skills, and creativity. Undoubtedly, attending workshops and training sessions will assist teachers in gaining confidence and competence in using AI tools. Professional development activities such as these and training at workshops will indeed help the teachers. Further, fostering a community of educators will create an opportunity for sharing practices, ideas, and success stories, emphasizing the seamless integration of AI technology in the classroom. This will likely raise the general skills and knowledge level across the school.

REFERENCES

Abimanto, D., & Sumarsono, W. (2024). Improving English Pronunciation With AI Speech-Recognition Technology. *Acitya Journal of Teaching & Education*, *6*(1), 146–156. DOI: 10.30650/ajte.v6i1.3810

Adıgüzel, T., Kaya, M. H., & Cansu, F. K. (2023). Revolutionizing education with AI: Exploring the transformative potential of ChatGPT. *Contemporary Educational Technology*, *15*(3), ep429. DOI: 10.30935/cedtech/13152

Ahmad, A., Andriani, F., Mulyani, M. Y. D., Sarita, R., & Anita, R. H. (2022). The Students' Difficulties in Essay Writing During Pandemic Covid- 19 in English Language Education of Universitas Islam Riau. *J-Shmic Journal of English for Academic*, *9*(2), 81–90. DOI: 10.25299/jshmic.2022.vol9(2).9770

Aithal, P. S. (2023). Optimizing the Use of Artificial Intelligence-Powered GPTs as Teaching and Research Assistants by Professors in Higher Education Institutions: A Study on Smart Utilization. *International Journal of Management Technology and Social Sciences*, 368–401. DOI: 10.47992/IJMTS.2581.6012.0326

Akbarani, R. (2024). Use of Artificial Intelligence in English Language Teaching. *International Journal of English Learning and Applied Linguistics (Ijelal)*, *4*(1), 14–23. DOI: 10.21111/ijelal.v4i1.10756

Alqaralleh, B. A. Y., & Aldhaban, F., A-Matarneh, F. M., & AlQaralleh, E. A. (. (2022). Automated Handwriting Recognition and Speech Synthesizer for Indigenous Language Processing. *Computers, Materials & Continua*, *72*(2), 3913–3927. DOI: 10.32604/cmc.2022.026531

Alsanousi, B., Albesher, A. S., Do, H., & Ludi, S. (2023). Investigating the User Experience and Evaluating Usability Issues in AI-Enabled Learning Mobile Apps: An Analysis of User Reviews. *International Journal of Advanced Computer Science and Applications*, *14*(6). Advance online publication. DOI: 10.14569/IJACSA.2023.0140602

Arafah, B., & Kaharuddin. (2019). The Idol: A Model for Incorporating Literature in Elt. *Kne Social Sciences*. DOI: 10.18502/kss.v3i19.4829

Baido-anu, D. (2023). Education in the Era of Generative Artificial Intelligence (AI). *Understanding the Potential Benefits of ChatGPT in Promoting Teaching and Learning.*, *7*(1), 52–62. DOI: 10.61969/jai.1337500

Barua, P. D., Vicnesh, J., Gururajan, R., Oh, S. L., Palmer, E. E., Azizan, M. M., Kadri, N. A., & Acharya, U. R. (2022). Artificial Intelligence Enabled Personalised Assistive Tools to Enhance Education of Children With Neurodevelopmental Disorders—A Review. *International Journal of Environmental Research and Public Health*, *19*(3), 1192. DOI: 10.3390/ijerph19031192 PMID: 35162220

Baskara, F. X. R. (2023). AI-Driven Dynamics: ChatGPT Transforming ELT Teacher-Student Interactions. *Lensa Kajian Kebahasaan Kesusastraan Dan Budaya*, *13*(2), 261. DOI: 10.26714/lensa.13.2.2023.261-275

Belda-Medina, J., & Goddard, M. B. (2024). AI-Driven Digital Storytelling: A Strategy for Creating English as a Foreign Language (EFL) Materials. *International Journal of Linguistics Studies*, *4*(1), 40–49. DOI: 10.32996/ijls.2024.4.1.4

Cantos, K. F. S. (2023). Artificial Intelligence in Language Teaching and Learning. *Ciencia Latina Revista Científica Multidisciplinar*, *7*(4), 5629–5638. DOI: 10.37811/cl_rcm.v7i4.7368

Chen, J., Lai, P., Chan, A., Man, V., & Chan, C.-H. (2022). AI-assisted enhancement of student presentation skills: Challenges and opportunities. *Sustainability (Basel)*, *15*(1), 196. DOI: 10.3390/su15010196

Dai, Y., Liu, A., & Lim, C. P. (2023). Reconceptualizing ChatGPT and generative AI as a student-driven innovation in higher education. *Procedia CIRP*, *119*, 84–90. DOI: 10.1016/j.procir.2023.05.002

Derakhshan, A., & Nazari, M. (2024). Examining teacher identity construction in action research: The mediating role of experience. *Educational Studies*, *50*(6), 1280–1299. DOI: 10.1080/03055698.2022.2073177

Dergaa, I., Chamari, K., Żmijewski, P., & Saad, H. B. (2023). From Human Writing to Artificial Intelligence Generated Text: Examining the Prospects and Potential Threats of ChatGPT in Academic Writing. *Biology of Sport*, *40*(2), 615–622. DOI: 10.5114/biolsport.2023.125623 PMID: 37077800

Falebita, O. S. (2024). Assessing the Relationship Between Anxiety and the Adoption of Artificial Intelligence Tools Among Mathematics Preservice Teachers. *Interdisciplinary Journal of Education Research*, *6*, 1–13. DOI: 10.38140/ijer-2024.vol6.20

Fathurrahman, A. Z., Utami, D. I. S., & Safitri, K. A. (2023). Utilization of Augmented Reality as a Solution for Vernacular Language Approaches to Recognize an Object Through Speech Recognition. *International Journal of Research and Applied Technology*, *3*(1), 79–86. DOI: 10.34010/injuratech.v3i1.9954

Fitria, T. N. (2021). Grammarly as AI-powered English Writing Assistant: Students' Alternative for Writing English. *Metathesis Journal of English Language Literature and Teaching*, *5*(1), 65. DOI: 10.31002/metathesis.v5i1.3519

George, B., & Wooden, O. (2023). Managing the Strategic Transformation of Higher Education Through Artificial Intelligence. *Administrative Sciences*, *13*(9), 196. DOI: 10.3390/admsci13090196

Ghafar, Z. N., Salh, H. F., Abdulrahim, M. A., Farxha, S. S., Arf, S. F., & Rahim, R. I. (2023). The Role of Artificial Intelligence Technology on English Language Learning: A Literature Review. *Canadian Journal of Language and Literature Studies*, *3*(2). Advance online publication. DOI: 10.53103/cjlls.v3i2.87

Guadaña, R. M. F. (2021). Transmedia Storytelling Towards an Expanded Teaching of Reading in Distance Learning. *Studies in Humanities and Education*, *2*(2), 47–56. DOI: 10.48185/she.v2i2.407

Gurrieri, L., & Drenten, J. M. (2019). Visual Storytelling and Vulnerable Health Care Consumers: Normalising Practices and Social Support Through Instagram. *Journal of Services Marketing*, *33*(6), 702–720. DOI: 10.1108/JSM-09-2018-0262

Gyawali, Y. P., & Mehandroo, M. (2022). Artificial Intelligence in English Language Teaching: Navigating the Future With Emerging Perspectives. *Journal of Language and Linguistics in Society*, *26*(26), 21–27. DOI: 10.55529/jlls.26.21.27

Hashem, R., Ali, N., El Zein, F., Fidalgo, P., & Abu Khurma, O. (2023). AI to the Rescue: Exploring the Potential of ChatGPT as a Teacher Ally for Workload Relief and Burnout Prevention. *Research and Practice in Technology Enhanced Learning*, *19*, 23. DOI: 10.58459/rptel.2024.19023

Hoang, N. T., Ngoc Han, D., & Le, D. H. (2023). Exploring Chatbot AI in Improving Vocational Students' English Pronunciation. *AsiaCALL Online Journal*, *14*(2), 140–155. DOI: 10.54855/acoj.231429

Huang, S. (2021). Design and Development of Educational Robot Teaching Resources Using Artificial Intelligence Technology. *International Journal of Emerging Technologies in Learning*, *16*(05), 116. DOI: 10.3991/ijet.v16i05.20311

Hwang, W., Nurtantyana, R., Purba, S. W. D., Hariyanti, U., Indrihapsari, Y., & Surjono, H. D. (2023). AI and Recognition Technologies to Facilitate English as a Foreign Language Writing for Supporting Personalization and Contextualization in Authentic Contexts. *Journal of Educational Computing Research*, *61*(5), 1008–1035. DOI: 10.1177/07356331221137253

Idham, A. Z., Rauf, W., & Rajab, A. (2024). Navigating the Transformative Impact of Artificial Intelligence on English Language Teaching: Exploring Challenges and Opportunities. *Jes*, *4*(1), 8–14. DOI: 10.56185/jes.v4i1.620

Jeong, K.-O. (2022). Facilitating Sustainable Self-Directed Learning Experience With the Use of Mobile-Assisted Language Learning. *Sustainability (Basel)*, *14*(5), 2894. DOI: 10.3390/su14052894

Jiang, R. (2022). How Does Artificial Intelligence Empower EFL Teaching and Learning Nowadays? A Review on Artificial Intelligence in the EFL Context. *Frontiers in Psychology*, *13*, 1049401. Advance online publication. DOI: 10.3389/fpsyg.2022.1049401 PMID: 36467167

Jiao, F., Song, J., Zhao, X., Zhao, P., & Wang, R. (2021). A Spoken English Teaching System Based on Speech Recognition and Machine Learning. *International Journal of Emerging Technologies in Learning*, *16*(14), 68. DOI: 10.3991/ijet.v16i14.24049

Kallinikou, E., & Nicolaidou, I. (2019). Digital Storytelling to Enhance Adults' Speaking Skills in Learning Foreign Languages: A Case Study. *Multimodal Technologies and Interaction*, *3*(3), 59. DOI: 10.3390/mti3030059

Khan, W. M. (2023). Examining the Transformative Role of Artificial Intelligence in Language Skill Enhancement: A Case Study of BS English Students in Okara, Pakistan. *Abbdm*, *3*(1), 190–196. DOI: 10.62019/abbdm.v3i1.88

Kholis, A. (2021). Elsa Speak App: Automatic Speech Recognition (ASR) for Supplementing English Pronunciation Skills. *Pedagogy Journal of English Language Teaching*, *9*(1), 1. DOI: 10.32332/joelt.v9i1.2723

Klímová, B., Pikhart, M., Poláková, P., Černá, M., Yayilgan, S. Y., & Shaikh, S. (2023). A Systematic Review on the Use of Emerging Technologies in Teaching English as an Applied Language at the University Level. *Systems*, *11*(1), 42. DOI: 10.3390/systems11010042

Koh, J., Cowling, M., Jha, M., & Sim, K. N. (2022). Collaborating With AIed for Better Student-Teacher Reconnection. *Ascilite Publications*, e22126. DOI: 10.14742/apubs.2022.126

Kuhail, M. A., Alturki, N., Alramlawi, S., & Alhejori, K. (2022). Interacting With Educational Chatbots: A Systematic Review. *Education and Information Technologies*, *28*(1), 973–1018. DOI: 10.1007/s10639-022-11177-3

Laurel, R. D., Belting, A. C., & Almansouri, E. O. (2021). Evaluation of the English Language Teaching Program of the Faculty of Education, University of Benghazi Using the Peacock Model: Towards Quality Education. *European Journal of Education Studies, 8*(10). Advance online publication. DOI: 10.46827/ejes.v8i10.3945

Lee, H. (2024). The rise of ChatGPT: Exploring its potential in medical education. *Anatomical Sciences Education, 17*(5), 926–931. DOI: 10.1002/ase.2270 PMID: 36916887

Leong, A. C. H., Abidin, M. J. Z., & Saibon, J. S. (2019). The Benefits and Drawbacks of Using Tablet-Based Digital Storytelling in Vocabulary Learning Among Malaysian Young English as a Second Language (ESL) Learners. *Asia Pacific Journal of Educators and Education, 34*, 17–47. DOI: 10.21315/apjee2019.34.2

Li, K. C., & Wong, B. (2023). Artificial Intelligence in Personalised Learning: A Bibliometric Analysis. *Interactive Technology and Smart Education, 20*(3), 422–445. DOI: 10.1108/ITSE-01-2023-0007

Liu, M. (2023). Exploring the application of artificial intelligence in foreign language teaching: Challenges and future development. *SHS Web of Conferences, 168*, 3025.

Lou, L., Xu, W., & Liu, R. (2024). A Bibliometric Approach and Meta-Analysis of Effects of Automatic Speech Recognition on Second Language Learning. *International Journal of Web-Based Learning and Teaching Technologies, 19*(1), 1–20. DOI: 10.4018/IJWLTT.349959

Luke, K. (2021). Twelve Tips for Using Synchronous Virtual Classroom Technologies in Medical Education. *MedEdPublish, 10*(1). Advance online publication. DOI: 10.15694/mep.2021.000066.1 PMID: 38486516

Luo, Y. (2024). Innovative Research on AI-assisted Teaching Models for College English Listening and Speaking Courses. *Applied and Computational Engineering, 69*(1), 155–160. DOI: 10.54254/2755-2721/69/20241493

Manggiasih, L. A., Loreana, Y. R., Azizah, A., & Nurjati, N. (2023). Strengths and Limitations of SmallTalk2Me App in English Language Proficiency Evaluation. *Tell Teaching of English Language and Literature Journal, 11*(2). Advance online publication. DOI: 10.30651/tell.v11i2.19560

Maqbool, F., Ansari, S., & Otero, P. véase además M. (2021). The Role of Artificial Intelligence and Smart Classrooms During Covid-19 Pandemic and Its Impact on Education. *Journal of Independent Studies and Research - Computing, 19*(1). DOI: 10.31645/JISRC.41.19.1.2

Maqsood, M., Zahid, A., Asghar, T., Farooqi, S.-H., & Shahbaz, M. (2024). Issues in Teaching English in a Cultural Context. *Migration Letters : An International Journal of Migration Studies, 21*(S4), 1020–1027. DOI: 10.59670/ml.v21iS4.7411

Maruf, N., & Halyna, K. (2023). Investigating EFL Teachers' Perceptions and Meanings on Digital Storytelling in Language Learning: A Narrative Approach. [Journal of English Education and Linguistics Studies]. *Jeels, 10*(2), 357–378. DOI: 10.30762/jeels.v10i2.912

Minh, A. N. (2024). Leveraging ChatGPT for Enhancing English Writing Skills and Critical Thinking in University Freshmen. *Journal of Knowledge Learning and Science Technology Issn 2959-6386 (Online), 3*(2), 51–62. DOI: 10.60087/jklst.vol3.n2.p62

Nassif, A. B., Shahin, I., Attili, I. B., Azzeh, M., & Shaalan, K. (2019). Speech Recognition Using Deep Neural Networks: A Systematic Review. *IEEE Access : Practical Innovations, Open Solutions, 7*, 19143–19165. DOI: 10.1109/ACCESS.2019.2896880

Nazari, M. (2022). Plan, act, observe, reflect, identity: Exploring teacher identity construction across the stages of action research. *RELC Journal, 53*(3), 672–685. DOI: 10.1177/0033688220972456

Ng, D. T. K., Leung, J. K. L., Su, J., Ng, R. C. W., & Chu, S. K. W. (2023). Teachers' AI digital competencies and twenty-first century skills in the post-pandemic world. *Educational Technology Research and Development, 71*(1), 137–161. DOI: 10.1007/s11423-023-10203-6 PMID: 36844361

Nguyen, T. X. (2024). English Majors' Perceptions of AI Tool Application in English Language Learning at Tertiary Level in Vietnam. *Journal of Knowledge Learning and Science Technology Issn 2959-6386 (Online), 3*(1), 179–193. DOI: 10.60087/jklst.vol3.n1.p193

Niu, S. J., Luo, J., Niemi, H., Li, X., & Lu, Y. (2022). Teachers' and Students' Views of Using an AI-Aided Educational Platform for Supporting Teaching and Learning at Chinese Schools. *Education Sciences, 12*(12), 858. DOI: 10.3390/educsci12120858

Parmaxi, A., & Demetriou, A. A. (2020). Augmented Reality in Language Learning: A State-of-the-art Review of 2014–2019. *Journal of Computer Assisted Learning, 36*(6), 861–875. DOI: 10.1111/jcal.12486

Pipiras, L., Maskeliūnas, R., & Damaševičius, R. (2019). Lithuanian Speech Recognition Using Purely Phonetic Deep Learning. *Computers, 8*(4), 76. DOI: 10.3390/computers8040076

Pratama, M. P., Sampelolo, R., & Lura, H. (2023). Revolutionizing Education: Harnessing the Power of Artificial Intelligence for Personalized Learning. *Klasikal Journal of Education Language Teaching and Science*, *5*(2), 350–357. DOI: 10.52208/klasikal.v5i2.877

Qasem, F., Ghaleb, M., Mahdi, H. S., Khateeb, A. A. A., & Fadda, H. A. (2023). Dialog chatbot as an interactive online tool in enhancing ESP vocabulary learning. *Saudi Journal of Language Studies*, *3*(2), 76–86. DOI: 10.1108/SJLS-10-2022-0072

Qiao, H., & Zhao, A. (2023). Artificial Intelligence-Based Language Learning: Illuminating the Impact on Speaking Skills and Self-Regulation in Chinese EFL Context. *Frontiers in Psychology*, *14*, 1255594. Advance online publication. DOI: 10.3389/fpsyg.2023.1255594 PMID: 38022973

Sabari, N. A. S., & Hashim, H. (2023). Sustaining Education With Digital Storytelling in the English Language Teaching and Learning: A Systematic Review. *International Journal of Academic Research in Business & Social Sciences*, *13*(4). Advance online publication. DOI: 10.6007/IJARBSS/v13-i4/16860

Saputra, D. I. S., Handani, S. W., Indartono, K., & Wijanarko, A. (2020). SMART-In English: Learn English Using Speech Recognition. *Journal of Robotics and Control (Jrc)*, *1*(4). Advance online publication. DOI: 10.18196/jrc.1423

Seo, K., Tang, J., Roll, I., Fels, S., & Yoon, D. (2021). The Impact of Artificial Intelligence on Learner–instructor Interaction in Online Learning. *International Journal of Educational Technology in Higher Education*, *18*(1), 54. Advance online publication. DOI: 10.1186/s41239-021-00292-9 PMID: 34778540

Sheng, J. (2023). Exploration on the Mode of College English Language Teaching Under the Background of Informatization. *International Journal of New Developments in Education*, *5*(8). Advance online publication. DOI: 10.25236/IJNDE.2023.050818

Shirin, A. (2022). Artificial Intelligence Technology on Teaching-Learning: Exploring Bangladeshi Teachers' Perceptions. *Embedded Selforganising Systems, 9*(4), 3–9. https://doi.org/DOI: 10.14464/ess.v9i4.553

Tew, Y., Lim, K.-G., & Joan, H. (2022). An Evaluation of Virtual Classroom Performance With Artificial Intelligence Components. *The Journal of the Institution of Engineers Malaysia*, *82*(3). Advance online publication. DOI: 10.54552/v82i3.116

Tian, W., Ge, J., Zhao, Y., & Zheng, X. (2024). AI Chatbots in Chinese Higher Education: Adoption, Perception, and Influence Among Graduate Students—an Integrated Analysis Utilizing UTAUT and ECM Models. *Frontiers in Psychology*, *15*, 1268549. Advance online publication. DOI: 10.3389/fpsyg.2024.1268549 PMID: 38384353

Tiwari, H. P. (2024). Artificial Intelligence in the Classroom: Revolutionizing English Language Teaching. [Jet Li]. *Journal of English Teaching and Linguistics Studies*, *6*(1), 42–59. DOI: 10.55215/jetli.v6i1.9757

Triyoga, A. (2018). Evaluating the Instructional Materials for Peer Assisted Learning Program (PALP). *Asian Social Science*, *15*(1), 37. DOI: 10.5539/ass.v15n1p37

Vadivel, B., Shaban, A. A., Ahmed, Z. A., & Saravanan, B. (2023). Unlocking English Proficiency: Assessing the Influence of AI-Powered Language Learning Apps on Young Learners' Language Acquisition. *International Journal of English Language Education and Literature Studies (Ijeel)*, *2*(6), 55–62. DOI: 10.22161/ijeel.2.6.7

Wang, C. (2024). *Exploring Students' Generative AI-Assisted Writing Processes: Perceptions and Experiences From Native and Non-native English Speakers*. Technology Knowledge and Learning., DOI: 10.1007/s10758-024-09744-3

Wang, S. (2022). Exploring the Teaching Mode of English Audiovisual Speaking in Multimedia Network Environment. *Advances in Multimedia*, *2022*, 1–9. DOI: 10.1155/2022/2424380

Wu, T. (2024). Virtual Research Laboratory in Foreign Language Teaching: Strategies and Role. *Scientific Bulletin of Mukachevo State University Series. Pedagogy and Psychology*, *10*(1), 107–115. DOI: 10.52534/msu-pp1.2024.107

Wu, Y. (2024). Study on the Impact of Utilizing ChatGPT and Other AI Tools for Feedback in EAP Writing Classrooms on the Discursive Writing Performance of English Major Students. *Tssehr*, *4*, 143–150. DOI: 10.62051/4se95x52

Yuen, C. L., & Schlote, N. (2024). Learner Experiences of Mobile Apps and Artificial Intelligence to Support Additional Language Learning in Education. *Journal of Educational Technology Systems*, *52*(4), 507–525. DOI: 10.1177/00472395241238693

Zhang, H., Lee, I., & Moore, K. (2024). An Effectiveness Study of Teacher-Led AI Literacy Curriculum in K-12 Classrooms. *Proceedings of the AAAI Conference on Artificial Intelligence*, *38*(21), 23318–23325. DOI: 10.1609/aaai.v38i21.30380

Zhang, Z. (2024). Advancements and Challenges in AI-driven Language Technologies: From Natural Language Processing to Language Acquisition. *Applied and Computational Engineering*, *57*(1), 146–152. DOI: 10.54254/2755-2721/57/20241325

Chapter 9
Preparing Educators for the Future:
Navigating AI Tools in English Language Teaching

Mustafa Kayyali
https://orcid.org/0000-0003-3300-262X
HE Higher Education Ranking, Idlib, Syria

ABSTRACT

The use of Artificial Intelligence (AI) in English Language Teaching (ELT) is set to transform educators' methodologies in language education and students' involvement in language learning. As AI technologies progress, they provide a diverse range of tools and resources aimed at improving teaching methods and learning results. To enable AI to significantly influence the future of language teaching, it is crucial to provide instructors with the knowledge to comprehend, maneuver, and proficiently incorporate these technologies into their classrooms. This chapter examines the diverse AI tools accessible to English language instructors, emphasizing their potential to provide customized, dynamic, and interactive learning experiences. By comprehending the function of AI, educators may adeptly maneuver through the difficulties of these technologies and leverage their capabilities to enhance the language acquisition process, cultivating a more efficient and stimulating educational atmosphere for learners.

DOI: 10.4018/979-8-3373-1952-0.ch009

INTRODUCTION

The educational environment is experiencing a significant transition, propelled by technology breakthroughs that are continually altering the methods of teaching, learning, and engagement with information (Kalyani, 2024). Nowhere is this more clear than in the field of English language teaching (ELT), where the incorporation of Artificial Intelligence (AI) is beginning to change established techniques of language learning. AI, long a concept relegated to science fiction, is now a palpable force in the classroom, enriching the learning experience for both educators and students alike. The significance of AI in education is not only a fleeting fad but a fundamental revolution in how teaching and learning are conducted. English, as a global lingua franca, is particularly ripe for such change, given its broad use across borders, countries, and sectors (Kecskes, 2019). In this chapter, we investigate how AI technologies are impacting the future of English language teaching, focusing on the potential they bring for better learning outcomes, improving teaching efficiency, and promoting more individualized and engaging educational experiences.

AI, at its core, offers a range of technologies that have the potential to significantly revolutionize how educators teach and how students acquire language. From natural language processing (NLP) and speech recognition to machine learning algorithms, AI delivers tools that can adapt to the particular needs of individual learners, enabling individualized educational experiences that were formerly impossible in traditional language classes (Sajja et al, 2024). These advancements promise not only to improve linguistic proficiency but also to offer richer, more interactive learning environments that can mimic real-world experiences, something that is especially important for language learners who may not have regular access to native speakers or immersive English-speaking contexts. With the potential of AI comes a series of difficulties and ethical issues that must be addressed as we embrace this new age in education. As AI technologies get more advanced, there are real worries about data privacy, algorithmic biases, and the possibility of over-reliance on technology at the expense of human involvement in the learning process. Furthermore, the integration of AI in ELT is not a one-size-fits-all approach (Pitychoutis & Al Rawahi, 2024). Educators must be prepared with the information, skills, and awareness to properly incorporate AI into their teaching practices, ensuring that it complements rather than replaces the fundamental human parts of education.

The objective of this chapter is to dive into the numerous ways AI is being utilized in English language instruction, highlighting both the benefits and the obstacles that occur as a result of its incorporation. Through an investigation of AI tools and their applications, we will investigate how these technologies may help language learners in their path toward fluency while also providing instructors with useful insights and resources to strengthen their teaching methods. Additionally, we will discuss the future of AI in ELT, identifying significant trends, breakthroughs, and prospective shifts in the pedagogical environment that will effect how English is taught and learned in the coming years. In investigating the convergence of AI and English language instruction, we are not only looking at a technology transformation but a paradigm shift in how we think about education itself. AI can break down traditional obstacles in language acquisition, making education more accessible, customized, and efficient. As such, this chapter seeks to present a complete overview of the role of AI in defining the future of ELT, giving educators, policymakers, and stakeholders the knowledge they need to navigate this fascinating and fast-growing topic.

Ultimately, as we continue to explore the possibilities of AI in education, it is vital to retain a balanced viewpoint, acknowledging both the great benefits and the possible drawbacks of new technologies. By adopting AI intelligently and responsibly, we can guarantee that it serves as a strong tool in producing more effective, inclusive, and engaging language learning experiences that are accessible to all learners, regardless of their background or environment. Through careful integration, continued professional development, and a dedication to pedagogical quality, AI has the potential to not just improve English language teaching but also influence the future of education as a whole.

THE ROLE OF AI IN SHAPING THE FUTURE OF ENGLISH LANGUAGE TEACHING

The importance of Artificial Intelligence (AI) in defining the future of English Language Teaching (ELT) is more clear as technology grows and affects many parts of modern life (Sharadgah & Sa'di, 2022). For decades, the area of education has been exposed to significant changes, spurred by technological breakthroughs. In the field of language education, AI has opened new paths for educators and learners alike, altering not just how English is taught but also how learners engage with the language and how professors may customize and improve their teaching tactics (Pokrivcakova, 2019). AI's role in determining the future of ELT is not only about boosting established approaches but also about rethinking and redesigning language teaching entirely.

At its heart, AI in ELT has the potential to develop more dynamic, customized, and efficient learning environments, making education more accessible to students from all backgrounds and learning levels (Kovalenko & Baranivska, 2024). The digital revolution brought on by AI has led to the creation of a vast array of tools, platforms, and apps meant to help instructors and students in ways that were formerly imagined. These technologies, which vary from voice recognition systems and chatbots to intelligent tutoring systems, are altering how language education is delivered, offering both instructors and students dynamic tools for progress and engagement. One of the most fundamental ways AI is affecting ELT is by supporting tailored learning experiences (Anis, 2023). Traditionally, language education was generally conducted in a one-size-fits-all paradigm, with instructors employing the same resources and procedures for every student in the classroom. While this paradigm works effectively for some, it does not address the different demands of learners with varying language skill levels, learning rates, or preferred learning methods. AI, however, has the opportunity to cater to these variances more effectively (Zhang & Tao, 2020). With AI-powered language learning systems, students may receive individualized teaching based on their unique learning profiles. These systems may change the pace, difficulty level, and kind of information delivered based on individual success, ensuring that students remain interested and challenged without feeling overwhelmed. Personalized learning environments empower students to take command of their learning experience, allowing them to work at their speed and repeat classes and activities as required. In turn, professors may monitor student development and change their instruction accordingly, ensuring that no one is left behind.

AI's impact extends beyond mere customization, giving greater possibilities for immersion and engagement, two crucial components of efficient language acquisition (Loor et al, 2024). Language learners need to engage with the language in real-world circumstances to gain competency, but this has historically been problematic, especially for individuals who lack access to native speakers or immersive surroundings. AI solutions, like chatbots and virtual assistants, bridge this gap by giving students opportunities to speak with an AI-powered entity in real-time, replicating realistic language use. These tools can offer a judgment-free zone for students to practice speaking, helping them to acquire confidence and fluency without the worry of making errors in front of others. Additionally, AI can replicate several real-world settings, ranging from informal talks to formal business dialogues, giving learners a greater range of language experiences that they may not otherwise encounter in the classroom. AI-driven systems also have the potential to aid with language assessment in ways that were previously unattainable (Arani, 2024). Automated writing assessment systems, for example, may provide quick feedback to students on their written work, indicating grammatical faults, recommending fixes, and even making stylistic ideas. This sort of feedback, supplied promptly and precisely, helps learners polish their language abilities and obtain a better knowledge of the norms and complexities of English. In addition, AI can aid instructors in measuring language competency more effectively, allowing them to focus on tailored training rather than spending excessive time on grading and evaluation. By automating repetitive chores, AI helps educators dedicate more of their focus to new teaching tactics and direct student involvement. As language learners increasingly seek flexibility in their education, AI has also made it feasible to integrate English language instruction into non-traditional venues. With the rise of mobile devices and the internet, AI-powered learning tools are available anywhere, anytime. This degree of accessibility is particularly crucial in the worldwide context of English language acquisition. Learners who are unable to attend traditional classes owing to geographic, budgetary, or time restrictions now have access to a multitude of AI-driven resources (Mishra, 2024). Mobile applications driven by AI algorithms can offer individualized lectures and activities, allowing students to learn English on their terms, wherever they may be. These technologies allow learners to practice language skills in their leisure time, leading to more flexible and self-directed learning experiences that supplement traditional classroom training.

Another key function AI plays in ELT is in providing instructors with increased support. Language teaching has historically been a very demanding profession, requiring educators to juggle a wide array of activities, from lesson planning and teaching to grading and student support. AI systems can relieve these pressures by reducing administrative processes and offering professors sophisticated data-driven insights into their students' development (Ahmad et al, 2023). AI-powered platforms can monitor how students are performing on various tasks, detect patterns in their learning, and even forecast future obstacles. This data helps instructors identify areas where students are underperforming, allowing for targeted solutions before issues become substantial. Additionally, AI's capacity to automate monotonous processes such as grading frees up time for professors to focus on developing more interesting classes, increasing classroom engagement, and delivering tailored feedback to students.

Despite the many benefits AI presents in the area of language instruction, the integration of AI into ELT is not without its hurdles. One of the most critical obstacles is the requirement for instructors to have the requisite skills and expertise to properly integrate AI tools into their classrooms (Dimitriadou & Lanitis, 2023). While AI has the potential to improve teaching and learning, it cannot replace the function of the instructor. Instead, AI should be considered as a powerful tool to complement the teaching process, allowing instructors new methods to engage students and promote their learning. For this reason, professional development programs must be designed to help instructors get familiar with the possibilities of AI and learn how to integrate it into their pedagogical methods successfully. Training should include everything from using AI technologies for individualized instruction and evaluation to comprehending the ethical implications of AI in education. There are ethical considerations concerning the use of AI in education (Kayyali, 2024). Data privacy and security are key concerns, particularly in the context of AI technologies that gather and analyze student data. The usage of AI-powered language learning systems demands the collecting of huge amounts of personal and performance data, which raises critical considerations regarding who owns this data and how it is utilized. Additionally, there is the topic of AI bias. Since AI systems are trained on big datasets, there is a concern that these systems may reflect the biases contained in the data, thus resulting in unequal treatment of some groups of students. Developers and educators must work together to address these ethical problems, ensuring that AI technologies are built and utilized ethically and openly.

Looking to the future, the use of AI in ELT is only going to increase. As AI technology continues to grow, new apps and tools will emerge that further enrich the language learning experience. For example, natural language processing (NLP) technologies are evolving at an incredible pace, enabling robots to better interpret and synthesize human language. Soon, NLP technologies may become more effective at understanding the difficulties of students' spoken language, allowing for even more precise feedback on pronunciation and fluency (Chandran et al, 2024). Additionally, machine learning algorithms may grow more complex, allowing AI systems to forecast students' future learning requirements with greater precision and offer targeted interventions. AI is playing a revolutionary role in influencing the future of English Language Teaching, generating new opportunities for both instructors and learners. By delivering individualized learning experiences, allowing interactive language practice, and generating data-driven insights, AI tools are boosting the teaching and learning of English in unprecedented ways. However, for AI to realize its full potential in the classroom, educators must be educated with the skills and knowledge necessary to integrate these technologies successfully into their teaching methods. As we move forward, it is crucial to ensure that AI is utilized ethically, responsibly, and in a way that complements the invaluable function of professors in facilitating language learning.

UNDERSTANDING AI TOOLS: AN OVERVIEW FOR EDUCATORS

In recent years, the landscape of education has experienced tremendous changes, with technology emerging as a potent instrument that modifies how information is taught and absorbed. One of the most fundamental revolutions has been the introduction of Artificial Intelligence (AI) into the educational arena (Chaka, 2023). AI is no longer simply a futuristic notion but a current reality, with tools and applications that have the potential to alter the way we teach and learn. For educators, this brings new opportunities and problems, notably in the domain of English Language Teaching (ELT). To properly harness the potential of AI technologies, educators need to first grasp what these tools are, how they function, and how they may be integrated into the classroom. Artificial intellect refers to the replication of human intellect in computers meant to think and act like humans. AI may be used to accomplish activities that traditionally require human intellect, such as learning, problem-solving, pattern recognition, and decision-making. In the context of education, AI solutions may enhance teaching techniques, create tailored learning experiences, and aid in automating administrative work. However, the most transformational component of AI in education is its capacity to adapt to the requirements of individual learners, making it a useful asset for educators wanting to improve the quality of teaching.

For educators to make the most of AI tools in their classrooms, they must first establish an awareness of the many types of AI applications available and how they may be deployed successfully. One of the most prevalent kinds of AI utilized in education nowadays is Intelligent Tutoring Systems ITS (Akyuz, 2020). These systems employ AI algorithms to deliver individualized feedback and teaching to students. They alter the content and complexity of classes based on a student's specific learning rate and development. ITS is particularly beneficial in language acquisition since it can alter exercises, quizzes, and feedback to meet the competency level of each learner, ensuring that they are continually pushed without feeling overwhelmed. Another AI technique often utilized in education is Natural Language Processing (NLP). NLP allows machines to perceive, interpret, and produce human language. In the context of ELT, NLP may be used to analyze and assess students' written or spoken language. AI-powered platforms that apply NLP may analyze grammar, vocabulary, pronunciation, and fluency, delivering rapid feedback to students. This allows students to enhance their language skills in real-time, which is particularly good for enhancing speaking and writing abilities. Moreover, NLP may also be utilized to support talks between students and AI-driven chatbots, giving students with opportunity to develop their language abilities in a low-pressure environment. These chatbots may imitate real-world discussions, helping students improve their conversational English by engaging them in dynamic and interactive dialogues.

AI techniques may also be utilized to assist language acquisition through gamification (AbuSahyon et al, 2023). Many AI-powered programs use game-like aspects to interest students in the learning process. These tools generally feature exams, challenges, and incentives that push students to continue learning and honing their language abilities. Gamification, along with AI, can assist students achieve improved retention of language skills by delivering courses in an engaging and pleasurable style (Rajak et al, 2024). For example, students can play educational games that evaluate their vocabulary knowledge, grammatical abilities, or listening comprehension, with AI algorithms altering the challenge level based on their success. This strategy guarantees that students remain engaged and committed to their language learning experience.

In addition to these student-facing technologies, AI may also support instructors in numerous aspects of education. One of the most significant advantages of AI is its capacity to automate time-consuming administrative activities (Parycek et al, 2024). Grading assignments, tracking student progress, and organizing classroom activities may be difficult for instructors, especially in big classrooms. AI systems can assist expedite these duties by automatically grading assignments, monitoring students' learning habits, and delivering extensive information on student performance. This frees up significant time for professors, allowing them to focus on more meaningful parts of teaching, such as boosting student engagement, designing engaging sessions, and delivering tailored feedback. AI technologies can also aid in identifying children who may require further support, allowing professors to intervene early and give focused guidance (Barua et al, 2022). For educators to successfully incorporate AI technologies into their teaching methods, it is vital to have a thorough knowledge of the pedagogical ideas underpinning these tools. AI is not a one-size-fits-all answer; it must be implemented into the educational process intelligently and strategically. The goal is to employ AI as a complementing tool rather than a replacement for traditional educational approaches (Chen, 2020). For example, AI may be utilized to deliver tailored education or offer more practice to students, while professors can focus on building an engaged and collaborative classroom atmosphere. In this approach, AI may enhance the learning experience without undermining the function of the instructor.

Educators must know that AI is not flawless. While AI tools can give significant insights and help, they are nevertheless constrained by the data and algorithms that drive them. AI is not capable of grasping the emotional or social components of teaching, and it cannot reproduce the human ties that are crucial to effective education (Latif et al, 2023). Professors must stay actively engaged in the learning process, employing AI as a tool to complement their efforts rather than depending exclusively on technology. By maintaining a balance between AI-driven technologies and conventional teaching approaches, instructors may create a more dynamic and effective learning environment.

In addition to grasping the potential of AI technologies, educators must also be cognizant of the ethical implications surrounding their usage. As AI systems collect and analyze vast volumes of data, it is vital to guarantee that student privacy and data security are maintained. Educators must be cautious of the sorts of data being gathered and how it is being utilized. For example, AI-powered language learning systems may track students' progress and gather data on their language abilities, but this data should be used purely to improve the learning experience and should not be shared without valid authorization. Professors should also be mindful of the possible biases in AI systems, which might unwittingly impair students' learning experiences (Gauthier et al, 2022). It is crucial to pick AI technologies that are honest about their data gathering and privacy methods and that are created with fairness and inclusion in mind. Another key factor is the digital divide. While AI technologies have the potential to transform education, not all students have equal access to the technology necessary to benefit from them. In many regions of the world, students may lack access to high-speed internet, cellphones, or laptops, making it difficult for them to engage with AI-powered learning platforms. Educators must be cognizant of these inequities and endeavor to ensure that all students have access to the resources they need to succeed. This may mean finding alternate alternatives, such as offline AI tools, or pressing for increased investment in educational technology infrastructure.

Despite these obstacles, the potential benefits of AI in education are apparent. For educators, AI tools provide the chance to better their teaching approaches, boost student engagement, and create more tailored learning experiences (Alam, 2023). By knowing the numerous types of AI tools available, identifying their strengths and limits, and incorporating them into their teaching practices, educators may create a more dynamic and effective learning environment. However, educators must approach AI with a critical eye, ensuring that technology is utilized ethically, responsibly, and in a way that benefits all students. With the correct approach, AI has the potential to reinvent English Language Teaching, making it more accessible, entertaining, and successful than ever before. AI technologies have the potential to change education, notably in the domain of English Language Teaching (Edmett et al, 2023). For educators, knowing the capabilities and limits of these technologies is vital to integrating them into their courses successfully. By employing AI to customize instruction, automate administrative duties, and boost student engagement, educators can create a more dynamic and inclusive learning environment. However, it is crucial to employ AI as a complimentary tool that complements existing teaching techniques rather than replacing them. Through intelligent integration and ethical concerns, AI may dramatically boost the quality of education and help prepare students for the future.

The Impact of AI on Language Acquisition and Teaching Methodologies

The integration of Artificial Intelligence (AI) into language acquisition and teaching approaches is altering how both educators and learners approach the process of learning languages, notably English (Kuddus, 2022). The fast development and acceptance of AI tools have opened up new opportunities for generating more customized, adaptable, and interactive language learning experiences. By utilizing the power of AI, educators may better address the different requirements of their students while delivering more individualized learning routes. For students, the reward resides in the potential to interact with language acquisition in ways that are more dynamic, helpful, and, perhaps most significantly, individualized. The conventional techniques of teaching and acquiring language, albeit successful, frequently confront constraints in terms of accessibility, flexibility, and real-time feedback. Professors have historically employed textbooks, grammar exercises, oral practice, and group work to aid language acquisition (Horwitz, 2020). While these approaches give essential exposure to the language, they frequently do not take into consideration the various learning speeds, abilities, or shortcomings of individual students. The introduction of AI in language teaching has begun to overcome these limits by producing tools that can instantaneously adjust to the requirements of the learner, offer rapid corrective feedback, and imitate real-world language experiences in ways that were previously inconceivable. AI's influence on language acquisition is most visible in its capacity to deliver individualized learning experiences. In traditional language programs, students follow a fixed curriculum, which may or may not suit their specific learning speed or style. With AI technologies, the curriculum becomes fluid and adaptive, responding to the learner's progress and obstacles. For example, AI-powered language learning software, such as Duolingo, Babbel, and Memrise, employ algorithms to analyze a learner's performance and modify the difficulty level of exercises appropriately (Eswaran et al, 2025). These systems track students' strengths and weaknesses, ensuring that information is neither too simple nor too challenging, but ideally linked with the learner's level of skill. This technique, which is focused on real-time data collecting and analysis, is a distinct break from typical classroom settings where students may either be left behind or not adequately pushed enough to make meaningful progress.

Another significant advantage of AI in language acquisition is its capacity to deliver individualized feedback (Sajja et al, 2024). Language learners typically struggle with self-assessment or receive delayed feedback from professors in traditional classroom settings. With AI-powered systems, feedback may be offered instantly after a student completes an activity or engages in a conversation. For instance, AI-driven programs may check grammar, pronunciation, word usage, and sentence structure, delivering rapid suggestions for improvement. These technologies utilize Natural Language Processing (NLP) algorithms to detect errors and deliver context-sensitive corrections, which dramatically boosts the pace at which students learn from their mistakes. Immediate feedback not only speeds the learning process but also develops student confidence by helping them realize their errors without the fear of criticism or shame. AI allows practicing language skills in circumstances that may not be easily recreated in a typical classroom (Martin, 2019). Language acquisition frequently entails a lot of repetition, which is crucial for reinforcing new vocabulary and grammatical structures. AI technologies excel at delivering limitless practice opportunities, allowing learners to engage with the language at any time, from any place. For example, AI-driven chatbots replicate real-world interactions, enabling learners to practice their speaking and listening abilities without the requirement for a human conversation partner. These bots are driven by powerful voice recognition and NLP algorithms, which allow them to interpret and respond to learner inputs in a way that simulates genuine interaction. This ongoing, on-demand access to conversational practice is particularly advantageous for learners who may not have the opportunity to practice speaking with native speakers in their regular lives. AI's function in language acquisition extends beyond the area of grammar, vocabulary, and speaking practice (Schmidt & Strasser, 2022). It also considerably boosts the cultural and contextual components of language acquisition. Understanding the difficulties of a language, including idiomatic phrases, colloquialisms, and cultural allusions, is crucial for acquiring fluency. AI technologies may give learners exposure to real-world settings through media such as video clips, chapters, and podcasts, helping them gain a deeper grasp of how language is utilized in diverse scenarios. AI-powered systems may assess the context of a conversation and give cultural insights, making learners more aware of the social and cultural components of language use.

Another essential element of AI in language learning is its potential to serve learners with unique needs or impairments (Zdravkova et al, 2022). Traditional language teaching approaches may not always be tailored to accommodate students with diverse learning issues, such as dyslexia, auditory processing abnormalities, or speech impairments. AI tools, however, may be modified to address the special demands of these children. For example, AI-powered text-to-speech systems can benefit learners with visual impairments, while voice recognition software can support learners with speech challenges by allowing them the option to practice pronunciation in a non-judgmental setting. This tailored approach guarantees that all children, regardless of their ability, have access to effective language learning tools. The growth of AI in language learning also brings about important modifications in teaching approaches (Fitria, 2021). As AI technologies get more advanced, instructors are realizing that they no longer need to be the exclusive producers of material or teaching. Instead, AI may take over regular chores, like as grading and testing, enabling professors to focus on the more creative and human parts of teaching. For instance, AI can automatically evaluate written assignments, offering thorough comments on grammar, vocabulary, and sentence structure. This saves instructors a tremendous amount of time, enabling them to focus on activities that develop critical thinking, creativity, and cooperation among students. In this approach, AI transforms the job of the professor from a content supplier to a facilitator of learning, allowing educators to focus on establishing a more engaging and dynamic classroom environment.

In addition to allowing tailored learning, AI may assist professors assess student performance data more efficiently. By tracking student development in real time, AI systems give instructors specific insights into how well individual students are performing, what areas they are struggling with, and what interventions might be needed. These insights enable professors to provide targeted help to students, either by delivering more practice or by altering lesson plans to better meet the requirements of the class. AI may also assist professors in recognizing trends in student behavior, such as frequent errors in a particular area of grammar or vocabulary, and make data-driven decisions on how to handle these difficulties in future sessions (Sajja et al, 2023). AI-powered solutions can facilitate collaborative language learning, which is increasingly acknowledged as an effective way for language acquisition. Collaborative learning enables students to work together, exchange ideas, and practice language in social circumstances. AI may enhance collaboration by offering platforms where students can connect in real time, either through chatbots, discussion forums, or virtual classrooms. AI-powered solutions may also give recommendations for group activities based on individual student profiles, ensuring that students are put in learning contexts where they can work most successfully. While AI's influence on language learning and teaching approaches is transformational, it is crucial to note the limitations and constraints connected with the incorporation of AI into education. One of the primary worries is that AI may lack the emotional intelligence essential to grasp the difficulties of human interactions. For instance, AI systems may not be able to recognize a student's dissatisfaction or give the degree of emotional support that a professor can offer in a typical classroom setting (Schiff, 2021). Furthermore, AI may not always be able to give the social and cultural background that is crucial for comprehending how language is utilized in real-world circumstances. In addition, the broad use of AI in education raises questions about data privacy and the ethical implications of utilizing personal data to train AI systems.

Despite these limitations, the future of AI in language acquisition appears promising (Kim et al, 2019). As AI continues to advance, its capacity to grasp and respond to human emotions, social cues, and cultural subtleties is expected to increase. Additionally, as AI tools become more accessible and inexpensive, the benefits of AI-powered language learning will be offered to a greater spectrum of learners, particularly those in disadvantaged or distant places. By augmenting traditional teaching techniques with AI-driven technologies, educators may build more inclusive, customized, and successful language learning environments that respond to the different requirements of their students. The influence of AI on language learning and teaching approaches is substantial and far-reaching. AI provides instructors and learners an unparalleled potential to tailor instruction, provide rapid feedback, and participate in real-world language practice. For language instructors, AI is a strong tool that may enhance their teaching techniques, increase student engagement, and promote data-driven decision-making. While problems exist, such as the ethical considerations around data protection and the need for emotional intelligence in teaching, AI has immense potential for changing language instruction. As technology continues to progress, the importance of AI in language acquisition will only continue to rise, making language learning more accessible, individualized, and successful than ever before.

Ethical Considerations in Integrating AI into English Language Teaching

The integration of Artificial Intelligence (AI) into English Language Teaching (ELT) has the potential to transform how educators teach and how students learn. It offers unparalleled options for tailored instruction, effective evaluation, and interactive language practice. However, like with any technical progress, the use of AI in education comes with a plethora of ethical problems that must be carefully addressed to ensure its responsible, fair, and inclusive usage. These issues touch upon different elements, ranging from data privacy to bias in algorithms, equity of access, and the preservation of human engagement in the learning process. Educators, politicians, and developers must examine these ethical concerns before completely integrating AI technologies into the classroom.

One of the biggest ethical issues in AI integration with ELT is data protection (Al-khresheh, 2024). AI-driven systems rely significantly on gathering and analyzing data from students to create individualized learning experiences. This data can include personal information, learning habits, language competence levels, and even contacts with other students or AI systems. With the rising quantity of sensitive data being gathered, there is a growing worry over who gets access to this data, how it is stored, and how it is utilized. The possibility of data breaches, abuse of personal information, and illegal sharing of data is a big worry. For example, AI technologies may store student data on cloud-based systems, which might be exposed to hacking or exploitation if sufficient security measures are not in place. Educators and institutions must guarantee that students' data is handled with the highest care and that stringent privacy policies are in place (Jones et al, 2020). This includes installing effective encryption, adopting anonymization techniques where available, and ensuring that children and their parents or guardians are properly informed about how their data will be used and kept. The acquisition of data also raises questions regarding informed consent. Students, particularly younger learners, may not completely comprehend the amount to which their data is being gathered, how it will be used, or the possible hazards connected with giving personal information. Educational institutions adopting AI technologies in language acquisition must give clear and accessible information about their data-gathering policies (Arani, 2024). Consent should not be assumed or implied; it should be sought clearly, and students should have the choice to opt out of data collection at any moment without incurring any negative implications for their learning experience. This ethical obligation extends to parents or guardians in circumstances where students are minors, ensuring that they are fully informed about the data-gathering procedures and may make decisions on behalf of their children.

Another important ethical concern in the use of AI in ELT is the possibility of prejudice in AI algorithms. AI systems are only as good as the data they are trained on. If the data used to train an AI tool is biased or unrepresentative, the technology itself can perpetuate these biases. For example, if an AI language model is trained predominantly on data from native English speakers, it may have trouble comprehending or accurately processing the language of non-native speakers. Similarly, if the data used to train the AI is not varied enough in terms of cultural, geographical, or socio-economic origins, the system might unintentionally promote preconceptions or deliver misleading linguistic input (Vučković & Sikimić, 2024). Bias in AI tools might show in numerous ways, such as mispronouncing non-native names, delivering erroneous translations, or favoring some dialects or linguistic types over others. The danger of bias in AI tools is particularly significant in the context of language acquisition since it might reinforce existing disparities and disfavor certain groups of learners. For example, students from underrepresented linguistic or cultural backgrounds could be unfairly penalized by AI technologies that have not been taught to comprehend the complexities of their language use. Educators must be aware of the possibility of prejudice and take action to mitigate it. This may be addressed by ensuring that AI systems are trained on varied, representative datasets and by routinely auditing and testing the tools for any biases. Moreover, developers should stress openness and explainability in AI models so that educators can better understand how the system makes judgments and guarantee that it is working in a fair and unbiased manner.

In addition to data privacy and prejudice, another ethical problem in the integration of AI into ELT is the question of fairness and access. Not all students have equal access to the technology necessary to benefit from AI-powered learning tools. In many parts of the world, especially in disadvantaged or rural regions, students may not have access to the internet, cellphones, or computers needed to participate in AI-driven language learning platforms. This digital gap might compound current inequities in education, placing some students at a substantial disadvantage. For AI technologies to be effective in advancing English language education, educators and policymakers must address the problem of access and guarantee that all students, regardless of their socio-economic status, have the chance to benefit from these breakthroughs (Chan, 2023). One answer to this difficulty is to guarantee that AI-powered tools are accessible across a range of platforms, including smartphones and low-cost laptops. Additionally, educational institutions should aim to offer students in underprivileged regions the appropriate tools, such as internet connection and hardware, to guarantee that no learner is left behind. However, access is not only about providing the required technology; it also requires giving the support and training that instructors and students need to utilize these tools successfully.

Professors must be prepared with the knowledge and abilities to incorporate AI technologies into their teaching techniques, and students must be taught how to utilize them effectively (Fitria, 2021). This involves continual professional development and support for both educators and learners, as well as coordination between colleges, technology providers, and governments to enable fair access to AI-powered learning opportunities. While AI may give several benefits in language instruction, it is necessary to maintain a balance between technology and human contact. One of the primary issues in the incorporation of AI into ELT is the possibility for technology to supplant the function of the instructor (Sharadgah & Sa'di, 2022). Language acquisition is not only about acquiring grammatical rules or vocabulary; it is a fundamentally social process that requires interaction, empathy, and cultural understanding. Professors have a critical role in mentoring students, giving emotional support, and establishing a sense of community in the classroom. AI, while strong in giving individualized feedback and practice opportunities, cannot replace the human touch that is crucial to the language acquisition process. The overreliance on AI technologies in the classroom might lead to a dehumanization of the learning experience. If students spend more time engaging with computers than with their peers or professors, they may lose out on essential social and communicative components of language acquisition. This might result in a more transactional and less meaningful learning experience. Ethical issues in this context are ensuring that AI is utilized as a supplement to, rather than a replacement for, human interaction in the classroom. Educators must carefully strike the balance between employing AI to boost learning and keeping the crucial human factors that make language instruction effective.

Another key ethical concern is the openness and accountability of AI systems (Díaz-Rodríguez et al, 2023). As AI technologies become more incorporated into the classroom, both instructors and students must understand how these tools operate and what judgments they are making. This includes being upfront about how AI algorithms assess language competency, how feedback is created, and how student data is utilized to tailor learning experiences. Without this openness, students may feel alienated or skeptical of the technology, which might weaken its usefulness. It is the obligation of both AI developers and educational institutions to guarantee that AI technologies are not only functional but also ethically developed and applied in a way that respects the rights and autonomy of students. AI in ELT raises worries about the long-term repercussions for instructors and the profession as a whole. While AI can automate many duties, such as grading and delivering feedback, it also raises issues about the future role of instructors. As AI technologies become more advanced, there is a risk that educators may lose their jobs or see their functions decrease. This can be an especially serious matter in locations where college resources are low and there is already pressure to minimize expenditures. However, rather than replacing instructors, AI has the potential to improve the teaching profession by allowing educators to focus on more creative, engaging, and meaningful parts of their work. The ethical dilemma, in this scenario, rests on how to guarantee that AI is utilized to supplement, rather than replace, the human aspect of education (Abulibdeh et al, 2024). The incorporation of AI into English Language Teaching has huge promise for boosting the language learning experience, but it also raises serious ethical problems that must be addressed. Data privacy, algorithmic bias, equity of access, the balance between technology and human connection, transparency, and the future of the teaching profession are just a few of the ethical difficulties that educators, legislators, and AI developers must negotiate. By tackling these difficulties with care, forethought, and a dedication to equality, we can guarantee that AI is utilized ethically and efficiently to enhance the teaching and learning of English. Ultimately, the objective should be to establish a learning environment where technology works to support and improve the human parts of education, ensuring that all learners have the chance to flourish in a fast-changing world.

AI-Driven Personalization in Language Learning: Opportunities and Challenges

Artificial Intelligence (AI) is rapidly affecting the way we approach education, notably in the field of language learning. One of the most significant contributions AI can bring to this field is through the process of customization (Anshari et al, 2019). AI-driven solutions may personalize language learning experiences to individual students, altering material, tempo, and difficulty levels to meet each learner's requirements, skills, and preferences. This degree of customization allows students to advance at their speed, get rapid feedback, and connect with learning resources that are most relevant to them. It marks a considerable transition from the old, one-size-fits-all teaching methodology to a more tailored approach that enhances learning potential. The prospects afforded by AI-driven customization in language learning are tremendous. For starters, customization can boost student engagement and motivation. When learners are provided with resources that fit with their current skill level and interests, they are more likely to stay engaged and invested in the learning process. AI systems are capable of assessing student data in real-time, detecting strengths and weaknesses, and giving personalized content that ensures learners are pushed just enough to keep them progressing without feeling overwhelmed. By giving tailored feedback and ideas for improvement, AI-driven technologies can inspire students to take ownership of their learning, making it a more active and self-directed process.

Another significant benefit of AI-driven customization is its capacity to accommodate varied learning styles (Kanchon et al, 2024). Language learners, like all students, have diverse preferences when it comes to how they learn best. Some students may flourish with visual help, while others may prefer aural input or tactile exercises. AI systems may change material delivery techniques depending on these choices, offering learners a more flexible and effective experience. For example, a student who suffers from reading comprehension may benefit from listening to audio versions of books or seeing films that reinforce the topic. A student who prefers a more hands-on approach may be given interactive activities and simulations. This sort of flexibility enables AI systems to adjust to individual requirements and learning preferences, encouraging students to feel more comfortable and confident in their language learning journey.

In addition, AI systems may deliver fast feedback, which is vital for language learners (Schmidt & Strasser, 2022). Traditionally, students would have to wait for a professor's answer before they could grasp what they did wrong and how to improve. With AI-driven systems, students may receive real-time criticisms and ideas, allowing them to alter their approach quickly. This rapid feedback can assist in reinforcing learning and prevent students from ingraining wrong habits or misconceptions. Moreover, it enables learners to measure their progress over time, giving them a sense of success and pushing them to continue. For instance, AI-powered programs may check pronunciation, grammar, and vocabulary usage, delivering corrections and explanations that assist learners in comprehending the issue and how to remedy it. The opportunity to practice and receive feedback at any time and from anywhere helps expedite learning, particularly for students who do not have access to a conventional classroom environment (Bender, 2023). AI-driven customization can help create more inclusion in language learning. In traditional classrooms, it can be tough for professors to satisfy the requirements of every student, particularly in big, varied classes. However, AI systems can accommodate a wide range of learners, including those with differing degrees of expertise, learning difficulties, or different native languages. For example, AI technologies may be trained to give additional help to students who struggle with pronunciation by providing visual feedback on lip motions or delivering repeating repetition in regions where they have difficulties. Similarly, learners with hearing impairments or other physical obstacles may benefit from AI technologies that give visual signals or subtitles, ensuring that they are not excluded from the learning process. By allowing students to get tailored attention, AI-driven solutions can contribute to more fair learning environments and create better opportunities for all learners to thrive.

Despite the tremendous benefits that AI-driven customization provides to language learning, there are also substantial hurdles that need to be solved to fully fulfill its promise. One of the most serious problems is the issue of data privacy and security. AI systems rely on gathering and analyzing enormous quantities of data from students to create individualized learning experiences (Murtaza et al, 2022). This data might include sensitive information such as a student's learning history, performance indicators, and even their personal preferences or behavioral tendencies. While this data is vital for personalizing the learning experience, it also raises questions about how that data is maintained, who has access to it, and how it is utilized. There is the possibility of breaches of privacy, abuse of personal information, or even the exploitation of data for commercial interests. Educational institutions and AI developers must guarantee that they have adequate security mechanisms in place to secure student data and that they are honest about how this data is being utilized.

Another problem is the potential for over-reliance on AI systems. While AI-driven customization might enhance the learning process, it should not replace the function of the instructor or human connection in language acquisition (Chen, 2024). Language acquisition is a social activity, and much of the benefit in learning a language comes from connection with others—whether via discussions, collaborative work, or cultural immersion. AI systems, albeit sophisticated, cannot mimic the emotional intelligence, sensitivity, and deep understanding that a human instructor brings to the classroom. In addition, students gain from the social and communicative components of learning, which AI systems cannot completely deliver. Therefore, while AI may serve as an excellent addition to language acquisition, it should be utilized in conjunction with, not as a substitute for, human-led education. The problem, then, is to achieve a balance between the employment of AI technologies and the continuous necessity of human engagement in the language acquisition process. While AI systems can deliver individualized learning experiences, they are not flawless. The efficacy of AI-driven customization is primarily reliant on the quality of the algorithms and the data they are trained on (Rehan, 2024). If the data utilized to train AI systems is biased or inadequate, the system may deliver erroneous or ineffective suggestions. For example, if an AI system is trained largely on data from native English speakers, it may fail to deliver individualized feedback for non-native speakers, or it may promote prejudices and biases. Additionally, some AI systems may be excessively basic or overly strict, giving personalized information that is not matched to the learner's requirements. This might lead to dissatisfaction or disengagement from the learner. To solve these difficulties, AI developers must continually enhance their algorithms, ensuring that their training data is varied and representative, and routinely test their systems to discover and rectify any limits.

Another problem in AI-driven language learning is ensuring that these tools are available to all learners, regardless of their socioeconomic status. While AI-driven customization has the potential to democratize language learning by offering access to tailored learning experiences, not all students have equal access to the equipment necessary to use these tools. In many regions of the world, students may not have dependable access to the internet, cellphones, or computers, which are necessary for engaging with AI-driven language learning platforms. This digital barrier might worsen current inequities in education, leaving underprivileged students without the opportunity to benefit from AI-powered learning. To solve this difficulty, governments and educational institutions need to offer fair access to the appropriate technology and infrastructure, so that all learners, regardless of their background, have the chance to benefit from tailored language learning experiences. The role of instructors in AI-driven individualized language learning also demands serious study (Strielkowski et al, 2024). Professors will need to adapt to new technology and incorporate them into their teaching approaches (Nilson & Goodson, 2021). This involves professional development and regular training to guarantee that educators can utilize AI technologies successfully and incorporate them into their teachings in a meaningful way. Professors must also be prepared to analyze the data supplied by AI systems and utilize it to inform their education. For example, AI technologies may give extensive data on a student's strengths and shortcomings, but it is up to the instructor to interpret this information and determine how best to utilize it to help the student's learning. While AI may give significant insights and recommendations, the professor's role in evaluating and using these findings is crucial (Chiu et al, 2023). This implies that AI should not be considered as a substitute for professors, but rather as a tool that may increase their efficacy and help them in fulfilling the requirements of their students. AI-driven customization in language learning provides a huge opportunity to improve the learning experience for students, making it more personalized, interesting, and successful. It provides for tailored learning routes, rapid feedback, and adjustments for diverse learning styles, creating increased motivation and inclusion. However, the incorporation of AI into language acquisition is not without its problems. Issues such as data privacy, over-reliance on technology, algorithmic bias, and accessibility must be properly addressed to fully fulfill the promise of AI in education. Furthermore, the human aspect of teaching should remain at the core of language acquisition, with AI functioning as a supplement to, rather than a replacement for, human education. By tackling these difficulties wisely and ethically, we can ensure that AI-driven customization becomes a strong and good force in the future of language teaching.

Training Educators: Developing Competence in AI Tools for Effective Teaching

In recent years, the integration of Artificial Intelligence (AI) in education has proven revolutionary, giving new tools and strategies that increase teaching and learning. However, as educators attempt to adapt to this transformation, it is vital to understand the need to fully teach them how to utilize these AI technologies effectively. While AI may offer a broad range of advantages—such as individualized learning experiences, real-time feedback, and adaptable learning pathways—it is only through the correct training of educators that the full potential of these technologies can be achieved. The route to incorporating AI into education begins with increasing educator expertise in deploying AI technologies in a way that enriches their pedagogy, helps student learning, and fosters deeper engagement in the classroom.

The environment of education is evolving, and as technology continues to grow, so too must the teaching tactics and abilities of educators (Basilotta-Gómez-Pablos et al, 2022). AI is becoming a crucial element of this transformation, allowing professors the capacity to give tailored training that adjusts to the particular requirements of their students. Yet, despite its rising presence in educational contexts, many professors still feel unprepared to deploy AI tools successfully. This unpreparedness originates from numerous issues, including a lack of training, an insufficient grasp of how AI works, and a fear of technology replacing the human part of education. To address these problems, it is vital to build a well-rounded training program that not only teaches educators how to utilize AI technologies but also enables them to comprehend and incorporate these tools into their existing teaching methods. Training educators with AI technologies begins with helping them acquire a solid grasp of the technology. This involves familiarizing instructors with the numerous types of AI tools available, their characteristics, and how these technologies might be deployed to enhance teaching and learning. There is no one-size-fits-all answer when it comes to AI tools for education; the correct tools rely on the unique environment, the requirements of the learners, and the aims of the educator. For example, AI-based language learning applications, such as Duolingo or Rosetta Stone, focus on language acquisition through individualized courses and gamified experiences. On the other side, AI-driven evaluation platforms, such as Gradescope, employ machine learning algorithms to analyze student work and give quick feedback. By knowing the numerous sorts of tools at their disposal, educators may make educated judgments about which ones will best suit their teaching techniques and the requirements of their students.

In addition to comprehending the operation of AI technologies, educators must also be educated to critically analyze the usefulness of these tools in the classroom (Dimitriadou & Lanitis, 2023). It is vital to note that AI, like any other educational technology, is not necessarily useful; its effectiveness relies on how it is employed. For example, certain AI solutions may give real-time analytics on student development, but these insights will be beneficial only if instructors know how to evaluate the data and take appropriate measures based on it. AI tools can also enhance cooperation among students, but instructors must develop activities and lesson plans that maximize this potential. By giving training that focuses on the critical assessment of AI tools, educators will be able to make better judgments regarding which tools to deploy and how to utilize them to fulfill their educational objectives. Equally crucial is teaching instructors how to integrate AI technologies seamlessly into their present curriculum (Kayyali, 2025 A). It is common for educators to feel overwhelmed by the thought of adopting new technology into their classrooms, particularly when they are already juggling multiple teaching obligations. However, AI tools should not be perceived as a replacement for traditional teaching techniques; rather, they should be viewed as an augmentation. For example, AI-driven tutoring systems can give additional help to difficult students, freeing up time for professors to focus on more sophisticated educational duties. By delivering training that highlights the integration of AI into established teaching processes, educators may understand how technology can compliment, rather than disrupt, their teaching approach.

One of the major worries when it comes to the deployment of AI technologies in the classroom is the idea that technology will overwhelm the human element of teaching (Ikedinachi et al, 2019). Educators may worry that AI technologies will replace face-to-face engagement with students, diminishing the chance for meaningful relationships to be built. However, AI solutions are supposed to improve the teaching process, not replace it. Professors are still needed to establish an engaging and supportive learning environment, nurture social-emotional growth, and adapt to the individual needs of their students. AI may help instructors by automating monotonous duties, such as grading or delivering quizzes, giving them more time to focus on the human components of teaching, such as offering feedback, stimulating creativity, and boosting student well-being. In teaching educators to utilize AI technologies effectively, it is crucial to highlight the role of the professor as a guide and facilitator in the learning process, rather than as a passive user of technology. One major part of educating educators in AI technologies is ensuring that they have the requisite technical abilities (Luckin et al, 2022). While educators do not need to become specialists in AI or machine learning, they should be comfortable navigating the platforms and technologies they utilize in their classrooms. This involves learning how to set up AI-based tools, fix typical difficulties, and make the most of the available capabilities. Educators should also be taught data privacy and security procedures, as AI systems typically need the gathering and analysis of student data. Professors need to know how to secure student information, preserve confidentiality, and comply with data protection rules. By training educators with the technical skills they need to utilize AI tools efficiently and ethically, we ensure that they can fully embrace the potential of emerging technologies while preserving ethical standards. The emotional preparedness of educators also plays a crucial influence in the adoption of AI technologies in the classroom. Many instructors are averse to change, particularly when it comes to the introduction of technology that may appear sophisticated or scary. Building educators' confidence in utilizing AI technologies is therefore a key component of training. This may be done by giving hands-on chances for instructors to interact with AI tools in a low-pressure atmosphere, enabling them to acquaint themselves with the technology at their speed. In addition, training programs should stress the benefits that AI can provide to both instructors and students, showing how AI technologies may make teaching more efficient, effective, and fun. By cultivating a favorable perspective toward technology, educators will be more ready to accept AI technologies and incorporate them into their teaching techniques.

Another key concern is providing continued assistance for educators after they have been educated in AI tools (Schiff, 2022). Professional development should not be a one-time event, but rather a continuous process that allows instructors to keep current on breakthroughs in AI technology and learn how to further enhance their use of these tools. Continuous professional learning possibilities can include seminars, online courses, peer collaboration, and involvement in AI-focused education networks. By delivering continuing support and opportunities for professional growth, educators may feel sure that they have the tools and advice they need to succeed in integrating AI into their teaching methods. It is vital to note that educating educators in AI tools is not a "one-size-fits-all" approach. Varied instructors have varied levels of technology skills, instructional methods, and topic areas. Therefore, training programs should be personalized to match the particular requirements and goals of individual instructors. For example, a language professor may require different training than a math instructor when it comes to employing AI technologies in the classroom. By giving individualized training that meets the particular requirements and problems of each educator, training programs may optimize the effect of AI technologies in the classroom and guarantee that all instructors are equipped with the skills they need to succeed. The integration of AI technologies into the classroom has great opportunities for increasing teaching and learning, but it is only through proper training that these tools can be used to their full potential. Educators must be supplied with the information, technical skills, and emotional preparation to properly use AI technologies in their teaching methods. Moreover, continual support and individualized training programs are vital to ensure that instructors stay confident and competent in utilizing AI technologies as the technology continues to grow. By investing in the professional development of educators and cultivating a favorable attitude toward AI, we can ensure that AI-driven educational technologies play a meaningful and useful role in defining the future of teaching and learning. Through this approach, educators will not only become adept in using AI technologies but will also be able to harness the potential of these tools to create more customized, engaging, and successful learning experiences for their students.

Case Studies: Successful Applications of AI Tools in English Language Classrooms

In recent years, Artificial Intelligence (AI) has progressively found its way into the field of education, bringing revolutionary prospects for instructors and learners alike. In English language classes, AI technologies are beginning to change how students acquire language skills, giving professors vital resources for customizing learning, raising engagement, and improving the entire educational experience. While the potential of AI in education is tremendous, it is via real-world applications that its worth truly becomes clear. Numerous case studies from across the world indicate how AI technologies have been effectively deployed in English language education, delivering extraordinary benefits in terms of student learning outcomes and instructional efficiency.

One such scenario comes from a high college in Singapore, where the college integrated an AI-powered language learning platform into its English curriculum (Kot & Nykyporets, 2024). The platform, developed to assist students improve their reading comprehension and vocabulary abilities, uses machine learning algorithms to analyze students' performance and adjust to their particular learning requirements. As students interacted with the platform, the system continually recorded their progress, delivering individualized suggestions for growth based on their unique areas of weakness. This allowed students to study at their own pace, with the system delivering increasingly complex material as their abilities grew. The data created by the platform enables professors to monitor each student's development in real time, giving them the insights necessary to offer targeted help and intervention when needed. What made this scenario distinctive was the method by which AI was effortlessly incorporated into the educational setting. Instead of replacing traditional teaching techniques, the AI tool operated as an additional resource that empowered both students and professors. For students, it provided an interactive and interesting approach to practice reading and vocabulary skills, while for instructors, it allowed them to assess individual progress, intervene more effectively, and give tailored feedback. The outcome was a considerable gain in student engagement and academic achievement, with students saying that the AI tool helped them feel more confident in their skills and encouraged them to continue studying. Professors, on the other hand, found that the platform made their teaching more efficient since it freed up time that would otherwise be spent on grading or specialized training.

In another example, a university in the United Kingdom deployed an AI-driven voice recognition system to enable non-native English speakers to improve their pronunciation (Mamun et al, 2024). The system uses natural language processing (NLP) and machine learning algorithms to analyze the correctness of students' spoken English, delivering real-time feedback on their pronunciation, intonation, and accent. This allowed students to practice speaking English without the direct presence of an instructor, allowing them the flexibility to make errors and progress at their speed. The system was developed to imitate a discussion with a native speaker, allowing students the opportunity to practice conversational English in a low-pressure atmosphere. For both instructors and students, this AI technology was a game-changer. Professors were able to track students' pronunciation improvement over time, finding patterns of frequent faults and delivering focused instruction to correct these concerns. Students loved the chance to practice speaking without feeling self-conscious, and many said that they felt more comfortable using English in real-world circumstances. The AI technology also gave significant insights into individual students' speech habits, which enabled professors to modify their lectures to better fit the requirements of each learner. As a consequence, students demonstrated considerable increases in both their speaking confidence and their pronunciation skills.

Similarly, in a big language college in Japan, AI-powered chatbots were utilized to assist conversational practice and increase students' speaking proficiency. The chatbots, built to simulate real-life discussions, allowed students to participate in discourse with an AI system that could interpret and respond to their inputs. These AI chatbots were available to students 24/7, providing them the option to practice speaking at any time outside of class hours. The chatbots were able to engage students in meaningful discussions, giving corrections and ideas for development based on their replies. This offered students a more involved and dynamic opportunity to develop their speaking abilities, outside the confines of standard classroom-based education. The usage of AI chatbots in this example proved to be very effective for students who suffered from speaking anxiety or lacked confidence in their abilities to communicate in English. Many students claimed that they found it simpler to communicate with the chatbot than with a human instructor or fellow student since it removed the worry of criticism or making errors in front of others. The AI system also gave quick feedback, allowing students to fix their mistakes in real-time and measure their progress over time. Professors felt that the chatbot integration allowed them to focus on more complicated parts of language acquisition, such as grammar and vocabulary development, while the chatbots handled conversational practice. As a consequence, the college noticed a rise in students' speaking skills, and the chatbot-based system became a vital element of the college's language learning method.

Another case study comes from a blended learning program at a middle college in the United States, where AI was utilized to tailor the learning experience for each student. In this initiative, students used an AI-powered platform to engage in personalized English classes that were suited to their learning style and competence level. The software examined data from students' interactions, such as the pace at which they completed tasks and the sorts of errors they made, to construct individualized learning pathways. These routes ensured that students were constantly engaged in content that was suitable for their ability level, eliminating irritation from activities that were too challenging or boredom from material that was too easy. One of the most surprising features of this example was how the platform's AI algorithms were able to recognize learning patterns and provide suggestions to improve student results. For example, if a student struggled with a certain grammatical idea, the platform would give extra tasks and materials to reinforce that subject. If a learner exhibited significant improvement in a specific area, the platform would provide more challenging content to keep them interested. Professors were able to monitor students' progress using a dashboard that gave real-time data, allowing them to step in and provide extra help when necessary. The results were outstanding, with students making faster progress and developing greater confidence in their talents. Professors also reported feeling more empowered, as the AI technology offered them vital insights about student performance and helped them focus on areas where they could make the biggest effect.

In each of these situations, the effective deployment of AI tools in English language colleges showed the significance of customization, real-time feedback, and constant progress tracking. AI technologies, such as machine learning, natural language processing, and speech recognition, were utilized to build tailored learning experiences that catered to individual students' requirements, while also giving professors useful information about student development. These case studies further indicate that AI does not replace the function of the instructor but rather acts as a strong tool that supports and enhances traditional teaching approaches. Professors are still vital in giving emotional support, promoting critical thinking, and creating meaningful relationships with students, but AI tools give additional resources that make the learning process more efficient and successful. While the scenarios cited above highlight the promise of AI in language education, it is vital to remember that the effective use of AI tools requires careful preparation and a clear knowledge of the individual requirements and goals of the learners. In each case, the AI tools were picked and created with the learners in mind, ensuring that the technology complimented the existing curriculum and teaching techniques. Moreover, continued assistance and professional development for instructors were critical components in ensuring that the technologies were used effectively. Professors needed to be prepared with the knowledge and abilities to incorporate AI tools into their lectures and make the most of the data and insights generated by these technologies.

The success stories from these case studies offer useful insights for educators and administrators considering the integration of AI into their classrooms. AI has the potential to change English language education, enabling individualized learning experiences, real-time feedback, and data-driven insights that can help both students and professors thrive (Loor et al, 2024). As AI continues to advance, probably, its role in education will only expand, creating even more potential for innovative and effective language learning. The successful implementations of AI technologies in English language classrooms illustrate the great potential of this technology to improve student learning outcomes and enhance teaching techniques. By incorporating AI technologies into the classroom, educators may develop more customized, engaging, and efficient learning experiences that respond to the different requirements of their students. These case studies serve as a compelling reminder that AI is not a replacement for the human aspect of education, but rather a complimentary tool that may help educators unlock new possibilities for student achievement. As AI continues to advance, the future of English language instruction will be molded by these transformational technologies, and educators will play a critical role in harnessing their potential to create more effective and meaningful learning experiences for their students.

The Future of AI in English Language Teaching: Trends, Innovations, and Opportunities

The future of English language education (ELT) is experiencing a spectacular transition (Chavez, 2022). At the center of this transition lies Artificial Intelligence (AI), a technology that is transforming how educators teach and students learn. With the tremendous breakthroughs in AI, the opportunities for boosting language teaching are nearly unlimited. The incorporation of AI into English language colleges promises to change traditional teaching approaches, bringing new options for tailored learning, interactive engagement, and better efficiency. However, while AI provides enormous potential, its future in ELT also poses crucial considerations regarding the ethical, pedagogical, and practical consequences of such a major transformation. As we look to the future, AI's position in English language instruction will surely expand in prominence. One of the most significant developments we can anticipate is the broad use of AI-powered solutions that focus on customizing learning experiences for individual students. Unlike traditional teaching approaches, where the information is generally developed for a “one-size-fits-all” approach, AI enables the production of highly personalized educational experiences (Makinde et al, 2024). AI-driven systems are already being used to evaluate student progress in real-time and change learning courses accordingly. By observing a student's interactions with the material, AI can discern areas of strength and weakness, giving individualized information and suggestions that suit the particular requirements of each learner. This degree of customization allows students to grow at their speed, ensuring they receive the correct level of challenge without becoming overwhelmed or distracted.

In addition to tailored learning, AI will also promote a deeper, more immersive approach to language acquisition. Technologies like natural language processing (NLP) and voice recognition are already being utilized to enhance students' pronunciation, grammar, and speaking abilities (Chandran et al, 2024). The future will certainly witness even more advanced implementations of these technologies. For instance, AI-powered systems will be able to offer real-time feedback on not just pronunciation, but also on tone, pitch, and emotional expression. These developments will help students enhance not just their linguistic correctness but also their capacity to communicate successfully in diverse circumstances, be it professional, casual, or emotional (Kayyali, 2025 B). AI will allow for more dynamic and engaging language learning experiences. Traditional language training frequently entails limited opportunities for students to practice speaking and listening in real-world circumstances. While classroom activities might imitate some of these experiences, there's a limit to how much real-life exposure children can get inside the boundaries of a regimented environment. However, with AI, language learners will be able to participate in fully interactive discussions with virtual assistants, chatbots, or even simulated native speakers, at any time and from any location. These tools will create a risk-free environment for children to practice speaking and listening skills, without the fear of criticism or shame. Over time, these encounters may expand from simple dialogues to complicated talks, allowing students to practice their abilities across a range of themes and settings.

This move toward more interactive and immersive learning environments is further boosted by the rise of AI in the domain of augmented reality (AR) and virtual reality (VR). In the future, we might witness immersive language learning experiences where students are digitally transferred to English-speaking areas. Imagine a student learning English through a VR experience where they travel to an English-speaking city, engage with local speakers, and complete language assignments based on real-life circumstances. These sorts of encounters would not only improve language abilities but also promote cultural awareness and offer a more thorough knowledge of the language in context. As AR and VR technology continues to progress, we may anticipate these immersive learning tools to become more accessible and integrated into ordinary language learning situations. AI's capacity to aid in language acquisition isn't restricted to delivering real-time feedback or creating individualized learning experiences. Another intriguing development in the future of AI in ELT is its role in automating administrative activities. Professors spend a large amount of time on tasks such as grading assignments, assessing student progress, and managing classroom logistics (Cooper et al, 2019). AI can assist lessen the stress of these activities, allowing educators to focus more on teaching and less on administrative labor. For example, AI-powered grading systems are already being used to analyze student writing and assignments, providing professors with a tool that can assess content, language, and structure in a fraction of the time it would take a person. Similarly, AI can automate progress monitoring and student reporting, giving professors precise insights into student performance without having to manually assess each student's work. As AI continues to improve, there will undoubtedly be a rising emphasis on its ability to help instructors in professional growth and cooperation. Professors will be able to utilize AI to access information and tools that help better their teaching methods, remain current on the latest research and advancements in ELT, and even connect with other educators across the world. For instance, AI systems might be used to recommend teaching tactics or resources based on a professor's prior lessons and student outcomes, helping educators enhance their ways and stay aligned with best practices. Moreover, AI might provide a platform for instructors to exchange materials, lesson plans, and experiences, building a worldwide community of educators devoted to continual learning and growth.

Despite the exciting possibilities that AI provides to English language instruction, some problems and issues must be addressed to fully fulfill its promise. One of the most significant challenges is the need to guarantee that AI technologies are created in a way that is culturally sensitive and linguistically suitable. While AI may be trained to comprehend and produce language, it must also be able to manage the complexity of diverse cultures, dialects, and regional variants of English. If AI technologies are not created with these aspects in mind, they risk reinforcing prejudices or offering erroneous feedback (Weidinger et al, 2021). For example, a voice recognition system trained exclusively in American English can have trouble recognizing or rating non-native English speakers from other places. To prevent these challenges, AI developers must guarantee that their systems are adaptive and able to identify the diversity of English language learners. Another issue is the potential for AI to widen the digital divide. While AI technologies offer the promise of transforming language acquisition, they also require access to technology and the internet. In many parts of the world, particularly in low-income communities, this access is limited or absent. As AI becomes more incorporated into education, there is a concern that students who lack access to essential equipment might be left behind. To overcome this difficulty, educational institutions, governments, and technology companies must work together to guarantee that AI technologies are available to all learners, regardless of their socioeconomic status.

Additionally, there is a concern about data privacy and security. AI systems in language learning create large volumes of data about students, including their progress, errors, and personal preferences. This data must be saved and managed appropriately, with robust protections in place to protect students' privacy. Educators must be mindful of the ethical implications of utilizing AI in the classroom and ensure that students' data is not exploited or disclosed to unauthorized parties. Looking ahead, one of the most intriguing prospects for AI in English language instruction is the possibility of lifelong learning. Language learning is not confined to a single age group or educational level. People of all ages are continuously learning new languages, whether for personal, professional, or academic reasons. AI can empower lifelong learners by delivering adaptable, on-demand language learning tools that respond to the needs of individuals at various phases of their language journey. Whether it's an adult learning English for the first time, a professional trying to better their business English, or a retiree studying English for travel purposes, AI can give individualized guidance to help learners reach their goals.

The future of AI in English language instruction is packed with promise (Celik et al, 2024). As AI continues to progress, we should expect increasingly more complex tools and breakthroughs that will alter how language is taught and learned. From individualized learning experiences and immersive settings to administrative automation and professional development, AI will provide new opportunities to revolutionize language teaching and empower both students and instructors. However, like with any technology innovation, it is necessary to approach AI integration wisely and ethically, ensuring that it serves to enhance the human components of education and create inclusion, accessibility, and equity. Ultimately, the future of AI in English language education will depend not just on the technology itself, but on how it is used to provide meaningful, successful, and engaging learning experiences for students throughout the world.

Recommendations

As we reflect on the integration of Artificial Intelligence in English Language Teaching (ELT), it becomes clear that while the potential is immense, the path forward must be navigated with care, foresight, and an unwavering commitment to the human dimension of education. AI is not merely a tool—it is a shift in the texture of teaching, a new kind of relationship between learner, knowledge, and machine. Therefore, any recommendation must honor the complexity of classrooms, the diversity of learners, and the lived realities of teachers. What follows is not a list of directives, but a set of thoughtfully grounded suggestions drawn from observation, dialogue, and the evolving practice of educators who are learning to teach differently.

First and foremost, educators must be at the heart of the AI conversation—not on the periphery. Too often, new technologies are introduced to classrooms without meaningful involvement from those who know the learners best: the teachers. When educators are treated as passive implementers rather than active designers of AI integration, the result is often superficial adoption or even resistance. Schools and institutions should commit to a culture of inclusion, where teachers are consulted early and often. This means involving them in pilot programs, seeking their feedback on tool usability, and genuinely listening to their concerns about practicality, workload, and pedagogical value. A teacher who feels respected and empowered is far more likely to embrace innovation with intention rather than hesitation. Second, professional development must evolve in both scope and spirit. It is not enough to offer one-off training sessions or technical walkthroughs. What educators need is sustained, context-sensitive support that meets them where they are. This includes ongoing mentorship, collaborative learning communities, and access to specialists who understand both technology and language pedagogy. Importantly, training should not focus solely on how to use AI tools, but also on when and why to use them. Teachers should feel confident making pedagogical decisions about which AI applications align with their goals, classroom dynamics, and student profiles. In many ways, this is about restoring agency to educators—not replacing their expertise with algorithmic logic, but complementing it with new capacities. Third, institutions should commit to ethical transparency. This is not a matter of ticking a compliance box but of building trust with both educators and learners. Every AI tool used in the classroom collects data, shapes learning pathways, and potentially influences student behavior. It is essential that students and their families understand what information is being gathered, how it is being used, and who has access to it. Similarly, educators must be informed about the limitations of these tools—their biases, their assumptions, and their boundaries. This transparency is particularly important in multilingual, multicultural classrooms where language is not only a skill to be mastered but an identity to be honored. AI must never become a hidden judge; it must remain an accountable partner in the learning process.

Another important recommendation is to foster critical digital literacy—not only among students, but among teachers and administrators as well. It is tempting to treat AI as a neutral force, a smart machine that simply delivers what the user needs. But AI is never neutral. Its "intelligence" is trained on data sets that reflect particular worldviews, languages, and power structures. Therefore, both teachers and students should be encouraged to question the content and feedback that AI tools provide. Why does the grammar checker flag this sentence? Why does the pronunciation app rate a particular accent as "less fluent"? These are not merely technical questions—they are cultural and pedagogical ones. By creating space for these discussions, classrooms become sites of empowerment rather than passive consumption. AI tools should be used to enhance—not replace—the most vital aspects of language learning: communication, creativity, and connection. Language is not merely a system of rules to be mastered but a human practice of meaning-making. While AI can support grammar drills or vocabulary practice, it cannot (and should not) replace the organic messiness of human conversation. Educators should prioritize activities that preserve this human core: group discussions, collaborative projects, storytelling, debate, improvisation. AI might offer a mirror, but it is people who offer the spark. It is the teacher who notices when a shy student finally speaks up; it is a classmate who asks a question that opens a new insight. No algorithm can replicate those moments of real learning. Equity must also be a guiding principle. The promise of AI is meaningless if it remains accessible only to those with high-speed internet, modern devices, or well-resourced schools. Policymakers, developers, and educational leaders must work together to close the digital divide. This includes investing in infrastructure for rural and underserved communities, designing tools that function offline or on low-end devices, and ensuring that interfaces are linguistically and culturally inclusive. At the same time, AI tools should not widen gaps by reinforcing linguistic norms that marginalize certain dialects, accents, or expressions. Language learners come from diverse backgrounds, and their voices deserve to be heard and affirmed—not "corrected" into homogeneity.

Another area that demands attention is research and evaluation. AI in ELT is still a relatively new field, and its impact needs to be assessed with rigor and nuance. Schools and institutions should invest in small-scale, practice-based research projects that involve teachers as co-investigators. What works in one context may not work in another, and it is only through grounded, iterative inquiry that meaningful patterns will emerge. These findings should then be shared openly, creating a living archive of what is possible, what is challenging, and what still needs to be understood. Emotional well-being must also be part of the equation. The introduction of AI tools can sometimes increase anxiety—for teachers who fear being replaced, for students who feel watched by an invisible evaluator, for parents unsure about data privacy. Schools should not rush to implement new tools without addressing these emotional landscapes. This could take the form of open forums, parent workshops, student-led feedback sessions, or even co-design opportunities where learners help shape how AI is used in their learning environment. When people feel involved, their anxiety diminishes. When they feel heard, their openness grows.

Lastly, we must retain a sense of humility. No matter how sophisticated the technology becomes, education remains a fundamentally human endeavor. It is shaped by curiosity, empathy, struggle, and transformation. AI can help us teach more efficiently, perhaps even more effectively—but it cannot teach us what it means to be in relationship with another mind, another voice, another life. That is the teacher's work. That is the learner's journey. And that is what must always be protected. The future of English language teaching will undoubtedly be influenced by Artificial Intelligence, but how that future unfolds depends on the choices we make today. If we approach this transformation with care, courage, and a deep respect for the people at its center, AI will not eclipse the classroom—it will illuminate it. Let us then proceed not with blind enthusiasm, nor with fear, but with the quiet, determined belief that technology, when guided by wisdom and shaped by human hands, can truly help us build better, more inclusive, more inspiring spaces for language learning.

CONCLUSION

As we conclude this chapter, it is obvious that Artificial Intelligence (AI) has enormous promise in the area of English Language Teaching (ELT), changing the future of education in deep and transformational ways. The incorporation of AI technologies into ELT is not only a technology trend but a significant step forward that challenges standard teaching paradigms and creates new opportunities for both instructors and learners alike. The road to incorporating AI in ELT is difficult, subtle, and full of both possibilities and problems, yet the potential for development and innovation is evident. One of the most striking elements of AI in ELT is its capacity to tailor learning experiences. Traditional language courses, albeit useful, sometimes work under a one-size-fits-all format that may not adequately meet the specific needs of each student. AI-powered technologies, such as intelligent tutoring systems, adaptive learning platforms, and voice recognition software, can adjust courses, feedback, and practice to suit individual learners. This customization enables a deeper, more interesting learning experience, where students may move at their speed, review difficult ideas, and receive prompt, individualized feedback. Such qualities are particularly important in language learning, where the acquisition of new vocabulary, grammar, and pronunciation requires constant repetition and specific attention.

Moreover, AI has the potential to boost professors' productivity by automating time-consuming administrative activities, such as grading and tracking student progress. This enables instructors to spend more time connecting with students, devising unique lesson plans, and delivering relevant feedback. In addition, AI may act as a great teaching aid, delivering resources and ideas that correspond with curricular objectives and helping professors remain informed with the newest pedagogical breakthroughs. This dynamic interplay between AI and educators produces a collaborative atmosphere where technology enhances rather than replaces the function of the instructor. Despite the evident benefits, the incorporation of AI in English language instruction is not without its hurdles. One of the biggest issues is the problem of data privacy and security. AI solutions generally rely on huge volumes of data to perform properly, including personal information, learning patterns, and interaction histories. Protecting this data is vital, and colleges, institutions, and developers must guarantee that AI systems are developed with effective security safeguards and conform to ethical norms. Furthermore, educators must be educated to recognize the ethical implications of AI in the classroom, such as the possibility of algorithmic bias and the necessity for openness in how AI makes judgments. These ethical issues are crucial in ensuring that AI is utilized properly and in ways that benefit all learners, regardless of their background or demographic.

Another problem is the possible over-reliance on technology. While AI can boost learning, it is vital to recognize that language acquisition is a fundamentally social and participatory process. The human parts of language instruction, such as cultural context, emotional support, and social connection, cannot be substituted by robots. As such, AI should be considered as a complement to, rather than a substitute for, human instructors. The role of the instructor in encouraging debates, promoting innovation, and offering emotional direction remains irreplaceable, and AI technologies must be understood as instruments that enhance rather than reduce these human attributes. As we move into the future, the role of AI in English language instruction is expected to develop and evolve. With breakthroughs in natural language processing (NLP), machine learning, and neural networks, AI systems will become increasingly intelligent, and capable of comprehending and reacting to students in more subtle and individualized ways. The development of AI-powered systems that can imitate real-world language contexts, such as virtual conversation partners or interactive cultural simulations, will significantly improve the language learning experience. Additionally, as AI tools become more widely adopted and refined, we can expect to see more seamless integration between classroom instruction and real-world applications, such as the ability to practice language skills in authentic settings, even if students are geographically distant from native speakers.

It is equally vital to note that the future of AI in ELT will be influenced by continuing research and cooperation. Educators, academics, and technology developers must work together to guarantee that AI technologies are not only successful in assisting language acquisition but also equitable and accessible to all students. This involves bridging the digital divide, ensuring that AI technologies are inexpensive and available to learners in varied contexts, and encouraging digital literacy among educators to guarantee they can successfully incorporate AI into their teaching techniques. By stressing inclusion and accessibility, we can guarantee that AI acts as a tool for empowerment, enabling learners from all backgrounds to accomplish their language learning goals. The effectiveness of AI in English language instruction ultimately depends on how it is incorporated into current educational systems and how instructors are equipped to use these technologies successfully. Professional development programs will be vital in helping instructors grow their skills in utilizing AI tools and understanding how these technologies might enhance their teaching. Furthermore, continuing reflection and adaptation will be crucial, as AI technologies are always growing. Professors must be open to learning and adjusting their techniques to accommodate new technologies, while also critically analyzing the impact of AI on student results. The future of English language instruction is closely related to the incorporation of AI, and while obstacles persist, the prospects are tremendous. As AI continues to advance, it has the potential to revolutionize not only how we teach and learn languages but also how we conceive about education itself. By adopting AI carefully, ethically, and responsibly, we may uncover new routes to language acquisition, encouraging more individualized, interesting, and successful learning experiences. As we navigate this fascinating new frontier, it is vital to remember that AI is not a goal in itself but a tool to increase the human connections, creativity, and critical thinking that lie at the heart of language acquisition. The future of AI-powered English language teaching is bright, and with careful study and planning, it will lead to more inclusive, efficient, and effective educational experiences for learners and educators alike.

REFERENCES

Abulibdeh, A., Zaidan, E., & Abulibdeh, R. (2024). Navigating the confluence of artificial intelligence and education for sustainable development in the era of industry 4.0: Challenges, opportunities, and ethical dimensions. *Journal of Cleaner Production, 437*, 140527. DOI: 10.1016/j.jclepro.2023.140527

AbuSahyon, A. S. A. E., Alzyoud, A., Alshorman, O., & Al-Absi, B. (2023). AI-driven technology and Chatbots as tools for enhancing English language learning in the context of second language acquisition: A review study. *International Journal of Membrane Science and Technology, 10*(1), 1209–1223. DOI: 10.15379/ijmst.v10i1.2829

Ahmad, K., Iqbal, W., El-Hassan, A., Qadir, J., Benhaddou, D., Ayyash, M., & Al-Fuqaha, A. (2023). Data-driven artificial intelligence in education: A comprehensive review. *IEEE Transactions on Learning Technologies*.

Akyuz, Y. (2020). Effects of intelligent tutoring systems (ITS) on personalized learning (PL). *Creative Education, 11*(06), 953–978. DOI: 10.4236/ce.2020.116069

Al-khresheh, M. H. (2024). The future of artificial intelligence in English language teaching: Pros and cons of ChatGPT implementation through a systematic review. *Language Teaching Research, 43*, 54–80. DOI: 10.32038/ltrq.2024.43.04

Alam, A. (2023). Harnessing the Power of AI to Create Intelligent Tutoring Systems for Enhanced Classroom Experience and Improved Learning Outcomes. In *Intelligent Communication Technologies and Virtual Mobile Networks* (pp. 571–591). Springer Nature Singapore. DOI: 10.1007/978-981-99-1767-9_42

Anis, M. (2023). Leveraging artificial intelligence for inclusive English language teaching: Strategies and implications for learner diversity. *Journal of Multidisciplinary Educational Research, 12*(6), 54–70.

Anshari, M., Almunawar, M. N., Lim, S. A., & Al-Mudimigh, A. (2019). Customer relationship management and big data enabled: Personalization & customization of services. *Applied Computing and Informatics, 15*(2), 94–101. DOI: 10.1016/j.aci.2018.05.004

Arani, S. M. N. (2024). Navigating the future of language learning: A Conceptual review of ai's role in personalized learning. *Computer-Assisted Language Learning Electronic Journal, 25*(3), 1–22.

Barua, P. D., Vicnesh, J., Gururajan, R., Oh, S. L., Palmer, E., Azizan, M. M., Kadri, N. A., & Acharya, U. R. (2022). Artificial intelligence enabled personalised assistive tools to enhance education of children with neurodevelopmental disorders—A review. *International Journal of Environmental Research and Public Health, 19*(3), 1192. DOI: 10.3390/ijerph19031192 PMID: 35162220

Basilotta-Gómez-Pablos, V., Matarranz, M., Casado-Aranda, L. A., & Otto, A. (2022). Teachers' digital competencies in higher education: A systematic literature review. *International Journal of Educational Technology in Higher Education, 19*(1), 8. DOI: 10.1186/s41239-021-00312-8

Bender, T. (2023). *Discussion-based online teaching to enhance student learning: Theory, practice and assessment.* Taylor & Francis.

Celik, I., Dindar, M., Muukkonen, H., & Järvelä, S. (2022). The promises and challenges of artificial intelligence for teachers: A systematic review of research. *TechTrends, 66*(4), 616–630. DOI: 10.1007/s11528-022-00715-y

Chaka, C. (2023). Fourth industrial revolution—a review of applications, prospects, and challenges for artificial intelligence, robotics and blockchain in higher education. Research and Practice in Technology Enhanced Learning, 18, 002-002.

Chan, C. K. Y. (2023). A comprehensive AI policy education framework for university teaching and learning. *International Journal of Educational Technology in Higher Education, 20*(1), 38. DOI: 10.1186/s41239-023-00408-3

Chandran, M., Wang, S. L., Dzulkifly, S., Ng, T. F., & Ghoneim, A. S. (2024). Enhancing English Pronunciation Learning in Primary Education through Natural Language Processing: A Quantitative Study. *Journal of ICT in Education, 11*(2), 1–17. DOI: 10.37134/jictie.vol11.2.1.2024

Chavez, J. (2022). Narratives of bilingual parents on the real-life use of English language: Materials for English language teaching curriculum. Arab World English Journals, 13(3).

Chen, L., Chen, P., & Lin, Z. (2020). Artificial intelligence in education: A review. *IEEE Access : Practical Innovations, Open Solutions, 8*, 75264–75278. DOI: 10.1109/ACCESS.2020.2988510

Chen, Y. (2024, May). Enhancing Language Acquisition: The Role of AI in Facilitating Effective Language Learning. In 2024 3rd International Conference on Humanities, Wisdom Education and Service Management (HWESM 2024) (pp. 593-600). Atlantis Press.

Chiu, T. K., Xia, Q., Zhou, X., Chai, C. S., & Cheng, M. (2023). Systematic literature review on opportunities, challenges, and future research recommendations of artificial intelligence in education. *Computers and Education: Artificial Intelligence, 4*, 100118. DOI: 10.1016/j.caeai.2022.100118

Cooper, L. J., Laster-Loftus, A., & Mandernach, B. J. (2019). Efficient online instruction: Maximum impact in minimal time. *Online Journal of Distance Learning Administration, 22*(3), 1–9.

Díaz-Rodríguez, N., Del Ser, J., Coeckelbergh, M., de Prado, M. L., Herrera-Viedma, E., & Herrera, F. (2023). Connecting the dots in trustworthy Artificial Intelligence: From AI principles, ethics, and key requirements to responsible AI systems and regulation. *Information Fusion, 99*, 101896. DOI: 10.1016/j.inffus.2023.101896

Dimitriadou, E., & Lanitis, A. (2023). A critical evaluation, challenges, and future perspectives of using artificial intelligence and emerging technologies in smart classrooms. *Smart Learning Environments, 10*(1), 12. DOI: 10.1186/s40561-023-00231-3 PMID: 40478141

Edmett, A., Ichaporia, N., Crompton, H., & Crichton, R. (2023). Artificial intelligence and English language teaching: Preparing for the future. British Council, 2024-08.

Eswaran, U., Eswaran, V., Murali, K., & Eswaran, V. (2025). AI-Powered Language Teaching and Learning: Innovations and Challenges. In Reimagining Intelligent Computer-Assisted Language Education (pp. 55-92). IGI Global.

Fitria, T. N. (2021). The use technology based on artificial intelligence in English teaching and learning. ELT Echo. *The Journal of English Language Teaching in Foreign Language Context, 6*(2), 213–223.

Fitria, T. N. (2021, December). Artificial intelligence (AI) in education: Using AI tools for teaching and learning process. In Prosiding Seminar Nasional & Call for Paper STIE AAS (Vol. 4, No. 1, pp. 134-147).

Gauthier, A., Rizvi, S., Cukurova, M., & Mavrikis, M. (2022). Is it time we get real? A systematic review of the potential of data-driven technologies to address teachers' implicit biases. *Frontiers in Artificial Intelligence, 5*, 994967. DOI: 10.3389/frai.2022.994967 PMID: 36304958

Horwitz, E. K. (2020). *Becoming a language teacher: A practical guide to second language learning and teaching*. Castledown Publishers.

Ikedinachi, A. P., Misra, S., Assibong, P. A., Olu-Owolabi, E. F., Maskeliūnas, R., & Damasevicius, R. (2019). Artificial intelligence, smart classrooms and online education in the 21st century: Implications for human development. [JCIT]. *Journal of Cases on Information Technology, 21*(3), 66–79. DOI: 10.4018/JCIT.2019070105

Jones, K. M., Asher, A., Goben, A., Perry, M. R., Salo, D., Briney, K. A., & Robertshaw, M. B. (2020). "We're being tracked at all times": Student perspectives of their privacy in relation to learning analytics in higher education. *Journal of the Association for Information Science and Technology, 71*(9), 1044–1059. DOI: 10.1002/asi.24358

Kalyani, L. K. (2024). The role of technology in education: Enhancing learning outcomes and 21st century skills. International journal of scientific research in modern science and technology, 3(4), 05-10.

Kanchon, M. K. H., Sadman, M., Nabila, K. F., Tarannum, R., & Khan, R. (2024). Enhancing personalized learning: AI-driven identification of learning styles and content modification strategies. *International Journal of Cognitive Computing in Engineering, 5*, 269–278. DOI: 10.1016/j.ijcce.2024.06.002

Kayyali, M. (2024). Future possibilities and challenges of AI in education. In *Transforming education with generative AI: Prompt engineering and synthetic content creation* (pp. 118–137). IGI Global. DOI: 10.4018/979-8-3693-1351-0.ch006

Kayyali, M. (2025 A). AI in Higher Education: Revolutionizing Curriculum and Administration. In AI Adoption and Diffusion in Education (pp. 31-62). IGI Global Scientific Publishing.

Kayyali, M. (2025 B). The Future of AI in Education: Predictions and Emerging Trends. Next-Generation AI Methodologies in Education, 367-406.

Kecskes, I. (2019). *English as a lingua franca: The pragmatic perspective.* Cambridge University Press.

Kim, N. Y., Cha, Y., & Kim, H. S. (2019). Future English learning: Chatbots and artificial intelligence. Multimedia-Assisted Language Learning, 22(3).

Kot, S. O., & Nykyporets, S. S. (2024). *Utilization of artificial intelligence in enhancing English language proficiency in tertiary education. Science and Education in the Third Millennium: Information Technology.* Education, Law, Psychology, Social Sphere, Management.

Kovalenko, I., & Baranivska, N. (2024). Integrating Artificial Intelligence in English Language Teaching: Exploring the potential and challenges of AI tools in enhancing language learning outcomes and personalized education. Європейські соціо-правові та гуманітарні студії, (1), 86-95.

Kuddus, K. (2022). Artificial intelligence in language learning: Practices and prospects. Advanced Analytics and Deep Learning Models, 1-17.

Latif, E., Mai, G., Nyaaba, M., Wu, X., Liu, N., Lu, G., . . . Zhai, X. (2023). Artificial general intelligence (AGI) for education. arXiv preprint arXiv:2304.12479, 1.

Loor, M. A. M., Solorzano, D. M. A., Katherine, A., & Moreira, V. (2024). Integration of Artificial Intelligence in English Teaching. *Journal of Cleaner Production*, *289*, 125834.

Luckin, R., Cukurova, M., Kent, C., & Du Boulay, B. (2022). Empowering educators to be AI-ready. *Computers and Education: Artificial Intelligence*, *3*, 100076.

Makinde, A. I., Adeleye, S. A., Oronti, A. O., & Jimoh, I. T. (2024). Revolutionizing education. Artificial Intelligence for Wireless Communication Systems: Technology and Applications, 103.

Mamun, K. A., Nabid, R. A., Pranto, S. I., Lamim, S. M., Rahman, M. M., Mahammed, N., Huda, M. N., Sarker, F., & Khan, R. R. (2024). Smart reception: An artificial intelligence driven bangla language based receptionist system employing speech, speaker, and face recognition for automating reception services. *Engineering Applications of Artificial Intelligence*, *136*, 108923. DOI: 10.1016/j.engappai.2024.108923

Martin, S. M. (2019). *Artificial intelligence, mixed reality, and the redefinition of the classroom*. Rowman & Littlefield.

Mishra, R. (2024). EMBRACING A PARADIGM SHIFT: TRANSITIONING FROM TRADITIONAL TEACHING METHODS TO AI-BASED NLP EDUCATION. Research and Reviews in Literature. *Social Sciences*, •••, 75.

Murtaza, M., Ahmed, Y., Shamsi, J. A., Sherwani, F., & Usman, M. (2022). AI-based personalized e-learning systems: Issues, challenges, and solutions. *IEEE Access : Practical Innovations, Open Solutions*, *10*, 81323–81342. DOI: 10.1109/ACCESS.2022.3193938

Nilson, L. B., & Goodson, L. A. (2021). *Online teaching at its best: Merging instructional design with teaching and learning research*. John Wiley & Sons.

Parycek, P., Schmid, V., & Novak, A. S. (2024). Artificial Intelligence (AI) and automation in administrative procedures: Potentials, limitations, and framework conditions. *Journal of the Knowledge Economy*, *15*(2), 8390–8415. DOI: 10.1007/s13132-023-01433-3

Pitychoutis, K. M., & Al Rawahi, A. (2024). Smart Teaching: The Synergy of Multiple Intelligences and Artificial Intelligence in English as a Foreign Language Instruction.

Pokrivcakova, S. (2019). Preparing teachers for the application of AI-powered technologies in foreign language education. *Journal of Language and Cultural Education*, *7*(3), 135–153. DOI: 10.2478/jolace-2019-0025

Rajak, L., Chauhan, S., & Bara, S. (2024). Transforming English Pedagogy with Artificial Intelligence: Enroute to Enhanced Language Learning. In Artificial Intelligence: A Multidisciplinary Approach towards Teaching and Learning (pp. 216-241). Bentham Science Publishers.

Rehan, H. (2024). Advancing Cancer Treatment with AI-Driven Personalized Medicine and Cloud-Based Data Integration. *Journal of Machine Learning in Pharmaceutical Research*, *4*(2), 1–40.

Sajja, R., Sermet, Y., Cikmaz, M., Cwiertny, D., & Demir, I. (2024). Artificial intelligence-enabled intelligent assistant for personalized and adaptive learning in higher education. *Information (Basel)*, *15*(10), 596. DOI: 10.3390/info15100596

Sajja, R., Sermet, Y., Cwiertny, D., & Demir, I. (2023). Integrating AI and Learning Analytics for Data-Driven Pedagogical Decisions and Personalized Interventions in Education. arXiv preprint arXiv:2312.09548.

Schiff, D. (2021). Out of the laboratory and into the classroom: The future of artificial intelligence in education. *AI & Society*, *36*(1), 331–348. DOI: 10.1007/s00146-020-01033-8 PMID: 32836908

Schiff, D. (2022). Education for AI, not AI for education: The role of education and ethics in national AI policy strategies. *International Journal of Artificial Intelligence in Education*, *32*(3), 527–563. DOI: 10.1007/s40593-021-00270-2

Schmidt, T., & Strasser, T. (2022). Artificial intelligence in foreign language learning and teaching: A CALL for intelligent practice. Anglistik. *International Journal of English Studies*, *33*(1), 165–184.

Sharadgah, T. A., & Sa'di, R. A. (2022). A systematic review of research on the use of artificial intelligence in English language teaching and learning (2015-2021): What are the current effects? *Journal of Information Technology Education*, •••, 21.

Strielkowski, W., Grebennikova, V., Lisovskiy, A., Rakhimova, G., & Vasileva, T. (2024). AI-driven adaptive learning for sustainable educational transformation. *Sustainable Development.*

Vučković, A., & Sikimić, V. (2024). Global justice and the use of AI in education: Ethical and epistemic aspects. *AI & Society*, •••, 1–18.

Weidinger, L., Mellor, J., Rauh, M., Griffin, C., Uesato, J., Huang, P. S., . . . Gabriel, I. (2021). Ethical and social risks of harm from language models. arXiv preprint arXiv:2112.04359.

Zdravkova, K., Krasniqi, V., Dalipi, F., & Ferati, M. (2022). Cutting-edge communication and learning assistive technologies for disabled children: An artificial intelligence perspective. *Frontiers in Artificial Intelligence*, *5*, 970430. DOI: 10.3389/frai.2022.970430 PMID: 36388402

Zhang, J., & Tao, D. (2020). Empowering things with intelligence: A survey of the progress, challenges, and opportunities in artificial intelligence of things. *IEEE Internet of Things Journal*, *8*(10), 7789–7817. DOI: 10.1109/JIOT.2020.3039359

Chapter 10
The Effect of Artificial Intelligence on English Learners' Anxiety Levels

Farzaneh Kazemi
https://orcid.org/0009-0003-2332-2301
University of Tabriz, Iran

ABSTRACT

With the development of communication, acquiring a second language different from one's first language has become of great significance. Moreover, as the current era is known for the prevalence of technology being an integral part of individual lifestyles, the phenomenon of artificial intelligence (AI) has turned into one of the central issues in language teaching and learning. The chapter explores the concept of second language anxiety as a key phenomenon. As per the literature, AI has been reported to have several benefits, such as lower cognitive load, improved language output, a higher level of motivation, adaptive learning environment, provision of personalized feedback, and reduced demotivation. However, it is not free from shortcomings, such as unfamiliarity with computer skills can cause even more L2 anxiety in language learners. Therefore, it is concluded that the over-reliance on this technology may not be as advantageous as it may seem. The chapter is set to provide practical implications for the stakeholders in the realm of language education.

INTRODUCTION

With the development of communication, acquiring a language different from one's first language or L1 has become of great significance. Moreover, considering English as a lingua franca, the demand to learn this language has grown exponen-

DOI: 10.4018/979-8-3373-1952-0.ch010

tially. This trend, being unquestionably beneficial in terms of interactions, has not been free from challenges. Language learners may struggle with numerous barriers, ranging from physical, such as the lack of access to high-quality materials, to mental ones, such as the sense of ambiguity, anxiety, lack of motivation, lack of access to the most appropriate and up-to-date teaching methods, and lack of self-confidence.

Beyond any doubt, among the abovementioned issues, anxiety and the stress students experience in their learning process are of paramount importance. The issue is so highlighted that the concept of Second or Foreign Language Anxiety has grabbed remarkable attention in recent decades. According to the definition provided by Young (1991), the anxiety linked to the learning of a second or foreign language is referred to as "second/foreign language anxiety". However, its multidimensional nature has made it rather more complicated than expected. According to McIntyre and Gardner (1994), "a subjective feeling of tension, apprehension, nervousness, and worry associated with an arousal of the automatic nervous system" is what we can consider as L2 learning anxiety. As per Horwitz et al., (1986), a 'mental block' may exist of part of learners to represent their foreign language ability in public, despite their desirable learning skills. Moreover, they mention that this sort of anxiety includes three main components: (1) communication anxiety, (2) negative social criticism, and (3) test or academic anxiety.

As the current era is known for the prevalence of technology being an integral part of individual lifestyles, terms such as computer-assisted language learning (CALL) and mobile-assisted language learning (MALL) have now turned into one of the widely concerned areas worldwide. More precisely, in the recent couple of years, the phenomenon of artificial intelligence (AI) has turned into one of the central issues in the entire discipline of language teaching and learning. As the name suggests, Artificial Intelligence refers to the development of computer systems for performing tasks that require human intelligence. In another definition, it is referred to as an unnatural object or entity that includes the capability and capacity to meet or exceed the needs and wants of the task it is assigned taking into account the cultural and demographic circumstances (Bringsjord, 2011; Dobrev, 2012; McLean and Osei-Frimpong, 2019; Omohundro, 2014). Put simply, the availability of numerous chatbots, which only require a simple short prompt to provide the user with a great body of knowledge makes the use of this advancement more common day by day. Having considered advantages, such as accessibility, easiness of use, and personalized learning environment, they should also be investigated in terms of both pros as well as cons they are prone to bring about for their users. Hence, phenomena, such as autonomy, motivation, anxiety, and willingness to communicate in the target language are some of the issues worth investigating.

As far as the present chapter is concerned, it probes into the intersection of the notion of second or foreign language learning anxiety and the use of artificial intelligence in the process of learning and teaching English language. To this end, it is set out to cover both advantageous and disadvantageous outcomes of the use of this technology along with a thorough elaboration on the topic. The chapter is hoped to provide practical pedagogical implications for the stakeholders in the industry in the modern era of technology.

UNDERSTANDING ANXIETY IN L2 LEARNING

As mentioned earlier, the concept of anxiety is now a mainstay of second language acquisition (L2A) research. From an overall perspective, the term anxiety has been defined as the state of feeling apprehension by a person, which stems from the consciousness of the autonomic nervous system (Spielberger, 1983). More specifically, to define Language anxiety, as mentioned by MacIntyre (1999), it is *the apprehension experienced when a situation requires the use of a second language with which the individual is not fully proficient ... the propensity for an individual to react in a nervous manner when speaking, listening, reading, or writing in the second language. (p. 5)*

This concept can be categorized into two classes trait anxiety (stable disposition) and state anxiety (transient, "moment-by-moment" experience). Whereas the former is a general, rather stable emotion that a person is constantly dealing with, the latter refers to the anxiety that one experiences in particular conditions and circumstances. To reach a more precise definition, trait anxiety can be referred as "a feature of an individual's personality and therefore is both stable over time and applicable to wide range of situations" (MacIntyre, 1999, p.217). On the other hand, state anxiety "varies in intensity and duration and fluctuates over time as a function of the amount of stress that impinges upon an individual and that individual's interpretation of the stressful situation as personally dangerous or threatening" (Spielberger, 1976, p. 5)

In a second language learning situation, anxiety can be caused by several known as well as unknown resources. Foreign language (classroom) anxiety (FLCA) can be a consequence of three representative anxieties, namely, communication apprehension and understanding, test anxiety, and fear of negative evaluation (Horwitz, 2017). As defined by Horwitz et al., (1986, p. 128) it is "a distinct complex of self-perceptions, beliefs, feelings, and behaviors related to classroom language learning arising from the uniqueness of the language learning process".

A large number interior along with exterior factors can be involved in FLCA. In other words, students in a typical foreign language classroom can feel anxious due to various reasons such as their fear of failure, e.g., fear of using inappropriate lexis choice or grammatical structure or incorrect pronunciation. Their anxiety also can have its roots in communication anxiety, when they find it much more difficult to express their thoughts and emotions in a language different from their L1. For instance, finding appropriate wording and structure which completely conveys the meaning they want to may put them under a lot of mental pressure. They also may be scared of being kid in cases of error or mistake. As known peer pressure, refers to the state in which 'peers' pressure one to do or not do something against their wishes in exchange for making them a member of, or affiliated with, the peer group (Clasen & Brown, 1985). For example, a case of mispronunciation, other learners may laugh at them and cause several negative feelings, such as anxiety. It can also be because of being tested in the target language, as they may not see themselves as capable of answering questions in another language, with the highest efficiency, representing their literacy level in that second or foreign language. This is mostly apparent in earlier levels, such as basic or elementary, when learners do possess a mastery over less sophisticated language concepts and elements.

It is worth-mentioning that this emotion has been found to be both a driving force and also a barrier to achieving success in the language learning process. To elaborate more, this chapter seeks to determine how the use of artificial intelligence acts as a facilitator or deteriorator in this journey.

AI Tools in L2 Learning

The current century has witnessed a gradual rather considerable integration of big data and natural language processing technology, and as a result, AI into education in general. Forming educational AI, known by technological diversification, personalized education, and intelligent assessment are among the renowned uses of AI in education (Qu et al., 2022). It is aimed to provide learners with a meticulous, personalized, flexible, and open education ecology (Cai et al., 2023) and promotes the development of education in the intelligent era.

With the evolution of speech recognition, intelligent writing correction, personalized recommendations, and other functions, AI has been widely used in language learning (Ling, 2023). Students can benefit from learning, individualized to their own pace and needs, regardless of time and location, and take advantage of feedback, which is tailored to their own performance. Moreover, those with hearing or vision impairments are also provided with a chance to acquire their dream language (Ghafar et al., 2023). This phenomenon is considered an opportunity in many regards so that AI-enhanced platforms such as chatbots and chat-based teaching systems have engaged a large number of audiences worldwide. To name some, ChatGPT and Duolingo are worldly-known applications, available to everyone, providing a chance to learn as many languages as possible, especially in Duolingo, which teaches language through diversified activities and even gamification. Learners can practice several macro kills, including reading, writing, listening and speaking and some micro skills such as spelling and pronunciation. They also have the opportunity to practice creativity and confidence in communicating with other people through recently learned content and benefit from authentic and real-world applications (Handini et al., 2022). It has also been found to keep students both interested and active in their learning process (Nugraha et al., 2023).

In addition, ChatGPT also can assist learners in many aspects such as helping with ambiguity points and clarifying language concepts and also act as a speaking partner, with whom they can practice speaking and other skills and sub-skills. For instance, as far as writing skill is concerned, it has been reported to be capable of answering an extensive range of questions with appropriate wording, tense, and voice (Fitria, 2023). Furthermore, it has the ability to recommend activities for more language practice (Bin-Hady et al., 2023). Other positive outcomes, such as attitude change, and learning motivation have also been reported in the literature (Songsiengchai, 2025).

AI and Anxiety Reduction: Potential Benefits

The use of artificial intelligence in teaching and learning has been proven to be advantageous by several means. For instance, language learners have been reported to obtain improved language output, and subsequently, as a result, experience a higher level of motivation, when using AI in their learning. As they see their receptive and productive skills in English have excelled to a considerable extent, they will probably get more motivated to follow the path with greater passion and enthusiasm. This technology also makes the access to grammatical checking of sentences by language users much more convenient, through options, such as Grammarly and ChatGPT.

Moreover, the students struggle with a much lower cognitive load as they are provided with an adaptive learning environment that is tailored to their desires. They can adjust the appearance of the AI chatbot they use the majority of the time. For instance, if they feel more comfortable in dark themes than light ones, simply a click can bring their desirable working space. One more example is the chance of choosing the voice by which the chatbot speaks, to achieve more comfort. In addition, the pace at which the chatbot is talking is also alterable, learners can either slow it down or increase the pace, most of the time by dragging on a spectrum of speed. More importantly, it can act as a tireless tutor. Put simply, the learner can ask for clarification and scaffolding over and over again, regardless of human impatience or time constriction in traditional and in-person classrooms. There is no concept is fatigue experienced by a chatbot. For one thing, if one does not quite take in when and where a particular structure and voice is applied, the bot can give an endless list of sample sentences in authentic materials, such as newspapers, magazines, TV shows, etc. They are no longer afraid of being judged by peers when they do not quite figure the concept being taught out. Even basic questions can be answered by this technology.

As mentioned earlier, time is not a constraining factor any longer as well. Learners can have access to the AI applications at 10 a.m. or. 3 p.m. or even 2 a.m. That being said, time is not an excuse anymore to not acquire a new language. Flexible learning schedules have paved the way to reach considerably desired outcomes in English learning. This mostly benefits those with hectic lifestyles and overwhelming schedules, such as employees and college and university students.

Learners also enjoy greater confidence levels, when using AI. Firstly, personalized feedback makes it possible for them to understand their potential weakness and strengths in a very detailed way. Then they can work on highlighting the strengths and attempt to get rid of challenging points. Supportive virtual tutoring systems also give them positive encouraging messages to keep them in tune.

In recent years, a growing body of literature has focused on the use of AI in language learning and teaching. For one thing, Kazu and Kuvvetli (2023) in their research titled "The Influence of Pronunciation Education via Artificial Intelligence Technology on Vocabulary Acquisition in Learning English" investigated the ways in which vocabulary learning with the help of pronouncing with artificial intelligence leads to a longer memory. Applying an experimental pattern, a pre-test and post-test control group design, and involving a number of 56 high school students they found that pronunciation practice using artificial intelligence enabled the words to linger in memory longer.

Moreover, in a systematic literature review, Peña-Acuña, et al., (2024), investigated a body of research papers published in the domain of using artificial intelligence (AI) in English as a second language learning. Their work revealed that emerging technologies, especially chat with artificial intelligence (AI), adaptative or interactive, combined with other technologies, as AR, or teaching methodologies, as gamification, are putting English language teaching into revolution from a teaching perspective (Huang, 2020; Mabuan, 2024).

More related to the subject of this chapter, several studies have investigated the impact of the use of AI on English as a second or foreign language learners' anxiety levels. To name some, Elsayed et al., (2024) involved 92 BA Management students to study the impact of teacher support in AI-assisted exams on L2 learners' demotivation, anxiety, L2 learning experience, and academic success. The study followed a quantitative quasi-experimental design and using the Foreign Language Classroom Anxiety Scale designed by Horwitz (1983) and as found by the researchers, there were significant positive effects of teacher support on reducing demotivation and anxiety, enhancing L2 learning experiences, and improving academic success in the experimental group compared to the control group. The research then concluded that embedding AI technology with human elements is highly crucial in building up an interactive and responsive learning atmosphere.

Furthermore, Wen et al., (2024), probed into the effectiveness of generative AI, particularly ChatGPT3.5, in increasing interaction skills and reducing second language (L2) anxiety in English language teaching settings. Including a number of 293 secondary school students in Beijing, China, the study analyzed the situation of AI anxiety among secondary school students. As per the findings, a significant reduction in L2 anxiety was seen in the participants of this study. According to the suggestions provided by the researchers, educators are advised to cultivate students' AI literacy through comprehensive AI education and help them to create correct emotions through scientific psychological interventions to achieve a better use of AI EFL learning tools.

In another work, Zhang et al., (2024) also investigated the influence of an AI-speaking assistant, Lora, on Chinese EFL students' foreign language enjoyment (FLE), foreign language anxiety (FLA), and willingness to communicate (WTC) in English. The findings revealed a noteworthy reduction in FLA among the experimental group. The paper offers a more widespread implementation of AI-driven technologies to form diverse language-learning opportunities, and the application of AI features to create a supportive classroom setting.

In addition, Biju et al., (2024) examined the impact of AI-assisted language assessment on L2 learners' foreign language anxiety (FLA). With a sequential exploratory mixed-methods design, and involving 70 intermediate English learners from two intact university classes in Bangladesh, the study found that AI-assisted assessment lowered FLA to a considerable extent, and raised learners' motivation, besides improving attitudes about language acquisition.

On the contrary, several studies have not found a significant impact of the use of AI in anxiety reduction. For instance, El Shazly (2021) explored the effect of AI-powered language learning tools on Egyptian EFL learners' speaking performance and foreign language anxiety. The latter was measured through a questionnaire developed by Horwitz et al. (1986) and the results reported that the use of the AI-assisted language applications in the learners' speaking activities did not diminish the learners' foreign language anxiety.

Later on, Liu et al. (2023) investigated the impact of AI-assisted image recognition technologies on EFL learners' vocabulary knowledge, self-regulation, and anxiety. With an experimental design, the learners in the experimental group were given AI-assisted image recognition technologies to demonstrate images along with the related vocabulary to develop the learners' vocabulary knowledge. According to the findings of the research, there were no statistically significant differences between the experimental and control groups with regard to their self-regulation and language learning anxiety.

AI and Anxiety Increase: Potential Risks

Despite the aforementioned pros of the use of AI in language education, it is not free from challenges and shortcomings, which still require further research. The imbalance poses disadvantages and challenges to education such as AI inducing negative emotions such as anxiety and burnout in language learners (Steenbergen-Hu & Cooper, 2013) and reduced students' initiative (Miao et al., 2021). Moreover, AI is accompanied by the potential hazards of algorithmic bias and privacy infringement (Miao et al., 2021). Students might be hesitant or even unwilling to use AI (Jeon, 2024), especially after the rise of large generative AI models such as ChatGPT (Chat Generative Pre-Trained Transformer) and Sora (A text-to-video AI model from OpenAI), thus hindering the potential application and development of AI in education.

With the growth in the use of AI, individuals find human interactions more needless. Rather than discussing an issue with a human being, they simply grab their cell phones and raise it with a chatbot to suggest possible solutions. Since the basic elements of these bots are just algorithms, the lack of emotional support can bring about several psychological demerits. That being said, a robot will judge the situation based on the algorithms it is given; biased algorithms are then prone to bring about biased interaction between humans and chatbots. Moreover, in occasions when the AI application does not quite understand or misunderstands the user, by the provision of irrelevant and even sometimes incorrect responses, the person is about to get disheartened.

Besides several challenges mentioned, AI anxiety has also become common. To get a big picture, a definition can pave the way. As defined by Chen et al., (2024), it can be defined as an excessive fear stemming from the repercussions of AI-induced changes in one's personal or societal existence. The fear one experiences when seeing the majority of the aspects of their life have changed or are going to change, a sort of feeling of losing control can lead to anxiety. More particular to the subject of this chapter, language learners also can suffer from anxiety in their learning process while using AI. As reported by Shen and Guo (2024), along with positive feelings, EFL students also are reported to experience negative emotions such as 'anxiety', 'stress', 'worry', and 'frustration' in their AI-based classes. In another work, Çakmak (2022) also found that L2 learners face challenges in being understood precisely, which might have contributed to higher anxiety in L2 speaking. That is to say, when they cannot fully convey their intended meaning through appropriate words and do not experience the safe feeling of being understood e.g., by the AI chatbot, they may sense anxiety. Take a person who intends to learn the meaning and the use of an idiom in English; in cases of misspelling or using incorrect wording, the bot may not quite take in the user, and eventually, asking for further clarification can put the user under a lot of mental pressure.

Furthermore, there are numerous ethical concerns as well. Plagiarism is another absolutely frequent issue, where students merely copy the content provided by the chatbot and do not involve creativity and brain work. For instance, when they are asked to compose an essay on a particular topic, be it general, specialized, or scientific, regardless of familiarity or unfamiliarity, they tend to ask AI to do so for them. Even in oral productive speaking, for instance preparing for standard English tests, such as the IELTS exam, some learners simply memorize the answers by AI applications, without any complete comprehension of its syntax and semantics. As a result, even if they produce grammatically and lexically correct sentences, issues such as intonation and pragmatics are suffering. Therefore, examiners recognize this phenomenon and reduce marks according to their performance.

Factors Involved in the Impact of AI on Second Language Anxiety

Taking the abovementioned contradicting effects of AI on the level of anxiety experienced by L2 learners into consideration, there are several factors that need to be discussed in greater detail.

Initially, the individual differences should not be taken for granted. For one thing, learners of different ages may feel varying anxiety degrees; the amount of anxiety experienced by an adult AI user is much different from that of an adolescent. More importantly, the extent to which a person is familiar with computer skills can also be a determining factor. Thus, as the younger generations have a greater mastery over the use of the internet and AI in their everyday activities and as an integral part of their lifestyles, they may feel more confident and less anxious about implementing this tool in their language learning process. On the contrary, those with less advanced skills may feel uncomfortable and find talking to an electronic device rather wired, even when they are practicing English speaking skills. Additionally, anxiety-coping strategies differ widely among various individuals. While some try to learn more in cases of unfamiliarity, or as known to be ambiguity-tolerant people, others may discontinue the path and quit the learning process. Ultimately, gender can also play a role in different contexts and cultures, although this factor requires further comprehensive research.

Furthermore, a concept known as the Unified Theory of Acceptance and Use of Technology (UTAUT) was proposed by Venkatesh and Davis et al. in 2003 and defined as users' behavioral intention to use information systems and their subsequent use behaviors (Wong et al., 2013) can be a determining factor in the extent to which one finds the use of AI in English learning more/less anxiety-provoking.

The second influential factor is the design and functionality of AI tools. For one thing, the degree to which these tools are user-friendly can be an incentive and motif to use them more frequently and with more interest. Therefore, as language learners get more engaged by the appearance and the extent of being "easy-to-use" of an AI chatbot, they would feel less anxious. To exemplify, among renowned applications, Duolingo tries to build up a colorful, attractive, and game-like environment so that users find the language learning process rather more fun and interesting than a tedious, demanding activity. It also uses a sense of humor in its reminder messages to persuade its users to follow more passionately. For instance, in some cases, it sends messages containing the sentence that we wanted to send you an email in the target language, but since you do not follow your learning process regularly, we noticed that you would not be able to understand that email.

Another aspect is the degree to which these tools are empathetic and provide support for their users. The greater the support, the less amount of anxiety will be experienced by the L2 learners. Chatbots with more supportive, positive feedback, tailored to each learner and user, are more likely to lower the level of foreign language learning anxiety. Avoiding the provision of one-size-fits-all feedback can help developers reach a greater audience.

The third group of factors are those related to the social context in which learning is taking place. The extent of teacher involvement, the required level of human interaction, and peer support, where individuals can get help from their counterparts are also of considerable significance. As in some cultures, a vast majority of classes have always been held teacher-centered, students may find it rather stressful to rely on an application on their cell phones. Moreover, a class where a student finds others involved with the same activity and even sees that others also are dealing with some challenges while using AI, can be a contributing factor to experience less anxiety. Moreover, as they have access to a guiding person who is there to support them, i.e., a teacher, they may even be more encouraged to employ this technology. However, teachers need to be wary of the degree of this guide, as they should not neglect the significance of autonomy.

Future Directions

When it comes to future prospects of AI in the EFL learning discipline, a number of possible directions seem to make sense. Initially, AI would be even more integrated into the English language curriculum and English classes would take advantage of the latest developments in the AI domain in the foreseeable future. Secondly, augmented teaching is going to be increased. This approach of teaching is the one in which the teaching environment gets adapted to the needs and wants of the learner. With the aid of AI, stakeholders would set the environment and teaching methodology and materials tailored to learners' needs, taking their areas of strength and weakness into consideration. Third, the use of AI has the potential to develop more diverse learning styles. With the increase in accessibility and wider use of AI, it is likely that while one learner may find audio-visual aid provided by chatbots more useful, others may find the answers to their questions in written form more understandable. This can help learners discover their learning styles and reach optimal efficiency and performance. Moreover, informal learning may be going to take the place of traditional in-person classes in a formal way. Furthermore, open-source learning language channels will also experience a soar in the number of audiences in upcoming years. Another possible prospect can be more frequent use of chatbots in English as a second or foreign language classrooms, where even some part of teaching would take place with the aid of these tools. Another direction can be aligning professional development for teachers using AI platforms with language curricula. Last but not least, a growth in the number of online international language institutions is not far from expectation in the not-so-distant future.

However, one significant point to bear in mind is to avoid over-reliance on technology. In other words, especially educators should consider the fact that neither are these tools and chatbots ideally developed nor are the students fully familiar with them. Under these circumstances, a class completely based on AI can lead to higher levels of anxiety and less desirable outcomes. That is to say, they can be used as a supplementary tool to act as a sort of complementary material. However, their further development has the potential to obviate existing issues and result in a more reliable educational system. Thus, at the current stage, putting a more balanced teaching and learning method into practice would be really pivotal for the advancement of education, especially in teaching the English language. Hence, taking advantage of both human interactions and AI-enhanced chatbots is more likely to result in effective learning, than merely making use of one of them.

Future studies can focus more on the teachers' perspectives towards the use of artificial intelligence and the extent to which they find it helpful in reducing negative feelings in themselves and fellow students. Moreover, future studies can take advantage of both quantitative as well as qualitative methods to measure the level of L2 anxiety on the part of English learners, a mixture of instruments such as surveys and scales, and qualitative procedures e.g., interviews can be highly recommended to elicit more precise data. More precisely, anxiety for each skill and sub-skill of the English language (e.g., reading, listening, speaking, and writing) can also be measured and the efficacy of using AI in reducing anxiety levels in each can be compared to the other. For instance, receptive skills and sub-skills can be compared to productive ones. Furthermore, creating culturally adaptive feedback mechanisms can also be worthwhile, as an important factor influencing anxiety. The feedback provided by an application or chatbot can evoke various reactions in different circumstances and settings, for example in Asian versus European cultures. Another area can be comparing the use of AI in learning various languages and its efficiency in reducing cognitive load and undesirable emotions. In this regard, the role played by the users' first language or L1, the degree of similarity with the target language, and its effect on the level of anxiety experienced by a learner can be worth investigating. Additionally, upcoming research can consider contextual factors such as the level of support and resources available to students, including access to technology and language practice opportunities, and the role they might play in learners' anxiety levels. Besides, future research can track students across time and the long-term effects of this technology utilization. In sum, according to its new and ever-evolving nature, the use of AI in language learning would require considerably greater research and investigation before any sort of generalization.

CONCLUSION

To summarize what this chapter covered, initially, the use of AI in second or foreign-language teaching settings was discussed. Several potential advantages, such as improved performance, increased motivation, and better accessibility to learning materials were mentioned in the opening sections of the chapter. Providing a background in L2 learning anxiety, the chapter highlighted a number of widely used AI technologies in the language education industry, such as Duolingo and ChatGPT. The following part discusses how AI can benefit its users in a large diversity of ways. Lower cognitive load, improved language output, a higher level of motivation, adaptive learning environment, lack of time constraints, provision of personalized feedback, reduced demotivation and anxiety, enhanced L2 learning experiences, improved academic success, and reduction in L2 anxiety were among some very common merits. However, as mentioned in the subsequent section of the chapter, it is not free from challenges and shortcomings. For instance, according to existing literature and studies, it is subject to taking the place of human interactions, as opposed to the fact that the very goal of learning a new language is to extend communication skills. Moreover, emotional support is one of the limitations AI is believed to have. Furthermore, especially for those with less advanced computer skills, as they may not find the process of using AI as smooth as others, this even leads to higher anxiety levels in this group of people. Several other concerns, such as plagiarism, algorithmic bias, and data security issues also are concerning areas, which need to be taken into account.

The chapter provides a number of worthwhile issues for future research. For instance, it is recommended for the upcoming studies to explore factors such as comparing the effect of using AI in English learning and other languages. The anxiety in different areas, e.g., speaking versus listening can also be an interesting subject. In addition, the role of one's mother tongue or L1 and cultural differences are open to further investigation as well.

Considering the fact that the intersection between artificial intelligence and English as a foreign language learning is a promising one, developers, and users are supposed to take into account its current drawbacks and aim at obviating them. More importantly, this technology should not be over-relied on. Put simply, the significance of the presence of a teacher or tutor should not be overlooked and it is recommended that, at the existing stage of its development, AI should be used as an additional aid, rather than the primary medium of instruction.

REFERENCES

Biju, N., Abdelrasheed, N. S. G., Bakiyeva, K., Prasad, K. D. V., & Jember, B. (2024). Which one? AI-assisted language assessment or paper format: An exploration of the impacts on foreign language anxiety, learning attitudes, motivation, and writing performance. *Language Testing in Asia*, *14*(1), 45. DOI: 10.1186/s40468-024-00322-z

Bin-Hady, W. R. A., Al-Kadi, A., Hazaea, A., & Ali, J. K. M. (2023). Exploring the dimensions of ChatGPT in English language learning: A global perspective. *Library Hi Tech*. Advance online publication. DOI: 10.1108/LHT-05-2023-0200

Bringsjord, S. (2011). Psychometric artificial intelligence. *Journal of Experimental & Theoretical Artificial Intelligence*, *23*(3), 271–277. DOI: 10.1080/0952813X.2010.502314

Cai, M. (2023). Research on Postgraduate Classroom Construction Framework from the Perspective of Smart Education. *Journal of Contemporary Educational Research*, *7*(3), 35–42. DOI: 10.26689/jcer.v7i3.4793

Çakmak, F. (2022). Chatbot-Human Interaction and Its Effects on EFL Students' L2 Speaking Performance and Anxiety. [Research on Youth and Language]. *Novitas-ROYAL*, *16*(2), 113–131.

Chen, M. Y., Chen, P., An, F. R., Sha, S., Feng, Y., Su, Z., Cheung, T., Ungvari, G. S., Ng, C. H., Zhang, L., & Xiang, Y. T. (2024). Depression, anxiety and suicidality among Chinese mental health professionals immediately after China's dynamic zero-COVID policy: A network perspective. *Journal of Affective Disorders*, *352*, 153–162. DOI: 10.1016/j.jad.2024.01.270 PMID: 38316260

Clasen, D. R., & Brown, B. B. (1985). The multidimensionality of peer pressure in adolescence. *Journal of Youth and Adolescence*, *14*(6), 451–468. DOI: 10.1007/BF02139520 PMID: 24301413

Dobrev, D. (2012). A definition of artificial intelligence. arXiv preprint arXiv:1210.1568.

El Shazly, R. (2021). Effects of artificial intelligence on English speaking anxiety and speaking performance: A case study. *Expert Systems: International Journal of Knowledge Engineering and Neural Networks*, *38*(3), e12667. DOI: 10.1111/exsy.12667

Elsayed, A. M., Kholikov, A., Abdullayeva, I., Al-Farouni, M., & Wodajo, M. R. (2024). Teacher support in AI-assisted exams: An experimental study to inspect the effects on demotivation, anxiety management in exams, L2 learning experience, and academic success. *Language Testing in Asia, 14*(1), 53. DOI: 10.1186/s40468-024-00328-7

Fitria, T. N. (2023, March). Artificial intelligence (AI) technology in OpenAI ChatGPT application: A review of ChatGPT in writing English essay. In ELT Forum. *Journal of English Language Teaching, 12*(1), 44–58.

Ghafar, Z. N., Salh, H. F., Abdulrahim, M. A., Farxha, S. S., Arf, S. F., & Rahim, R. I. (2023). The role of artificial intelligence technology on English language learning: A literature review. *Canadian Journal of Language and Literature Studies, 3*(2), 17–31.

Handini, B. S., Nurhasanah, N., & Panly, F. I. (2022). The effect of artificial intelligent technology used (Duolingo application) to enhance English learning. ELLITE. *Journal of English Language, Literature, and Teaching, 7*(2), 86–94. DOI: 10.32528/ellite.v7i2.8354

Horwitz, E. K. (1983). Foreign language classroom anxiety scale. *Revista Argentina de Clínica Psicológica.*

Horwitz, E. K. (2017). On the misreading of Horwitz, Horwitz, and Cope (1986) and the need to balance anxiety research and the experiences of anxious language learners. *New insights into language anxiety: Theory, research and educational implications, 31*, 47.

Horwitz, E. K., Horwitz, M. B., & Cope, J. (1986). Foreign language classroom anxiety. *Modern Language Journal, 70*(2), 125–132. DOI: 10.1111/j.1540-4781.1986.tb05256.x

Huang, Z. (2020). Thirteen years since the first iPhone: A systematic review on the effectiveness of language learning apps on smart devices (Doctoral dissertation, University of Oxford).

Jeon, J. (2024). Exploring AI chatbot affordances in the EFL classroom: Young learners' experiences and perspectives. *Computer Assisted Language Learning, 37*(1-2), 1–26. DOI: 10.1080/09588221.2021.2021241

Kazu, I. Y., & Kuvvetli, M. (2023). The Influence of Pronunciation Education via Artificial Intelligence Technology on Vocabulary Acquisition in Learning English. *International Journal of Psychology and Educational Studies, 10*(2), 480–493. DOI: 10.52380/ijpes.2023.10.2.1044

Ling, Z., & Mohammed, A. L. (2023). The Influence of Multimodal Learning Methods on English Language Competence in Higher Vocational Colleges. *Advances in Vocational and Technical Education*, *5*(13), 100–105.

Liu, H. C., Lin, M. H., Chang, W. C., Zeng, R. C., Wang, Y. M., & Sun, C. W. (2023). Rapid on-site AI-assisted grading for lung surgery based on optical coherence tomography. *Cancers (Basel)*, *15*(22), 5388. DOI: 10.3390/cancers15225388 PMID: 38001648

Mabuan, R. A. (2024). ChatGPT and ELT: Exploring Teachers' Voices. International journal of technology in education, 7(1), 128-153.

MacIntyre, A. (1999). Social structures and their threats to moral agency. *Philosophy (London, England)*, *74*(3), 311–329. DOI: 10.1017/S0031819199000431

MacIntyre, P. D. (1999). Language anxiety: A review of the research for language teachers. Affect in foreign language and second language learning: A practical guide to creating a low-anxiety classroom atmosphere, 24(1), 34-70.

MacIntyre, P. D., & Gardner, R. C. (1994). The effects of induced anxiety on cognitive processing in second language learning. *Studies in Second Language Acquisition*, *16*, 1–17. DOI: 10.1017/S0272263100012560

McLean, G., & Osei-Frimpong, K. (2019). Hey Alexa… examine the variables influencing the use of artificial intelligent in-home voice assistants. *Computers in Human Behavior*, *99*, 28–37. DOI: 10.1016/j.chb.2019.05.009

Miao, F., Holmes, W., Huang, R., & Zhang, H. (2021). *AI and education: A guidance for policymakers*. Unesco Publishing.

Miao, H., Guo, X., & Yuan, F. (2021). Research on identification of potential directions of artificial intelligence industry from the perspective of weak signal. *IEEE Transactions on Engineering Management*, *71*, 465–480. DOI: 10.1109/TEM.2021.3123639

Nugraha, D. N. S., Simatupang, E. C., Sari, P., Gunawan, H., Dianita, D., & Rusyan, S. (2023). Duolingo as an artificial intelligence technology-based learning system in English. *Jurnal Sinestesia*, *13*(2), 1085–1089.

Omohundro, S. (2014). Autonomous technology and the greater human good. *Journal of Experimental & Theoretical Artificial Intelligence*, *26*(3), 303–315. DOI: 10.1080/0952813X.2014.895111

Peña-Acuña, B., & Corga Fernandes Durão, R. (2024, November). Learning English as a second language with artificial intelligence for prospective teachers: A systematic review. []). Frontiers Media SA.]. *Frontiers in Education, 9*, 1490067. DOI: 10.3389/feduc.2024.1490067

Qu, C., & Kim, E. (2022). Dynamic capabilities perspective on innovation ecosystem of China's universities in the age of artificial intelligence: Policy-based analysis. Journal of Infrastructure. *Policy and Development*, *6*(2), 1661. DOI: 10.24294/jipd.v6i2.1661

Shen, Y., & Guo, H. (2024). "I feel AI is neither too good nor too bad": Unveiling Chinese EFL teachers' perceived emotions in generative AI-Mediated L2 classes. *Computers in Human Behavior, 161*, 108429. DOI: 10.1016/j.chb.2024.108429

Songsiengchai, S. (2025). Implementation of Artificial Intelligence (AI): Chat GPT for Effective English Language Learning among Thai Students in Higher Education. *International Journal of Education and Literacy Studies, 13*(1), 302–312. DOI: 10.7575/aiac.ijels.v.13n.1p.302

Spielberger, C. D. (1983). *Manual for the state-trait anxiety inventory: STAI (Form Y)*. Consulting Psychologists Press.

Steenbergen-Hu, S., & Cooper, H. (2013). A meta-analysis of the effectiveness of intelligent tutoring systems on K–12 students' mathematical learning. *Journal of Educational Psychology, 105*(4), 970–987. DOI: 10.1037/a0032447

Venkatesh, V., Morris, M. G., Davis, G. B., & Davis, F. D. (2003). User acceptance of information technology: Toward a unified view. *Management Information Systems Quarterly, 27*(3), 425–478. DOI: 10.2307/30036540

Wen, F., Li, Y., Zhou, Y., An, X., & Zou, Q. (2024). A study on the relationship between AI anxiety and AI behavioral intention of secondary school students learning English as a foreign language. [JETDE]. *Journal of Educational Technology Development and Exchange, 17*(1), 130–154. DOI: 10.18785/jetde.1701.07

Wong, K., Teo, T., & Russo, S. (2013). Interactive whiteboard acceptance: Applicability of the UTAUT model to student teachers. *The Asia-Pacific Education Researcher, 22*(1), 1–10. DOI: 10.1007/s40299-012-0001-9

Young, D. J. (1991). Creating a low-anxiety classroom environment: What does language anxiety research suggest? *Modern Language Journal, 75*(4), 426–439.

Zhang, C., Meng, Y., & Ma, X. (2024). Artificial intelligence in EFL speaking: Impact on enjoyment, anxiety, and willingness to communicate. *System, 121*, 103259. DOI: 10.1016/j.system.2024.103259

ADDITIONAL READING

Almaiah, M. A., Alfaisal, R., Salloum, S. A., Hajjej, F., Thabit, S., El-Qirem, F. A., Lutfi, A., Alrawad, M., Al Mulhem, A., Alkhdour, T., Awad, A. B., & Al-Maroof, R. S. (2022). Examining the impact of artificial intelligence and social and computer anxiety in e-learning settings: Students' perceptions at the university level. *Electronics (Basel), 11*(22), 3662. DOI: 10.3390/electronics11223662

Azizimajd, H. (2023). Investigating the impacts of voice-based student-chatbot interactions in the classroom on EFL learners' oral fluency and foreign language speaking anxiety. *Technology Assisted Language Education, 1*(2), 61–83. DOI: 10.22126/tale.2023.2732

Çakmak, F. (2022). Chatbot-human interaction and its effects on EFL students' L2 speaking performance and anxiety. https://hdl.handle.net/20.500.12868/2272

Fathi, J., Rahimi, M., & Derakhshan, A. (2024). Improving EFL learners' speaking skills and willingness to communicate via artificial intelligence-mediated interactions. *System, 121*, 103254. DOI: 10.1016/j.system.2024.103254

Hapsari, I. P., & Wu, T. T. (2022, August). AI chatbots learning model in English speaking skill: Alleviating speaking anxiety, boosting enjoyment, and fostering critical thinking. In *International conference on innovative technologies and learning* (pp. 444-453). Cham: Springer International Publishing. https://doi.org/DOI: 10.1007/978-3-031-15273-3_49

Hawanti, S., & Zubaydulloevna, K. M. (2023). AI chatbot-based learning: Alleviating students' anxiety in English writing classroom. *Bulletin of Social Informatics Theory and Application*, 7(2), 182–192. DOI: 10.31763/businta.v7i2.659

Hopcan, S., Türkmen, G., & Polat, E. (2024). Exploring the artificial intelligence anxiety and machine learning attitudes of teacher candidates. *Education and Information Technologies, 29*(6), 7281–7301. DOI: 10.1007/s10639-023-12086-9

Klos, M. C., Escoredo, M., Joerin, A., Lemos, V. N., Rauws, M., & Bunge, E. L. (2021). Artificial intelligence–based chatbot for anxiety and depression in university students: Pilot randomized controlled trial. *JMIR Formative Research, 5*(8), e20678. DOI: 10.2196/20678 PMID: 34092548

Nazari, N., Shabbir, M. S., & Setiawan, R. (2021). Application of Artificial Intelligence powered digital writing assistant in higher education: Randomized controlled trial. *Heliyon, 7*(5), e07014. Advance online publication. DOI: 10.1016/j.heliyon.2021.e07014 PMID: 34027198

Wang, Y. M., Wei, C. L., Lin, H. H., Wang, S. C., & Wang, Y. S. (2024). What drives students' AI learning behavior: A perspective of AI anxiety. *Interactive Learning Environments, 32*(6), 2584–2600.

KEY TERMS AND DEFINITIONS

Artificial Intelligence: An unnatural object or entity that includes the capability and capacity to meet or exceed the needs and wants of the task it is assigned taking into account the cultural and demographic circumstances (Bringsjord, 2011; Dobrev, 2012; McLean and Osei-Frimpong, 2019; Omohundro, 2014)

Language Anxiety: It is "*the apprehension experienced when a situation requires the use of a second language with which the individual is not fully proficient ... the propensity for an individual to react in a nervous manner when speaking, listening, reading, or writing in the second language.*" *(*MacIntyre, 999; *p. 5)*

Foreign language (classroom) anxiety (FLCA): It is "a distinct complex of self-perceptions, beliefs, feelings, and behaviors related to classroom language learning arising from the uniqueness of the language learning process" (Horwitz et al., 1986; p. 128)

AI Anxiety: It can be defined as an excessive fear stemming from the repercussions of AI-induced changes in one's personal or societal existence (Chen et al., 2024).

Trait Anxiety: It is "a feature of an individual's personality and therefore is both stable over time and applicable to a wide range of situations" (MacIntyre, 1999, p.217).

State Anxiety: It "varies in intensity and duration and fluctuates over time as a function of the amount of stress that impinges upon an individual and that individual's interpretation of the stressful situation as personally dangerous or threatening" (Spielberger, 1976, p. 5)

Unified Theory of Acceptance and Use of Technology (UTAUT): It is users' behavioral intention to use information systems and their subsequent use behaviors (Wong et al., 2013)

Compilation of References

Abimanto, D., & Sumarsono, W. (2024). Improving English Pronunciation With AI Speech-Recognition Technology. *Acitya Journal of Teaching & Education, 6*(1), 146–156. DOI: 10.30650/ajte.v6i1.3810

Abobaker, R., & Moleta, S. (2024). *ESL 4.0* (pp. 71–134). DOI: 10.4018/979-8-3693-5443-8.ch004

Abulibdeh, A., Zaidan, E., & Abulibdeh, R. (2024). Navigating the confluence of artificial intelligence and education for sustainable development in the era of industry 4.0: Challenges, opportunities, and ethical dimensions. *Journal of Cleaner Production, 437*, 140527. DOI: 10.1016/j.jclepro.2023.140527

AbuSahyon, A. S. A. E., Alzyoud, A., Alshorman, O., & Al-Absi, B. (2023). AI-driven technology and Chatbots as tools for enhancing English language learning in the context of second language acquisition: A review study. *International Journal of Membrane Science and Technology, 10*(1), 1209–1223. DOI: 10.15379/ijmst.v10i1.2829

Adıgüzel, T., Kaya, M. H., & Cansu, F. K. (2023). Revolutionizing education with AI: Exploring the transformative potential of ChatGPT. *Contemporary Educational Technology, 15*(3), ep429. DOI: 10.30935/cedtech/13152

Adler, H. (2002). *Handbook of NLP: A manual for professional communicators*. Gower Publishing Limited.

Afiliani, A., Tanasale, I. O., & Rijoly, H. M. A. (2024). The use of Google Translate in the translation class at English Education Study Program Pattimura University. *Journal of English Language Teaching and Linguistics, 9*(1), 95–109. DOI: 10.21462/jeltl.v9i1.1299

Agata Majchrowska, A., Tarkowski, A., Alamäki, A., Butler, D., Baten, D., Van Den Broek, E., Noto La Diega, G., Muukkonen Van Der Meer, H., Molenaar, I., Vie, J.-J., Kaplan, J., Giraldo Ospino, J. P., Estevez, J., Quille, K., Kralj, L., Crosta, L., Karliuk, M., Wirzberger, M., Montebello, M., . . . Slavov, V. (2022). *Ethical guidelines on the use of artificial intelligence (AI) and data in teaching and learning for educators*. Publications Office of the European Union. https://school-education.ec.europa.eu/system/files/2023-12/ethical_guidelines_on_the_use_of_artificial_intelligence-nc0722649enn_0.pdf

Ahmad, A., Andriani, F., Mulyani, M. Y. D., Sarita, R., & Anita, R. H. (2022). The Students' Difficulties in Essay Writing During Pandemic Covid- 19 in English Language Education of Universitas Islam Riau. *J-Shmic Journal of English for Academic*, *9*(2), 81–90. DOI: 10.25299/jshmic.2022.vol9(2).9770

Ahmad, K., Iqbal, W., El-Hassan, A., Qadir, J., Benhaddou, D., Ayyash, M., & Al-Fuqaha, A. (2023). Data-driven artificial intelligence in education: A comprehensive review. *IEEE Transactions on Learning Technologies*.

Ahmad, K., & Rashid, T. (2023). Adaptive language learning systems: A systematic review of implementation models and outcomes. *Educational Technology Research and Development*, *71*(3), 512–537.

Ahmed Abdel-Al Ibrahim, K., Cuba Carbajal, N., Zuta, M. E. C., & Bayat, S. (2023). Collaborative learning, scaffolding-based instruction, and self-assessment: Impacts on intermediate EFL learners' reading comprehension, motivation, and anxiety. *Language Testing in Asia*, *13*(1), 16. DOI: 10.1186/s40468-023-00229-1

Aithal, P. S. (2023). Optimizing the Use of Artificial Intelligence-Powered GPTs as Teaching and Research Assistants by Professors in Higher Education Institutions: A Study on Smart Utilization. *International Journal of Management Technology and Social Sciences*, 368–401. DOI: 10.47992/IJMTS.2581.6012.0326

Aiybirdi, N. (2023). Revolutionizing English language teaching: The role of artificial intelligence. In Kabadayi, A., & Eraslan, M. (Eds.), *Conceptual change theories and practice examples in education*. Livre de Lyon.

Akbarani, R. (2024). Use of Artificial Intelligence in English Language Teaching. *International Journal of English Learning and Applied Linguistics (Ijelal)*, *4*(1), 14–23. DOI: 10.21111/ijelal.v4i1.10756

Akcayir, M., & Akcayir, G. (2017). Advantages and challenges associated with augmented reality for education: A systematic review of the literature. *Educational Research Review*, *20*, 1–11. DOI: 10.1016/j.edurev.2016.11.002

Akyuz, Y. (2020). Effects of intelligent tutoring systems (ITS) on personalized learning (PL). *Creative Education, 11*(06), 953–978. DOI: 10.4236/ce.2020.116069

Al-Abdullatif, A. M., Al-Dokhny, A. A., & Drwish, A. M. (2023). Implementing the Bashayer chatbot in Saudi higher education: Measuring the influence on students' motivation and learning strategies. *Frontiers in Psychology, 14*, 1129070. DOI: 10.3389/fpsyg.2023.1129070 PMID: 37255522

Alam, A. (2021). Possibilities and Apprehensions in the Landscape of Artificial Intelligence in Education. *2021 International Conference on Computational Intelligence and Computing Applications (ICCICA)*, 1–8. DOI: 10.1109/ICCICA52458.2021.9697272

Alam, A. (2023). Harnessing the Power of AI to Create Intelligent Tutoring Systems for Enhanced Classroom Experience and Improved Learning Outcomes. In *Intelligent Communication Technologies and Virtual Mobile Networks* (pp. 571–591). Springer Nature Singapore. DOI: 10.1007/978-981-99-1767-9_42

Al-Ansi, A. M., Jaboob, M., Garad, A., & Al-Ansi, A. (2023). Analyzing augmented reality (AR) and virtual reality (VR) recent development in education. *Social Sciences & Humanities Open, 8*(1), 100532. DOI: 10.1016/j.ssaho.2023.100532

AlGerafi, M. A. M., Zhou, Y., Oubibi, M., & Wijaya, T. T. (2023). Unlocking the potential: A comprehensive evaluation of augmented reality and virtual reality in education. *Electronics (Basel), 12*(18), 3953. DOI: 10.3390/electronics12183953

Alharbi, W. (2023). AI in the foreign language classroom: A pedagogical overview of automated writing assistance tools. *Education Research International, 1*, 1–15. Advance online publication. DOI: 10.1155/2023/4253331

Al-khresheh, M. H. (2024). The future of artificial intelligence in English language teaching: Pros and cons of ChatGPT implementation through a systematic review. *Language Teaching Research, 43*, 54–80. DOI: 10.32038/ltrq.2024.43.04

Allen, G. (2020). *Understanding AI technology.* https://apps.dtic.mil/sti/pdfs/AD1099286.pdf

Allioui, H., & Mourdi, Y. (2023). Exploring the full potentials of IoT for better financial growth and stability: A comprehensive survey. *Sensors (Basel), 23*(19), 8015. DOI: 10.3390/s23198015 PMID: 37836845

Al-Maroof, R. S., Salloum, S. A., Al Hamadand, A. Q., & Shaalan, K. A. (2020). Understanding an extension technology acceptance model of Google Translation: A multi-cultural study in United Arab Emirates. *International Journal of Interactive Mobile Technologies (iJIM, 14)*(03), 157. https://doi.org/DOI: 10.3991/ijim.v14i03.11110

Alqaralleh, B. A. Y., & Aldhaban, F., A-Matarneh, F. M., & AlQaralleh, E. A. (. (2022). Automated Handwriting Recognition and Speech Synthesizer for Indigenous Language Processing. *Computers, Materials & Continua*, *72*(2), 3913–3927. DOI: 10.32604/cmc.2022.026531

Alrabai, F. (2022). The role of mixed emotions in language learning and teaching: A positive psychology teacher intervention. *System*, *107*, 102821. DOI: 10.1016/j.system.2022.102821

Al-Saadawi, H. F. T., Das, B., & Das, R. (2024). A systematic review of trimodal affective computing approaches: Text, audio, and visual integration in emotion recognition and sentiment analysis. *Expert Systems with Applications*, *255*, 124852. DOI: 10.1016/j.eswa.2024.124852

AlSaied, N., & Akhtar, F. (2021). Media students using mobile phones in the Arabian Gulf to improve English writing and video production skills. *Learning and Teaching in Higher Education: Gulf Perspectives*, *17*(1), 4–15. DOI: 10.1108/LTHE-09-2020-0038

Alsanousi, B., Albesher, A. S., Do, H., & Ludi, S. (2023). Investigating the User Experience and Evaluating Usability Issues in AI-Enabled Learning Mobile Apps: An Analysis of User Reviews. *International Journal of Advanced Computer Science and Applications*, *14*(6). Advance online publication. DOI: 10.14569/IJACSA.2023.0140602

Alshehri, A. A. (2024). *Building the medical lexicon: A corpus-based approach to optimising medical terminology acquisition for pre-health science students*. Forum for Linguistic Studies., DOI: 10.30564/fls.v6i6.7400

Amirjalili, F. (2024). Exploring the efficacy of ChatGPT in personalized language learning: An intervention study in Iranian ESL classrooms. [Formerly Journal of Teaching Language Skills]. *Teaching English as a Second Language Quarterly*, *43*(3), 1–26.

Anggraini, A., & Faisal, F. (2024). The use of artificial intelligence based technology in English language teaching. *Golden Ratio of Data in Summary*, *4*(2), 950–957. DOI: 10.52970/grdis.v4i2.749

Anis, M. (2023). Leveraging artificial intelligence for inclusive English language teaching: Strategies and implications for learner diversity. *Journal of Multidisciplinary Educational Research*, *12*(6), 54–70.

Annamalai, N., Rashid, M., Eltahir, M., & Zyoud, S. (2023). Exploring English language learning via chatbot: A case study from a self-determination theory perspective. *Computers and Education: Artificial Intelligence*, *5*, 100148. DOI: 10.1016/j.caeai.2023.100148

Anshari, M., Almunawar, M. N., Lim, S. A., & Al-Mudimigh, A. (2019). Customer relationship management and big data enabled: Personalization & customization of services. *Applied Computing and Informatics*, *15*(2), 94–101. DOI: 10.1016/j.aci.2018.05.004

Arafah, B., & Kaharuddin. (2019). The Idol: A Model for Incorporating Literature in Elt. *Kne Social Sciences*. DOI: 10.18502/kss.v3i19.4829

Arani, S. M. N. (2024). Navigating the future of language learning: A conceptual review of AI's role in personalized learning. *Computer-Assisted Language Learning Electronic Journal*, *25*(3), 1–22.

Arani, S. M. N. (2024). Navigating the future of language learning: A Conceptual review of ai's role in personalized learning. *Computer-Assisted Language Learning Electronic Journal*, *25*(3), 1–22.

Ardiny, H., & Khanmirza, E. (2018). The role of AR and VR technologies in education developments: Opportunities and challenges. *2018 6th RSI International Conference on Robotics and Mechatronics (IcRoM)*, Tehran, Iran, 482–487. DOI: 10.1109/ICRoM.2018.8657615

Arnab, S. (2020). *Game Science in Hybrid Learning Spaces*. Routledge., DOI: 10.4324/9781315295053

August, D., Carlo, M., Dressler, C., & Snow, C.The Division for Learning Disabilities of the Council for Exceptional Children. (2005). The critical role of vocabulary development for English language learners. *Learning Disabilities Research & Practice*, *20*(1), 50–57. DOI: 10.1111/j.1540-5826.2005.00120.x

Ayanwale, M. A., Adelana, O. P., Molefi, R. R., Adeeko, O., & Ishola, A. M. (2024). Examining artificial intelligence literacy among pre-service teachers for future classrooms. *Computers and Education Open*, *6*, 100179. DOI: 10.1016/j.caeo.2024.100179

Aydın, Ö., & Karaarslan, E. (2023). Is ChatGPT leading generative AI? What is beyond expectations? *Academic Platform Journal of Engineering and Smart Systems*, *11*(3), 118–134. DOI: 10.21541/apjess.1293702

Azuma, R., Baillot, Y., Behringer, R., Feiner, S., Julier, S., & MacIntyre, B. (2001). Recent advances in augmented reality. *IEEE Computer Graphics and Applications*, *21*(6), 34–47. DOI: 10.1109/38.963459

Baido-anu, D. (2023). Education in the Era of Generative Artificial Intelligence (AI). *Understanding the Potential Benefits of ChatGPT in Promoting Teaching and Learning.*, *7*(1), 52–62. DOI: 10.61969/jai.1337500

Bailey, D., & Lee, A. R. (2020). An exploratory study of Grammarly in the language learning context: An analysis of test-based, textbook-based and Facebook corpora. *TESOL International Journal*, *15*(2), 4–27.

Barua, P. D., Vicnesh, J., Gururajan, R., Oh, S. L., Palmer, E. E., Azizan, M. M., Kadri, N. A., & Acharya, U. R. (2022). Artificial Intelligence Enabled Personalised Assistive Tools to Enhance Education of Children With Neurodevelopmental Disorders—A Review. *International Journal of Environmental Research and Public Health*, *19*(3), 1192. DOI: 10.3390/ijerph19031192 PMID: 35162220

Basilotta-Gómez-Pablos, V., Matarranz, M., Casado-Aranda, L. A., & Otto, A. (2022). Teachers' digital competencies in higher education: A systematic literature review. *International Journal of Educational Technology in Higher Education*, *19*(1), 8. DOI: 10.1186/s41239-021-00312-8

Baskara, F. X. R. (2023). AI-Driven Dynamics: ChatGPT Transforming ELT Teacher-Student Interactions. *Lensa Kajian Kebahasaan Kesusastraan Dan Budaya*, *13*(2), 261. DOI: 10.26714/lensa.13.2.2023.261-275

Begum, S., Vimochana, M., Arunadevi, V., Dhivya, A. C. A., Vuyyuru, V. A., & Faizal, M. M. (2024, December). Using AI for personalized English writing feedback on educational platforms. In *2024 International Conference on Artificial Intelligence and Quantum Computation-Based Sensor Application (ICAIQSA)* (pp. 1–6). IEEE. DOI: 10.1109/ICAIQSA64000.2024.10882334

Belda-Medina, J., & Goddard, M. B. (2024). AI-Driven Digital Storytelling: A Strategy for Creating English as a Foreign Language (EFL) Materials. *International Journal of Linguistics Studies*, *4*(1), 40–49. DOI: 10.32996/ijls.2024.4.1.4

Bender, T. (2023). *Discussion-based online teaching to enhance student learning: Theory, practice and assessment.* Taylor & Francis.

Betaubun, M., Laila Rokhmah, D. E., & Budiasto, J. (2023). Personalized pathways to proficiency: Exploring the synergy of adaptive learning and artificial intelligence in English language learning. *Technium*, •••, 17.

Bhutoria, A. (2022). Personalized education and artificial intelligence in the United States, China, and India: A systematic review using a human-in-the-loop model. *Computers and Education: Artificial Intelligence*, *3*, 100068. DOI: 10.1016/j.caeai.2022.100068

Bierstaker, J. L., Brink, W. D., Khatoon, S., & Thorne, L. (2024). Academic fraud and remote evaluation of accounting students: An application of the fraud triangle. *Journal of Business Ethics*, *195*(2), 425–447. Advance online publication. DOI: 10.1007/s10551-024-05628-9

Biju, N., Abdelrasheed, N. S. G., Bakiyeva, K., Prasad, K. D. V., & Jember, B. (2024). Which one? AI-assisted language assessment or paper format: An exploration of the impacts on foreign language anxiety, learning attitudes, motivation, and writing performance. *Language Testing in Asia*, *14*(1), 45. DOI: 10.1186/s40468-024-00322-z

Bilad, M. R., Yaqin, L. N., & Zubaidah, S. (2023). Recent progress in the use of artificial intelligence tools in education. *Jurnal Penelitian dan Pengkajian Ilmu Pendidikan e-Saintika*, *7*(3). https://doi.org/DOI: 10.36312/esaintika.v7i3.1377

Bin-Hady, W. R. A., Al-Kadi, A., Hazaea, A., & Ali, J. K. M. (2023). Exploring the dimensions of ChatGPT in English language learning: A global perspective. *Library Hi Tech*. Advance online publication. DOI: 10.1108/LHT-05-2023-0200

Bonina, C., Koskinen, K., Eaton, B., & Gawer, A. (2021). Digital platforms for development: Foundations and research agenda. *Information Systems Journal*, *31*(6), 869–902. DOI: 10.1111/isj.12326

Boonsuk, Y., Ambele, E. A., & McKinley, J. (2021). Developing awareness of Global Englishes: Moving away from 'native standards' for Thai university ELT. *System*, *99*, 102511. DOI: 10.1016/j.system.2021.102511

Booton, S. A., Hodgkiss, A., & Murphy, V. A. (2023). The impact of mobile application features on children's language and literacy learning: A systematic review. *Computer Assisted Language Learning*, *36*(3), 400–429. DOI: 10.1080/09588221.2021.1930057

Brezzi, M., González, S., Nguyen, D., & Prats, M. (2021). An updated OECD framework on drivers of trust in public institutions to meet current and future challenges. *OECD working papers on public governance*, (48), 0_1-60.

Bringsjord, S. (2011). Psychometric artificial intelligence. *Journal of Experimental & Theoretical Artificial Intelligence, 23*(3), 271–277. DOI: 10.1080/0952813X.2010.502314

Brożek, B., Furman, M., Jakubiec, M., & Kucharzyk, B. (2024). The black box problem revisited. Real and imaginary challenges for automated legal decision making. *Artificial Intelligence and Law, 32*(2), 427–440. DOI: 10.1007/s10506-023-09356-9

Buckingham Shum, S., Lim, L. A., Boud, D., Bearman, M., & Dawson, P. (2023). A comparative analysis of the skilled use of automated feedback tools through the lens of teacher feedback literacy. *International Journal of Educational Technology in Higher Education, 20*(1), 40. DOI: 10.1186/s41239-023-00410-9

Bundgaard, K., & Møller, A. K. (2024). Use of AI-powered technologies in upper secondary language learning. *Learning Tech – Tidsskrift for læremidler, didaktik-ogteknologi, 14*, 14–35. https://doi.org/DOI: 10.7146/lt.v9i14.136900

Bu, Q. (2022). Ethical Risks in Integrating Artificial Intelligence into Education and Potential Countermeasures. *Science Insights, 41*(1), 561–566. DOI: 10.15354/si.22.re067

Busso, A., & Sanchez, B. (2024). Advancing communicative competence in the digital age: A case for AI tools in Japanese EFL education. *Technology in Language Teaching & Learning, 6*(3), 1–17. DOI: 10.29140/tltl.v6n3.1211

Cai, M. (2023). Research on Postgraduate Classroom Construction Framework from the Perspective of Smart Education. *Journal of Contemporary Educational Research, 7*(3), 35–42. DOI: 10.26689/jcer.v7i3.4793

Çakmak, F. (2022). Chatbot-Human Interaction and Its Effects on EFL Students' L2 Speaking Performance and Anxiety. [Research on Youth and Language]. *Novitas-ROYAL, 16*(2), 113–131.

Cambria, E., & White, B. (2014). Jumping NLP curves: A review of natural language processing research. *IEEE Computational Intelligence Magazine, 9*(2), 48–57. DOI: 10.1109/MCI.2014.2307227

Campbell, C., & Olteanu, A. (2024). The Challenge of Postdigital Literacy: Extending Multimodality and Social Semiotics for a New Age. *Postdigital Science and Education, 6*(2), 572–594. DOI: 10.1007/s42438-023-00414-8

Cantos, K. F. S. (2023). Artificial Intelligence in Language Teaching and Learning. *Ciencia Latina Revista Científica Multidisciplinar, 7*(4), 5629–5638. DOI: 10.37811/cl_rcm.v7i4.7368

Carnegie Learning. (n.d.). Meet MATHia. Retrieved from https://discover.carnegielearning.com/meet-mathia

Casal-Otero, L., Catala, A., Fernández-Morante, C., Taboada, M., Cebreiro, B., & Barro, S. (2023). AI literacy in K-12: A systematic literature review. *International Journal of STEM Education, 10*(1), 29. DOI: 10.1186/s40594-023-00418-7

Catalán, P. C. M. (2024). *Generative AI's Influence on Design Thinking: Enhancing Empathy Through Extreme Users and Parallel Universes* (Master's thesis, Universidade NOVA de Lisboa (Portugal)).

Celaj, D., & Jani, G. (2023). NLP applications in vocabulary acquisition: Enhancing ESL learning through intelligent tools. *Journal of Educational Technology & Society, 25*(1), 15–34.

Celik, I., Dindar, M., Muukkonen, H., & Järvelä, S. (2022). The promises and challenges of artificial intelligence for teachers: A systematic review of research. *TechTrends, 66*(4), 616–630. DOI: 10.1007/s11528-022-00715-y

Chaka, C. (2023). Fourth industrial revolution—a review of applications, prospects, and challenges for artificial intelligence, robotics and blockchain in higher education. Research and Practice in Technology Enhanced Learning, 18, 002-002.

Chamot, A. U., & O'Malley, J. M. (1994). *The CALLA handbook: Implementing the cognitive academic language learning approach.* Addison-Wesley Publishing Company.

Chan, C. K. Y. (2023). A comprehensive AI policy education framework for university teaching and learning. *International Journal of Educational Technology in Higher Education, 20*(1), 38. DOI: 10.1186/s41239-023-00408-3

Chandran, M., Wang, S. L., Dzulkifly, S., Ng, T. F., & Ghoneim, A. S. (2024). Enhancing English Pronunciation Learning in Primary Education through Natural Language Processing: A Quantitative Study. *Journal of ICT in Education, 11*(2), 1–17. DOI: 10.37134/jictie.vol11.2.1.2024

Chavez, J. (2022). Narratives of bilingual parents on the real-life use of English language: Materials for English language teaching curriculum. Arab World English Journals, 13(3).

Chen, Y. (2024, May). Enhancing Language Acquisition: The Role of AI in Facilitating Effective Language Learning. In 2024 3rd International Conference on Humanities, Wisdom Education and Service Management (HWESM 2024) (pp. 593-600). Atlantis Press.

Chen, F. (2024). Exploring blended learning models supported by mobile interactive technologies in higher education. *International Journal of Interactive Mobile Technologies, 18*(11).

Chen, J. J., & Perez, C. (2023). Enhancing assessment and personalized learning through artificial intelligence. *Childhood Education, 99*(6), 72–79. DOI: 10.1080/00094056.2023.2282903

Chen, J., Lai, P., Chan, A., Man, V., & Chan, C.-H. (2022). AI-assisted enhancement of student presentation skills: Challenges and opportunities. *Sustainability (Basel), 15*(1), 196. DOI: 10.3390/su15010196

Chen, L., Chen, P., & Lin, Z. (2020). Artificial intelligence in education: A review. *IEEE Access : Practical Innovations, Open Solutions, 8*, 75264–75278. DOI: 10.1109/ACCESS.2020.2988510

Chen, M. Y., Chen, P., An, F. R., Sha, S., Feng, Y., Su, Z., Cheung, T., Ungvari, G. S., Ng, C. H., Zhang, L., & Xiang, Y. T. (2024). Depression, anxiety and suicidality among Chinese mental health professionals immediately after China's dynamic zero-COVID policy: A network perspective. *Journal of Affective Disorders, 352*, 153–162. DOI: 10.1016/j.jad.2024.01.270 PMID: 38316260

Chen, X., Zou, D., Cheng, G., & Xie, H. (2021, July). Artificial intelligence-assisted personalized language learning: Systematic review and co-citation analysis. In *2021 International Conference on Advanced Learning Technologies (ICALT)* (pp. 241–245). IEEE. DOI: 10.1109/ICALT52272.2021.00079

Chen, X., Zou, D., Xie, H., & Cheng, G. (2021). Twenty years of personalized language learning. *Journal of Educational Technology & Society, 24*(1), 205–222.

Chen, X., Zou, D., Xie, H., & Wang, F. L. (2022). Engagement patterns and learning outcomes in AI-enhanced language learning environments: A 24-week longitudinal study. *System, 107*, 102795.

Chiu, T. K., Xia, Q., Zhou, X., Chai, C. S., & Cheng, M. (2023). Systematic literature review on opportunities, challenges, and future research recommendations of artificial intelligence in education. *Computers and Education: Artificial Intelligence, 4*, 100118. DOI: 10.1016/j.caeai.2022.100118

Clasen, D. R., & Brown, B. B. (1985). The multidimensionality of peer pressure in adolescence. *Journal of Youth and Adolescence, 14*(6), 451–468. DOI: 10.1007/BF02139520 PMID: 24301413

Cohen, L., Manion, L., & Morrison, K. (2007). *Research methods in education* (6th ed.). Routledge., http://repository.unmas.ac.id/medias/journal/EBK-00127.pdf DOI: 10.4324/9780203029053

Cooper, L. J., Laster-Loftus, A., & Mandernach, B. J. (2019). Efficient online instruction: Maximum impact in minimal time. *Online Journal of Distance Learning Administration, 22*(3), 1–9.

Crompton, H., & Burke, D. (2023). Artificial intelligence in higher education: The state of the field. *International Journal of Educational Technology in Higher Education, 20*(1), 2–22. DOI: 10.1186/s41239-023-00392-8

Curtin, M., Wakefield, T., Herman, R., Morgan, G., & Cruice, M. (2024). "It doesn't matter if we're the most amazing professionals in the world…" A qualitative study of professionals' perspectives on parent-child interaction assessment with deaf infants. *Frontiers in Psychology, 15*, 1315220. DOI: 10.3389/fpsyg.2024.1315220 PMID: 38500650

D'Ignazio, C., & Klein, L. (2023). Introducing Data Feminism. In *Women's Empowerment and Its Limits: Interdisciplinary and Transnational Perspectives Toward Sustainable Progress* (pp. 139–151). Springer International Publishing. DOI: 10.1007/978-3-031-29332-0_8

Dai, Y., Liu, A., & Lim, C. P. (2023). Reconceptualizing ChatGPT and generative AI as a student-driven innovation in higher education. *Procedia CIRP, 119*, 84–90. DOI: 10.1016/j.procir.2023.05.002

Damşa, C., Langford, M., Uehara, D., & Scherer, R. (2021). Teachers' agency and online education in times of crisis. *Computers in Human Behavior, 121*, 106793. DOI: 10.1016/j.chb.2021.106793 PMID: 36568039

Danylchenko-Cherniak, O. (2024). Phililogical perspectives of design thinking and artificial intelligence in the Education 5.0-7.0 era.

Dede, C. J., Jacobson, J., & Richards, J. (2017). Introduction: Virtual, augmented, and mixed realities in education. In Liu, D., Dede, C., Huang, R., & Richards, J. (Eds.), *Virtual, augmented, and mixed realities in education* (pp. 1–9). Springer., DOI: 10.1007/978-981-10-5490-7_1

Dempere, J., Modugu, K., Hesham, A., & Ramasamy, L. K. (2023, September). The impact of ChatGPT on higher education. [). Frontiers Media SA.]. *Frontiers in Education, 8*, 1206936. DOI: 10.3389/feduc.2023.1206936

Derakhshan, A., & Nazari, M. (2024). Examining teacher identity construction in action research: The mediating role of experience. *Educational Studies*, *50*(6), 1280–1299. DOI: 10.1080/03055698.2022.2073177

Dergaa, I., Chamari, K., Żmijewski, P., & Saad, H. B. (2023). From Human Writing to Artificial Intelligence Generated Text: Examining the Prospects and Potential Threats of ChatGPT in Academic Writing. *Biology of Sport*, *40*(2), 615–622. DOI: 10.5114/biolsport.2023.125623 PMID: 37077800

Deslauriers, L., McCarty, L. S., Miller, K., Callaghan, K., & Kestin, G. (2019). Measuring actual learning versus feeling of learning in response to being actively engaged in the classroom. *Proceedings of the National Academy of Sciences of the United States of America*, *116*(39), 19251–19257. DOI: 10.1073/pnas.1821936116 PMID: 31484770

Dey, D. (2025). *Enhancing educational tools through artificial intelligence in the perspective of need of AI.* https://doi.org/DOI: 10.2139/ssrn.5031275

Díaz-Rodríguez, N., Del Ser, J., Coeckelbergh, M., de Prado, M. L., Herrera-Viedma, E., & Herrera, F. (2023). Connecting the dots in trustworthy Artificial Intelligence: From AI principles, ethics, and key requirements to responsible AI systems and regulation. *Information Fusion*, *99*, 101896. DOI: 10.1016/j.inffus.2023.101896

Dichev, C., Dicheva, D., Angelova, G., & Agre, G. (2015). From gamification to gameful design and gameful experience in learning. *Cybernetics and Information Technologies*, *14*(4), 80–100.

Dimitriadis, Y., Er, E., & Gasevic, D. (2021). Collaborative peer feedback and learning analytics: theory-oriented design for supporting class-wide interventions.

Dimitriadou, E., & Lanitis, A. (2023). A critical evaluation, challenges, and future perspectives of using artificial intelligence and emerging technologies in smart classrooms. *Smart Learning Environments*, *10*(1), 12. DOI: 10.1186/s40561-023-00231-3 PMID: 40478141

Dja'far, V. H., & Hamidah, F. N.Veri Hardinansyah Dja'farFitria Nur Hamidah. (2024). The effectiveness of AI technology in improving academic English writing skills in higher education. *Journal of Language and Literature Studies*, *4*(3), 579–593. DOI: 10.36312/jolls.v4i3.2031

Dobrev, D. (2012). A definition of artificial intelligence. arXiv preprint arXiv:1210.1568.

Dong, Y. (2023). Revolutionizing academic English writing through AI-powered pedagogy: Practical exploration of teaching process and assessment. *Journal of Higher Education Research, 4*(2), 52. DOI: 10.32629/jher.v4i2.1188

Double, K. S., McGrane, J. A., & Hopfenbeck, T. N. (2020). The impact of peer assessment on academic performance: A meta-analysis of control group studies. *Educational Psychology Review, 32*(2), 481–509. DOI: 10.1007/s10648-019-09510-3

Druckman, D. (1988). Enhancing human performance: Issues, theories, and techniques. In Druckman, D. (Ed.), *Enhancing human performance* (pp. 138–139). National Academy Press.

Dwivedi, Y. K., Kshetri, N., Hughes, L., Slade, E. L., Jeyaraj, A., Kar, A. K., Baabdullah, A. M., Koohang, A., Raghavan, V., Ahuja, M., Albanna, H., Albashrawi, M. A., Al-Busaidi, A. S., Balakrishnan, J., Barlette, Y., Basu, S., Bose, I., Brooks, L., Buhalis, D., & Wright, R. (2023). Opinion Paper:"So what if ChatGPT wrote it?" Multidisciplinary perspectives on opportunities, challenges and implications of generative conversational AI for research, practice and policy. *International Journal of Information Management, 71*, 102642. DOI: 10.1016/j.ijinfomgt.2023.102642

Edmett, A., Ichaporia, N., Crompton, H., & Crichton, R. (2023). Artificial intelligence and English language teaching: Preparing for the future. British Council, 2024-08.

Edmett, A., Ichaporia, N., Crompton, H., & Crichton, R. (2024). *Artificial intelligence and English language teaching: Preparing for the future* (2nd ed.). British Council., DOI: 10.57884/78ea-3c69

Eguchi, A., Okada, H., & Muto, Y. (2021). Contextualizing AI Education for K-12 Students to Enhance Their Learning of AI Literacy Through Culturally Responsive Approaches. *KI - Künstliche Intelligenz, 35*(2), 153–161. DOI: 10.1007/s13218-021-00737-3

El Gazi, S., & Ibrahimi, A. (2024). *Personalized Learning*., DOI: 10.4018/979-8-3693-1206-3.ch014

El Shazly, R. (2021). Effects of artificial intelligence on English speaking anxiety and speaking performance: A case study. *Expert Systems: International Journal of Knowledge Engineering and Neural Networks, 38*(3), e12667. DOI: 10.1111/exsy.12667

Elkhatat, A. M., Elsaid, K., & Almeer, S. (2023). Evaluating the efficacy of AI content detection tools in differentiating between human and AI-generated text. *International Journal for Educational Integrity, 19*(1), 17. Advance online publication. DOI: 10.1007/s40979-023-00140-5

Elsayed, A. M., Kholikov, A., Abdullayeva, I., Al-Farouni, M., & Wodajo, M. R. (2024). Teacher support in AI-assisted exams: An experimental study to inspect the effects on demotivation, anxiety management in exams, L2 learning experience, and academic success. *Language Testing in Asia*, *14*(1), 53. DOI: 10.1186/s40468-024-00328-7

Emon, M. M. H., Khan, T., Rahman, M. A., Hamid, A. B. A., & Yaakub, N. I. (2025). GreenTech Revolution: Navigating Challenges and Seizing Opportunities. In *AI and Green Technology Applications in Society* (pp. 63–90). IGI Global Scientific Publishing. DOI: 10.4018/979-8-3693-9879-1.ch003

Emon, M. M. H., & Khan, T. (2025). The mediating role of attitude towards the technology in shaping artificial intelligence usage among professionals. *Telematics and Informatics Reports*, *17*, 100188. DOI: 10.1016/j.teler.2025.100188

Emon, M. M. H., Khan, T., Rahman, M. A., & Siam, S. A. J. (2024). Factors Influencing the Usage of Artificial Intelligence among Bangladeshi Professionals: Mediating role of Attitude Towards the Technology. *2024 IEEE International Conference on Computing, Applications and Systems (COMPAS)*, 1–7. DOI: 10.1109/COMPAS60761.2024.10796110

Eronen, J., Lee, S., & Prefectural University of Kumamoto. (2024). Improving English education in Japan: Leveraging large language models for personalized and skill-diverse learning. In *The 9th Linguistic and Cognitive Approaches to Dialog Agents Workshop* [Conference proceeding]. Kyoto University.

Er-radi, H., Touis, B., & Aammou, S. (2023). *Machine Learning in Adaptive Online Learning for Enhanced Learner Engagement.*, DOI: 10.4018/979-8-3693-3132-3.ch003

Eslit, E. (2023). Integrating multiple intelligence and artificial intelligence in language learning: Enhancing personalization and engagement.

Essafi, M., Belfakir, L., & Moubtassime, M. (2024). Investigating mobile-assisted language learning apps: Babbel, Memrise, and Duolingo as a case study. *Journal of Curriculum and Teaching*, *13*(2), 197–210. DOI: 10.5430/jct.v13n2p197

Eswaran, U., Eswaran, V., Murali, K., & Eswaran, V. (2025). AI-Powered Language Teaching and Learning: Innovations and Challenges. In Reimagining Intelligent Computer-Assisted Language Education (pp. 55-92). IGI Global.

Falebita, O. S. (2024). Assessing the Relationship Between Anxiety and the Adoption of Artificial Intelligence Tools Among Mathematics Preservice Teachers. *Interdisciplinary Journal of Education Research*, *6*, 1–13. DOI: 10.38140/ijer-2024.vol6.20

Familoni, N. B. T., & Onyebuchi, N. N. C. (2024). Augmented and virtual reality in U.S. education: A review: Analyzing the impact, effectiveness, and future prospects of AR/VR tools in enhancing learning experiences. *International Journal of Applied Research in Social Sciences*, *6*(4), 642–663. DOI: 10.51594/ijarss.v6i4.1043

Fathurrahman, A. Z., Utami, D. I. S., & Safitri, K. A. (2023). Utilization of Augmented Reality as a Solution for Vernacular Language Approaches to Recognize an Object Through Speech Recognition. *International Journal of Research and Applied Technology*, *3*(1), 79–86. DOI: 10.34010/injuratech.v3i1.9954

Finnish Institute for Educational Research (FIER). (2023). Trends and issues of promoting digital learning in Finland. University of Jyväskylä., 10.978-951-39-8913-2.

Fitria, T. N. (2021, December). Artificial intelligence (AI) in education: Using AI tools for teaching and learning process. In Prosiding Seminar Nasional & Call for Paper STIE AAS (Vol. 4, No. 1, pp. 134-147).

Fitrianto, I., Setyawan, C. E., & Saleh, M. (2024). Utilizing artificial intelligence for personalized Arabic language learning plans. *International Journal of Post Axial: Futuristic Teaching and Learning*, 30–40.

Fitria, T. N. (2021). The use technology based on artificial intelligence in English teaching and learning. ELT Echo. *The Journal of English Language Teaching in Foreign Language Context*, *6*(2), 213–223.

Fitria, T. N. (2021a). The use of technology based on artificial intelligence in English teaching and learning. *ELT Echo: The Journal of English Language Teaching in Foreign Language Context*, *6*(2). Advance online publication. DOI: 10.24235/eltecho.v6i2.9299

Fitria, T. N. (2021b). "Grammarly" as AI-powered English writing assistant: Students' alternative for English writing. *Metathesis Journal of English Language Literature and Teaching*, *5*(1), 65–78. DOI: 10.31002/metathesis.v5i1.3519

Fitria, T. N. (2023, March). Artificial intelligence (AI) technology in OpenAI ChatGPT application: A review of ChatGPT in writing English essay. In ELT Forum. *Journal of English Language Teaching*, *12*(1), 44–58.

Foltynek, T., Bjelobaba, S., Glendinning, I., Khan, Z. R., Santos, R., Pavletic, P., & Kravjar, J. (2023). ENAI recommendations on the ethical use of artificial intelligence in education. *International Journal for Educational Integrity*, *19*(1), 12. DOI: 10.1007/s40979-023-00133-4

Freeman, Y. S., Freeman, D. E., & Marzano, R. J. (2009). *Academic language for English language learners and struggling readers: How to help students succeed across content areas*. Heinemann.

Galindo, L., Perset, K., & Sheeka, F. (2021). *An overview of national AI strategies and policies. OECD Going Digital Toolkit Notes, 14*. OECD Publishing., DOI: 10.1787/c05140d9-

Gaoat, K. E. F., Caligan, M. J. A., Butel, M. A. S., & Domingo, M. J. A. (2022). *Learning Strategies that Predict Success in Overcoming English Language Learning Anxiety*. International Journal of Research in Education., DOI: 10.26877/ijre.v2i1.11089

Gauthier, A., Rizvi, S., Cukurova, M., & Mavrikis, M. (2022). Is it time we get real? A systematic review of the potential of data-driven technologies to address teachers' implicit biases. *Frontiers in Artificial Intelligence*, *5*, 994967. DOI: 10.3389/frai.2022.994967 PMID: 36304958

Gawate, S. (2019). Artificial intelligence (AI) based instructional programs in teaching-learning of English language. *International Journal of English Language* [IJELR]. *Literature and Translation Studies*, *6*(4), 69–70. DOI: 10.33329/ijelr.64.69

George, B., & Wooden, O. (2023). Managing the Strategic Transformation of Higher Education Through Artificial Intelligence. *Administrative Sciences*, *13*(9), 196. DOI: 10.3390/admsci13090196

Ghafar, Z. N., Salh, H. F., Abdulrahim, M. A., Farxha, S. S., Arf, S. F., & Rahim, R. I. (2023). The role of artificial intelligence technology on English language learning: A literature review. *Canadian Journal of Language and Literature Studies*, *3*(2), 17–31.

Ghafar, Z. N., Salh, H. F., Abdulrahim, M. A., Farxha, S. S., Arf, S. F., & Rahim, R. I. (2023). The Role of Artificial Intelligence Technology on English Language Learning: A Literature Review. *Canadian Journal of Language and Literature Studies*, *3*(2). Advance online publication. DOI: 10.53103/cjlls.v3i2.87

Gholami, V., Attaran, A., & Morady Moghaddam, M., & Young Researchers and Elite Club, Mashhad Branch, Islamic Azad University. (2014). Towards an interactive EFL class: Using active learning strategies. *Research on Humanities and Social Sciences*, *4*(19), 190–191.

Global Educational Studies Review. (2020). Global Educational. *Studies and Reviews (General Fisheries Commission for the Mediterranean)*. Advance online publication. DOI: 10.31703/gesr

Gm, D., Goudar, R. H., Kulkarni, A. A., Rathod, V. N., & Hukkeri, G. S. (2024). A digital recommendation system for personalized learning to enhance online education: A review. *IEEE Access : Practical Innovations, Open Solutions, 12*, 34019–34041. DOI: 10.1109/ACCESS.2024.3369901

Godwin-Jones, R. (2021). Evolving technologies for language learning. *Language Learning & Technology, 25*(3), 1–14.

Goldenberg, C., & Coleman, R. (2010). *Promoting academic achievement among English learners: A guide to the research*. Corwin Press. DOI: 10.4135/9781452219073

Guadaña, R. M. F. (2021). Transmedia Storytelling Towards an Expanded Teaching of Reading in Distance Learning. *Studies in Humanities and Education, 2*(2), 47–56. DOI: 10.48185/she.v2i2.407

Guo, X., Guo, Y., & Liu, Y. (2021b). The development of extended reality in education: Inspiration from the research literature. *Sustainability (Basel), 13*(24), 13776. DOI: 10.3390/su132413776

Guo, Y. (2021a). A study of English informative teaching strategies based on deep learning. *Journal of Mathematics, 2021*, 1–8. DOI: 10.1155/2021/5364892

Gurrieri, L., & Drenten, J. M. (2019). Visual Storytelling and Vulnerable Health Care Consumers: Normalising Practices and Social Support Through Instagram. *Journal of Services Marketing, 33*(6), 702–720. DOI: 10.1108/JSM-09-2018-0262

Gyawali, Y. P., & Mehandroo, M. (2022). Artificial Intelligence in English Language Teaching: Navigating the Future With Emerging Perspectives. *Journal of Language and Linguistics in Society, 26*(26), 21–27. DOI: 10.55529/jlls.26.21.27

Hakim, A., & Anggraini, P. (2023). Artificial intelligence in teaching Islamic studies: Challenges and opportunities. *Molang Journal Islamic Education, 1*(2), 57–69. DOI: 10.32806/6ynvg541

Hallarte, D. K., Camaongay, Q. M., Congson, J., Cuamag, S., Datosme, J., Laude, V. K. B., Milano, M. L., Gonzales, R., & Gonzales, G. (2024). Modeling self-regulation in learning mathematics through teacher-promoting interaction and parental support among STEM learners: The mediating role of intrinsic motivation. *Social Sciences & Humanities Open, 10*, 101135. DOI: 10.1016/j.ssaho.2024.101135

Handini, B. S., Nurhasanah, N., & Panly, F. I. (2022). The effect of artificial intelligent technology used (Duolingo application) to enhance English learning. ELLITE. *Journal of English Language, Literature, and Teaching, 7*(2), 86–94. DOI: 10.32528/ellite.v7i2.8354

Han, G. T., Heavner, H. S., Rains, T. R., Hoang, A. H., & Stone, A. L. (2024). Chronic pain in autistic youth: Clinical prevalence and reflections on tailoring evidence-based interventions from an interdisciplinary treatment team. *Children (Basel, Switzerland), 11*(3), 312. DOI: 10.3390/children11030312 PMID: 38539347

Haristiani, N. (2019). Artificial intelligence (AI) chatbot as language learning medium: An inquiry. *Journal of Physics: Conference Series, 1387*(1), 012020. Advance online publication. DOI: 10.1088/1742-6596/1387/1/012020

Harmer, J. (2007). *The practice of English language teaching* (4th ed.). Pearson Longman.

Harris, C. R., Millman, K. J., Van Der Walt, S. J., Gommers, R., Virtanen, P., Cournapeau, D., Wieser, E., Taylor, J., Berg, S., Smith, N. J., Kern, R., Picus, M., Hoyer, S., van Kerkwijk, M. H., Brett, M., Haldane, A., del Río, J. F., Wiebe, M., Peterson, P., & Oliphant, T. E. (2020). Array programming with NumPy. *Nature, 585*(7825), 357–362. DOI: 10.1038/s41586-020-2649-2 PMID: 32939066

Hasan, R. (2024). Enhancing stakeholder engagement in project management through ai-driven predictive modeling.

Hashem, R., Ali, N., El Zein, F., Fidalgo, P., & Abu Khurma, O. (2023). AI to the Rescue: Exploring the Potential of ChatGPT as a Teacher Ally for Workload Relief and Burnout Prevention. *Research and Practice in Technology Enhanced Learning, 19*, 23. DOI: 10.58459/rptel.2024.19023

Hassan, F., Khaled Amin, M., Khan, T., Mehedi Hasan Emon, M., & Amin, A. (2020). Roles of social influence in expediting online learning acceptance: A preliminary study on Bangladeshi learners. *ACM International Conference Proceeding Series.* DOI: 10.1145/3377049.3377087

Hassija, V., Chamola, V., Mahapatra, A., Singal, A., Goel, D., Huang, K., Scardapane, S., Spinelli, I., Mahmud, M., & Hussain, A. (2024). Interpreting Black-Box Models: A Review on Explainable Artificial Intelligence. *Cognitive Computation, 16*(1), 45–74. DOI: 10.1007/s12559-023-10179-8

Hitchcock, G., & Hughes, D. (1995). *Research and the teacher: A qualitative introduction to school-based research* (2nd ed.). Routledge., DOI: 10.4324/9780203424605

Hoang, N. T., Ngoc Han, D., & Le, D. H. (2023). Exploring Chatbot AI in Improving Vocational Students' English Pronunciation. *AsiaCALL Online Journal, 14*(2), 140–155. DOI: 10.54855/acoj.231429

Hodson, D. (2020). Going Beyond STS Education: Building a Curriculum for Sociopolitical Activism. *Canadian Journal of Science, Mathematics and Technology Education = Revue Canadienne de l'Enseignement des Sciences, des Mathématiques et de la Technologie, 20*(4), 592–622. DOI: 10.1007/s42330-020-00114-6

Hong, J.-C., Hwang, M.-Y., Liu, Y.-H., & Tai, K.-H. (2022). Effects of gamifying questions on English grammar learning mediated by epistemic curiosity and language anxiety. *Computer Assisted Language Learning, 35*(7), 1458–1482. DOI: 10.1080/09588221.2020.1803361

Hood, N., & Littlejohn, A. (2016). Quality in MOOCs: Surveying the terrain.

Hoque, K. E., & Bt Kenayathulla, H. B., D/O Subramaniam, M. V., & Islam, R. (. (2020). Relationships Between Supervision and Teachers' Performance and Attitude in Secondary Schools in Malaysia. *SAGE Open, 10*(2). Advance online publication. DOI: 10.1177/2158244020925501

Horwitz, E. K. (2017). On the misreading of Horwitz, Horwitz, and Cope (1986) and the need to balance anxiety research and the experiences of anxious language learners. *New insights into language anxiety: Theory, research and educational implications, 31*, 47.

Horwitz, E. K. (1983). Foreign language classroom anxiety scale. *Revista Argentina de Clínica Psicológica*.

Horwitz, E. K. (2020). *Becoming a language teacher: A practical guide to second language learning and teaching*. Castledown Publishers.

Horwitz, E. K., Horwitz, M. B., & Cope, J. (1986). Foreign language classroom anxiety. *Modern Language Journal, 70*(2), 125–132. DOI: 10.1111/j.1540-4781.1986.tb05256.x

Huang, Z. (2020). Thirteen years since the first iPhone: A systematic review on the effectiveness of language learning apps on smart devices (Doctoral dissertation, University of Oxford).

Huang, A. Y. Q., Lu, O. H. T., & Yang, S. J. H. (2022). Effects of artificial intelligence–enabled personalised recommendations on learners' learning engagement, motivation, and outcomes in a flipped classroom. *Computers & Education, 194*, 104684. DOI: 10.1016/j.compedu.2022.104684

Huang, S. (2021). Design and Development of Educational Robot Teaching Resources Using Artificial Intelligence Technology. *International Journal of Emerging Technologies in Learning, 16*(05), 116. DOI: 10.3991/ijet.v16i05.20311

Huang, W., Hew, K. F., & Fryer, L. K. (2022). Chatbots for language learning—Are they really useful? A systematic review of chatbot-supported language learning. *Journal of Computer Assisted Learning*, *38*(1), 237–257. DOI: 10.1111/jcal.12610

Hwang, W. Y., Nurtantyana, R., Purba, S. W. D., Hariyanti, U., Indrihapsari, Y., & Surjono, H. D. (2023). AI and recognition technologies to facilitate English as foreign language writing for supporting personalization and contextualization in authentic contexts. *Journal of Educational Computing Research*, *61*(5), 1008–1035. DOI: 10.1177/07356331221137253

Idham, A. Z., Rauf, W., & Rajab, A. (2024). Navigating the Transformative Impact of Artificial Intelligence on English Language Teaching: Exploring Challenges and Opportunities. *Jes*, *4*(1), 8–14. DOI: 10.56185/jes.v4i1.620

Ikedinachi, A. P., Misra, S., Assibong, P. A., Olu-Owolabi, E. F., Maskeliūnas, R., & Damasevicius, R. (2019). Artificial intelligence, smart classrooms and online education in the 21st century: Implications for human development. [JCIT]. *Journal of Cases on Information Technology*, *21*(3), 66–79. DOI: 10.4018/JCIT.2019070105

Ito, T., Yamashita, N., Kuribayashi, T., Hidaka, M., Suzuki, J., Gao, G., Jamieson, J., & Inui, K. (2023). Use of an AI-powered rewriting support software in context with other tools: A study of non-native English speakers. *36th Annual ACM Symposium on User Interface Software and Technology (UIST '23),* San Francisco, CA, USA. https://doi.org/DOI: 10.1145/3586183.3606810

Jamshed, M., Manjur Ahmed, A. S. M., Sarfaraj, M., & Warda, W. U. (2024). The Impact of ChatGPT on English Language Learners' Writing Skills: An Assessment of AI Feedback on Mobile. *International Journal of Interactive Mobile Technologies*, *18*(19), 18–36. DOI: 10.3991/ijim.v18i19.50361

Jayakumar, V. M., Rajakumari, R., Alapati, P. R., Manchanda, M., Vimochana, M., & Bala, B. K. (2024, December). Applying artificial intelligence in English language learning for customized education. In *2024 International Conference on Artificial Intelligence and Quantum Computation-Based Sensor Application (ICAIQSA)* (pp. 1–6). IEEE. DOI: 10.1109/ICAIQSA64000.2024.10882275

Jeong, K.-O. (2022). Facilitating Sustainable Self-Directed Learning Experience With the Use of Mobile-Assisted Language Learning. *Sustainability (Basel)*, *14*(5), 2894. DOI: 10.3390/su14052894

Jeon, J. (2024). Exploring AI chatbot affordances in the EFL classroom: Young learners' experiences and perspectives. *Computer Assisted Language Learning*, *37*(1-2), 1–26. DOI: 10.1080/09588221.2021.2021241

Jiang, R. (2022). How does artificial intelligence empower EFL teaching and learning nowadays? A review on artificial intelligence in the EFL context. *Frontiers in Psychology, 13*, 1049401. Advance online publication. DOI: 10.3389/fpsyg.2022.1049401 PMID: 36467167

Jian, M. J. K. O. (2023). Personalised learning through AI. *Advances in Engineering Innovation, 5*(1), 16–19. DOI: 10.54254/2977-3903/5/2023039

Jiao, F., Song, J., Zhao, X., Zhao, P., & Wang, R. (2021). A Spoken English Teaching System Based on Speech Recognition and Machine Learning. *International Journal of Emerging Technologies in Learning, 16*(14), 68. DOI: 10.3991/ijet.v16i14.24049

Jing, Y., & Jia, G. (2024, July). Application of artificial intelligence (AI) technology in intelligent recommendation of English personalized learning system. In *2024 3rd International Conference on Artificial Intelligence and Autonomous Robot Systems (AIARS)* (pp. 455–460). IEEE.

Jomaa, N. J. (2025). *Corrective Feedback of AI Tools in Writing and Translation.*, DOI: 10.4018/979-8-3693-9511-0.ch010

Jones, K. M., Asher, A., Goben, A., Perry, M. R., Salo, D., Briney, K. A., & Robertshaw, M. B. (2020). "We're being tracked at all times": Student perspectives of their privacy in relation to learning analytics in higher education. *Journal of the Association for Information Science and Technology, 71*(9), 1044–1059. DOI: 10.1002/asi.24358

Kallinikou, E., & Nicolaidou, I. (2019). Digital Storytelling to Enhance Adults' Speaking Skills in Learning Foreign Languages: A Case Study. *Multimodal Technologies and Interaction, 3*(3), 59. DOI: 10.3390/mti3030059

Kalyani, L. K. (2024). The role of technology in education: Enhancing learning outcomes and 21st century skills. International journal of scientific research in modern science and technology, 3(4), 05-10.

Kamalov, F., Santandreu Calonge, D., & Gurrib, I. (2023). New era of artificial intelligence in education: Towards a sustainable multifaceted revolution. *Sustainability (Basel), 15*(16), 12451. DOI: 10.3390/su151612451

Kamarulzaman, L. M., Abdul Ghani, M. T., & Wan Daud, W. A. A. (2018). The effect of active learning strategies on students' attitudes towards English: A study at Universiti Teknologi Petronas. *INSANIAH: Online Journal of Language, Communication, and Humanities, 1*(2).

Kanchon, M. K. H., Sadman, M., Nabila, K. F., Tarannum, R., & Khan, R. (2024). Enhancing personalized learning: AI-driven identification of learning styles and content modification strategies. *International Journal of Cognitive Computing in Engineering*, *5*, 269–278. DOI: 10.1016/j.ijcce.2024.06.002

Kantan, P. R. (2024). Orchestrating Motion: Real-Time Sonification Tools and Methods to Support Movement Rehabilitation.

Kara, Y., Kamata, A., Ozkeskin, E. E., Qiao, X., & Nese, J. F. (2023). Predicting oral reading fluency scores by between-word silence times using natural language processing and random forest algorithm. *Psychological Test and Assessment Modeling*, *65*(1), 36–54.

Kayyali, M. (2025 A). AI in Higher Education: Revolutionizing Curriculum and Administration. In AI Adoption and Diffusion in Education (pp. 31-62). IGI Global Scientific Publishing.

Kayyali, M. (2025 B). The Future of AI in Education: Predictions and Emerging Trends. Next-Generation AI Methodologies in Education, 367-406.

Kayyali, M. (2024). Future possibilities and challenges of AI in education. In *Transforming education with generative AI: Prompt engineering and synthetic content creation* (pp. 118–137). IGI Global. DOI: 10.4018/979-8-3693-1351-0.ch006

Kazu, I. Y., & Kuvvetli, M. (2023). The Influence of Pronunciation Education via Artificial Intelligence Technology on Vocabulary Acquisition in Learning English. *International Journal of Psychology and Educational Studies*, *10*(2), 480–493. DOI: 10.52380/ijpes.2023.10.2.1044

Kecskes, I. (2019). *English as a lingua franca: The pragmatic perspective.* Cambridge University Press.

Khan, T., & Hasan Emon, M. M. (2024). Determinants of AI Image Generator Adoption Among Marketing Agencies: The Mediating Effects of Perceived Usefulness. *2024 IEEE 3rd International Conference on Robotics, Automation, Artificial-Intelligence and Internet-of-Things (RAAICON)*, 177–182. DOI: 10.1109/RAAICON64172.2024.10928548

Khan, T., Emon, M. M. H., & Rahman, S. (2024). Marketing Strategy Innovation via AI Adoption: A Study on Bangladeshi SMEs in the Context of Industry 5.0. *2024 6th International Conference on Sustainable Technologies for Industry 5.0 (STI)*, 1–6. DOI: 10.1109/STI64222.2024.10951050

Khan, T., Emon, M. M. H., Rahman, M. A., Hamid, A. B. A., & Yaakub, N. I. (2025). Bridging the Gap: Realizing GreenTech Potential. In *AI and Green Technology Applications in Society* (pp. 91–122). IGI Global Scientific Publishing. DOI: 10.4018/979-8-3693-9879-1.ch004

Khan, W. M. (2023). Examining the Transformative Role of Artificial Intelligence in Language Skill Enhancement: A Case Study of BS English Students in Okara, Pakistan. *Abbdm*, *3*(1), 190–196. DOI: 10.62019/abbdm.v3i1.88

Kholis, A. (2021). Elsa Speak App: Automatic Speech Recognition (ASR) for supplementing English pronunciation skills. *Pedagogy Journal of English Language Teaching, 9*(1), 01. https://doi.org/DOI: 10.32332/joelt.v9i1.2723

Kim, N. Y., Cha, Y., & Kim, H. S. (2019). Future English learning: Chatbots and artificial intelligence. Multimedia-Assisted Language Learning, 22(3).

Kim, J., & Lee, H. (2023). Teacher roles in AI-enhanced language classrooms: An activity theory analysis. *CALICO Journal*, *40*(1), 86–110.

Klayklung, P., Chocksathaporn, P., Limna, L., Kraiwanit, T., & Jangjarat, K. (2023). Revolutionizing education with ChatGPT: Enhancing learning through conversational AI. *Universal Journal of Educational Research*, *2*(3), 217–225.

Klímová, B., Pikhart, M., Poláková, P., Černá, M., Yayilgan, S. Y., & Shaikh, S. (2023). A Systematic Review on the Use of Emerging Technologies in Teaching English as an Applied Language at the University Level. *Systems*, *11*(1), 42. DOI: 10.3390/systems11010042

Koh, J., Cowling, M., Jha, M., & Sim, K. N. (2022). Collaborating With AIed for Better Student-Teacher Reconnection. *Ascilite Publications*, e22126. DOI: 10.14742/apubs.2022.126

Komljenovic, J. (2021). The rise of education rentiers: Digital platforms, digital data and rents. *Learning, Media and Technology*, *46*(3), 320–332. DOI: 10.1080/17439884.2021.1891422

Kot, S. O., & Nykyporets, S. S. (2024). *Utilization of artificial intelligence in enhancing English language proficiency in tertiary education. Science and Education in the Third Millennium: Information Technology*. Education, Law, Psychology, Social Sphere, Management.

Kovalenko, I., & Baranivska, N. (2024). Integrating artificial intelligence in English language teaching: Exploring the potential and challenges of AI tools in enhancing language learning outcomes and personalized education. *Європейські соціо-правові та гуманітарні студії, (1)*, 86–95.

Kovalenko, I., & Baranivska, N. (2024). Integrating Artificial Intelligence in English Language Teaching: Exploring the potential and challenges of AI tools in enhancing language learning outcomes and personalized education. Європейські соціо-правові та гуманітарні студії, (1), 86-95.

Krashen, S. D. (1982). *Principles and Practice in Second Language Acquisition*. Pergamon Press. Retrieved from https://www.sdkrashen.com/content/books/principles_and_practice.pdf

Krashen, S. D. (1985). *The Input Hypothesis: Issues and Implications*. Longman.

Kuddus, K. (2022). Artificial intelligence in language learning: Practices and prospects. Advanced Analytics and Deep Learning Models, 1-17.

Kuddus, K. (2022). Artificial intelligence in language learning: Practices and prospects. In *Advanced Analytics and Deep Learning Models* (pp. 1–17).

Kuddus, K. (2022). Artificial Intelligence in Language Learning: Practices and Prospects. In *Advanced Analytics and Deep Learning Models* (pp. 1–17). Wiley. DOI: 10.1002/9781119792437.ch1

Kuhail, M. A., Alturki, N., Alramlawi, S., & Alhejori, K. (2022). Interacting With Educational Chatbots: A Systematic Review. *Education and Information Technologies*, *28*(1), 973–1018. DOI: 10.1007/s10639-022-11177-3

Kung, T. H., Cheatham, M., Medenilla, A., Sillos, C., De Leon, L., Elepaño, C., Madriaga, M., Aggabao, R., Diaz-Candido, G., Maningo, J., & Tseng, V. (2023). Performance of ChatGPT on USMLE: Potential for AI-assisted medical education using large language models. *PLOS Digital Health*, *2*(2), e0000198. DOI: 10.1371/journal.pdig.0000198 PMID: 36812645

Labadze, L., Grigolia, M., & Machaidze, L. (2023). Role of AI chatbots in education: Systematic literature review. *International Journal of Educational Technology in Higher Education*, *20*(1), 56. DOI: 10.1186/s41239-023-00426-1

Lai, C. C., & Kritsonis, W. A. (2006). The advantages and disadvantages of computer technology in second language acquisition. *Online Submission, 3*(1).

Landers, R. N. (2015). Developing a theory of gamified learning: Linking serious games and gamification of learning. *Simulation & Gaming*, •••, 1–17. DOI: 10.1177/1046878114563660

Latif, E., Mai, G., Nyaaba, M., Wu, X., Liu, N., Lu, G., . . . Zhai, X. (2023). Artificial general intelligence (AGI) for education. arXiv preprint arXiv:2304.12479, 1.

Laurel, R. D., Belting, A. C., & Almansouri, E. O. (2021). Evaluation of the English Language Teaching Program of the Faculty of Education, University of Benghazi Using the Peacock Model: Towards Quality Education. *European Journal of Education Studies, 8*(10). Advance online publication. DOI: 10.46827/ejes.v8i10.3945

Lee, H. (2024). The rise of ChatGPT: Exploring its potential in medical education. *Anatomical Sciences Education, 17*(5), 926–931. DOI: 10.1002/ase.2270 PMID: 36916887

Lehikko, A., & Nykänen, M. (2024, August). A Mixed-Methods Study on Learner-IVR Interactivity, Agency, Cognitive Load and Learning Outcomes. In *European Association for Research on Learning and Instruction SIG 6 & 7 Conference 2024*. Instructional Design, Technology-Enhanced Learning and Instruction.

Leong, A. C. H., Abidin, M. J. Z., & Saibon, J. S. (2019). The Benefits and Drawbacks of Using Tablet-Based Digital Storytelling in Vocabulary Learning Among Malaysian Young English as a Second Language (ESL) Learners. *Asia Pacific Journal of Educators and Education, 34*, 17–47. DOI: 10.21315/apjee2019.34.2

Levi, E. I. (2024). *Technology in Lifelong Language Learning*., DOI: 10.4018/979-8-3693-1410-4.ch012

Lewers, K. K. (2024). Comparative Methods for Building Chatbots: Open Source, Hybrid, and Fully Integrated Large Language Models. *Biodiversity Information Science and Standards, 8*, 8. DOI: 10.3897/biss.8.143032

Li, K. C., & Wong, B. (2023). Artificial Intelligence in Personalised Learning: A Bibliometric Analysis. *Interactive Technology and Smart Education, 20*(3), 422–445. DOI: 10.1108/ITSE-01-2023-0007

Li, K. C., & Wong, B. T. (2021). A literature review of augmented reality, virtual reality, and mixed reality in language learning. *International Journal of Mobile Learning and Organisation, 15*(2), 164–178. DOI: 10.1504/IJMLO.2021.114516

Limna, P., Kraiwanit, T., Jangjarat, K., Klayklung, P., & Chocksathaporn, P. (2023). The use of ChatGPT in the digital era: Perspectives on chatbot implementation. *Journal of Applied Learning and Teaching, 6*(1), 64–74.

Lin, C., & Mubarok, H. (2021). Artificial intelligence in intelligent tutoring systems toward sustainable education. *Smart Learning Environments, 8*(1), 1–11. https://slejournal.springeropen.com/articles/10.1186/s40561-023-00260-y

Ling, Z., & Mohammed, A. L. (2023). The Influence of Multimodal Learning Methods on English Language Competence in Higher Vocational Colleges. *Advances in Vocational and Technical Education, 5*(13), 100–105.

Litman, D. (2016). Natural language processing for enhancing teaching and learning. *Proceedings of the AAAI Conference on Artificial Intelligence, 30*(1), •••. DOI: 10.1609/aaai.v30i1.9879

Liu, M. (2023). Exploring the application of artificial intelligence in foreign language teaching: Challenges and future development. *SHS Web of Conferences, 168*, 3025.

Liu, H. C., Lin, M. H., Chang, W. C., Zeng, R. C., Wang, Y. M., & Sun, C. W. (2023). Rapid on-site AI-assisted grading for lung surgery based on optical coherence tomography. *Cancers (Basel), 15*(22), 5388. DOI: 10.3390/cancers15225388 PMID: 38001648

Liu, X. (2024). Online Learning Based on Learning Analytics in Big Data for College English Language Teaching. *International Journal of Computational Intelligence Systems, 17*(1), 192. DOI: 10.1007/s44196-024-00594-6

Liu, Y., & Quan, Q. (2022). AI recognition method of pronunciation errors in oral English speech with the help of big data for personalized learning. *Journal of Information & Knowledge Management, 21*(Supp02), 2240028. DOI: 10.1142/S0219649222400287

Liu, Y., Wang, Y., & Zheng, P. (2024). Equity challenges in AI-enhanced language education: A global perspective. *TESOL Quarterly, 58*(1), 123–148.

Li, X. (2024). A personalized teaching system for college English based on big data and artificial intelligence. *Scalable Computing: Practice and Experience, 25*(6), 5477–5485. DOI: 10.12694/scpe.v25i6.3341

Llorens-Largo, F., Gallego-Durán, F. J., Villagrá-Arnedo, C. J., Compañ-Rosique, P., Satorre-Cuerda, R., & Molina-Carmona, R. (2016). *Gamification of the learning process: Lessons learned.* RevistaIberoamericana De Tecnologias Del Aprendizaje., DOI: 10.1109/RITA.2016.2619138

Long, M. H. (1996). The role of the linguistic environment in second language acquisition. In Ritchie, W. C., & Bhatia, T. K. (Eds.), *Handbook of Second Language Acquisition* (pp. 413–468). Academic Press.

Loor, M. A. M., Solorzano, D. M. A., Katherine, A., & Moreira, V. (2024). Integration of Artificial Intelligence in English Teaching. *Journal of Cleaner Production, 289*, 125834.

Lou, L., Xu, W., & Liu, R. (2024). A Bibliometric Approach and Meta-Analysis of Effects of Automatic Speech Recognition on Second Language Learning. *International Journal of Web-Based Learning and Teaching Technologies, 19*(1), 1–20. DOI: 10.4018/IJWLTT.349959

Luckin, R., Cukurova, M., Kent, C., & Du Boulay, B. (2022). Empowering educators to be AI-ready. *Computers and Education: Artificial Intelligence, 3*, 100076.

Luczaj, K., Leonowicz-Bukala, I., & Kurek-Ochmanska, O. (2022). English as a lingua franca? The limits of everyday English-language communication in Polish academia. *English for Specific Purposes, 66*, 3–16. DOI: 10.1016/j.esp.2021.11.002

Luke, K. (2021). Twelve Tips for Using Synchronous Virtual Classroom Technologies in Medical Education. *MedEdPublish, 10*(1). Advance online publication. DOI: 10.15694/mep.2021.000066.1 PMID: 38486516

Luo, B. (2020). The influence of teaching learning techniques on students' long-term learning behavior. *Computer Assisted Language Learning, 33*(4), 388–412. DOI: 10.1080/09588221.2019.1567557

Luo, Q. Z., & Hsiao-Chin, L. Y. (2023). The influence of AI-powered adaptive learning platforms on student performance in Chinese classrooms. *Journal of Education, 6*(3), 1–12. DOI: 10.53819/81018102t4181

Luo, Y. (2024). Innovative Research on AI-assisted Teaching Models for College English Listening and Speaking Courses. *Applied and Computational Engineering, 69*(1), 155–160. DOI: 10.54254/2755-2721/69/20241493

Mabuan, R. A. (2024). ChatGPT and ELT: Exploring Teachers' Voices. International journal of technology in education, 7(1), 128-153.

MacIntyre, P. D. (1999). Language anxiety: A review of the research for language teachers. Affect in foreign language and second language learning: A practical guide to creating a low-anxiety classroom atmosphere, 24(1), 34-70.

MacIntyre, A. (1999). Social structures and their threats to moral agency. *Philosophy (London, England), 74*(3), 311–329. DOI: 10.1017/S0031819199000431

MacIntyre, P. D., & Gardner, R. C. (1994). The effects of induced anxiety on cognitive processing in second language learning. *Studies in Second Language Acquisition, 16*, 1–17. DOI: 10.1017/S0272263100012560

Maghsudi, S., Lan, A., Xu, J., & van der Schaar, M. (2021). Personalised education in the artificial intelligence era: What to expect next. *IEEE Signal Processing Magazine, 38*(3), 37–50. Advance online publication. DOI: 10.1109/MSP.2021.3055032

Mahmoud, C., & Sørensen, J. T. (2024). Artificial intelligence in personalized learning with a focus on current developments and future prospects. *Research and Advances in Education, 3*(8), 25–31. DOI: 10.56397/RAE.2024.08.04

Makinde, A. I., Adeleye, S. A., Oronti, A. O., & Jimoh, I. T. (2024). Revolutionizing education. Artificial Intelligence for Wireless Communication Systems: Technology and Applications, 103.

Mamun, K. A., Nabid, R. A., Pranto, S. I., Lamim, S. M., Rahman, M. M., Mahammed, N., Huda, M. N., Sarker, F., & Khan, R. R. (2024). Smart reception: An artificial intelligence driven bangla language based receptionist system employing speech, speaker, and face recognition for automating reception services. *Engineering Applications of Artificial Intelligence, 136*, 108923. DOI: 10.1016/j.engappai.2024.108923

Manggiasih, L. A., Loreana, Y. R., Azizah, A., & Nurjati, N. (2023). Strengths and Limitations of SmallTalk2Me App in English Language Proficiency Evaluation. *Tell Teaching of English Language and Literature Journal, 11*(2). Advance online publication. DOI: 10.30651/tell.v11i2.19560

Maqbool, F., Ansari, S., & Otero, P. véase además M. (2021). The Role of Artificial Intelligence and Smart Classrooms During Covid-19 Pandemic and Its Impact on Education. *Journal of Independent Studies and Research - Computing, 19*(1). DOI: 10.31645/JISRC.41.19.1.2

Maqsood, M., Zahid, A., Asghar, T., Farooqi, S.-H., & Shahbaz, M. (2024). Issues in Teaching English in a Cultural Context. *Migration Letters : An International Journal of Migration Studies, 21*(S4), 1020–1027. DOI: 10.59670/ml.v21iS4.7411

Markus, A. F., Kors, J. A., & Rijnbeek, P. R. (2021). The role of explainability in creating trustworthy artificial intelligence for health care: A comprehensive survey of the terminology, design choices, and evaluation strategies. *Journal of Biomedical Informatics, 113*, 103655. DOI: 10.1016/j.jbi.2020.103655 PMID: 33309898

Marouf, A., Al-Dahdooh, R., Abu Ghali, M. J., Mahdi, A. O., Abunasser, B. S., & Abu-Naser, S. S. (2024). Enhancing education with artificial intelligence: The role of intelligent tutoring systems. *International Journal of Engineering and Information Systems (IJEAIS, 8)*(8), 10–16. https://www.ijeais.org/ijeais

Martinez-Lopez, R., & Chung, S. (2024). Multimodal feedback mechanisms in AI language tutors: Effects on learner motivation and self-regulation. *Language Teaching Research, 28*(2), 243–267.

Martin, S. M. (2019). *Artificial intelligence, mixed reality, and the redefinition of the classroom*. Rowman & Littlefield.

Maruf, N., & Halyna, K. (2023). Investigating EFL Teachers' Perceptions and Meanings on Digital Storytelling in Language Learning: A Narrative Approach. [Journal of English Education and Linguistics Studies]. *Jeels, 10*(2), 357–378. DOI: 10.30762/jeels.v10i2.912

Marzuki, W., Widiati, U., Rusdin, D., Darwin, , & Indrawati, I. (2023). The impact of AI writing tools on the content and organization of students' writing: EFL teachers' perspective. *Cogent Education, 10*(2), 2236469. Advance online publication. DOI: 10.1080/2331186X.2023.2236469

Mavropoulou, E., Koutsoukos, M., & Oikonomou, A. (2023). Integration of artificial intelligence on teaching the course of didactic methodology: A case study. *European Journal of Social Science Education and Research.* https://revistia.com/ejser/article/view/542

Mayer, R. E. (2009). *Multimedia learning* (2nd ed.). Cambridge University Press., DOI: 10.1017/CBO9780511811678

Mayer, R. E. (Ed.). (2014). *The Cambridge handbook of multimedia learning* (2nd ed.). Cambridge University Press., http://molwave.chem.auth.gr/sigalas_edu/files/Multimedia_Learning.pdf#page=43 DOI: 10.1017/CBO9781139547369

Mazur, J., & Serafin, M. (2023). Stalling the State: How Digital Platforms Contribute to and Profit From Delays in the Enforcement and Adoption of Regulations. *Comparative Political Studies, 56*(1), 101–130. DOI: 10.1177/00104140221089651

McCullough, L. E. (2024). Examining the Lived Experiences of Educators Using Different Levels of Support for Teaching Math to Students with Learning Disabilities in Math Computation and Problem-Solving for Teachers at Public Cyber Charter High Schools in the Northeastern United States: A Transcendental Phenomenological Study.

McLean, G., & Osei-Frimpong, K. (2019). Hey Alexa… examine the variables influencing the use of artificial intelligent in-home voice assistants. *Computers in Human Behavior, 99*, 28–37. DOI: 10.1016/j.chb.2019.05.009

Medvedev, G. (2016). Google Translate in teaching English. *The Journal of Teaching English for Specific and Academic Purposes, 4*(1), 181–193.

Meera, S., & Geerthik, S. (2022). Natural language processing. In *Artificial Intelligent Techniques for Wireless Communication and Networking* (pp. 139–153). Wiley., DOI: 10.1002/9781119821809.ch10

Meirbekov, A., Nyshanova, S., Meiirbekov, A., Kazykhankyzy, L., Burayeva, Z., & Abzhekenova, B. (2024). Digitisation of English language education: Instagram and TikTok online educational blogs and courses vs. traditional academic education. How to increase student motivation? *Education and Information Technologies, 29*(11), 13635–13662. DOI: 10.1007/s10639-023-12396-y

Meng, X., Yang, B., Yang, L., Zhang, J., & Liu, Y. (2025). A Novel AI-Empowered, Student-Centered Teaching Strategy for Large Classes in Higher Education. *International Journal of Science and Mathematics Education*. Advance online publication. DOI: 10.1007/s10763-025-10573-8

Meurers, D., & Dickinson, M. (2023). Natural language processing for learner language: Current capabilities and future directions. *Annual Review of Applied Linguistics, 43*, 78–97.

Miao, F., Holmes, W., Huang, R., & Zhang, H. (2021). *AI and education: A guidance for policymakers*. Unesco Publishing.

Miao, H., Guo, X., & Yuan, F. (2021). Research on identification of potential directions of artificial intelligence industry from the perspective of weak signal. *IEEE Transactions on Engineering Management, 71*, 465–480. DOI: 10.1109/TEM.2021.3123639

Michel-Villarreal, R., Vilalta-Perdomo, E., Salinas-Navarro, D. E., Thierry-Aguilera, R., & Gerardou, F. S. (2023). Challenges and opportunities of generative AI for higher education as explained by ChatGPT. *Education Sciences, 13*(9), 856. DOI: 10.3390/educsci13090856

Miller, J. A., & Cooper, S. (2021). Case Studies in Game-Based Complex Learning. *Multimodal Technologies and Interaction, 5*(12), 72. DOI: 10.3390/mti5120072

Minh, A. N. (2024). Leveraging ChatGPT for Enhancing English Writing Skills and Critical Thinking in University Freshmen. *Journal of Knowledge Learning and Science Technology Issn 2959-6386 (Online), 3*(2), 51–62. DOI: 10.60087/jklst.vol3.n2.p62

Ministry of Education and Culture. Finland. (2023). *Digital learning and AI in Finnish schools: Challenges and opportunities*. Helsinki: Government Printing Office.

Mishra, R. (2024). EMBRACING A PARADIGM SHIFT: TRANSITIONING FROM TRADITIONAL TEACHING METHODS TO AI-BASED NLP EDUCATION. Research and Reviews in Literature. *Social Sciences*, •••, 75.

Mohammad Ali, A. (2023). An intervention study on the use of artificial intelligence in the ESL classroom: English teacher perspectives on the effectiveness of ChatGPT for personalized language learning.

Morkun, V. S., Morkun, N. V., & Pikilnyak, A. V. (2020). Augmented reality as a tool for visualization of ultrasound propagation in heterogeneous media based on the k-space method. *International Workshop on Augmented Reality in Education.* DOI: 10.31812/123456789/3757

Murtaza, M., Ahmed, Y., Shamsi, J. A., Sherwani, F., & Usman, M. (2022). AI-based personalized e-learning systems: Issues, challenges, and solutions. *IEEE Access : Practical Innovations, Open Solutions, 10*, 81323–81342. DOI: 10.1109/ACCESS.2022.3193938

Namazi, M., & Raiessi, Z. (n.d.). Stem accounting: Effects of traditional and significant data education, learning and intelligence on the accounting student's achievement. [No journal or DOI provided]

Nassif, A. B., Shahin, I., Attili, I. B., Azzeh, M., & Shaalan, K. (2019). Speech Recognition Using Deep Neural Networks: A Systematic Review. *IEEE Access : Practical Innovations, Open Solutions, 7*, 19143–19165. DOI: 10.1109/ACCESS.2019.2896880

National Academic Integrity Network. (2023). *Generative artificial intelligence: Guidelines for educators.* https://www.qqi.ie/sites/default/files/2023-09/NAIN%20Generative%20AI%20Guidelines%20for%20Educators%202023.pdf

Nazari, M. (2022). Plan, act, observe, reflect, identity: Exploring teacher identity construction across the stages of action research. *RELC Journal, 53*(3), 672–685. DOI: 10.1177/0033688220972456

Negrila, A. M. C. (2023). The new revolution in language learning: The power of artificial intelligence and Education 4.0. *Bulletin of "Carol I". National Defence University, 12*(2), 16–27. DOI: 10.53477/2284-9378-23-17

Ng, D. T. K., Leung, J. K. L., Su, J., Ng, R. C. W., & Chu, S. K. W. (2023). Teachers' AI digital competencies and twenty-first century skills in the post-pandemic world. *Educational Technology Research and Development, 71*(1), 137–161. DOI: 10.1007/s11423-023-10203-6 PMID: 36844361

Nghi, T. T., Phuc, T. H., & Thang, N. T. (2019). Applying AI chatbot for teaching a foreign language: An empirical research. *International Journal of Scientific and Technology Research, 8*(12), 897–902.

Nguyen, T. X. (2024). English Majors' Perceptions of AI Tool Application in English Language Learning at Tertiary Level in Vietnam. *Journal of Knowledge Learning and Science Technology Issn 2959-6386 (Online), 3*(1), 179–193. DOI: 10.60087/jklst.vol3.n1.p193

Nguyen, A., Ngo, H. N., Hong, Y., Dang, B., & Nguyen, B.-P. T. (2023). Ethical principles for artificial intelligence in education. *Education and Information Technologies, 28*(4), 4221–4241. DOI: 10.1007/s10639-022-11316-w PMID: 36254344

Nguyen, T. T. H., & Hwang, W. Y. (2022). The impact of AI-powered speaking practice on learner anxiety and performance: Evidence from East Asian contexts. *Language Learning, 72*(2), 389–421.

Nicolaidou, I., Pissas, P., & Boglou, D. (2021). Comparing immersive virtual reality to mobile applications in foreign language learning in higher education: A quasi-experiment. *Interactive Learning Environments, 31*(4), 2001–2015. DOI: 10.1080/10494820.2020.1870504

Nilson, L. B., & Goodson, L. A. (2021). *Online teaching at its best: Merging instructional design with teaching and learning research.* John Wiley & Sons.

Niu, S. J., Luo, J., Niemi, H., Li, X., & Lu, Y. (2022). Teachers' and Students' Views of Using an AI-Aided Educational Platform for Supporting Teaching and Learning at Chinese Schools. *Education Sciences, 12*(12), 858. DOI: 10.3390/educsci12120858

Nkadimeng, M., & Ankiewicz, P. (2022). The Affordances of Minecraft Education as a Game-Based Learning Tool for Atomic Structure in Junior High School Science Education. *Journal of Science Education and Technology, 31*(5), 605–620. DOI: 10.1007/s10956-022-09981-0

Novik, K. (2024). From chatbots to adaptive learning: The role of AI in personalized English language education. In *Collection of scientific papers "SCIENTIA"* (November 1, 2024; Lisbon, Portugal), 161–164.

Nugraha, D. N. S., Simatupang, E. C., Sari, P., Gunawan, H., Dianita, D., & Rusyan, S. (2023). Duolingo as an artificial intelligence technology-based learning system in English. *Jurnal Sinestesia, 13*(2), 1085–1089.

Nurmatova, S., & Noori, N. (2023). Examining the synergistic impact of cross-cultural communication and virtual reality on young adults' English language proficiency. *International Journal of Social Sciences and Educational Studies, 11*(1). Advance online publication. DOI: 10.23918/ijsses.v11i1p18

Omohundro, S. (2014). Autonomous technology and the greater human good. *Journal of Experimental & Theoretical Artificial Intelligence*, *26*(3), 303–315. DOI: 10.1080/0952813X.2014.895111

Ooi, K. B., Tan, G. W. H., Al-Emran, M., Al-Sharafi, M. A., Capatina, A., Chakraborty, A., Dwivedi, Y. K., Huang, T.-L., Kar, A. K., Lee, V.-H., Loh, X.-M., Micu, A., Mikalef, P., Mogaji, E., Pandey, N., Raman, R., Rana, N. P., Sarker, P., Sharma, A., & Wong, L. W. (2025). The potential of generative artificial intelligence across disciplines: Perspectives and future directions. *Journal of Computer Information Systems*, *65*(1), 76–107. DOI: 10.1080/08874417.2023.2261010

Owoc, M. L., Sawicka, A., & Weichbroth, P. (2019). Artificial intelligence technologies in education: Benefits, challenges, and strategies of implementation. *IFIP International Workshop on Artificial Intelligence for Knowledge Management*, 37–58.

Özer, M. (2024). Potential benefits and risks of artificial intelligence in education. *Bartın University Journal of Faculty of Education*, *13*(2), 232–244. DOI: 10.14686/buefad.1416087

Pahuja, A., Kaur, S., Budhraja, K., & Kathuria, S. (2024). Examining the impact of AI on education: Ethical, psychological, and pedagogical perspectives. In *Ethical AI and Data Management Strategies in Marketing* (pp. 208–225). IGI Global., DOI: 10.4018/979-8-3693-6660-8.ch015

Pan, J. (2024). AI-driven English language learning program and academic writing integrity in the era of intelligent interface. *English Language Teaching and Linguistics Studies*, *6*(4), 120. DOI: 10.22158/eltls.v6n4p120

Park, S. M., & Kim, Y. G. (2022). A metaverse: Taxonomy, components, applications, and open challenges. *IEEE Access : Practical Innovations, Open Solutions*, *10*, 4209–4251. DOI: 10.1109/ACCESS.2021.3140175

Parmaxi, A., & Demetriou, A. A. (2020). Augmented Reality in Language Learning: A State-of-the-art Review of 2014–2019. *Journal of Computer Assisted Learning*, *36*(6), 861–875. DOI: 10.1111/jcal.12486

Parraga, A. P. B., Ramírez, E. A. C., Macias, K. J. A., Madrid, C. A. C., Espinoza, B. D. C. V., Alcivar, J. G. V., & Cedeño, J. U. C. (2025). The impact of artificial intelligence on personalized learning in English language education. *Ciencia Latina Revista Científica Multidisciplinar*, *9*(1), 5500–5518. DOI: 10.37811/cl_rcm.v9i1.16234

Partners, T. (2023). *Time for class 2023: Bridging student and faculty perspectives on digital learning*. https://tytonpartners.com/app/uploads/2023/06/Time-for-Class-2023-Report_Final.pdf

Parycek, P., Schmid, V., & Novak, A. S. (2024). Artificial Intelligence (AI) and automation in administrative procedures: Potentials, limitations, and framework conditions. *Journal of the Knowledge Economy*, *15*(2), 8390–8415. DOI: 10.1007/s13132-023-01433-3

Peña-Acuña, B., & Corga Fernandes Durão, R. (2024, November). Learning English as a second language with artificial intelligence for prospective teachers: A systematic review. [). Frontiers Media SA.]. *Frontiers in Education*, *9*, 1490067. DOI: 10.3389/feduc.2024.1490067

Perdana, I., Manullang, S. O., & Masri, F. A. (2021). Effectiveness of online Grammarly application in improving academic writing: Review of experts' experience. *The International Journal of Social Sciences (Islamabad)*, *4*(1), 122–130. DOI: 10.31295/ijss.v4n1.1444

Peterson, M., & Yamashita, T. (2024). Conversational agents in second language acquisition: A comparative analysis of learner interactions and outcomes. *ReCALL*, *36*(2), 178–195.

Phillips Galloway, E., McClain, J. B., & Uccelli, P. (2020). Broadening the Lens on the Science of Reading: A Multifaceted Perspective on the Role of Academic Language in Text Understanding. *Reading Research Quarterly*, *55*(S1). Advance online publication. DOI: 10.1002/rrq.359

Pipiras, L., Maskeliūnas, R., & Damaševičius, R. (2019). Lithuanian Speech Recognition Using Purely Phonetic Deep Learning. *Computers*, *8*(4), 76. DOI: 10.3390/computers8040076

Pitychoutis, K. M., & Al Rawahi, A. (2024). Smart Teaching: The Synergy of Multiple Intelligences and Artificial Intelligence in English as a Foreign Language Instruction.

Pokrivcakova, S. (2019). Preparing teachers for the application of AI-powered technologies in foreign language education. *Journal of Language and Cultural Education*, *7*(3), 135–153. DOI: 10.2478/jolace-2019-0025

Pratama, M. P., Sampelolo, R., & Lura, H. (2023). Revolutionizing Education: Harnessing the Power of Artificial Intelligence for Personalized Learning. *Klasikal Journal of Education Language Teaching and Science*, *5*(2), 350–357. DOI: 10.52208/klasikal.v5i2.877

Prather, J., Denny, P., Leinonen, J., Becker, B. A., Albluwi, I., Craig, M., & Savelka, J. (2023). The robots are here: Navigating the generative ai revolution in computing education. In *Proceedings of the 2023 working group reports on innovation and technology in computer science education* (pp. 108-159). DOI: 10.1145/3623762.3633499

Qasem, F., Ghaleb, M., Mahdi, H. S., Khateeb, A. A. A., & Fadda, H. A. (2023). Dialog chatbot as an interactive online tool in enhancing ESP vocabulary learning. *Saudi Journal of Language Studies, 3*(2), 76–86. DOI: 10.1108/SJLS-10-2022-0072

Qassrawi, N. R. M., ElMashharawi, N. A., Itmeizeh, N. M., & Tamimi, N. M. H. M. (2024). AI-powered applications for improving EFL students' speaking proficiency in higher education. *Forum for Linguistic Studies*, *6*(5), 535–549. DOI: 10.30564/fls.v6i5.6966

Qiao, H., & Zhao, A. (2023). Artificial intelligence-based language learning: Illuminating the impact on speaking skills and self-regulation in the Chinese EFL context. *Frontiers in Psychology*, *14*, 1255594. Advance online publication. DOI: 10.3389/fpsyg.2023.1255594 PMID: 38022973

Qu, C., & Kim, E. (2022). Dynamic capabilities perspective on innovation ecosystem of China's universities in the age of artificial intelligence: Policy-based analysis. Journal of Infrastructure. *Policy and Development*, *6*(2), 1661. DOI: 10.24294/jipd.v6i2.1661

Qureshi, R., Hajare, S., & Verma, P. (2024, July). A review on the role of artificial intelligence in personalized learning. In *2024 Asia Pacific Conference on Innovation in Technology (APCIT)* (pp. 1–5). IEEE. DOI: 10.1109/APCIT62007.2024.10673706

R'boul, H. (2024). English medium instruction in Moroccan universities: Implications for multilingualism, linguistic dependency and epistemic justice. *Journal of Multilingual and Multicultural Development*, *45*(7), 2770–2784. DOI: 10.1080/01434632.2022.2069250

Radu, B., & Schneider, B. (2023). How augmented reality (AR) can help and hinder collaborative learning: A study of AR in electromagnetism education. *IEEE Transactions on Visualization and Computer Graphics*, *29*(9), 3734–3745. DOI: 10.1109/TVCG.2022.3169980 PMID: 35500084

Rajak, L., Chauhan, S., & Bara, S. (2024). Transforming English Pedagogy with Artificial Intelligence: Enroute to Enhanced Language Learning. In Artificial Intelligence: A Multidisciplinary Approach towards Teaching and Learning (pp. 216-241). Bentham Science Publishers.

Rasheed, A., San, O., & Kvamsdal, T. (2020). Digital twin: Values, challenges and enablers from a modeling perspective. *IEEE Access : Practical Innovations, Open Solutions*, *8*, 21980–22012. DOI: 10.1109/ACCESS.2020.2970143

Rasheed, Z., Ghwanmeh, S., & Abualkishik, A. Z. (2023). Harnessing artificial intelligence for personalized learning: A systematic review. *Data and Metadata*, *2*, 146–146. DOI: 10.56294/dm2023146

Rehan, H. (2024). Advancing Cancer Treatment with AI-Driven Personalized Medicine and Cloud-Based Data Integration. *Journal of Machine Learning in Pharmaceutical Research*, *4*(2), 1–40.

Reunanen, T., & Nieminen, N. (2024). Artificial Intelligence as a Catalyst: A Case Study on Adaptive Learning in Programming Education. *Human Factors, Business Management and Society, 135*(135).

Revell, J., & Norman, S. (1997). *In your hands: NLP in ELT*. Saffire Press.

Rinaepi, R., Triwardani, H. R., & Azi, R. N. (2022). The effectiveness of ELSA speak application to improve pronunciation ability. *Jurnal Fakultas Keguruan Dan Ilmu Pendidikan*, *3*(1), 28–33.

Rismawati, D., Suryana, Y., & Agustiana, V. (2021). The effectiveness of ELSA speaking application in improving English pronunciation. *Journal of Language and Learning*, *29*(1), 55–69.

Rodriguez-Garcia, M., & Smith, B. (2023). Multimodal approaches to language learning with immersive technologies: A meta-analysis. *Modern Language Journal*, *107*(1), 228–251.

Rojas-Sánchez, M. A., Palos-Sánchez, P. R., & Folgado-Fernández, J. A. (2023). Systematic literature review and bibliometric analysis on virtual reality and education. *Education and Information Technologies*, *28*(1), 155–192. DOI: 10.1007/s10639-022-11167-5 PMID: 35789766

Roy, K., & Swargiary, K. (2024). *Exploring the impact of AI integration in education: A mixed-methods study*. https://doi.org/DOI: 10.2139/ssrn.4857648

Ruan, S., Jiang, L., Xu, Q., Liu, Z., Davis, G. M., Brunskill, E., & Landay, J. A. (2021). EnglishBot: An AI-Powered Conversational System for Second Language Learning. *26th International Conference on Intelligent User Interfaces*, 434–444. DOI: 10.1145/3397481.3450648

Ruelmann, M., Charalambous, C. Y., & Praetorius, A. K. (2023). The representation of feedback literature in classroom observation frameworks: An exploratory study. *Educational Assessment, Evaluation and Accountability, 35*(1), 67–104. DOI: 10.1007/s11092-022-09403-0

Rukiati, E., Wicaksono, J. A., Taufan, G. T., & Suharsono, D. D. (2023). AI on learning English: Application, benefit, and threat. *Journal of Language Communication and Tourism, 1*(2), 32–40. DOI: 10.25047/jlct.v1i2.3967

Rusmiyanto, R., Huriati, N., Fitriani, N., Tyas, N. K., Rofi'i, A., & Sari, M. N. (2023). The role of artificial intelligence (AI) in developing English language learner's communication skills. *Journal of Education, 6*(1), 750–757.

Sabari, N. A. S., & Hashim, H. (2023). Sustaining Education With Digital Storytelling in the English Language Teaching and Learning: A Systematic Review. *International Journal of Academic Research in Business & Social Sciences, 13*(4). Advance online publication. DOI: 10.6007/IJARBSS/v13-i4/16860

Sajja, R., Sermet, Y., Cwiertny, D., & Demir, I. (2023). Integrating AI and learning analytics for data-driven pedagogical decisions and personalized interventions in education. *arXiv preprint arXiv:2312.09548.*

Sajja, R., Sermet, Y., Cwiertny, D., & Demir, I. (2023). Integrating AI and Learning Analytics for Data-Driven Pedagogical Decisions and Personalized Interventions in Education. arXiv preprint arXiv:2312.09548.

Sajja, R., Sermet, Y., Cikmaz, M., Cwiertny, D., & Demir, I. (2024). Artificial intelligence-enabled intelligent assistant for personalized and adaptive learning in higher education. *Information (Basel), 15*(10), 596. DOI: 10.3390/info15100596

Saleem, A. N., Noori, N. M., & Ozdamli, F. (2022). Gamification applications in e-learning: A literature review. *Tech Know Learn, 27*(1), 139–159. DOI: 10.1007/s10758-020-09487-x

Sallam, M. (2023, March). ChatGPT utility in healthcare education, research, and practice: Systematic review on the promising perspectives and valid concerns. []. MDPI.]. *Health Care, 11*(6), 887. PMID: 36981544

Saputra, D. I. S., Handani, S. W., Indartono, K., & Wijanarko, A. (2020). SMART-In English: Learn English Using Speech Recognition. *Journal of Robotics and Control (Jrc), 1*(4). Advance online publication. DOI: 10.18196/jrc.1423

Saraswathi, T., Karthikeyan, M., Balakrishnan, C., Nithya, T., Maheswari, B., & Subramanian, R. S. (2023). Artificial intelligence in human resource management: Advancements, implications and future prospects. *International Journal on Recent and Innovation Trends in Computing and Communication, 11*(11), 266–281.

Schiff, D. (2021). Out of the laboratory and into the classroom: The future of artificial intelligence in education. *AI & Society, 36*(1), 331–348. DOI: 10.1007/s00146-020-01033-8 PMID: 32836908

Schiff, D. (2022). Education for AI, not AI for education: The role of education and ethics in national AI policy strategies. *International Journal of Artificial Intelligence in Education, 32*(3), 527–563. DOI: 10.1007/s40593-021-00270-2

Schlamp, C. (2024). *Effect of Virtual Learning on Middle School English and Mathematics Scores* (Doctoral dissertation, Walden University).

Schmidt, R., & Thompson, A. (2023). Data privacy and ethics in educational AI: Regulatory frameworks and best practices. *Journal of Computing in Higher Education, 35*(2), 267–292.

Schmidt, T., & Strasser, T. (2022). Artificial intelligence in foreign language learning and teaching: A CALL for intelligent practice. Anglistik. *International Journal of English Studies, 33*(1), 165–184.

Schmidt, T., & Strasser, T. (2022). Artificial intelligence in foreign language learning and teaching: A CALL for intelligent practice. *Anglistik: International Journal of English Studies, 33*(1), 165–184. DOI: 10.33675/ANGL/2022/1/14

Schwanenflugel, P. J., Hamilton, A. M., Kuhn, M. R., Wisenbaker, J. M., & Stahl, S. A. (2004). Becoming a fluent reader: Reading skill and prosodic features in the oral reading of young readers. *Journal of Educational Psychology, 96*(1), 119–129. DOI: 10.1037/0022-0663.96.1.119 PMID: 19777077

Selwyn, N. (2022). The future of AI and education: Some cautionary notes. *European Journal of Education, 57*(4), 620–631. DOI: 10.1111/ejed.12532

Seo, K., Tang, J., Roll, I., Fels, S., & Yoon, D. (2021). The Impact of Artificial Intelligence on Learner–instructor Interaction in Online Learning. *International Journal of Educational Technology in Higher Education, 18*(1), 54. Advance online publication. DOI: 10.1186/s41239-021-00292-9 PMID: 34778540

Seyedi, A., Yeganeh, M. A. A., Noorzad, D., Firouzi, S., Qurbani, M., Shakeri, E., & Osati, K. (2024). How artificial intelligence helps students to learn English in depth. *Advances in Social Sciences Research Journal, 11*(10), 414–440. DOI: 10.14738/assrj.1110.17803

Shahri, N., & Karizmeh, M. S. (2025). Inventing a Language Online: The Practice of Edutainment in English Teaching Instagram Posts. *International Journal of Applied Linguistics, 35*(2), 756–767. DOI: 10.1111/ijal.12645

Shaik, T., Tao, X., Li, Y., Dann, C., McDonald, J., Redmond, P., & Galligan, L. (2022). A review of the trends and challenges in adopting natural language processing methods for education feedback analysis. *IEEE Access : Practical Innovations, Open Solutions, 10*, 56720–56733. DOI: 10.1109/ACCESS.2022.3177752

Shakeel, A. (2024). *The Role of ChatGPT in Academic Writing: An Exploratory Study* (Master's thesis, Oslo Metropolitan University).

Sharadgah, T. A., & Sa'di, R. A. (2022). A systematic review of research on the use of artificial intelligence in English language teaching and learning (2015-2021): What are the current effects? *Journal of Information Technology Education*, •••, 21.

Sheng, J. (2023). Exploration on the Mode of College English Language Teaching Under the Background of Informatization. *International Journal of New Developments in Education, 5*(8). Advance online publication. DOI: 10.25236/IJNDE.2023.050818

Shen, H., DeVos, A., Eslami, M., & Holstein, K. (2021). Everyday Algorithm Auditing: Understanding the Power of Everyday Users in Surfacing Harmful Algorithmic Behaviors. *Proceedings of the ACM on Human-Computer Interaction, 5*(CSCW2), 1–29. DOI: 10.1145/3479577

Shen, Y., & Guo, H. (2024). "I feel AI is neither too good nor too bad": Unveiling Chinese EFL teachers' perceived emotions in generative AI-Mediated L2 classes. *Computers in Human Behavior, 161*, 108429. DOI: 10.1016/j.chb.2024.108429

Shirin, A. (2022). Artificial Intelligence Technology on Teaching-Learning: Exploring Bangladeshi Teachers' Perceptions. *Embedded Selforganising Systems, 9*(4), 3–9. https://doi.org/DOI: 10.14464/ess.v9i4.553

Sienes, M. J. V., & Sarsale, J. C. S. (2024). *Revisiting AI in an English classroom.* Atlantis Highlights in Social Sciences, Education and Humanities., DOI: 10.2991/978-94-6463-396-2_4

Singh, H., Chauhan, U., Chauhan, S. P. S., Saxena, A., & Kumari, P. (2024). *Adaptive and Personalized Learning in Industry 5.0 Education* (pp. 1–19). DOI: 10.4018/979-8-3693-0782-3.ch001

Singh, H., Mohammad, S., Yaseen, A., Molawade, M., Mohite, S. G., Jadhav, V., & Jadhav, R. (2024, April). Multilingual education through optical character recognition (OCR) and AI. In 2024 MIT Art, Design and Technology School of Computing International Conference (pp. 1-6). IEEE. https://doi.org/DOI: 10.1109/MITADTSoCiCon51479.2024.1234567

Solak, E. (2024). Revolutionizing language learning: How ChatGPT and AI are changing the way we learn languages. *International Journal of Technology in Education, 7*(2), 353–372. DOI: 10.46328/ijte.732

Song, C., & Song, Y. (2023). Enhancing academic writing skills and motivation: Assessing the efficacy of ChatGPT in AI-assisted language learning for EFL students. *Frontiers in Psychology, 14*, 1260843. Advance online publication. DOI: 10.3389/fpsyg.2023.1260843 PMID: 38162975

Songsiengchai, S. (2025). Implementation of Artificial Intelligence (AI): Chat GPT for Effective English Language Learning among Thai Students in Higher Education. *International Journal of Education and Literacy Studies, 13*(1), 302–312. DOI: 10.7575/aiac.ijels.v.13n.1p.302

Songsiengchai, S., Sereerat, B. O., & Watananimitgul, W. (2023). Leveraging artificial intelligence (AI): Chat GPT for effective English language learning among Thai students. *English Language Teaching, 16*(11), 68–79. DOI: 10.5539/elt.v16n11p68

Soper, K. N. (2024). *A Phenomenological Study of Teacher Experiences Personalizing Learning in English Language Arts*. Liberty University.

Sosa Díaz, M. J. (2021). Emergency Remote Education, Family Support and the Digital Divide in the Context of the COVID-19 Lockdown. *International Journal of Environmental Research and Public Health, 18*(15), 7956. DOI: 10.3390/ijerph18157956 PMID: 34360248

Spielberger, C. D. (1983). *Manual for the state-trait anxiety inventory: STAI (Form Y)*. Consulting Psychologists Press.

Spratt, M., Pulverness, A., & Williams, M. (2011). *The TKT teaching knowledge test course: Modules 1, 2, 3*. Cambridge University Press.

Steenbergen-Hu, S., & Cooper, H. (2013). A meta-analysis of the effectiveness of intelligent tutoring systems on K–12 students' mathematical learning. *Journal of Educational Psychology, 105*(4), 970–987. DOI: 10.1037/a0032447

Strielkowski, W., Grebennikova, V., Lisovskiy, A., Rakhimova, G., & Vasileva, T. (2024). AI-driven adaptive learning for sustainable educational transformation. *Sustainable Development*.

Subhash, S., & Cudney, E. A. (2018). Gamified learning in higher education: A systematic review of the literature. *Computers in Human Behavior*, *87*, 192–206. DOI: 10.1016/j.chb.2018.05.028

Sunengko, S. (2024) The Impact of CEFR-Aligned Writing Assessments on Enhancing ESL/EFL Learners' Writing Competence: A Comparative Analysis. doi: https://core.ac.uk/download/642342304.pdf

Tafazoli, D., & Gómez, E. (2019). Intelligent language tutoring system: Integrating intelligent computer-assisted language learning into language education. *International Journal of Information and Communication Technology Education*, *15*(3), 15–26. https://www.igi-global.com/article/intelligent-language-tutoring-system/229018. DOI: 10.4018/IJICTE.2019070105

Tahiru, F. (2021). AI in education: A systematic literature review. *Journal of Cases on Information Technology*, *23*(1), 1–20. DOI: 10.4018/JCIT.2021010101

Tanaka, H., Brown, D., & Oliveira, F. (2023). Cross-cultural adaptations of AI language learning tools: A comparative study across five countries. *Applied Linguistics*, *44*(4), 381–405.

Tao, Y. (2019). On the construction of active learning teaching model in college English classroom. *Francis Academic Press*. https://www.semanticscholar.org/paper/On-the-Construction-of-Active-Learning-Teaching-in-Yeqing/277e51b7230c44018b7e95292cb60c7a09f5bc73

Tariq, M. U. (2024). Generative AI in Curriculum Development in Higher Education. In Fields, Z. (Ed.), *Impacts of Generative AI on Creativity in Higher Education* (pp. 227–258). IGI Global., DOI: 10.4018/979-8-3693-2418-9.ch009

Tariq, M. U. (2025). AI-Driven Research Methodologies: Revolutionizing Data-Driven Discoveries in Engineering and Physical Sciences. In Basha, J., Alade, T., Al Khazimi, M., Vasudevan, R., & Khan, J. (Eds.), *Optimizing Research Techniques and Learning Strategies With Digital Technologies* (pp. 97–122). IGI Global Scientific Publishing., DOI: 10.4018/979-8-3693-7863-2.ch004

Tariq, M. U. (2025). AI-Enhanced Project-Based Learning: Revolutionizing Commerce Education With Generative AI. In ElSayary, A. (Ed.), *Prompt Engineering and Generative AI Applications for Teaching and Learning* (pp. 125–142). IGI Global Scientific Publishing., DOI: 10.4018/979-8-3693-7332-3.ch008

Tariq, M. U. (2025). Bridging Cultures and Languages: Innovative Literacy Strategies for Inclusive and Engaged Classrooms. In Tussey, J., & Haas, L. (Eds.), *Supporting Cultural Differences Through Literacy Education* (pp. 257–282). IGI Global Scientific Publishing., DOI: 10.4018/979-8-3693-9271-3.ch010

Tariq, M. U. (2025). Integrating ICT for Enhanced Organizational Resilience: Strategies and Case Studies. In Carvalho, L., Reis, L., Neves de Almeida Baptista Figueiredo, A., & Russo, N. (Eds.), *Leveraging Technology for Organizational Adaptability* (pp. 59–80). IGI Global Scientific Publishing., DOI: 10.4018/979-8-3693-6045-3.ch004

Tew, Y., Lim, K.-G., & Joan, H. (2022). An Evaluation of Virtual Classroom Performance With Artificial Intelligence Components. *The Journal of the Institution of Engineers Malaysia, 82*(3). Advance online publication. DOI: 10.54552/v82i3.116

Tian, W., Ge, J., Zhao, Y., & Zheng, X. (2024). AI Chatbots in Chinese Higher Education: Adoption, Perception, and Influence Among Graduate Students—an Integrated Analysis Utilizing UTAUT and ECM Models. *Frontiers in Psychology, 15*, 1268549. Advance online publication. DOI: 10.3389/fpsyg.2024.1268549 PMID: 38384353

Tiwari, H. P. (2024). Artificial Intelligence in the Classroom: Revolutionizing English Language Teaching. [Jet Li]. *Journal of English Teaching and Linguistics Studies, 6*(1), 42–59. DOI: 10.55215/jetli.v6i1.9757

Tolentino, R., Baradaran, A., Gore, G., Pluye, P., & Abbasgholizadeh-Rahimi, S. (2024). Curriculum frameworks and educational programs in AI for medical students, residents, and practicing physicians: Scoping review. *JMIR Medical Education, 10*(1), e54793. DOI: 10.2196/54793 PMID: 39023999

Toseeb, U., Gibson, J. L., Newbury, D. F., Orlik, W., Durkin, K., Pickles, A., & Conti-Ramsden, G. (2020). Play and prosociality are associated with fewer externalizing problems in children with developmental language disorder: The role of early language and communication environment. *International Journal of Language & Communication Disorders, 55*(4), 583–602. DOI: 10.1111/1460-6984.12541 PMID: 32497383

Triyoga, A. (2018). Evaluating the Instructional Materials for Peer Assisted Learning Program (PALP). *Asian Social Science, 15*(1), 37. DOI: 10.5539/ass.v15n1p37

Troussas, C., Papakostas, C., Krouska, A., Mylonas, P., & Sgouropoulou, C. (2023, May). Personalized feedback enhanced by natural language processing in intelligent tutoring systems. In *International Conference on Intelligent Tutoring Systems* (pp. 667–677). Cham: Springer Nature Switzerland. DOI: 10.1007/978-3-031-32883-1_58

Tusher, H., Nazir, S., & Mallam, S. (2022). Ethical considerations for the application of virtual reality in education and training. In Nazir, S. (Ed.), *Training, Education, and Learning Sciences* (Vol. 59). AHFE International., DOI: 10.54941/ahfe1002396

Umar. (2024). Advancements in English language teaching: Harnessing the power of artificial intelligence. *FLIP: Foreign Language Instruction Probe*. https://jurnal.stit-buntetpesantren.ac.id/index.php/flip

Uwosomah, E. E., & Dooly, M. (2025). It is not the huge enemy: Preservice teachers' evolving perspectives on AI. *Education Sciences*, *15*(2), 152. DOI: 10.3390/educsci15020152

Vadivel, B., Shaban, A. A., Ahmed, Z. A., & Saravanan, B. (2023). Unlocking English Proficiency: Assessing the Influence of AI-Powered Language Learning Apps on Young Learners' Language Acquisition. *International Journal of English Language Education and Literature Studies (Ijeel)*, *2*(6), 55–62. DOI: 10.22161/ijeel.2.6.7

Venkatesh, V., Morris, M. G., Davis, G. B., & Davis, F. D. (2003). User acceptance of information technology: Toward a unified view. *Management Information Systems Quarterly*, *27*(3), 425–478. DOI: 10.2307/30036540

Vijayakumar, N. M., & Chellapandiyan, N. G. (2024). Language learning through AI technology – LLA (Language Learning Apps). *Deleted Journal*, *2*(04), 957–962. DOI: 10.47392/IRJAEM.2024.0127

Vučković, A., & Sikimić, V. (2024). Global justice and the use of AI in education: Ethical and epistemic aspects. *AI & Society*, •••, 1–18.

Vygotsky, L. S. (1978). *Mind in Society: The Development of Higher Psychological Processes*. Harvard University Press.

Wamalwa, E. J., & Wamalwa, E. W. (2014). Towards the utilization of instructional media for effective teaching and learning of English in Kenya.

Wang, C. (2024). *Exploring Students' Generative AI-Assisted Writing Processes: Perceptions and Experiences From Native and Non-native English Speakers*. Technology Knowledge and Learning., DOI: 10.1007/s10758-024-09744-3

Wang, J.-C., & Wang, T. H. (2023). Learning effectiveness of energy education in junior high schools: Implementation of action research and the predict–observe–explain model to STEM course. *Heliyon*, *9*(3), e14058. Advance online publication. DOI: 10.1016/j.heliyon.2023.e14058 PMID: 36915494

Wang, S. (2022). Exploring the Teaching Mode of English Audiovisual Speaking in Multimedia Network Environment. *Advances in Multimedia, 2022*, 1–9. DOI: 10.1155/2022/2424380

Wang, Y., Liu, C., & Tu, Y.-F. (2021). Factors affecting the adoption of AI-based applications in higher education: An analysis of teachers' perspectives using structural equation modeling. *Journal of Educational Technology & Society*, *24*(3), 116–129. https://www.jstor.org/stable/27032860

Warschauer, M., & Garcia, P. (2023). Critical digital literacy in the era of generative AI: Implications for language education. *Journal of Language and Education*, *9*(4), 512–530.

Webb, M. E., Prasse, D., Phillips, M., Kadijevich, D. M., Angeli, C., Strijker, A., ... & Laugesen, H. (2018). Challenges for IT-enabled formative assessment of complex 21st century skills. *Technology, knowledge and learning, 23*, 441-456.

Weber-Wulff, D., Anohina-Naumeca, A., Bjelobaba, S., Foltýnek, T., Guerrero-Dib, J., Popoola, O., Šigut, P., & Waddington, L. (2023). Testing of detection tools for AI-generated text. *International Journal for Educational Integrity*, *19*(1), 26. DOI: 10.1007/s40979-023-00146-z

Weidinger, L., Mellor, J., Rauh, M., Griffin, C., Uesato, J., Huang, P. S., . . . Gabriel, I. (2021). Ethical and social risks of harm from language models. arXiv preprint arXiv:2112.04359.

Wei, L. (2023). Artificial intelligence in language instruction: Impact on English learning achievement, L2 motivation, and self-regulated learning. *Frontiers in Psychology*, *14*, 1261955. DOI: 10.3389/fpsyg.2023.1261955 PMID: 38023040

Wen, F., Li, Y., Zhou, Y., An, X., & Zou, Q. (2024). A study on the relationship between AI anxiety and AI behavioral intention of secondary school students learning English as a foreign language. [JETDE]. *Journal of Educational Technology Development and Exchange*, *17*(1), 130–154. DOI: 10.18785/jetde.1701.07

Wong, K., Teo, T., & Russo, S. (2013). Interactive whiteboard acceptance: Applicability of the UTAUT model to student teachers. *The Asia-Pacific Education Researcher*, *22*(1), 1–10. DOI: 10.1007/s40299-012-0001-9

Woo, J. H., & Choi, H. (2021). Systematic review for AI-based language learning tools. *Journal of Digital Contents Society*, *22*(11), 1783–1792. DOI: 10.9728/dcs.2021.22.11.1783

Woo, J. H., & Choi, I. (2021). Systematic review for AI-based language learning tools. Retrieved from https://arxiv.org/abs/2111.04455

World Economic Forum. (2016). *The fourth industrial revolution: What it means and how to respond*. https://www.weforum.org/agenda/2016/01/the-fourth-industrial-revolution-what-it-means-and-how-to-respond/

World Economic Forum. (2023). *Future of jobs report 2023*. https://www3.weforum.org/docs/WEF_Future_of_Jobs_2023.pdf

Wu, L., Li, K., Yu, M., & Lin, Y. (2024). Application of Artificial Intelligence in Teaching English as a Foreign Language: Progress, Challenges, and Trends. *English Language Teaching and Linguistics Studies*, *6*(4), 215. DOI: 10.22158/eltls.v6n4p215

Wu, T. (2024). Virtual Research Laboratory in Foreign Language Teaching: Strategies and Role. *Scientific Bulletin of Mukachevo State University Series. Pedagogy and Psychology*, *10*(1), 107–115. DOI: 10.52534/msu-pp1.2024.107

Wu, Y. (2024). Study on the Impact of Utilizing ChatGPT and Other AI Tools for Feedback in EAP Writing Classrooms on the Discursive Writing Performance of English Major Students. *Tssehr*, *4*, 143–150. DOI: 10.62051/4se95x52

Xiong, W. (2024, July). Artificial intelligence in English language education: The path to personalized learning. In *Proceedings of the 2nd International Conference on Educational Knowledge and Informatization* (pp. 72–77). DOI: 10.1145/3691720.3691733

Xu, W., & Ouyang, F. (2022). A systematic review of AI role in the educational system based on a proposed conceptual framework. *Education and Information Technologies*, *27*(3), 4195–4223. DOI: 10.1007/s10639-021-10774-y

Yadav, G., Carvalho, P. F., McLaughlin, E. A., & Koedinger, K. R. (2024, July). Beyond Repetition: The Role of Varied Questioning and Feedback in Knowledge Generalization. In *Proceedings of the Eleventh ACM Conference on Learning@ Scale* (pp. 451-455). DOI: 10.1145/3657604.3664688

Yağcı, M. (2022). Educational data mining: Prediction of students' academic performance using machine learning algorithms. *Smart Learning Environments*, *9*(1), 11. DOI: 10.1186/s40561-022-00192-z

Yang, T. (2024). Impact of artificial intelligence software on English learning motivation and achievement. *SHS Web of Conferences, 193*. https://doi.org/DOI: 10.1051/shsconf/202419302011

Yang, L., Johnson, K., & Patel, R. (2023). Personalization algorithms in adaptive language learning: Balancing efficiency and inclusivity. *International Journal of Artificial Intelligence in Education*, *33*(1), 92–114.

Yan, L., Sha, L., Zhao, L., Li, Y., Martinez-Maldonado, R., Chen, G., Li, X., Jin, Y., & Gašević, D. (2024). Practical and ethical challenges of large language models in education: A systematic scoping review. *British Journal of Educational Technology*, *55*(1), 90–112. DOI: 10.1111/bjet.13370

Yeşilçınar, S. (2023). Personalized learning through gamification: A ChatGPT approach to English language learning. In *Transforming the language teaching experience in the age of AI* (pp. 44–64). IGI Global. DOI: 10.4018/978-1-6684-9893-4.ch003

Yong, Q. (2020). Application of artificial intelligence to higher vocational English teaching in the information environment. *Journal of Physics: Conference Series*, *1533*(3), 032030. Advance online publication. DOI: 10.1088/1742-6596/1533/3/032030

York, E. J. (2021). Digital surveillance in online writing instruction: Panopticism and simulation in learning management systems. *Computers and Composition*, *62*, 102680. DOI: 10.1016/j.compcom.2021.102680

Young, D. J. (1991). Creating a low-anxiety classroom environment: What does language anxiety research suggest? *Modern Language Journal*, *75*(4), 426–439.

Yuan, Y. (2024). An empirical study of the efficacy of AI chatbots for English as a foreign language learning in primary education. *Interactive Learning Environments*, *32*(10), 6774–6789. DOI: 10.1080/10494820.2023.2282112

Yuen, C. L., & Schlote, N. (2024). Learner Experiences of Mobile Apps and Artificial Intelligence to Support Additional Language Learning in Education. *Journal of Educational Technology Systems*, *52*(4), 507–525. DOI: 10.1177/00472395241238693

Zavalevskyi, Y., Kyrilenko, S., Kijan, O., Bessarab, N., & Mosyakova, I. (2024). The role of AI in individualizing learning and creating personalized programs. *Amazonia Investiga*, *13*(73), 200–208. DOI: 10.34069/AI/2024.73.01.16

Zawacki-Richter, O., Marín, V., Bond, M., & Gouverneur, F. (2019). Systematic review of research on artificial intelligence applications in higher education. *International Journal of Educational Technology in Higher Education*, *16*(1), 1–27. DOI: 10.1186/s41239-019-0171-0

Zdravkova, K., Krasniqi, V., Dalipi, F., & Ferati, M. (2022). Cutting-edge communication and learning assistive technologies for disabled children: An artificial intelligence perspective. *Frontiers in Artificial Intelligence*, *5*, 970430. DOI: 10.3389/frai.2022.970430 PMID: 36388402

Zhai, X., Chu, X., Chai, C. S., Jong, M. S. Y., Istenic, A., Spector, M., Liu, J.-B., Yuan, J., & Li, Y. (2021). A review of Artificial Intelligence (AI) in education from 2010 to 2020. *Complexity*, *2021*(1), 8812542. DOI: 10.1155/2021/8812542

Zhang, H., Cui, Y., Shan, H., Qu, Z., Zhang, W., Tu, L., & Wang, Y. (2020, June). Hotspots and trends of virtual reality, augmented reality and mixed reality in education field. In *2020 6th International Conference of the Immersive Learning Research Network (iLRN)* (pp. 215–219). IEEE. DOI: 10.23919/iLRN47897.2020.9155170

Zhang, J. (2025). Integrating chatbot technology into English language learning to enhance student engagement and interactive communication skills. *Journal of Computational Methods in Sciences and Engineering*. DOI: 10.1177/14727978241312992

Zhang, C., Meng, Y., & Ma, X. (2024). Artificial intelligence in EFL speaking: Impact on enjoyment, anxiety, and willingness to communicate. *System*, *121*, 103259. DOI: 10.1016/j.system.2024.103259

Zhang, H., Lee, I., & Moore, K. (2024). An Effectiveness Study of Teacher-Led AI Literacy Curriculum in K-12 Classrooms. *Proceedings of the AAAI Conference on Artificial Intelligence*, *38*(21), 23318–23325. DOI: 10.1609/aaai.v38i21.30380

Zhang, J., & Tao, D. (2020). Empowering things with intelligence: A survey of the progress, challenges, and opportunities in artificial intelligence of things. *IEEE Internet of Things Journal*, *8*(10), 7789–7817. DOI: 10.1109/JIOT.2020.3039359

Zhang, J., & Zhang, L. J. (2024). The effect of feedback on metacognitive strategy use in EFL writing. *Computer Assisted Language Learning*, *37*(5–6), 1198–1223. DOI: 10.1080/09588221.2022.2069822

Zhang, M. (2024). Enhancing MALL with artificial intelligence: Personalized learning paths in EFL teaching. *Research and Advances in Education*, *3*(8), 49–61. DOI: 10.56397/RAE.2024.08.07

Zhang, Y. (2022). Construction of English language autonomous learning center system based on artificial intelligence technology. *Mathematical Problems in Engineering*, *2022*, 1–12. Advance online publication. DOI: 10.1155/2022/7900493

Zhang, Y. (2024). A lesson study on a MOOC-based and AI-powered flipped teaching and assessment of EFL writing model: Teachers' and students' growth. *International Journal for Lesson & Learning Studies*, *13*(1), 28–40. DOI: 10.1108/IJLLS-07-2023-0085

Zhang, Y., & Dong, C. (2024). Unveiling the dynamic mechanisms of generative AI in English language learning: A hybrid study based on fsQCA and system dynamics. *Behavioral Sciences (Basel, Switzerland)*, *14*(11), 1015. DOI: 10.3390/bs14111015 PMID: 39594315

Zhang, Z. (2024). Advancements and Challenges in AI-driven Language Technologies: From Natural Language Processing to Language Acquisition. *Applied and Computational Engineering*, *57*(1), 146–152. DOI: 10.54254/2755-2721/57/20241325

Zhan, H., & Chen, L. (2018). Performing WeChat recording tasks in mixed-ability study abroad content courses. *Journal of Technology and Chinese Language Teaching*, *9*(1), 15.

Zhao, H., & Lai, C. (2022). Culturally responsive AI for language learning: Challenges and approaches. *Computer Assisted Language Learning*, *35*(8), 1403–1427.

Zhao, Y., & Liu, S. (2022). A deep learning model with virtual reality technology for second language acquisition. *Mobile Information Systems*, *2022*, 1–7. DOI: 10.1155/2022/9686725

Zheng, C., Zhang, T., Chen, X., Zhang, H., Wan, J., & Wu, B. (2024). Assessing learners' English public speaking anxiety with multimodal deep learning technologies. *Computer Assisted Language Learning*, •••, 1–29. DOI: 10.1080/09588221.2024.2351129

Zheng, Y., Wang, Y., Liu, K. S.-X., & Jiang, M. Y.-C. (2024). Examining the moderating effect of motivation on technology acceptance of generative AI for English as a foreign language learning. *Education and Information Technologies*, *29*(17), 23547–23575. DOI: 10.1007/s10639-024-12763-3

Zou, B., Du, Y., Wang, Z., Chen, J., & Zhang, W. (2023). An Investigation Into Artificial Intelligence Speech Evaluation Programs With Automatic Feedback for Developing EFL Learners' Speaking Skills. *SAGE Open*, *13*(3), 21582440231193818. Advance online publication. DOI: 10.1177/21582440231193818

Холбаев, Ф. (2025). Transforming English language teaching: The dual impact of artificial intelligence on personalized learning and educational challenges. *Лингвоспектр*, *2*(1), 371 381.

About the Contributors

Ankit Shukla is an accomplished educator and researcher with a robust background in the hospitality and tourism industry. His career spans various roles, from frontline food and beverage service to academic leadership and extensive research contributions. Ankit's journey exemplifies a blend of practical experience, academic acumen, and a passion for advancing knowledge in his field. Early Career and Industry Experience Ankit's career in the hospitality industry began at the Hyatt Regency Chandigarh in September 2015, where he worked in the Food & Beverage Service department. His responsibilities included taking room service orders, managing point-of-sale systems, and setting up banquets for events. This role provided Ankit with hands-on experience in the operational aspects of the hospitality industry. Following his time at the Hyatt Regency, Ankit transitioned into academia, joining Kumaun University Nainital as a teaching personnel in September 2016. He took on multiple responsibilities, including lecturing MBA Tourism students, overseeing practical training, and designing course curricula. This marked the beginning of his journey in education, where he contributed to shaping the next generation of hospitality professionals. Academic Leadership and Teaching Ankit's academic career continued to flourish as he assumed the role of Assistant Professor at SIHMCT & AN Tehri Garhwal in July 2017. He became the head of the Food & Beverage Service department, where he coordinated events, designed course curricula, and managed the department's overall functioning. From February 2018 to April 2022, Ankit served as an Assistant Professor at Shoolini University Solan. Here, he expanded his responsibilities to include training and placement coordination, NAAC coordination for the Hospitality Management department, and handling operations of a hotel with eight rooms. His leadership skills and ability to manage complex tasks were instrumental in the smooth functioning of the university's hospitality department. Contributions to Research and Academia Ankit's passion for research is evident through his significant contributions to academic literature. He has presented research papers at various international conferences, focusing on topics such as ecology, local and regional food in destination marketing, and the influence of technological amenities on hotel guest satisfaction. His research has been published in reputable journals, with manuscripts addressing safety and security measures in hotels, tobacco consumption in India, and the role of Indian spices in Indian history. In addition to his research publications, Ankit has filed 40 patents, copyrights, and utility applications, with several already granted. His commitment to innovation and intellectual property rights underscores his dedication to advancing knowledge in his field. Current Role and Future Endeavors As of July 2023, Ankit is a lecturer at Raja Mangala University of Technology Thanyaburi in Thailand. In this role, he continues to inspire and educate students in the field of hospitality while pursuing his research interests. Ankit's extensive experience in both industry and academia, coupled with his passion for teaching and research, positions him as a key figure in the ongoing development of the hospitality and tourism sector. Ankit Shukla's journey from industry practitioner to esteemed academic is a testament to his dedication, expertise, and unwavering commitment to excellence in hospitality and education.

Benjaporn Meeprom is a seasoned educator and researcher specializing in Computer-Assisted Language Learning(CALL), digital game-based language learning, and English for Specific Purposes (ESP). With a Ph.D. from the University of Newcastle, Australia, her expertise lies in integrating technology into language education to foster learner autonomy and enhance curriculum design. She has led innovative projects such as the Erasmus Plus"GreenEdAsia" initiative and spearheaded the development of online language assessment systems. As an award-winning faculty supervisor and curriculum innovator at Rajamangala University of Technology Thanyaburi (RMUTT), Dr. Meeprom has transformed English language programs by incorporating AI-driven tools and methodologies. Her research on digital learning tools and strategies for TOEIC and IELTS preparation has contributed to bridging gaps in English language proficiency among Thai learners.A prolific conference speaker and workshop facilitator, she advocates for leveraging AI to personalize learning experiences and improve teaching effectiveness. Friendly and approachable, Dr. Meeprom's work inspires educators to embrace cutting-edge technologies in empowering students to thrive in global communication. Dr. Meeprom's contribution in this book reflects her lifelong commitment to advancing English language teaching through AI innovation, underscoring her passion for creating meaningful, tech-enabled educational experience.

Kongkiat Khunasathitchai is the Head of the Department of Western Languages and a distinguished expert in TOEIC preparation and English language instruction. With a strong academic foundation and years of hands-on experience, he has played a key role in advancing English education both in the classroom and at the institutional level. As a seasoned English educator, Mr. Kongkiat is known for his engaging teaching methods, deep knowledge of language assessment, and his ability to help students achieve outstanding TOEIC results. He is deeply committed to enhancing students' communication skills and building their confidence in using English in real-world contexts. In his administrative role, Mr. Kongkiat has led numerous curriculum development initiatives, teacher training programs, and international collaboration projects. His leadership has contributed significantly to the growth and modernization of the department, ensuring that students receive a well-rounded and globally relevant education. Widely respected by peers and students alike, Mr. Kongkiat continues to serve as a mentor, innovator, and advocate for excellence in English language teaching and academic leadership.

Nagendra Yadav is an 11th-year academia professional with a master's degree in hotel management from Kurukshetra University. With a passion for culinary arts and management, Nagendra has dedicated his career to enhancing guests' culinary dining and hospitality experience worldwide. His expertise spans various facets of hotel operations, including culinary innovation, guest services, and management practices. As an educator, Nagendra shares his knowledge and experience with the next generation of hospitality professionals, inspiring them to pursue excellence and creativity in their careers. He continues to explore new trends and innovations in the industry, aiming to elevate the standards of hospitality and enrich the experiences of guests and clients. He extensively researched promoting local and authentic culinary offerings in destinations. His work has contributed to a broader understanding of how culinary experiences can drive tourism and support local economies.

***

Deepak Dharrao, currently working as an Assistant Professor in the Department of CSE at Symbiosis Institute of Technology, Symbiosis International (Deemed University), Pune Maharashtra, India. He is having 16 years of experience in research and academics. He has authored or co-authored over 50 technical articles in reputed journals and conference proceedings. He published 2 patents and 1 Book on current demanding research topics. Dr. Deepak is member of IEEE, ACM & Life Member of ISTE professional organizations. His research interests include the areas of image and real-time video processing, FinTech, Data Science, Artificial Intelligence and Machine Learning.

Mehedi Hasan Emon is a research practitioner specializing in business and management, supply chain management, and digital transformation. His work has significantly contributed to the fields of marketing, artificial intelligence, and supply chain analytics, with a strong focus on sustainable business practices. Through his research, he explores the intersection of technology and business, aiming to enhance operational efficiency, digital marketing strategies, and sustainable supply chain practices. As an active researcher, he has authored numerous publications in Scopus and Web of Science-indexed journals. His research covers areas such as artificial intelligence adoption, digital marketing strategies, sustainable supply chain management, and the economic implications of technological advancements. His work has gained wide recognition, reflecting his growing influence within the academic community. He has been involved in multiple research projects, including those funded by the University Grants Commission of Bangladesh and European Union-funded initiatives. His research aligns with his vision of leveraging technology to drive sustainability, efficiency, and innovation in business ecosystems. Additionally, he has contributed to academia as a peer reviewer for high-impact journals, ensuring rigorous academic standards and fostering knowledge dissemination in his field.

Deepak Gupta is a distinguished academician with over 20 years of teaching experience and expertise in Computer Science and Engineering. He holds a Ph.D. in Computer Engineering and has an extensive research portfolio, including many international journal papers, multiple conference proceedings, and several books. His research interests span machine learning, artificial intelligence, and data mining. Currently, Dr. Gupta serves as an Associate Professor and Academic Coordinator in the Department of Computer Science & Engineering at ITM Gwalior, MP, India. He has also contributed significantly to the field through patents and copyrights and actively engages as a reviewer, conference chair and editor.

Manjiri Joshi serves as an Assistant Professor at Dr. D. Y. Patil B-School, bringing over 15 years of diverse experience across academia and industry. Her academic and research interests are centered on Human Resource Management and Hospitality Management. She is currently pursuing her Ph.D., furthering her commitment to scholarly advancement in the field of management. Prof. Joshi has been the recipient of notable honors, including the Best Young Faculty Award (2022) and the Innovative Research National Award—Excellence in Academics (2023), in recognition of her contributions to teaching and research. She has delivered sessions as a resource person in academic workshops and is the co-author of the book Managing Transport Operations, published by Himalaya Publications for Chandigarh University. Her academic portfolio includes publications in Scopus-indexed, UGC Care-listed, and peer-reviewed journals, along with contributions to book chapters and conference proceedings. She continues to engage in impactful research and academic discourse.

Shahjahan Kabir is a professor of English Discipline, Khulna University. Now, he is the head of English Discipline, Khulna University. He is an enthusiastic academic with profound teaching interest in English language, linguistics and literature. As an articulate English teacher, he is quite able to effectively communicate with students from diverse backgrounds or varying degrees of ability. He believes in committed and dedicated professional ability to teach, motivate and direct students to maximum performance by encouraging a positive and energetic environment. He has thirteen published articles in renowned journals. His research interests include linguistics, ELT, CALT, CALL, TALT, MALT, MALL, Curriculum, Poetry and drama.

Bhavana S. Karmore working as Assistant Professor and Dean at BCA and MCA Department of G. H. Raisoni University, Amravati for U.G. and P. G. Department . Total Years of Experience 15+ . She publish more than 20+ Papers in International Journals . She work as International Expert at International Conferences. She worked as a Editorial Board Members in 5+ International Journals and Reviewer in 10+ International Journals and International Conferences . Project Guided 10+ PG students and 10+ UG Students . She publish more than 10+ books of Electronics and Computer Engg. subjects. 3 Design patent, 2 copyright .

Sushant Kishore teaches English Language, Technical Communication, Literature and Cultural Studies at VIT, Vellore, Tamil Nadu. His doctoral research delved into the performative politics of Ethnic Nationalism in India, showcasing a keen interest in the politics of identity. He is interested in tinkering with technology and finding the best ways to make them useful in a classroom.

Yogita Deepak Mane is an Associate Professor in the Department of Artificial Intelligence and Data Science at Thakur College of Engineering and Technology. She holds a Master's degree in Computer Engineering from the University of Mumbai and earned her Ph.D. from the same institution in April 2022. Dr. Mane has published over 25 research papers in renowned national and international Journals, Conferences and holds a patent to her name. Dr. Mane has contributed as a reviewer in various National and International conferences and also serve as session chair. With 18 years of experience, she has demonstrated exceptional expertise and leadership in education, excelling in both academic and administrative roles.

Neeta Prashant Patil is an Associate Professor in the Department of Information Technology at Thakur College of Engineering and Technology. She holds a Master's in Engineering and a Ph.D. in Technology from the University of Mumbai. Dr. Patil has authored over 18 research papers in esteemed national and international journals and has actively participated in numerous conferences at both levels. As a reviewer for reputed international journals, she contributes significantly to the academic community. With more than 16 years of experience teaching undergraduate and postgraduate students, she has excelled in various academic and administrative roles, showcasing remarkable expertise and leadership in the field of education.

Vivit Rosmayanti, S.Pd.I., M.Pd was born in Botta on June 26, 1987. She has over 10 years of experience teaching at the University. She obtained a bachelor's degree in English Education from Alauddin State Islamic University. She completed her master's and doctoral degrees in English Education from Makassar State University. She is currently a lecturer in the Post Graduate Program, Department of English Education at Makassar State University, South Sulawesi, Indonesia. She is also actively writing research articles to be published in nationally and internationally accredited journals. She has written in some chapter books, monographs, and reference books. She is interested in teaching methods for teaching English. Her research interests include language teaching methodology, ICT instruction, and ESP teaching.

Muhammad Usman Tariq has more than 16+ year's experience in industry and academia. He has authored more than 200+ research articles, 110+ case studies, 130+ book chapters and several books other than 4 patents. He is founder and CEO of The Case HQ, a unique repository for courses, narrative and video case studies. He has been working as a consultant and trainer for industries representing six sigma, quality, health and safety, environmental systems, project management, and information security standards. His work has encompassed sectors in aviation, manufacturing, food, hospitality, education, finance, research, software and transportation. He has diverse and significant experience working with accreditation agencies of ABET, ACBSP, AACSB, WASC, CAA, EFQM and NCEAC. Additionally, Dr. Tariq has operational experience in incubators, research labs, government research projects, private sector startups, program creation and management at various industrial and academic levels. He is Certified Higher Education Teacher from Harvard University, USA, Certified Online Educator from HMBSU, Certified Six Sigma Master Black Belt and has been awarded PFHEA, SFSEDA, SMIEEE, and CMBE.

Farhana Yeasmin has been working as a faculty in the department of English at Jashore University of Science and Technology, Bangladesh since March 2017.

Her fascination and passion for teaching always motivate her to achieve extensive analytical skills in the English language and literature. To acquire the level of quality, she focuses on developing enthusiasm and confidence among the students and tries to instruct them according to their individual needs. She has twenty published articles in different journals of home and abroad. Her research interests include English language teaching and testing, Language Policy, TALT, MALT, World Literature etc.

Shraddha N. Zanjat currently serves as an Assistant Professor in the EEE Department at the School of Engineering and Technology (SOET), Sandip University, Nashik. With 10 years of teaching experience and 2 years of industry exposure, she brings a wealth of knowledge to her role. She holds a post-graduation degree, a Master of Technology in Electronics and Communication, from RTMN University. Additionally, she is pursuing her PhD at Sandip University, Nashik. Prof. Shraddha N. Zanjat has presented ten conference papers at both national and international levels and has published five papers in esteemed international journals such as IEEE, UGC, and others. Furthermore, she has obtained five Indian design patents. She is also a member of two technical association bodies. Prof. Shraddha N. Zanjat has registered four copyrights under her name and has published two book chapters in Scopus-indexed publications. Additionally, she has authored more than 50 books with international publications and has received royalties of about 20k.

Index

A

B

C

D

E

F

G

I

L

M

N

P

R

S

V

www.ingramcontent.com/pod-product-compliance
Ingram Content Group UK Ltd.
Pitfield, Milton Keynes, MK11 3LW, UK
UKHW050948290926
15470UKWH00005B/1708

9 798337 319520